More Than 20 Great Road Trips

SO-BEZ-546

THE
ULTIMATE
Tailgater's
TRAVEL
GUIDE

STEPHEN LINN

[interactive blvd]™

An Interactive Blvd Book
interactiveblvd.com

RUTLEDGE HILL PRESS®
Nashville, Tennessee

A Division of Thomas Nelson Publishers
www.ThomasNelson.com

theultimatetailgater.com

An Interactive Blvd Book. Interactive Blvd is a division of 4964 Productions, LLC., www.interactiveblvd.com.

Published by Rutledge Hill Press, a Division of Thomas Nelson, Inc., P.O. Box 141000, Nashville, Tennessee 37214.

This book is sold without warranties, expressed or implied, and the publisher and author disclaim any liability for injury, loss, or damage caused by the contents of this book.

Rutledge Hill Press Books may be purchased in bulk for educational, business, fundraising, or sales promotional use. For information, please email SpecialMarkets@ThomasNelson.com.

Special thanks to Barb Rishaw and Karen Williams.

Front cover photo: KCPix.com

Back cover photo: Tim Tadder

Photos pp. iii –iv, Ed Rode; p. v, Ravenstailgating.com; p. 1, Pantherfanz.net; p. 9, Carine Lutz Photography © Ann Arbor Convention & Visitors Bureau; p. 20, Dan Herron; p. 28, Baltimore Area Convention & Visitors Association; p. 39, Greater Boston Convention & Visitors Bureau; p. 49, Brandon Schauf; p. 57, Asten Rathbun; p. 71, Roger Lorenz; p. 86, Denver Metro Convention & Visitors Bureau; p. 96, Ed Rode; p. 107, Kansas City Convention & Visitors Association; p. 119, VISIT FLORIDA; p. 127, Ed Rode; p. 137, Central Park Conservancy; p. 149, Mark Matthews; p. 157, Melenie Ottosen; p. 165, Joanne DiBone; p. 172, David Goldberg; p.189, Seattle Convention & Visitors Bureau; p.197, centralPACVB.org; p. 205, JakeMcGuire.com

Design: Karen Williams [intudesign.net]

All trademarks, service marks, and trade names referenced in this book are the property of their respective owners. All rights reserved.

Library of Congress Cataloging-in-Publication Data

Linn, Stephen, 1964–
  The ultimate tailgater's travel guide : more than 20 great road trips
/ Stephen Linn.
      p. cm.
  "An Interactive Blvd. book."
  ISBN 1-4016-0258-4 (trade paper) 1. Football
fans—Travel—United States—Guidebooks. 2. Tailgate parties—United
States—Guidebooks. 3. Football—United States—Guidebooks.
4. Football stadiums—United States—Guidebooks. 5. Automobile
racing—United States—Guidebooks. 6. Racetracks (Automobile
racing)—United States—Guidebooks. 7. United States—Tours.
8. Automobile travel—United States—Guidebooks. I. Title.
  GV959.L63 2006
  796.332'06873—dc22
                          2006012660

Printed in the United States of America

06 07 08 09 10 — 5 4 3 2 1

Contents

"ROAD TRIP!"

Two simple words, but when put together, they make your pulse quicken, your mind wander, and your lips turn up in a grin. Add a game or race to the sentence, and you're ready to pack your bags and scamper to the car.

But hold on. First there's some planning to do. Not a lot, but some. If you're going to make a weekend out of this, you need to know what to do—and where to do it—once they turn off the stadium lights. This book will make that easy for you.

The Ultimate Tailgater's Travel Guide includes more than 20 great road trips. Sure, there are more than that, but there are only so many pages in this book. So we've picked some of the best trips for this first edition. We chose some of these trips simply because they are great places to spend a long weekend. Others were chosen because the tailgating there is something special. Most of them are both.

We realize there are plenty more places to see and things to do in these towns than what we've listed. But this is a tailgating weekend, so we've provided some local favorites to enjoy before and after the game—favorites that you'll still be talking about after you get home. But don't stop there. Explore and have fun. (And if you know of a great place not included in this book, tell us about it; we might feature it on *The Ultimate Tailgater* Web site or on our podcast. Go to theultimatetailgater.com to e-mail us.)

A note about what you won't find here: lists of chain grocery stores, chain hotels, shopping malls, and the like. We figure you're an adult; you can find those kinds of places on your own. What we've done is carefully pick some of the places that make these cities unique and fun destinations.

In each chapter we've listed hotels, restaurants, and attractions that are within a 40-mile radius of the city's center. We've also included tailgating guides and some city information for venues within 60 miles. The idea is to make it easy for you to get from place to place within an hour or so. Heck, you spent enough travel time getting there; now you deserve to enjoy yourself.

Let's spend a few moments on the topic of icons, several of which are in the book.

You'll see many icons in the venue guides, telling you what you can and can't do in the parking lots. Explanations for these icons are on page 8. Also shown there is a key to the dollar signs you'll see. These indicate how expensive it is to eat at a profiled restaurant or to visit one of the listed destinations.

Michigan Wolverines fans show up early in Ann Arbor. (Photo: Perry Calandrino)

All contact information, pricing, and similar attraction information was updated through the time this book went to press, but always call ahead to see if anything has changed.

On the road to Boulder, CO. (Photo: Jim Spittler)

While you will find tips for tailgating in each of the cities in this book, you'll find everything you need to know about tailgating in *The Ultimate Tailgater's Handbook*; it's the ultimate how-to book for the person who wants to throw the best party in the parking lot. The *Handbook* is available in stores and at theultimatetailgater.com.

Now, get your suitcase from the attic, gas up the car, and get ready to hit the road!

Planning Your Trip

You don't just decide to take off for a weekend, jump in your car, and go.

Okay, so maybe you did that in college, but you learned your lesson and did it only that one time. Well, maybe twice.

The point is, if you don't plan for your trip, you'll run into obstacles that will prevent you from having fun. You're going to forget things. And chances are, you're going to need those things.

This is not to say you have to write a minute-by-minute script for your road trip and hold to that plan. Think like Ike (Eisenhower, that is), who once said: "In preparing for battle I have always found that plans are useless, but planning is indispensable." That philosophy got him to the White House; it will get you to the game and back.

The first two steps to planning are the easy ones:

1. Where are you going?

2. How are you getting there?

Step three is where it can start to get tricky. Now, we know it's not like you've never traveled somewhere before. But tailgating trips are a little different from spring break in Destin. That's why we're here for you.

First a few general tips, then we'll get to flying, driving, and the ultimate in road trip tailgate travel: the RV. (You'll find checklists to help you with all of this beginning on page 5.)

As soon as you have answered those first two questions, make your reservations. Be sure to look for special deals and discounts you qualify for. These include AAA, frequent-flier programs, alumni organizations, and the like. Not sure if you qualify? Ask when booking the reservation. What have you got to lose? Just 10 percent or so off the cost, perhaps.

Also, check to make sure your car insurance is up to date and covers options such as rental cars. Failing to do this can end up costing you much more than you saved using that AAA card on the hotel room.

Whatever your mode of travel, you're going to need luggage. When buying new luggage, be on the lookout for a few things, that is, if you want your stuff to arrive in the same condition you packed it.

Look for bags with wheels, preferably ones that have a bearing system and are recessed into the actual frame of the bag. You know how much you prefer rolling to lugging, but when wheels are not retracted, there's a good chance they might break off. Then you'll find yourself lugging the rolling bag.

Second, if you're buying soft-sided luggage, know that the better frames use a highly resilient corrugated plastic that is wider and more flexible than common support systems. These are called "honeycomb memory frames." The more common narrow, metal-band supports with plastic "boots" on the rest of the bag are usually called "cheaper."

PLANNING YOUR TRIP   **1**

Grilling outside Washington's FedEx Field. (Photo: TheHogs.net)

Then there's the fabric, or denier. The number used for denier measures the weight of the thread: the higher the count, the heavier the thread. Nylons and polyesters hold up best. The word *ballistic*, if used in the manufacturer's description, refers to a type of weave. It resists tearing better, but it's not bulletproof.

Handles? Get the recessed kind.

Zippers? Look for the brand names (YKK is a good one).

Size? Get what you think will suit your needs for seasons to come, not just for this road trip. Keep in mind carry-on size restrictions for airplanes, too. You can find a chart of sizes for most major airlines at luggagebase.com/airline_carryons.aspx.

When packing your bag, remember this is a tailgating trip, not a vacation.

Pack light. Take only what you need, and coordinate your outfits so you can mix and match your wardrobe to save luggage space. Of course, check the weather forecast to make sure you include attire suitable for whatever kind of weather you are likely to encounter.

Pack tight. Roll your T-shirts, jeans, and other casual clothes. Put socks and underwear in your shoes to save space. Use miniature toiletry items and samples whenever possible so as to save even more space and leave room for the important things, like your Cheesehead.

When it comes to packing, the main difference between flying or driving to your destination is, of course, how much tailgating gear you can take with you. Tents, grills, chairs, and coolers won't fit into the overhead too well.

That doesn't mean, however, that a flying tailgate road trip has to be without accoutrements.

Of course, you're packing clothes that celebrate your team. Shirts, hats, and the like travel anywhere. So do car flags (they fit on rental cars, too, you know), small banners, pom-poms, cups and plates, blankets, and maybe even that inflatable chair (deflated, of course).

To spread your cheer from the luggage carousel to the bellman's cart, decorate your luggage to support your team or race-car driver and announce your arrival.

You can also decorate yourself, but be advised that many airlines and airport security officers might have something to say about passengers who have traded in their shirts for painted chests.

If you drive, you have miles and miles to go in which you can spread your spirit. From stickers, to shoe-polished windows, to car flags, to your personalized license plate, you can start your rolling tailgate before you hit the state line. Depending on your vehicle, you can also pack most of your usual tailgate gear. Even your grill.

A few words about that grill.

If you load it into your car, be sure it is firmly secured, and make sure the lid is closed and somehow locked down. If the grill is inside your vehicle and you're in an accident, all those metal pieces flying around can be hazardous to your health. If the grill is stashed in your trunk, you don't want to hear it rattling around for the entire eight hours it takes to get to Boston, either.

You can also travel with your grill *outside* your car. There are grills designed to attach to your bumper or hitch and lock into place. Freedom Grill offers a couple of good ones. The great thing about their grills is that they rest on a movable arm—you can swivel it away from the car and use it at your tailgate party without having to lift it into or out of your car.

No matter where you store your grill, be sure to take special care transporting the propane tank. While tanks are now equipped with an overflow protection device and are designed to be filled only to a certain level (which allows the fuel to expand into the vapor space as the temperature rises—a good thing) they are still flammable. They should always be turned off/closed and protected while traveling.

You should also protect yourself while driving. Start by getting enough rest. According to one government study, 20 percent of vehicle crashes in the U.S. are due to fatigued drivers.

If you find yourself yawning, restless, bored, missing road signs, or, of course, nodding off, then you are fatigued and should let someone else slide behind the wheel. In fact, it's a good idea to switch off drivers every hour or two to be safe.

And remember, caffeine is a short-term buzz. It won't keep your energy level up for very long. A good night's sleep before you hit the road is a better bet.

RVs: The Ultimate Tailgate Travel

There's a reason you see so many RVs parked in tailgate lots across the country. After all, the RV offers many of the comforts of home. Topping the list: the bathroom.

Tailgating with an RV means you're on your own schedule, and you can take your parking-lot setup with you anywhere. It also means you have a good chance of making new friends with your parking-lot neighbors. Your on-board bathroom trumps whatever their Explorers and BMWs might offer in terms of creature comforts.

But don't head straight to the dealer and buy just any RV for tailgating. Your needs are different from the guy who plans to camp at the national park for a week or who plans to tour the country this summer.

Mini–motor homes (aka Class C RVs) are the best chioce for weekend tailgating travelers. (Photo: Camping World)

To help us recommend the best RV for the tailgater, and the accessories to go with it, we turned to Cindy McCaleb at Camping World, the RV Supercenter, since she deals with this every day. (Expert help is good.)

Her answer: look for a Class C RV, also known as a mini–motor home.

"These are the RVs with the van nose and the bed over the cab," Cindy explains. "They're smaller than the Class A vehicles, but they have gotten bigger in the last 10 years. They average 28 to 30 feet long and are great for people who take weekend trips for tailgating and one or two vacations a year."

Cindy says you can expect to pay $70,000 for a new mini–motor home, so they aren't cheap. But if you look around, you can find a good used one for around $35,000 and up. (Camping World's Web site is a good place to start your search: campingworld.com/rvs.)

Step one to figuring out which specific RV to buy is to think about how many people will usually be traveling with you. From that, you can determine the features you want.

If you have a lot of people in your tailgating crew, you'll want to steer away from those cushy, swivel chairs. Sure, they're great once you get there, but for traveling with a group, they don't work so well. "You'll want to get one with a couch that folds out into a bed," Cindy suggests.

Of course, you'll get an RV with a bathroom and kitchen. In regards to the latter, make sure it includes a microwave and a 6- to 8-cubic-foot refrigerator. Most of that comes standard, but not on all units. Be sure to get a cook-top, but an oven is optional. You can decide on that based on your usual tailgate menus.

Some other RV features you'll want (usually included but not always):

Travel trailers offer most of the features of an RV, but are less expensive. (Photo: Camping World)

- A storage area under the floor. Make sure it has ample room so you can stow your grill, folding chairs, etc., there.
- Air conditioner
- LP furnace
- Hardwired generator – 4.0 and up
- A video back-up system. Remember, there are no back windows, so you can't see behind you.
- An awning. These attach to the side of the RV and are great for setting up your tailgate party under.

Another option Cindy offers for tailgaters, if budget is a concern, is to get a travel trailer. These units are towed behind your vehicle and have most of the features of the mini–motor home without the monster price tag. You can get a new travel trailer for $25,000–$45,000.

There are drawbacks to the travel trailer.

"You have two vehicles to deal with when using a travel trailer," Cindy points out, "so maneuvering and parking can be a problem, since you're now 40 feet long or longer. Plus, you can't carry people in it; everyone still has to fit in your car."

What brands should you look for? Cindy says Winnebago, Fleetwood, and Coachmen are good brands, each with several models and price points. If budget isn't an issue for you, she says to take a look at Airstream.

Whether you choose a Class C RV or a travel trailer, Cindy says don't take the keys and head straight to the game or race. You need to practice driving. We know, you're not a kid of 16, but driving one of these isn't the same as driving your car.

"Practice driving in a parking lot or other place where you have a lot of open space," Cindy says. "Practice turning, backing up, and parking, since you'll be doing a lot of that when tailgating. It isn't as easy as it looks."

Once you've mastered how to park your RV, there are a couple of things to keep in mind about where to park it.

Most race tracks and stadiums have specific areas for RVs to park. Check the venue guides we've included in this book for details. Also, check the stadium's Web site before you leave to see if there's anything else you should know. But these spots are for the game; you might get to stay the night before, but if your road trip is for the duration of the weekend, you'll need to find an RV park. We list some for every city featured.

If you're in a bind, most Wal-Marts will let you park overnight for free. It's not a company policy and each store manager makes that call, but most allow it. Call ahead to be sure.

The Ultimate Tailgater's Travel Guide

Ultimate Tailgater's Traveling Checklist

The first tip for a great tailgate road trip is the same as for a great tailgate party: use a checklist. Just as no one wants that burger put together on the asphalt because someone forgot a plate (go to theultimatetailgater.com to download the Ultimate Tailgater's Checklist), no one wants to be hoofing it to Denver because someone forgot to check the spare tire.

TWO WEEKS OUT

❏ Reconfirm lodging reservations.

❏ Check ATM and debit cards to learn if there are any daily limits and plan accordingly. You don't want to be stuck without cash.

❏ Check with your destination venue to learn their rules and costs for tailgating and plan accordingly (venue guides are included for the trips in this book; a complete venue guide for the NFL, NASCAR, and Division 1-A NCAA football can be found in *The Ultimate Tailgater's Handbook*).

❏ If traveling with a group, decide who will bring what items for your tailgate party. Go ahead and divvy up the food, the serving items, the drinks and coolers.

ONE WEEK OUT

❏ Review your food recipes and make sure you have all the ingredients.

❏ Review your tailgate gear list and make sure you have all the items.

❏ Buy new camera batteries, film, and/or digital cards.

❏ Make sure your luggage is identified inside and out with your current contact information.

❏ Buy or download maps, directions, and road atlases you may need.

❏ Make reservations for restaurants and attractions in town you don't want to miss (if it's a big game weekend, you may want to do this sooner to make sure you get in).

DAY BEFORE YOU LEAVE

❏ Prepare any food, drink, or other items that can be made ahead of time and properly stored on your trip.

❏ Charge your cell phone.

❏ Check your first-aid kit and make sure it's stocked (see page 6).

❏ Make sure you have your bags packed and ready to load into the vehicle.

❏ Gas up your vehicle (even if you're just heading to the airport).

❏ Make sure you have your game tickets.

TRAVEL DAY

❏ Load up the vehicle (make sure your coolers won't be in the sun).

❏ Make sure you have your driver's license, credit cards, etc. with you.

❏ Make sure your home is locked and secure.

❏ Hit the road.

IF FLYING

❏ Check your airline's luggage restrictions before packing.

❏ Make sure you have with you a valid driver's license or passport ID for airport security.

❏ Reconfirm your flights the day before you leave.

❏ If available from your airline, check in online the night before, or morning of, your trip to save time at the airport.

❏ Carry with you, or in your carry-on bag, your wallet, insurance cards, credit cards and travelers checks, plane and game tickets, your itinerary with confirmation numbers and phone numbers.

IF DRIVING

❏ Two weeks before you leave, have your vehicle checked, oil changed, etc.

❏ Two days before you leave, make sure your vehicle's spare tire is safe and properly inflated.

❏ The day before you leave, make sure your tires are properly inflated.

❏ Pack an Ultimate Tailgater's Vehicle Bag including: car door de-icer, car flags, first-aid kit (see below), Fix-a-Flat (or similar brand), flare, jumper cables, rags, water, blanket.

❏ Before you leave, check the road conditions for your trip: fhwa.dot.gov/trafficinfo.

IF DRIVING IN AN RV

❏ Two weeks before you leave, check that the electrical and sewer systems are working.

❏ A few days before you leave, check LP level in tank.

❏ The day before you leave, fill the fresh water tank.

❏ The day before you leave, pre-treat black water and gray water tanks.

❏ Make sure trash cans are on board the day before you leave (the collapsible container model is great for traveling).

❏ Before you leave, check that you have enough toilet paper on board and that it is approved for RV use (you can't just toss any toilet paper in there—RV paper dissolves quicker; check the RV manufacturer's specifications).

FIRST-AID KIT

As important as packing the grill, food, trash bags, and ice is having a stocked first-aid kit with you at your tailgate party. Whether driving or flying, be sure to pack a clearly marked first-aid kit and keep it with you in the parking lot (read: don't leave it at the hotel).

While your cell phone may be the first thing you reach for in an emergency, chances are you'll need at least some of these other items before help arrives.

❏ Alcohol swabs/antiseptic wipes.

❏ Triple antibiotic ointment.

❏ Hydrocortisone cream.

❏ Adhesive bandages.

- ❏ Sterile gauze pads
- ❏ First-aid tape
- ❏ Scissors (may not be able to take on airplanes)
- ❏ One or two elastic bandages
- ❏ Burn creams (including sunburn creams)
- ❏ Ibuprofen or acetaminophen
- ❏ Aspirin
- ❏ Antacids
- ❏ Tweezers
- ❏ Disposable instant cold pack
- ❏ Thermometer
- ❏ Plastic/latex gloves

Venue Guides and Pricing

For every city in the book, we've provided a venue guide for the stadiums and tracks. We've also included pricing keys for restaurants and attractions.

Each venue guide displays icons describing what you'll find, along with contact information and notes on each location. As of print time, all entries were correct. However, things can change. When in doubt, call the contact numbers listed to be sure the information you need is still current. Below is a key to what each icon means.

Remember—if you don't see an icon listed, that activity is forbidden entirely, restricted in some way, or doesn't apply to that location. Read the entry and call for further clarification, if necessary.

 Decorations are allowed, excluding banners and signs that are advertising services or goods.

 Alcohol is permitted for those of legal drinking age.

 Grills or cookers are permitted for noncommercial use only.

 Parking is more than $50 per day for cars or larger vehicles.

 Parking is between $30 and $50 per day for cars or larger vehicles.

 Parking is no more than $30 per day for any vehicle.

 RVs may park overnight before or after the game.

 Number of hours you can tailgate before game. Times exceeding 4 hours are included in "4" icon.

 Number of hours you may remain after the event. Usually this includes tailgating, but read the entry to be sure.

 RVs, limos, and other oversized vehicles are allowed.

 Tents may be erected.

 Tables, chairs, and other tailgating furniture are allowed.

 Venue offers visible security presence in parking and tailgating areas.

 Venue offers at least one paved parking lot.

 Shuttle service is available from parking or tailgating areas to the event and back again.

Pricing Guide for Restaurants and Attractions

Restaurants (based on average entrée price):
$ $1–$19
$$ $20–$39
$$$ $40+

Attractions (based on average general admission price):
$ $1–$9
$$ $10–$19
$$$ $20+

Michigan Stadium. The Big House. Capacity: 107,501. That's how many people can squeeze in to watch the Wolverines. It's the largest college football stadium in the country.

Big House begets big-time tailgating here.

Michigan has a rich and successful football legacy, which has created loyal and vocal fans. When you have enough fans turning up to create the state's third largest "city," you know you're going to have a great parking-lot party. The tough part is finding a place to park.

Parking at the stadium is for permit holders. Chances are you aren't one. But you can park in one of a dozen or so nearby lots for $15–$40 ($125 for buses and RVs). Several are within walking distance of the stadium, but some will be closed if it's raining or snowing. (You can get game-day weather and parking information on 1600-AM WAAM, 760-AM WJR, and 1050-AM WTKA. Also, you can get a list of lots and fees at mgoblue.com—click on "Facilities," then on "Michigan Stadium," "Traffic & Parking Information," and, finally, on "Football Parking Inventory.")

There's no overnight parking for cars, and Michigan enforces the tailgate rules you've come to expect—stay in your space, keep grills away from vehicles, etc.

RVs must park at Pioneer High School's Purple Lot on the southwest corner of Main Street and Stadium Boulevard. It's first-come, first-served, and the lot opens at 5:00 p.m. the day before the game. Call (734) 994-2277 for details. If you have questions about the other lots, call (734) 764-0247.

If you don't want to hassle with the parking, you can take a shuttle to the stadium to join your friends. It's called Football Ride, and it runs between the stadium and several lots and hotels in Ann Arbor. A round trip ticket costs $4. Call the Ann Arbor Transit Authority with questions at (734) 973-6500.

Just a few minutes away, in Ypsilanti, is Eastern Michigan University—the Eagles. It's quite a contrast.

EMU is a smaller school, as you might have guessed, and they play at Rynearson Stadium, which seats 30,200. They also don't have as good a team. Case in point: Michigan beat Eastern Michigan, 55-0, in 2005.

It shouldn't come as a surprise to you that tailgating isn't as big here. Parking is free, and you won't have trouble finding a spot. (There is no overnight parking at stadium lots.) You will find that the tailgaters next to you are a loyal bunch, proud to cheer their Eagles.

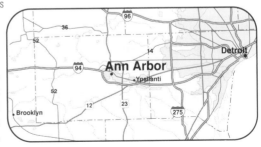

UNIVERSITY OF MICHIGAN
Michigan Stadium
Ann Arbor, Michigan
(734) 647-BLUE

RVs park at Pioneer High School's Purple Lot, southwest corner of Main St. and Stadium Blvd. Cost for RV parking $125. Lot available for RVs 5 p.m. day before game, ending noon next day. No advance reservations made: first-come, first-served.

Shuttle Info: Football Ride provides shuttles from several locations in Ann Arbor to Michigan Stadium. $2 one-way; $4 round trip. Call (734) 973-6500 for details.

Wolverines Media Partners: 760-AM WJR, 1050-AM WTKA, 1600-AM WAAM

They have been known as the Eagles only since 1991. For the 62 years prior to that, they were the Eastern Michigan Hurons, named for a Native-American tribe. Before that they were known as the Normalites and the Men from Ypsi. I don't know about you, but I'd go with the Eagles, too.

About Ann Arbor and Ypsilanti

Ann Arbor was incorporated as a village in 1833, and 40 acres of land were set aside to become the state capital. Instead, Lansing eventually became the capital city. In 1837 the 40 acres were sold to the University of Michigan, which until then had been located in Detroit.

Besides being a college town, Ann Arbor was a regional transportation hub in the mid-1800s. It also was a stop on the Underground Railroad during the Civil War and later a part of the anti-war movement of the 1960s.

Nearby Ypsilanti was originally a trading post in the early 1800s. It is best known as the place where, in 1960, Tom Monaghan borrowed $500 to buy DomiNick's, a small pizza store in town. Five years later he renamed his place Domino's. You know the rest of the story.

Where to Stay

RV PARKS

KC Campground: Country setting 12 miles from Ann Arbor, with 100 campsites, plus picnic areas, arcade, playground, swimming pool, and bath house. There's also a small camp store on-site. It will cost you $25 to stay here. (*14048 Sherman Rd., Milan, (734) 439-1076, kccampgroundmilan.com*)

KOA Detroit/Greenfield: On a private spring-fed lake, this campsite offers 207 sites, fishing, mini golf, and groceries for your last minute tailgate supplies. Daily rates run $30–$36. Kamping Kabins available. (*6680 Bunton Rd., Ypsilanti, (734) 482-7722, koa.com/where/mi/22178*)

Wayne County Fairgrounds and RV Park: Just a few miles from Ypsilanti, and a half hour from downtown Detroit, this park has 120 sites. It has the usual amenities, a dump station, and sports field/basketball court. Rates are $18–$22 for four people. (*10871 Quirk Rd., Belleville, (734) 697-7002, waynecountyfair.net*)

For more information: For additional RV parks and campsites visit campingworld.com/campsearch.

HOTELS

Bell Tower Hotel: Awarded the Outstanding Historic Preservation award, this hotel offers Old

World elegance and is decorated in classic English style. The hotel has standard rooms and suites. If you want to work out, you can use the University of Michigan's fitness facility. Rates run $191–$297. (*300 S. Thayer, Ann Arbor, (800) 562-3559, belltowerhotel.com*)

Lamp Post Inn: Close to campus, rooms here feature microwave ovens and refrigerators, or a full kitchenette. They must do something right; they say 90 percent of their guests are repeat customers. Rooms cost $45–$60, or $75–$90 when there are events in town. (*2424 E. Stadium Ave., Ann Arbor, (734) 971-8000, lamppostinn.com*)

Ypsilanti Marriott: We're breaking our rule about chain hotels here, but we don't have much of a choice. This is the only hotel in Ypsilanti. It's part of the **Eagle Crest Conference Resort,** which also includes Eastern Michigan University's conference center and a golf course. Rooms run $149 weekdays, and $89 on weekends. (*1275 S. Huron St., Ypsilanti, (734) 487-2000, eaglecrestresort.com*)

For more information: To learn about more hotels in the area visit tripadvisor.com for listings and guest reviews.

EASTERN MICHIGAN UNIVERSITY
Rynearson Stadium
Ypsilanti, Michigan
(734) 487-2282

Parking is free; leave glass containers and kegs at home. Leave by nightfall. Not many people tailgate here, so plenty of room for you.

Eagles Media Partners: 89.1-FM WEMU, 1600-AM WAAM

B&BS

Ann Arbor Bed and Breakfast: This 1962 contemporary chalet overlooks the Michigan campus and has nine uniquely furnished guest rooms, all with private baths. Most rooms have a private patio or balcony, and two have kitchenettes. They also have covered parking. No children under 10 years old. Rooms cost $129–$159. (*921 E. Huron St., Ann Arbor, (734) 994-9100, annarborbedandbreakfast.com*)

Parish House Inn: *Inn Traveler Magazine* named this B&B one of the top 15 located near a college or university. The Queen Anne–style house was built as a parsonage in 1893, and it was moved to its current location in 1987. The house has eight guest rooms with private baths. There's also a river-walk garden on the property. Rooms run $93–$165. (*103 S. Huron St., Ypsilanti, (800) 480-4866, parishhouseinn.com*)

For more information: To learn about more B&Bs in the area visit bedandbreakfast.com for a detailed directory.

Where to Eat

TAILGATER GROCERIES

Zingerman's Delicatessen: Located near the year-round **Ann Arbor Farmers' Market,** where you'll also find items for your tailgate, Zingerman's is a local institution. It stocks hearth-baked breads, farmhouse cheeses, estate-bottled olive oils, smoked fish, salami, coffee, tea, and more. (*422 Detroit St., Ann Arbor, (734) 663-3354, zingermans.com*)

Carving the bird in Ann Arbor. (Photo: Perry Calandrino)

SPORTS BARS

The Arena Sports Bar: They call themselves "the Restaurant of Champions." The Arena's menu has burgers and such, as you would expect from a sports bar. It also has seafood, pasta, and steak. Of course, it's a sports bar, so they have the requisite TVs. (*$, 203 E. Washington St., Ann Arbor, (734) 222-9999, thearenasportsbar.com*)

Enzo's Sports Bar & More: Three projection screens and 20 other TVs throughout the bar, as well as pool tables and video games, provide the ambiance. Pretty typical sports bar menu. If you're here during the week, Monday is poker night, Tuesday is karaoke, and live bands play fairly often. (*$, 3965 S. State St., Ann Arbor, (734) 665-1600, enzossportsbarandmore.com*)

RESTAURANTS

Aubree's: Aubree's is really three places in one. On the main floor of this historic 1870s building is, well, Aubree's itself, a popular hangout for students and locals that serves everything from pasta to burgers to salads. Upstairs is **Sticks Pool & Pub,** where you can play on one of six pool tables. If you go out back and up another level, you'll find the **Tiki Rooftop Bar,** which is open from March until it's too cold. (*$, 39-41 E. Cross St., Ypsilanti, (734) 483-1870, aubrees.com*)

Bella Ciao: The regional Italian menu here offers both heart-healthy choices and richer dishes in a cozy dining room. Try the lobster ravioli, pancetta-wrapped shrimp, or the roasted chicken. The wine list covers just about every region of Italy. (*$$, 118 W. Liberty St., Ann Arbor, (734) 995-2107, bellaciao.com*)

Zingerman's Roadhouse: The menu here covers everything from burgers and steak, to pasta and blue plate specials. But it's their fish they are most proud of. They offer selections as varied as escolar, shad, and walleye—plus salmon and other fish with which you might be more familiar. This locale is part of the local Zingerman restaurant "empire" that include a deli (see page 11), a bakehouse, coffee wholesaler, and more. (*$, 2501 Jackson Ave., Ann Arbor, (734) 663- 3663, zingermansroadhouse.com*)

For more information: For a directory of additional places to eat in the area visit opentable.com. You can also book a reservation for many restaurants on the site.

What to Do

DURING THE DAY

Matthaei Botanical Gardens & Nichols Arboretum: This 300-acre site offers outdoor display gardens, miles of nature trails, and a spacious indoor conservatory of three distinct climates: tropical rainforest, Mediterranean, and desert. The Nichols Arboretum is a 123-acre living museum nestled in the hills next to the University of Michigan's central campus. (*$, 1800 N. Dixboro, University of Michigan campus, Ann Arbor, (734) 998-7061, sitemaker.umich.edu/mbgna*)

Michigan Firehouse Museum: From horse-drawn pumps to bright red fire engines, the museum preserves Michigan's firefighting history and promotes fire safety. Exhibits also include bells, equipment, and even toy fire trucks. (*$, 110 W. Cross St., Ypsilanti, (734) 547-0663, michiganfirehousemuseum.org*)

University of Michigan Museum of Art: This is one of the top 10 university art museums in the country. It houses pieces from Picasso to Rembrandt, Whistler to Cézanne. Exhibits also include African sculpture, contemporary photography, and a Japanese gallery. It's current location—the 1910 Beaux Arts–style Alumni Memorial Hall—is undergoing renovation, so until mid-2008 the museum is exhibiting from a temporary location adjacent to campus. (*Free, Temporary location: 1301 S. University Ave., [Permanent location: 525 S. State St.], Ann Arbor, (734) 764-0395, umma.umich.edu*)

AT NIGHT

Conor O'Neill's: To find this traditional Irish Pub, just look for the storefront that looks like it should be in Dublin. That's not by accident. The owners had the pub designed and built in Ireland. Irish food on the menu and beers such as Guinness, Murphy's, and Newcastle are on tap. Come on Sundays to hear Irish music. (*$, 318 S. Main, Ann Arbor, (734) 665–2968, conoroneills.com*)

Divine: This is Ypsilanti's hip nightspot. Theme nights, DJs playing Top 40 dance music, and a popular bar beckon. Upstairs is a VIP Lounge. You can also eat here. Open Wednesdays–Saturdays. (*$, 23 N. Washington St., Ypsilanti, (734) 485-4444, club-divine.com*)

The Matthaei Botanical Gardens & Nichols Arboretum. (Photo: Carine Lutz/Ann Arbor CVB)

Firefly Club: You'll find live jazz and blues here seven nights a week. The interior is subdued and comfortable, and, with touches like exposed brick, it has the feel of a nostalgic club. Full bar, but limited menu of appetizers and sandwiches. Smoking is allowed only in the bar. (*$, 207 S. Ashley St., Ann Arbor, (734) 665-9090, fireflyclub.com*)

SHOPPING

Main Street and State Street: Both are near the University of Michigan and in the downtown area. These blocks offer a variety of shops, eateries, and sightseeing. Main Street also has a number of galleries and museums. You can also print coupons for Main Street merchants from the Web site. (*Ann Arbor, mainstreetannarbor.org, a2state.com*)

Kerrytown District: Just north of downtown Ann Arbor, you'll find the **Farmers' Market** and the **Artisan Market,** as well as a variety of shops, restaurants, galleries, and a children's museum. (*Ann Arbor, www.kerrytown.org*)

Depot Town: This restored nineteenth-century shopping destination has scores of antique shops, boutiques, and other merchants. You'll also find restaurants, clubs, and a theater. There are a couple of places where you can get your hair cut, too, if you need it. (*E. Cross St. and Huron St., Ypsilanti, depottown.org*).

For more information: To learn more about things to do in the area visit cityguide.aol.com/annarbormi.

BROOKLYN

Brooklyn is primarily a small tourist town of historical interest. And it loves its racing.

When the Michigan International Speedway opened in 1968, it had a 12,000-seat grandstand overlooking the track, with a couple of smaller grandstands on either side. It sat 25,000, and track founder Lawrence LoPatin drew compliments for that fact, as well as for bringing racing to the Irish Hills.

Today the Speedway seats 137,243, and since 1992 its NEXTEL Cup races have been the state's largest, single-day, paid-admission sporting event. It's also one of the biggest campsites you'll ever see.

There are seven campgrounds for RV tailgaters, plus the Speedway infield. Parking there will run you $75–$400 depending on which campground you choose. One thing to keep in mind is not all of the campgrounds are available for IRL race events. MIS will let you roll in early in the week to get the most out of your racing tailgating. Call (800) 354-1010 for details for specific lots and to reserve your space—that is a must. No drive-up sales here.

If you're not staying for the week, you can tailgate in the parking lot on race day. It's free, but there is no overnight parking. If you put up tents, set out chairs, and the like, be sure to pack them up before heading to your seats. If you don't, there's a really good chance they'll be gone when you get back. Security will confiscate it all.

Free trams run from the perimeter parking lots to drop-off spots on the north and south sides of the track. Once there, you'll want to visit the AAA Motorsports Fan Plaza. The Plaza encompasses 26 acres and includes interactive display areas, vendors, activities, and the Walk of Champions.

Where to Stay

RV PARKS

Greenbriar RV Park and Golf Course: Located just five miles from the Speedway, and close to **Mystery Hill** (see page 15) and several lakes for fishing, this RV park has the usual amenities. It also features a heated pool, nature trails, and golf (of course). Rates run $27–$45. (*14820 Wellwood Rd., Brooklyn, (517) 592-6943, greenbriarcampground.com*)

For more information: For additional RV parks and campsites visit campingworld.com/campsearch.

HOTELS

Super 8: We know, it's a chain, but it's the only hotel in Brooklyn. It's just three miles from the Speedway. Rooms run $139–$151, but do your booking via some online sites and you can get rooms for as little as $57. (*155 Wamplers Lake Rd., Brooklyn, (517) 592-0888, super8.com*)

For more information: To learn about more hotels in the area visit tripadvisor.com for listings and guest reviews.

B&BS

Bed of Roses: Decorated in the Victorian style, the house has four rooms and offers massages (by appointment). It's close to the Speedway and to several lakes for boating and fishing. Rooms cost $89–$149. (*10926 U.S. Hwy 12, Brooklyn, (888) 356-5325, bedofroses.us*)

Chicago Street Inn: This Queen Anne–style home was built in 1886 and still has some of the original touches such as English stained-glass windows and fireplace tile. There are three rooms with Jacuzzi tubs and fireplaces. All have private baths. The inn is just north of the Speedway. Rooms run $159–$169 based on the season. (*219 Chicago St., Brooklyn, (517) 592-3888, chicagostreetinn.com*)

For more information: To learn about more B&Bs in the area visit bedandbreakfast.com for a detailed directory.

Where to Eat

RESTAURANTS

Note: For the most part, restaurants in Brooklyn are chains. You will find places such as **Marco's Pizza** and **Poppa's Place,** but you might want to drive toward Ann Arbor if you're looking for more of a dining-style meal.

For more information: For a directory of additional places to eat in the area visit opentable.com. You can also book a reservation for many restaurants on the site.

What to Do

DURING THE DAY

Mystery Hill: They say it's mystifying. Baffling. You'll see water flow uphill and a chair that balances on a wall. You can decide for yourself how amazing that really is, but Mystery Hill can be a day of fun. In addition to the Mystery Hill tour, there's miniature golf and remote-control car racing. (*7611 U.S. Hwy. 12, Irish Hills, (517) 467-2517, mystery-hill.com*)

Fans at Michigan International Speedway. (Photo: MIS Archives)

Stagecoach Stop: It began 40 years ago as an antique museum, saloon, and restaurant, and it is now a "western resort and family fun park." There are rooms and cabins, restaurants, children's rides, and other activities to take you back to the Old West. (*$–$$, 7203 U.S. Hwy. 12 Irish Hills, Onsted, (517) 467-2300, stagecoachstop.com*)

For more information: To learn more about things to do in the area visit villiageofbrooklyn.com.

DETROIT

After three failed efforts to bring an NFL team to Motor City, Detroit radio executive George Richards in 1934 shelled out $8,000 (a jaw-dropping amount in those days) to buy the Portsmouth Spartans and move them from a little river town in Ohio to the big city. With the move came a new name: the Detroit Lions.

DETROIT LIONS

Ford Field
Detroit, Michigan
(800) 616-ROAR
(313) 831-5236 Handy, Mobile
(586) 784-1005 Park Right
(313) 832-8154 Eastern Market

All public parking handled by private companies. Each has own rules, which differ. The Lions' Web site recommends Eastern Market, as there's a shuttle. Get spaces in advance from city's Parking Department. More info at www.ci.detroit.mi.us/municipalpark/EasternMarket Tailgating2005.htm.

Shuttle Info: Detroit's bus system runs routes by Ford Field; log on to ci.detroit.mi.us/ddot/about.htm for details. You can also use the Detroit People Mover to get to the game from 13 stops in the downtown area; the fare is $0.50. Visit peoplemover.com for details and stop locations.

Lions Media Partner: 97.1-FM WKRK

The team shared a stadium (Tiger Stadium) with baseball's Detroit Tigers until 1975, when they moved to the suburbs to play in the enclosed Pontiac Silverdome. In 2002 they moved back downtown and into the state-of-the-art Ford Field.

Ford Field seats 65,000 and is in the heart of the downtown entertainment district.

Most of the lots nearest to Ford Field are reserved, but there are dozens of privately owned lots close by that sell spots to tailgaters on a first-come, first-served basis. Cost for these spaces varies based on how close they are to the stadium and what the owner thinks his space is worth.

The city also offers tailgating areas at the Eastern Market for $30 per space. If you have an RV or trailer that takes another space or two, it will cost you another $30–$60. You have to reserve these spots in advance (get the form at ci.detroit.mi.us/municipalpark). They do not sell spots for preseason games.

If you're not taking your car to the game, you can get to Ford Field on the Detroit People Mover. There are 13 stops in the downtown area. Get off at the Greektown, Broadway, or Grand Circus stations—they're closest to the stadium. The fare ranges from free to $0.50; log on to thepeoplemover.com for details. The city's bus service runs routes by Ford Field, too; visit ci.detroit.mi.us/ddot/about.htm to see the routes and fares.

Ford Field is home to the Detroit Lions. (Photo: Vito Palmisano)

About Detroit

In 1701 a French officer named Antoine de la Mothe Cadillac founded a fort and settlement on a strait along the Great Lakes waterway. No, he didn't build the car of the same name, but it turns out the settlement he built eventually became the city that built a lot of cars.

Detroit was incorporated as a city in 1815, and later that century a thriving carriage trade laid the groundwork for Henry Ford to build his first automobile in 1896. Later, people with names such as Dodge and Chevrolet came along and turned Detroit into Motor City.

Detroit also was home to Motown Records, which launched the Motown Sound. It is also home to companies such as Borders Books and Little Caesars Pizza.

Where to Stay

RV PARKS

Note: There aren't any RV parks in Detroit, as you might expect, but you can find some outside the city limits. In addition to the one below, the parks listed for Ann Arbor and Ypsilanti are similar distances from Detroit, just on the U.S. side of the Canadian border.

Wildwood Golf and R.V. Resort: Just across the border (remember to bring a passport or proper ID) in the Windsor, Ontario, area is this "Florida Style Resort" in Canada. There's an 18-hole golf course, as well as 385 RV sites. Wildwood accepts only full hookup units. It has the usual amenities as well as a controlled-access gate for security. Daily rates are $32 CAN. (*11112, 11th Concession Rd., RR#1, McGregor, Ontario, (866) 994-9699, golfwindsorweb.com—click on "Windsor Directory"*)

For more information: For additional RV parks and campsites visit campingworld.com/campsearch.

HOTELS

Hotel Pontchartrain: Built on the site of Detroit's first permanent settlement, Fort Pontchartrain, rooms here have views of the skyline and the Detroit River. The rooms have the amenities you'd expect, and the building has a restaurant and a fitness center and is close to a People Mover station. It's about a five-minute walk from Ford Field. Rooms average $129–$139. (*Two Washington Blvd., Detroit, (313) 965-0200, hotelpontch.com*)

The Antheneum: This all-suite hotel is in downtown's Greektown, steps away from shopping, restaurants, and bars. It's also adjacent to **Greektown Casino** (see page 19). Rooms offer skyline views, marble bathrooms with whirlpool or deep soaking tubs, and the amenities you'd expect from a four-diamond hotel. It's a short walk to Ford Field, but you can also take the hotel's shuttle. A room costs $179–$325. (*1000 Brush Ave., Detroit, (800) 772-2323, atheneumsuites.com*)

For more information: To learn about more hotels in the area visit tripadvisor.com for listings and guest reviews.

B&BS

The Inn on Ferry Street.
(Photo: Inn on Ferry Street)

Inn on Ferry Street: Located in Detroit's cultural district, which is currently undergoing a renaissance, this group of restored Victorian homes built in the late 19th century offers 40 rooms and two carriage houses. Many of the amenities are more like a hotel than many B&Bs. Rooms run $105–$159. (*84 E. Ferry St., Detroit, (313) 871-6000, innonferrystreet.com*)

The Woodbridge STAR: Located in one of the oldest neighborhoods in Detroit, this 1891 Victorian home began its life as a private residence, then became a church. Around 1970 it became a residence again. There are three guest rooms and three suites, all with private baths. Rates are discounted by how many nights you stay, but if you stay two nights they'll run $105–$150. (*3985 Trumbull Ave., Detroit, (313) 831-9668, woodbridgestar.com*)

For more information: To learn about more B&Bs in the area visit bedandbreakfast.com for a detailed directory.

Where to Eat

TAILGATER GROCERIES

Eastern Market: Just a few blocks from Ford Field, this 200-year-old market is open every day but Sunday—on game-day Sundays they use the lots for tailgating (see page 16). This historic open-air market offers everything from fresh produce and meats to condiments and candy. (*2934 Russell St., Detroit, (313) 833-1560, easternmarket.org*)

SPORTS BARS

Cobo Joe's Sports Bar & Grill: This place was rocking for Super Bowl XL. Why? Because the Steelers were in town, and Cobo Joe's bills itself as a "black and gold establishment." It provides a typical sports bar menu and TVs to watch games featuring teams other than the Steelers, too. (*$, 422 W. Congress, Detroit, (313) 965-0840, cobojoes.com*)

The Karras Bros. Tavern: This is a smoke-free sports bar just a couple of blocks from the river near downtown. It has a 7-foot big screen and other TVs. The tavern offers a basic bar menu and a diverse beer selection. (*$, 225 Joseph Campau, Detroit, (313) 259-2767, karrasbros.com*)

RESTAURANTS

Magnolia: This popular restaurant serves up honest-to-goodness soul food in a downtown supper-club setting. Generous servings are offered of traditional favorites such as baby back ribs, chicken-fried steak, and pork loin chops, with fried okra, yams, or greens on the side. (*$, 1440 E. Franklin St., Detroit, (313) 393-0018, magnoliaofdetroit.com*)

Rattlesnake Club: This riverside restaurant features great views of the skyline and riverfront. The menu is creative, with dishes such as Porcini Crusted Hawaiian Yellowfin Tuna and Cabernet Glazed Prime Angus Beef Short Ribs. You might also want to try their original martinis. (*$$, 300 River Place Dr., Detroit, (313) 567-4400, rattlesnakeclub.com*)

Roma Café: This is Detroit's oldest Italian restaurant; it's been open since the 1890s. Located in the **Eastern Market,** Roma Café is in a pretty nondescript building, but it serves traditional Italian favorites, prepared fresh. If you've been open for more than 100 years, you've been doing something right. (*$–$$, 3401 Riopelle St., Detroit, (313) 831-5940, romacafe.com*)

For more information: For a directory of additional places to eat in the area visit opentable.com. You can also book a reservation for many restaurants on the site.

What to Do

DURING THE DAY

Automotive Hall of Fame: Truly a feast for car lovers, this museum—adjacent to the **Henry Ford Museum and Greenfield Village** (see page 19)—has profiles of the men behind the machines, a mural of automotive history, and a replica of the world's first gas-powered car. Organized in 1939, the Hall of Fame honors inductees ranging from Henry Ford, to Mario Andretti, to Ferdinand von Zeppelin (yep, that Zeppelin). (*$, 21400 Oakwood Blvd., Dearborn, (888) 298-4748, automotivehalloffame.org*)

Detroit Institute of Arts: This is the fifth largest fine arts museum in the United States, with more

The Ultimate Tailgater's Travel Guide

than 100 galleries filling 600,000 square feet (and an expansion underway as of 2006 to add 77,000 more). Founded in 1885, it moved into its current Beaux-Arts building location in 1927. A hallmark of the museum is the diversity of its collection, from van Gogh, to a rare Korean Head of Buddha, to Diego Rivera's *Detroit Industry*. (*$, 5200 Woodward Ave., Detroit, (313) 833-7900, dia.org*)

The Greenfield Village at the Henry Ford Museum. (Photo: The Henry Ford)

Henry Ford Museum and Greenfield Village: Billed as a history destination that brings the American experience to life, these are two separate entities that occupy the same space. Greenfield Village charts 300 years of American history by preserving famous historic structures, while the Henry Ford Museum showcases the people and ideas that have changed the course of our lives—and not just with cars. Exhibits include everything from homes to planes. Includes an IMAX Theater. (*$$–$$$, 20900 Oakwood Blvd., Dearborn, (313) 271-1620, hfmgv.org*)

AT NIGHT

Bert's Jazz Marketplace: Five minutes from downtown in the **Eastern Market,** Bert's is a late-night club that's straight-up jazz. It's a pretty small venue, but the club has a reputation for attracting some of the best jazz musicians in the world. The menu is soul food, along with barbecue ribs. (*Admission varies, 2727 Russell, Detroit, (313) 567-2030*)

Greektown Casino: You'll find Vegas-style gaming, dining, and entertainment at this casino located in historic Greektown. It's near a number of restaurants and other attractions, too. (*555 E. Lafayette Ave., Detroit, (888) 771-4386, greektowncasino.com*)

The Majestic Theater Center: What you have here is a city block with a restaurant, a pizza joint, two live music venues, five bars, and bowling. **Garden Bowl** is the nation's oldest active bowling center and home to Rock 'N' Bowl (the kind with the neon lights). (*$–$$, 4120-4140 Woodward Ave., Detroit, (313) 833-9700, majesticdetroit.com*)

SHOPPING

Pewabic Pottery: Founded in 1903 during the Arts and Crafts Movement, brilliantly glazed ceramic Pewabic tiles can be found in buildings throughout the nation, including the Detroit Public Library and Washington's National Cathedral. You can buy items for your house or visit the shop for unique gifts. (*10125 E. Jefferson Ave., Detroit, (313) 822-0954, pewabic.com*)

GM Renaissance Center: The world headquarters of General Motors is located in five glass towers that also house a hotel, offices, homes, restaurants, and shops. There are two levels of shops. The **Ren Cen Shops** include national brands and local merchants. There's also a theater and a food court. (*E. Jefferson Ave. at Beaubien St., Detroit, (313) 568-5600, property-website.com/sites/82/live/—click on "Property Directory"*)

For more information: To learn more about things to do in the area visit cityguide.aol.com/detroit.

Austin

This place rocked at football games long before the Texas Longhorns became national champions for the fourth time by winning the 2006 Rose Bowl. Football is huge in Texas—from Pop Warner to high school, from college to the pros—and no place has the fever like Austin.

More than 50,000 students roam the UT campus, and the school is highly regarded for its academic rankings. But the football rankings are why Texas, Bevo, and those Hook 'em Horns are known across America.

Bevo might be the best-known mascot in the country. At least the heaviest. You know the legend of how the Longhorn mascot got his name, about how a group of rival Texas A&M pranksters branded the score of a game the Aggies won on the Texas mascot. The score was 13-0. UT students, to avoid prolonged embarrassment, converted the 13 into a B, the dash into an e, stuck in a v, and with the 0 it spelled Bevo.

Never happened.

Actually, the original Bevo was presented to the students and alumni of the university in 1916 at halftime of a Texas A&M–Texas game won by the 'Horns, 22-7. The editor of the *Texas Exes Alcalae* magazine, in his rushed-to-press story celebrating the new, live mascot, wrote: "His name is Bevo. Long may he reign!" There are several theories why he picked that name, but no one is sure.

In 1917 some A&M students did in fact brand the steer with the famous 13-0 score (which was from the 1915 game), but it had nothing to do with naming it Bevo.

Bevo now roams the field at the Darrell K. Royal–Memorial Stadium, which officially seats 80,082, although they often squeeze in another 3,000 or so for big games.

All those people, including you, have several parking options. (There's a map of parking lots at utexas.edu/parking/maps.) There are five surface lots that cost from $8 to $10. If you're not setting up your own tailgate party, you can also park in one of three garages for $8.

RV parking is allowed in Lots 110, 113, and 114, but the Longhorn Foundation controls these lots, so unless you're a member you'll have a tough time getting a spot. (No harm giving it a shot: call The Longhorn Foundation at (512) 471-4439.)

However, you can reserve a spot in Lot 115 for $100. To get an application, go to mackbrown-texasfootball.com, click on "Gameday/Parking," then click on the link in the RV Parking section.

If you don't have a car, $2 will get you a round-trip

ticket on one of two shuttles running to the stadium. The 51st Street Shuttle picks up riders at the UT Intramural Fields parking lot, and the Barton Creek Shuttle boards in front of Dillard's at the Barton Creek Mall. Log onto capmetro.org for details.

About Austin

Nestled in the heart of the Texas Hill Country—arguably the prettiest landscape in the state, with hills, valleys, lakes, and rivers forming the geography—the area was originally a buffalo-hunting ground. The first Anglo colonists—led by Texas's founding father Stephen F. Austin—settled here in 1822 on the lower Colorado River. They picked a locale near a large underground spring that was the site of an old sixteenth-century Spanish mission. But it wasn't until Texas President Mirabeau B. Lamar (Texas wasn't a state then, it was a country, the Republic of Texas) decided to move the seat of government from Houston to the settlement then known as Waterloo in 1838 that things really took off.

UNIVERSITY OF TEXAS
Darrell K Royal—Texas Memorial Stadium
Austin, Texas
(800) 982-2386 ticket office
(512) 471-4441 UT police

Lots surrounding stadium reserved for Longhorn Foundation members. Visitor parking $8; RVs stay in Lot 115; cost is $100.

Shuttle Info: Capital Metro runs two shuttle routes for games: the 51st Street Shuttle and the Barton Creek Shuttle. Round trip will cost you $2; children under six ride free. Visit capmetro.org for complete details and schedules.

Longhorns Media Partners: 98.1-FM and 1300-AM KVET, 1440-AM KELG (Spanish)

Renamed Austin (as in Stephen F.), work on a capitol building began in 1839. That was the same year the Congress of the Republic ordered the establishment of a college and set aside land for what would become the University of Texas.

The population of Austin has doubled every twenty years since its establishment, making it now the sixteenth-largest city in the United States, with 675,000 people living within the city limits, and 1.2 million in the total metropolitan area. The city is consistently found on "Best City" lists. Credit that to the nice climate, low unemployment, low cost of living, and a famed laid-back lifestyle that's lured both business (including Dell Computers) and culture. It's also known as the Live Music Capital of the World, a reputation born in the jazz and blues clubs of the 1920s and '30s. It continues today in the clubs along Sixth Street and other areas, where you can hear just about any kind of sound you like.

Where to Stay

RV PARKS

Austin Lone Star RV Resort: Located five miles south of downtown on I-35, the sites here are spacious pull-throughs with full hookups. Phone hookup is available on premium sites, and WiFi access is available for an added fee. Other features include an on-site lodge with full-service restaurant, heated swimming pool, and enclosed hot tub. A great plus for tailgaters is the mini-grocery store, where you can pick up supplies on the way to the stadium. All of this will cost you $26–$47. (*7009 S. Interstate Hwy. 35, Austin, (512) 444-6322, austinlonestar.com*)

La Hacienda RV Resort and Cabins: La Hacienda offers 49 standard and 4 deluxe sites. The park has the basic amenities, WiFi, and daily trash pick up at your site. They also offer a concierge service, a

Bevo has been the UT mascot since 1916.
(Photo: University of Texas at Austin)

business center, and shower facilities built to ADA standards. Cabins are available, too. Rates here run $39–$47. (*5320 Hudson Bend Rd., Austin, (888) 378-7275, campingfriend.com/LaHaciendaRVPark*)

Oak Forest RV Park: There actually is a forest adjoining Oak Forest, even if it's only 15 acres. The park has a fenced-in dog play area, swimming pool, hot tub, game room, and handicapped-accessible shower facilities, as well as daily trash pickup, two laundries, and a library. Rates are $40, but discounts are available. (*8207 Canoga Ave., Austin, (512) 926-8984, oakforest-rvpark.com*)

Royal Palms RV Community: Royal Palms sits five miles from the Austin central business district and the University of Texas. The park offers standard amenities as well as paved and lighted streets with sidewalks, and lots of shade trees. The perimeter is fenced for enhanced security. Plenty of recreational options are offered, including a tennis/basketball/volleyball court. Daily rates are $26 for up to four people; add $4 per day for each additional person. (*7901 E. Ben White Blvd., Austin, (512) 385-2211, royalpalms.net*)

For more information: For additional RV parks and campsites visit campingworld.com/ campsearch.

HOTELS

Austin Motel: A throwback to another era (think 1950s), this funky little motel was built in 1938. Although it's been renovated, it retains its retro feel, including the bean-shaped pool. Located downtown, the motel is near a number of shops, and from here you can see the **State Capitol** building and the "bat bridge" (see page 26). Each room is individually decorated, and the adjacent Mexican restaurant is a popular spot for locals. Rooms run $85–$148. (*1220 S. Congress Ave., Austin, (512) 441-1157, austinmotel.com*)

The Driskill: Built in 1886 as the showplace of a cattle baron, this National Historic Register hotel has a phenomenal history of famous guests and events. A massive renovation in 1999 kept the cattle baron feel and decor of its original owner (including the stained-glass dome ceiling in the lobby), while putting modern technology in every room (including WiFi). There are two on-site restaurants run by chef David Bull; if he looks familiar, it might be because you saw him on *Iron Chef America* battling Bobby Flay. 24-hour room service, pool, spa, and health club. Rooms run $205–$300. (*604 Brazos St. (Sixth St.), Austin, (800) 252-9367, driskillhotel.com*)

Hotel San José: This 1930s motor court has been completely remodeled into an ultra-cool boutique hotel, with Mexico-meets-Zen decor. Because it is located just across the street from the fabled **Continental Club,** lots of musicians stay here. It's also just blocks from where the Colorado River cuts through the city. The rooms have individual patios, and you can hang out in the hotel gardens. Rates run $90–$200. (*1316 S. Congress Ave., Austin, (512) 444-7322, sanjosehotel.com*)

The Mansion at Judges Hill: The hotel encompasses a Victorian-era mansion originally presented as a wedding gift by Thomas Dudley Wooten, one of the founders of the University of Texas. It's within walking distance of the campus. Loaded with amenities, there is also a restaurant and lounge on-site. Rooms will run you $99–$299. (*1900 Rio Grande, Austin, (800) 311-1619, mansionatjudgeshill.com*)

For more information: To learn about more hotels in the area visit tripadvisor.com for listings and guest reviews.

B&BS

Austin Folk House Bed and Breakfast: This charming B&B has been consistently voted "Best of Austin," and offers everything you'd expect, including high-speed Internet access and much more. If you don't want to sleep alone, the house cocker spaniel makes an excellent sleeping partner, if you don't mind his snoring and taking up most of the bed—but he does cost $20 per night. Rooms run $85–$225 (without the dog). (*506 W. 22nd St., Austin, (866) 472-6700, austinfolkhouse.com*)

Inn at Pearl Street: A good choice if you want to add a little romantic getaway to your road trip. Be sure to request a room with a Jacuzzi or private balcony. There are plenty of pampering packages available. Rooms are available inside the main house or in separate cottages on the walled property for $89–$200. (*809 West MLK, Jr. Blvd. at Pearl St., Austin, (800) 494-2261, innpearl.com*)

For more information: To learn about more B&Bs in the area visit bedandbreakfast.com for a detailed directory.

The Driskill Hotel. (Photo: Austin CVB)

Where to Eat
TAILGATER GROCERIES

Central Market: Fresh produce, meats, seafood, and flowers, specialty food items, full-service deli, baked goods, and imports from all over the world can be found at both locations. You can also get meals to go for your tailgate. (*4001 N. Lamar Blvd., Austin, (512) 206-1000 and 4477 S. Lamar Blvd. (Westgate), Austin, (512) 899-4300, centralmarket.com*)

SPORTS BARS

Cain and Abel's: Sitting near the Greek fraternity area of the UT campus, this bar is considered by many to be the best place in town to watch a game. There are more than a dozen TVs, as well as pool and foosball tables, an upstairs deck, and a downstairs patio. The menu is typical sports bar. This is a college hangout, so expect a crowd that can get loud. (*$, 2313 Rio Grande St., Austin, (512) 476-3201, cainandabels.com*)

Fox and Hound Smokehouse & Tavern: Put simply, you're not going to miss any of the game here. They have big screens in the dining area and bar—and somewhat smaller screens in the bathrooms. Really. The menu is what you'd expect in a sports bar, but with names like Voodoo Jerk Chicken. And they have 30 beers on tap. You can play pool and darts, too. (*$, 401 Guadalupe St., Austin 78701, (512) 494-1200, tentcorp.com*)

Lavaca Street Bar: Located in the Warehouse District, Lavaca has a laid-back, informal

PEACH COBBLER

Austin is in the Texas Hill Country, which is also peach country. Your tailgate menu needs a dessert, right? Well, run by Central Market (see page 23), pick up some fresh peaches, and treat your friends to a traditional peach cobbler. (Make this dish the day before the game; you can use your grill—on low heat—to warm it up if you don't have access to an oven in an RV.)

4 tablespoons margarine

2 cups peeled, sliced peaches
 (about 3 medium peaches)

1 cup sugar (divided)

1/2 cup water

1/2 cup flour

1 1/2 teaspoons baking powder

1/2 teaspoon salt

1/2 cup milk

Preheat oven to 375°.

Place margarine in baking dish and melt in oven. Remove the baking dish from the oven when the margarine has melted.

Meanwhile, in a saucepan, heat the peaches, 1/2 cup sugar, and water until the sugar is dissolved. Bring to a boil. Mix the flour, baking powder, salt, rest of the sugar, and milk together in a mixing bowl and stir until smooth.

Blend the flour mixture into the melted margarine in the baking dish. Mix in the peach mixture, and bake for 20 to 30 minutes, until done.

Makes 8 –12 servings

atmosphere. You'll find plenty of televisions scattered around, along with pool tables and shuffleboard. (*$, 405 Lavaca St., Austin 78701, (512) 469-0106, lavacastreet.com*)

The Tavern: An Austin institution since 1916 (and built with European plans to look like a German public house), this tavern even serves breakfast. There are TVs everywhere, because the Tavern is headquarters for almost every sports fan club in town. Upstairs are the pool tables and video games. (*$, 912 W. 12th St., Austin, (512) 320-8377, austintavern.com*)

Texas Showdown Saloon: This place looks like a saloon should. Not a lot of TVs, but plenty of atmosphere, pool tables, and an outside beer garden. Plus, during football season, you get free hot dogs on game days. Close to UT. (*$, 2610 Guadalupe St., Austin, (512) 472-2010, showdownsoftexas.com/austin/games.cfm*)

RESTAURANTS

Dan McKlusky's Sixth Street: An Austin fixture since 1979, the menu features aged steaks, fresh seafood, and a variety of interesting side dishes. Parking can be tricky downtown, so take advantage of the valet. (*$$$, 301 E. Sixth St., Austin, (512) 473-8924, danmckluskys.com*)

Earl Campbell's BBQ Restaurant & Bar: This legendary gridiron star has filled his restaurant with memorabilia, including his Heisman Trophy (from 1977). The food's hearty, the portions are large, and there's more than barbecue on the menu. (*$, 212 W. Sixth, Austin, (512) 397-3275*)

Fino Restaurant Patio & Bar: The folks behind Austin's well-known **Asti** restaurant opened this casual Spanish place that features a spacious open dining room and a room with tall bistro tables. Tapas rule the menu. The creamy fried goat cheese with onion jam and honey is often recommended. Fino's has a good wine list, too. (*$, 2905 San Gabriel St., Austin, (512) 474-2905*)

Las Palmas: This traditional Mexican restaurant serves top-notch enchiladas—recently voted "Best of Austin"—and other northern Mexican favorites. You'll be able to spot Las Palmas by all the Christmas lights strung around the outside of the building. Well, at least you'll be able to notice that at night. *($, 1209 E. Seventh, Austin, (512) 457-4944)*

Manuel's: This isn't your usual Mexican place. The chile relleno covered in walnut-brandy-cream sauce will prove it. The menu features interior Mexican dishes (no Tex-Mex here). Sit in the back room, away from the lively bar, for a quieter meal. *($$, 310 Congress Ave., Austin, (512) 472-7555)*

Thistle Café on 6th: Tall ceilings, white tablecloths, and sleek. Thistle offers everything from crab cakes, to chicken enchiladas, to filet mignon. Locals will suggest finishing off your meal with the white chocolate and bing cherry bread pudding with a crème anglais. There's also a second location in the Davenport Village. *($$, 300 W. 6th St., Suite 103, Austin, (512) 275-9777, thistlecafe.com)*

For more information: For a directory of additional places to eat in the area visit opentable.com. You can also book a reservation for many restaurants on the site.

What to Do
DURING THE DAY

Aquarena Center: This nonprofit environmental learning center is dedicated to protecting and conserving the environment, as well as educating the public on the important role that water plays in daily life. The San Marcos Springs lake area is home to five endangered species, featured in a natural aquarium on the grounds. Other activities include nature trails and wetlands boardwalks, scientific diving, environmental education tours, and daily glass-bottomed boat tours. *($, 921 Aquarena Springs Dr., San Marcos, (512) 245-7570, aquarena.txstate.edu)*

The Texas State Capitol building. (Photo: Austin CVB)

Austin Duck: The Austin Duck is an amphibious vehicle that tours downtown Austin (the **State Capitol,** governor's mansion, historic Congress Avenue, and more) and then drives straight into Lake Austin for a floating view of the city. Tours fill up quickly, so call ahead for reservations. *($$, 1605 W. Fifth St., Austin, (512) 477-5274. Tickets are also sold inside the Austin Visitor Information Center, 209 E. Sixth St., austin-ducks.com)*

Austin Museum of Art: There are two museum locations. The original site is known as Laguna Gloria. It is in a 1916 Mediterranean-style lakeside villa and 14 acres of rolling, tree-shaded land surround it. The second location, downtown, is temporarily housed in an old bank building, while they raise money for a larger, permanent downtown location (that won't open until at least 2009). Inside both museums you'll find a collection of twentieth-century and contemporary paintings, sculptures, photographs, prints, and drawings, and temporary exhibits and programs. Each year the AMOA includes a show of new Texas artists, a children's exhibit, and multicultural exhibits. *($, Laguna Gloria: 3809 W. 35th, Austin, (512) 458-8191; Downtown: 823 Congress Ave., Austin, (512) 495-9224, amoa.org)*

Austin Zoo: The Austin Zoo is like most zoos in that you can enjoy the outdoors and get a close-up look at exotic animals from around the world. But it's unlike most zoos because it's a "rescue zoo"—more than 90 percent of the zoo's residents have been rescued from circuses, improper residences, and research laboratories. There's a shady picnic area for a family lunch, too. (*$, 10807 Rawhide Trail, Austin, (512) 288-1490, austinzoo.org*)

Congress Avenue Bridge: Why are we sending you to a bridge? Well, because one of the most amazing sights in Austin—or anywhere, for that matter—takes place every evening from March to early November here. That's when 1.5 million Mexican free-tailed bats emerge from their roosts under the Congress Avenue Bridge. Bats have lived in the bridge for years. When it was refurbished in 1980, so many bats came to roost that it is now the largest urban bat colony in North America. There are several great viewing spots, and a bat-watching boat cruise on Town Lake is available. Take an umbrella when you go, since the bats have a tendency to relieve themselves as they leave the bridge. (*Free, Downtown*)

Lyndon Baines Johnson Library and Museum: The LBJ Library houses 40 million pages of historical documents including papers from the entire public career of the 36th president of the United States, as well as documents from his close associates. The museum also has permanent historical and cultural exhibits, as well as changing exhibitions and special activities. (*Free, 2313 Red River St., Austin, (512) 721-0200, lbjlib.utexas.edu*)

State Capitol: Yep, things are bigger in Texas. The 1888 Texas State Capitol Building is the largest in gross square footage of all state capitols, and is taller, by some 15 feet, than the U.S. Capitol Building. The Renaissance Revival–style building is made of Texas pink granite and native limestone, and it was placed on the National Register of Historic Places in 1970, and then designated a National Historic Landmark in 1986. There are about 22 acres of surrounding grounds and 17 historic monuments. Be sure to stand in the center of the Rotunda and look up to see the Lone Star! (*Free, 1100 Congress at 11th St., Austin, (512) 475-3070, tspb.state.tx.us/SPB/Capitol/TexCap*)

University of Texas Tower: This 307-foot-tall historic monument is one of the tallest structures on the Austin skyline. The 27-story tower is located in the middle of the 40-acre college campus and houses 56 bells that chime on the quarter hour and hour. Longhorn victories are celebrated by bathing the tower with orange and white lights at night. The observation deck of the tower offers a spectacular view of the campus and the Austin area in all directions. Observation deck tours are available by reservation only through the Texas Union Information Center. (*$, 23rd St. and Guadalupe, Austin, 78705, (877) 475-6633, utexas.edu/tower*)

Wonder World: Texas's most visited cave has guided tours through the nation's only earthquake-formed cave. As you exit, ride the elevator to the peak of the 110-foot Tejas Observation Tower for a fantastic view of the Texas Hill Country. You can also take a train ride through the waterfalls of Mystery Mountain into the wildlife petting park, play in the Anti-Gravity House, shop in the Mexico World Import Marketplace, or just picnic on the grounds. (*$$, 100 Prospect St., San Marcos, take I-35 south to San Marcos, exit at mile marker 202, and follow the signs, (877) 492-4657, wonderworldpark.com*)

AT NIGHT

Antone's: A local institution, Antone's might well be Austin's most famous music venue. While they book

The LBJ Library and Museum.
(Photo: Austin CVB)

legendary blues and funk acts, the club also supports local artists. Live music seven nights a week. (*Admission varies, 213 W. 5th St., Austin, (512) 320-8424, antones.net*)

Elephant Room: This cozy bar below street level is consistently voted "Best Jazz Bar" in Austin. Drawing a hip, upscale crowd for live music every night of the year, the Elephant Room features local and national acts. (*$, 315 Congress Ave., Austin (512) 473-2279, natespace.com/elephant*)

Fadó: This is home to what might be Austin's largest Irish whiskey selection. The classic Irish pub also offers a variety of Irish brews and pub grub, including authentic fish and chips. Fadó's televisions are often tuned to live satellite feeds for Gaelic Games, Rugby, and English Premiere League Soccer for that authentic Irish sports fan in you. (*$, 214 W. 4th St., Austin, (512) 457-0172, fadoirishpub.com/fado_pub_main.php?city=austin*)

Oslo: *Condé Nast Traveler* says Oslo's is "a bastion of cool sophistication and Nordic serenity." Long and narrow, with minimalist retro '60s decor, this bar offers hip drinks and a diverse menu—including fondue. It's a more grown-up crowd than some of the other clubs nearby. Wednesday is all-day happy hour. (*$, 310 W. 6th St., Austin, (512) 480-9433, osloaustin.com*)

Sixth Street and the Warehouse Entertainment District: This is where the town comes alive when the sun goes down. There are a myriad of restaurants and live music nightspots from which to choose, including some of Austin's best live music venues like **Emo's, Stubb's,** and the **Red-Eyed Fly.** These are great blocks to hop from place-to-place for the night.

SHOPPING

SoCo: Its name is short for South Congress Avenue, and it's Austin's hottest, hippest area. Once just an empty warehouse district, it's been revitalized as artists and galleries have moved in to take advantage of cheap and plentiful space. Now SoCo is home to artisans (**Austin Art Glass** offers handblown glass), funky antiques (**New Bohemia** is like a garage sale, only better), and vintage clothing shops, interesting boutiques, restaurants, and clubs. Stop by **Amy's Ice Creams** for a treat.

Sixth Street at night. (Photo: Austin CVB)

The Drag: This is what the locals call the strip of business along Guadalupe Street, which borders the University of Texas. Many of Austin's coolest shops are here, including music stores, vintage clothing, and a variety of locally owned shops and restaurants. The outdoor **Renaissance Market** here has jewelry, clothing, and gifts made by Austin artisans.

26 Doors: This collection of quaint boutique stores is a cozy little shopping center with a variety of interesting shops and restaurants in Austin's Midtown shopping district. Pick up a cool gift for kids at **Root and Ridge Toymakers,** an unusual knickknack at **Telfair at Home,** and when you're ready for a break, stop in the **Waterloo Ice House.** (*1206 W. 38th St., Austin, (512) 451-8331*)

For more information: To learn more about things to do in the area visit cityguide.aol.com/austin.

Baltimore

The Baltimore Ravens helped heal a wound in the city that had been festering for 12 years. When they took the field in 1996, they helped ease the pain left over from how their beloved Colts had been snatched from them, literally packed up by the team owner and moved without warning to Indianapolis in 1984, shocking the city. When the Ravens, who used to be the Cleveland Browns before being moved to Baltimore (what goes around . . .), won Super Bowl XXXV, many in the city finally accepted their fate and embraced the Ravens.

Baltimore has had a colorful football history, which mirrors the city itself. More about the city in a bit, but let's start with the football.

After one failed attempt to launch an NFL team in the city, Baltimore got a second chance in 1953, when the league rewarded Baltimore with the downtrodden franchise that had been known as the Dallas Texans. The deal was, the NFL promised Baltimore that if it could sell 15,000 season tickets in six weeks, it would get the Texans. Within four weeks, the mission was accomplished and Baltimore had an NFL team once again.

For the next 30 years, the Colts captured the hearts of Baltimore football fans, winning several NFL championships behind the leadership of legendary quarterback Johnny Unitas and a cast of greats that also included Lenny Moore, Tom Matte, and Jim Parker. The Colts would eventually make it to the Super Bowl in 1969 and again in 1971, losing to Joe Namath and the Jets in the first game but coming back two years later to beat the Dallas Cowboys on a late field goal. No Colts team, to include the Indy version, has ever made it back to the Super Bowl, although Baltimore returned years later thanks to the Ravens.

When Baltimore got its third pro-football franchise, fans named it the Ravens, drawn from the best-known work of Baltimore's Edgar Allan Poe. The names it beat out: Marauders and Americans.

The Ravens play in M&T Bank Stadium, which seats 69,000 and is also home to the Marching Ravens, the largest marching band in the NFL. It's bigger than some college bands, too.

Tailgaters have 13 lots on-site, but you'll need a pass ahead of time, and you can't save spots for friends who might be coming later. If you want to tailgate together, you'd better show up together.

RVs park in Lot H (on the south side of the lot) and must arrive at least 3 hours before kickoff to get in. RVs are required to have two parking passes. If you have only one, you can buy the second when you enter the lot for $25.

No matter which lot you're in, you can't cook within

2 feet of your vehicle. There's also a 20-pound tank limit for gas grills. If you opted for charcoal, there are red barrels scattered throughout the lots for disposing of coals and ash. If you have questions about tailgating rules and regulations here, call (410) 230-8017.

If you're not parking and tailgating, there are bus shuttles and Light Rail trains to the stadium. Log on to mtamaryland.com for details.

But no matter how you get to the stadium, if you want to join a big party, amble over to the Ravens Walk. You'll find it along the walkway between the stadium and Oriole Park. You can't miss it. Just look for the Ravens cheerleaders (they're there to sign autographs and such). You'll also find face painting, food, drinks, and contests. You can also take your picture beside a three-foot-tall replica of the Lombardi Trophy, emblematic of the Super Bowl victory, or you can sit in a giant replica of the Ravens Super Bowl XXXV ring.

About Baltimore

Baltimore is home to a dazzling array of marine species and wildlife. It's been the site of ferocious battles and events that define our history and national identity. Here is the nation's *other* Ellis Island, with as many as two million immigrants landing in Baltimore to begin new lives. Here, also, is where, from 1808 to 1861, thousands of Africans were sold, or shipped to be resold, as slaves.

Like its football team, Baltimore has had a colorful past. In the 18th and 19th centuries Baltimore was the place to find a fast-sailing ship. In fact, the city turned out so many privateer vessels (aka "government-sanctioned pirate ships") at the end of the 1700s that Baltimore was on the British Navy's hit list. When the War of 1812 started, the top item on every admiral's agenda was "Burn Baltimore to the ground." Despite heavy fire, Baltimore refused to fall.

What the British Navy couldn't accomplish, fire did when Baltimore's business district was almost leveled by the Great Baltimore Fire in 1904. Since then, the city has weathered its share of booms and busts, such as the renewal of its charred business district and, on the other hand, the poverty of the Great Depression.

Right now the city is experiencing a boom. Its latest rebirth started during the 1970s and continues today as more than 14 million tourists visit "Bal'mer" and its surrounding attractions. Its progress has set a national standard for reclaiming troubled urban areas.

Today Baltimore's leading industries include shipbuilding, sugar and food processing, oil refining, and biotechnology. It's still a busy port, too.

BALTIMORE RAVENS
M&T Bank Stadium
Baltimore, Maryland
(410) 261-RAVE

There are 13 on-site lots at the stadium controlled by Maryland Stadium Authority. Tailgating is allowed on all on-site lots. Due to limited space, on-site parking sold by permit only. Visit Ravens Walk for pregame fun, various sponsored activities.

Shuttle Info: Light Rail train and shuttle bus service is provided to the stadium. Fares vary, but the Park & Ride Express Bus runs $12 round trip. Visit mtamaryland.com for details (click on "Sports/Special Event Services" and then on "Ravens").

Ravens Media Partners: 1300-AM ESPN Radio, 102.7-FM WQSR (Jack FM), WBFF-TV Channel 45 (FOX)

Ravens fans tailgating outside M&T Bank Stadium.
(Photo: RavensTailgating.com)

Where to Stay

RV PARKS

Bar Harbor RV Park & Marina: This small park, with 93 spots, is about a half-hour's drive from downtown Baltimore. You're close to the water here, with RV sites both next to and set back from the waterfront. Sites are a bit on the smallish side. A waterfront site will run you $40, and off-waterfront sites go for $37. Extra people over the age of five are an additional $4 per day. (*4228 Birch Ave., Abingdon, (800) 351-CAMP (2267), barharborrvpark.com*)

Patapsco Valley State Park (Hollofield Area): This 14,000-acre state park has 73 campsites available for RVs (some with electric hookups), a pet loop, and a camp store. It's just 15 minutes or so from downtown Baltimore. The upside here is that the rates are relatively cheap—$25 with electricity—and Hollofield allows pets with some restrictions. The downside is overnight camping ends at the end of October. (*8020 Baltimore National Pike, Ellicott City, (888) 432-2267, dnr.state.md.us/publiclands/central/patapscovalley.html*)

Ramblin' Pines Campground: Big sites and 200 of them. Ramblin' Pines is about 30 minutes from downtown Baltimore and it is a park that tries to always have activities for kids. Rate for full hookup is $40 with $5 for an extra person. A minimum two-night stay is required during weekends. (*801 Hoods Mill Rd., Woodbine, (800) 550-8733, ramblinpines.com*)

For more information: For additional RV parks and campsites visit campingworld.com/campsearch.

HOTELS

Admiral Fell Inn: This inn spans eight buildings built between 1790 and 1996. It was first a boardinghouse for sailors, later a YMCA, and then a vinegar bottling plant. Now it's an 80-room hotel with individually decorated rooms featuring Federal period furnishings. The inn offers some unusual aspects, like the three "resident ghosts" who lead children's activities or host ghost tours. There are also unofficial, but more authentic, ghosts residing on the third and fourth floors. The inn's rate for rooms is $219–$249. (*888 S. Broadway, Baltimore, (866) 583-4162, harbormagic.com*)

Brookshire Suites: This is a good place for families. The suites have smallish bedrooms but large sitting areas. Rates are calculated in packages, ranging from the $182 family package (a two-room suite with breakfast for two adults and two kids) to the deluxe romance package for $357 (a two-room suite and a bunch of added amenities). Want a room without the family or romance? That'll run you $172. (*120 E. Lombard St, Baltimore, (866) 583-4162, harbormagic.com*)

Harbor Court: One of the most prestigious hotels in Baltimore, the Harbor Court is decorated in English country opulence, with a grand spiral staircase dominating the lobby. All guests get TVs in the bathrooms. Higher-end rooms get 6-foot marble tubs with separate shower. If you're a sound sleeper, get a room with a harbor view. Light sleepers will be happier with the quieter courtyard rooms. Rooms run $340–$390, and suites range from $540 to $780. (*550 Light St., Baltimore, (800) 824-0076, harborcourt.com*)

For more information: To learn about more hotels in the area visit tripadvisor.com for listings and guest reviews.

B&BS

Gramercy Mansion: A Tudor-style mansion on 45 manicured acres, Gramercy has 11 guest rooms, ranging in price from $75 to $350. The cheaper rooms are just fine, but the high-end rooms look like something out of a movie. A good movie. (*1400 Greenspring Valley Rd., Baltimore, (800) 553-3404, gramercymansion.com*)

Inn at 2920: The Inn is a brick townhouse located in Baltimore's Canton neighborhood, and it offers four rooms and one two-room suite. All are contemporary designs and have hypoallergenic bedding, WiFi, and a personal beta fish. Rooms go for $155–$255. (*2920 Elliott St., Baltimore, (800) 774-2920, theinnat2920.com*)

The Ravens Tailgating group includes live music at its parking lot parties. (Photo: RavensTailgating.com)

Wilson House Bed and Breakfast: This is a rambling, four-story Victorian mansion with 10 guest rooms. However, while Victorian, it looks more like it would've been built from 1900 to the 1930s—a mix of Victorian and Edwardian furniture, assorted paintings on the walls, and oriental rugs covering wood floors. Rooms run $85–$125. One note: the Wilson House does not take credit cards. (*2100 Mt. Royal Terrace, Baltimore, (410) 383-6267, wilson-house.net*)

For more information: To learn about more B&Bs in the area visit bedandbreakfast.com for a detailed directory.

Where to Eat

TAILGATER GROCERIES

Lexington Market: Founded in 1782, the Lexington Market bills itself as the world's largest, continuously running market. The market houses 140 merchants and in 2006 was preparing to undergo another major renovation. You'll find fish markets, bakeries, delicatessens, grocers, international food purveyors, fresh produce, and much more here. (*400 W. Lexington St., Baltimore, (410) 685-6169, lexingtonmarket.com*)

SPORTS BARS

ESPN Zone: Like other cities with an ESPN Zone, this one is a bit of a tourist spot, but it takes its sports seriously and you'll be able to watch the games while eating from a menu a couple notches up from what most sports bars offer. (*$$, 601 E. Pratt St., Baltimore, (410) 685-3776, espnzone.com*)

Looney's Pub: It's everything a sports bar should be: casual, loud, and fun. Oh, lots of TVs, too—34 of them hooked to satellites; three of them are big-screen. Baskets of shrimp simmered in beer and encrusted with Baltimore's ever-present Old Bay seasoning highlight the local-flavored menu. (*$, 2900 O'Donnell St., Canton, (410) 675-9235, looneyspub.com*)

Mother's Federal Hill Grille: Big window, big-screen TVs, pool tables, and a short walk from M&T Bank Stadium make this a winning spot. When the Ravens play, the party spills out onto a small deck and the parking lot for a tailgate party. The menu offers everything from vegan veggie wraps, chicken marsala, and sandwiches, to homemade ice cream. (*$, 1113 S. Charles St., Baltimore, (410) 244-8686, federalhillrestaurants.com*)

FRIED SOFT SHELL CRABS

The folks at Cantler's Riverside Inn know crabs. Annapolis watermen bring a fresh catch in daily here, and you can have them prepared any number of ways (see page 37). Here's a quick, easy recipe from the chefs at Cantler's for soft shell crabs you can prepare at your tailgate party. (Be sure to carefully dispose of the remaining oil.)

1 cup pancake flour
1 teaspoon seafood seasoning
12 Maryland soft shell crabs
Cooking oil

Mix together the pancake flour and seafood seasoning. Dredge the crabs in the flour mixture to coat well.

In a large frying pan (or an electric skillet) heat about 1 inch of cooking oil to 375°. Carefully place the crabs into the oil and cook until browned, about 5 minutes on each side.

Makes 6 to 10 servings

RESTAURANTS

Bertha's Restaurant & Bar: It's fun, it's funky, and it's the real thing—a waterfront tavern full of memorabilia and knickknacks. Bertha's is famous for serving huge bowls of tasty, steamed wild mussels accompanied by a variety of dipping sauces, but you can get other things, of course. Bertha's serves afternoon tea (reservation only) and Sunday brunch, too. The bar area features live blues and jazz. (*$, 734 S. Broadway, Baltimore, (410) 327-5795, berthas.com*)

Brass Elephant: Known as a newshound's watering hole, this regal relic is a throwback to another era—in a good way. After all, you'll be dining under Tiffany skylights. The menu includes dishes such as coq au vin and filet of beef. And in keeping with that other era theme—guys, you have to wear a jacket to get in (and we don't mean the one with the Ravens logo on it). (*$$, 924 N. Charles St., Baltimore, (410) 547-8485, brasselephant.com*)

The Helmand: A perennial on Baltimore "Best of" lists, the Helmand is owned by Qayum Karzai, brother of Afghanistan President Hamid Karzai. But don't go just for the gee-whiz factor. The Helmand serves Afghan fare such as the *chopan* (charcoaled rack of lamb) and the *kaddo* appetizer (a sweet-and-pungent pumpkin dish). Beautiful woven textiles and traditional dresses adorn the walls, adding spice to the pure white table settings. (*$$, 806 N. Charles St., Baltimore, (410) 752-0311, helmand.com*)

Mama's on the Half Shell: This is just good, down-home seafood. Of course, one glance at the name and you know the main dish. And there're a million ways to get your oysters here: grilled, Rockefeller, wrapped in bacon, raw, deep-fried, done up as a shooter—okay, not a million, but you get the idea. Sit downstairs at the ultra-casual bar or upstairs in the dining room. Mama's is filled with unique memorabilia that gives it an eccentric touch. (*$, 2901 O'Donnell St., Baltimore, (410) 276-3160, mamasonthehalfshell.com*)

Obrycki's Crab House: You're in Baltimore, which means you have to eat crab. You just do. And this is a good place to do it. Located in the historic-yet-hip Fell's Point neighborhood, this is the quintessential crab house, where you can crack open steamed crabs or choose crab soup, crab cocktail, crab balls, crab cakes, crab imperial, or soft-shell crabs. They have other things on the menu—but you're not going to care. One note, Obrycki's is a seasonal restaurant, opening in mid-March and closing between mid-November and mid-December, based on whenever the owner wants to shut the doors for the year. (*$–$$, 1727 E. Pratt St., Baltimore, (410) 732-6399, obryckis.com*)

For more information: For a directory of additional places to eat in the area visit opentable.com. You can also book a reservation for many restaurants on the site.

What to Do

DURING THE DAY

Fort McHenry. (Photo: Baltimore Area CVA)

American Visionary Art Museum: This isn't your normal art museum. This is a museum dedicated to "outsider" art: visual works by largely self-taught and occasionally unbalanced, or at the very least eccentric, folks. Some pieces might strike you as amateurish, some will intrigue you with their strange beauty, and some are just plain weird. (*$, 800 Key Hwy., Baltimore, (410) 244-1900, avam.org*)

Fell's Point Ghostwalk: There are some ghost stories, but the Ghostwalk is just another way of telling Fell's Point's history as a shipbuilding town and port of entry for immigrants for more than a century. The entertaining tour is intertwined with stories about black ship caulkers, typhoid outbreaks, Edgar Allan Poe, and the War of 1812. Tours run February–November. (*$$, 731 S. Broadway, Baltimore, (410) 522-7400, fellspointghost.com*)

Fort McHenry: Yes, this is the fort where the banner still waved, even after a night of heavy bombing and artillery fire during the War of 1812 (although it was 1814 by then) and inspired Francis Scott Key to write "The Star-Spangled Banner." The massive, vaguely star-shaped earthworks surrounding the fort are impressive. (*$, 2400 East Fort Ave., Baltimore, (410) 962-4290, nps.gov/fomc*)

National Aquarium in Baltimore: If you have time to hit just one attraction, this would be a good choice. From the glass floors with skates gliding underfoot, to the shark tanks, to the upland rain forest, this is a wonderful aquarium. In addition to the fish, there are numerous birds, including puffins, as well as turtles, lizards and other reptiles, and even two-toed sloths. If you decide to make a day of it, there's a food court and two cafés. (*$$, 501 E. Pratt St., Baltimore, (410) 576-3800, aqua.org*)

Port Discovery: This three-story interactive museum is designed for kids 2–12 years old, but parents will manage to have a good time, too. The exhibits are all interactive and educational, and they cover everything from math and science to the arts. There's also a three-story, climbable urban tree house. (*$, 35 Market Pl., Baltimore, (410) 727-8120, portdiscovery.org*)

AT NIGHT

Fell's Point: By day, it's a neighborhood full of great shops, stores, coffee houses, restaurants, and architectural details. (And also a few ghost stories—see above.) At night the neighborhood becomes a pub hub of live music, pool, and great restaurants. **Bertha's** is known for its mussels and brew, as well as the live music. (If you want to make a meal of it, see page 32 for our take.) **The Horse You Came in On,** known by regulars as simply "The Horse," is a dimly lit, wharf-side tavern, built in 1775, with 65 different beers (including microbrews) and local rock and folk musicians performing nightly. **Cat's Eye Pub** is an Irish bar best known for both its nightly music programming and its group-friendly atmosphere.

O'Donnell Square in Canton: The Canton Neighborhood was a blue-collar immigrant neighborhood. Today, it's one of the city's most diverse. O'Donnell Square has a great mix of restaurants and pubs with a merchant or two. Eat Irish at **Claddagh Pub,** local at **Mama's on the Half Shell** (see page 32), or Mexican at **Nacho Mamas.** If you're feeling more upscale, the **Cosmopolitan Bar and Grill** is Canton's exclusive martini bar, featuring 25 different martini creations.

Power Plant Live: Here you'll find two city blocks of entertainment, just two blocks north of the Inner Harbor. This mini-district is a collection of fifteen different entertainment venues. There's a wide range of restaurants, bars, comedy venues, dance clubs, and dueling pianos. The whole thing's anchored by a 1,600-seat music venue, **Ram's Head Live.** While the outdoor scene closes down at the end of October, all the other places, such as the **Havana Club, Have a Nice Day Café, Bar Baltimore, Ruth's Chris Steak House,** and the **Babalu Grill** are open all year. *(34 Market Pl., Baltimore, (410) 752-LIVE, powerplantlive.com)*

SHOPPING

Antique Row: About a mile from the Inner Harbor, in the Otterbein neighborhood, there is a single block (the 800 block) of Howard Street that is ground zero for antiquing. At **Connoisseur's Connection** you'll find a selection eclectic enough to provide items for locally produced movies, most recently *Gods and Generals.* **Antique Row Stalls** is an 8,000-square-foot space where antique dealers gather to sell, well, just about anything and everything. A note: many of the shops keep their doors locked, though most are open from 11 a.m. to 5 p.m.; just ring the doorbell.

Fell's Point: It's just as much fun during the daytime as at night, with a bunch of cool places to explore. The area has shops selling clothes, gifts, toys, records, and more. Restaurants dot the area, too.

For more information: To learn more about things to do in the area visit cityguide.aol.com/baltimore.

ANNAPOLIS

There might not be a better-known college football rivalry than Army-Navy, which is renewed annually in late autumn when the two service academies face off at a neutral site. But fans also crowd the streets around Navy-Marine Corps Memorial Stadium when the Midshipmen are back at home playing other opponents.

Midshipmen line up for food before a Navy game. (Photo: Connie Stimpert)

It took two decades for Navy to get this stadium. For years the Naval Academy had wanted to replace Thompson Field, the team's original home built in 1912. They bought land in 1939, eager to start building, but all plans were put on hold two years later when America was drawn into another war, and all steel and concrete went to America's efforts in World War II (not to fields and bleachers). In 1957 the call went out to raise $3 million to finally build a new stadium, and money came in from all over. Most came from sources you'd expect: military personnel, alumni, and the like. But money also came from some surprising sources, such as alumni and friends of Notre Dame, the legendary football power that has played

Navy every year since 1927. Even West Point's Corps of Cadets reportedly chipped in to help. The result was the 35,000-seat Navy-Marine Corps Memorial Stadium, which hosted its first game in 1959. The next season one of its own Middies, Joe Bellino, would go on to win the prestigious Heisman Trophy (a feat repeated in 1963 by a spit-and-polish quarterback by the name of Roger Staubach).

On game days the neighborhood near the stadium is crowded with cars and RVs, many of which fill the 4,400 parking spaces available. To park in one of these spots, you must buy parking passes before the game, either online at navysports.com or by calling 1-800-US4-NAVY. Tailgaters will want to get there at least 2 hours before the game, before parking lot attendants start directing traffic and perhaps preventing you from tailgating where you want to.

If you find yourself in Annapolis without a parking pass, you can park at Germantown Elementary, located across the street from the stadium off Cedar Park Drive. There are also several downtown parking garages, and you can hop on an Annapolis Transit Bus (free with a game ticket) to the stadium. The Naval Academy Athletic Association provides a free shuttle from the Harry Truman Park-and-Ride, too.

RVs and other oversized vehicles must park in the Gold Lot (Northeast corner). An individual game pass is $30, and you have to purchase it prior to the game.

UNITED STATES NAVAL ACADEMY (NAVY)

Navy-Marine Memorial Stadium

Annapolis, Maryland

(800) 874-6289 ticket office

Stadium parking sold season pass first, then single game passes. Parking sold on first-come, first-served basis, but not on game day. All passes bought in advance. RVs only $30. No overnight parking, saving spaces, or fireworks.

Shuttle Info: Annapolis Transit offers free bus service to games for game ticket holders (you must show your ticket when you board). Take the Gold "B" route. The NAAA also offers free shuttles from the Harry Truman Park-and-Ride.

Midshipmen Media Partner: 1430-AM WNAV

About Annapolis

Annapolis is full of history. That's because so much was written here. It's home to the oldest state capitol building in continuous legislative use in the United States. St. John's College (the nation's third oldest college) and, of course, the U.S. Naval Academy (founded in 1845) are also here. Plus, the nation's last surviving Liberty Tree, a 400-year-old tulip poplar, lived on St. John's College campus until 1999, when Hurricane Isabel finally conquered this last witness to the American Revolution.

Annapolis has that peace and tranquility many Colonial-era towns possess—it's part of time and history, but sits just a little outside it, as well. Annapolites love their ocean with its coves and bays, and their town's quirky independence.

Where to Stay

RV PARKS

There aren't any RV parks in Annapolis, so look for some of the parks mentioned earlier for Baltimore, or log on to campingworld.com/campsearch.

HOTELS

Historic Inns of Annapolis: What you'll find are actually three separate, historic (hence the name) buildings, run as a single enterprise. No matter which of the three inns you choose, you'll check in at the Governor Calvert House. Shuttles will take you to the appropriate building. Rooms run $139–$269 depending on day of the week and season. If you'd like a specific amenity (some rooms have antique fireplaces; a building might have carved wooden banisters or wide porches for enjoying the evening), ask when making reservations. (*58 State Cir., Annapolis, (800) 847-8882, annapolisinns.com*)

O'Callahan Hotel Annapolis: Formerly the Holiday Inn Annapolis, the O'Callahan is the closest hotel to Navy-Marine Corps Memorial Stadium. Since its conversion, the new owners have spruced up the place, adding a marble-floored lobby and custom contemporary Euro-style furniture in guest rooms. Prices vary with the seasons, but range from $129 to $259. The hotel has a restaurant, the **Commodore John Barry,** which offers lunch and dinner. (*174 West St., Annapolis, (410) 263-7700*)

For more information: To learn about more hotels in the area visit tripadvisor.com for listings and guest reviews.

B&BS

Eastport House: This is the oldest standing house in Eastport, a suburb of Annapolis. As you might expect, it's been well maintained and has five guest rooms. All rooms have private baths, except the two third-floor rooms that share one. The house is just a block from the waterfront and a short walk from downtown Annapolis. Rates run $120–$175. (*101 Severn Ave., Annapolis, (410) 295-9710, eastporthouse.com*)

The Schooner Woodwind: This is a fun place. It's a *Boat* & Breakfast with a 2-hour sunset sail, and a continental-plus breakfast served on deck the following morning. Guests stay in one of the 74-foot sailing yacht's four double-occupancy staterooms. The rooms are simple but come with reading lamps, a port window, and enough headroom to stand up straight—not necessarily a given on a boat. Yes, you will share one of two onboard bathrooms (called "heads") with other guests. But both heads include built-in showers and, even with full occupancy, you shouldn't have to wait long. This unique lodging will cost you $260. (*80 Compromise St., Annapolis, (410) 263-7837, schooner-woodwind.com; Off-Season/Postal Address: 1930-A Lincoln Drive, Annapolis*)

For more information: To learn about more B&Bs in the area visit bedandbreakfast.com for a detailed directory.

Where to Eat

TAILGATER GROCERIES

Pennsylvania Dutch Farmers' Market: Also called the Amish Market, it's located at the Annapolis Harbour Center, just a short drive from downtown Annapolis. The market features a large selection of fresh and prepared foods, as well as various candies, homemade snacks, and desserts. All the Amish merchants are from Lancaster County, PA, the heart of Pennsylvania Dutch country. (*2472 Solomons Island Rd., Annapolis, (410) 573-0770, padutchfarmmarket.com*)

SPORTS BARS

Dock Street Bar: Outside it's all sunny, yellow-painted brick. Inside it's a cozy little tavern with six HDTVs. It's also frequently full of midshipmen taking advantage of Dock Street's affordable specials. While this little pub doesn't bill itself as a sports bar, per se, those TVs will be on anytime there's a sports event taking place. (*$, 136 Dock St., Annapolis, (410) 269-8999, dockstreetbar.net*)

Heroes Pub: This humble one-story, white building has 48 beers on tap, satellite TV, and lots of rabid sports fans. This is a great neighborhood bar that loves sports and its community. The menu offers snacks and entrées, at very good prices. (*$, 1 Riverview Ave, Annapolis, (410) 573-1996, heroespub.com*)

T.K. Sharkey's Rock'n Sports Lounge: They claim to have "the most TVs under one roof." That's 50 TVs, including one with a 10-foot screen. You'll also find 30 pool tables, multiple Golden Tee games, a dance floor with a DJ, live music on weekend nights, a cigar bar, and a lounge area. (*$, 2072 Somerville Rd., Annapolis, (410) 841-5599, no URL*)

RESTAURANTS

Cantler's Riverside Inn: Local watermen provide fresh-caught crabs and seafood daily to this 30-plus-year-old institution. Don't let the casual crab-house surroundings (butcher paper on the tables, paper menus, etc.) fool you; Cantler's is regarded as having the best steamed crab and seafood in Annapolis. But seafood is not all that is offered. The menu includes landlocked fare such as filet mignon, chicken, and more. (*$, 458 Forest Beach Rd., Annapolis, (410) 757-1311, cantlers.com*)

Chick and Ruth's Delly: This tiny Jewish delicatessen serves huge piles of delicious, cheap food. It's cramped, it's busy, and the decor looks like it was time-warped in from the early '60s. But that's part of the fun. The most expensive item on the breakfast menu is the "Colonel David B. Mitchell" special—a one-pound T-bone steak, two eggs, fried potatoes, and toast—all for $8.45. Not sure who Col. Mitchell was, but he sure could eat. (*$, 165 Main St., Annapolis, (410) 269-6737, chickandruths.com*)

Davis's Pub: You won't find this tavern in the guidebooks, but if you want to know where the locals go, this is it. It's been here, in one form or another, since the late 1930s. Davis's is full of crusty old watermen and sailors crewing racing ships as well as younger professionals and residents. They're known for their chili, crab cakes, and crab pretzels. (*$, 400 Chester Ave., Annapolis (410) 268-7432*)

For more information: For a directory of additional places to eat in the area visit opentable.com. You can also book a reservation for many restaurants on the site.

What to Do

DURING THE DAY

Annapolis City Dock: The dock looks pretty much like it did a century ago, with shops, and places to eat, drink beer, or sip rum punch. The dock circles around a deep-water inlet called Spa Creek, but nicknamed "Ego Alley," since this is where the area's rich keep their yachts. There are all manner of other ships, work boats, and tour boats in the inlet, too. At the foot of the dock is a life-size sculpture of Alex Haley reading to children, which is part of the **Kunte Kinte–Alex Haley Memorial.** (*East Side: Dock Street; North Side: Randall Street; West Side: Compromise Street*)

The William Paca House and Gardens. (Photo: Annapolis Visitors Bureau)

U.S. Naval Academy: Security is tighter these days, but a tour of the Naval Academy is still worth your time. Enter the Naval Academy on foot at Gate 1 at the corner of Randall and King George Streets. Start your visit at the Armel-Leftwich Visitor Center, where you can sign up for a guided tour. You'll get to walk the grounds, see a sample midshipman's room, and visit the crypt of John Paul Jones beneath the Navy Chapel. (*$, 121 Blake Rd., Annapolis, (410) 293-2109, usna.edu*)

William Paca House and Gardens/Hammond-Harwood House: We've lumped these two sites together for a couple of reasons. Both are outstanding examples of colonial architecture and history, and since they lie adjacent to one another, you can buy combination tickets to see both.

The Paca House was built shortly before the Revolutionary War and has the austere lines one would expect of a colonial structure. But since its owner was once governor of Maryland and a signer of the Declaration of Independence, it's pretty grand by the standards of its day. Behind the house you'll see a series of formal gardens, with a fish-shaped pond, a two-story summer house, and other buildings. (*$, 186 Prince George St., Annapolis, (410) 263-5553, annapolis.org*)

The Hammond-Harwood House is another matter entirely. The architecture is amazing. A five-part Georgian home, this house has semi-octagonal wings and carved moldings. It now exhibits furniture, silver, and decorative arts of the home's three centuries. The fine arts collection, which includes works by the Peale family of artists, is one of Maryland's finest. (*$, 19 Maryland Ave., Annapolis, (410) 263-4683, hammondharwoodhouse.org*)

AT NIGHT

Ram's Head Tavern: Ram's Head hosts national acts that play to a small room jammed with fans. The club offers tableside service for drinks, top-notch pub fare, and entertainment that has included Aaron Neville, Lyle Lovett, Ralph Stanley, John Hiatt, and David Byrne. There's also a large and popular restaurant here. (*$$–$$$, 33 West St., Annapolis, (410) 268-4545, ramsheadtavern.com*)

49 West Coffeehouse and Wine Bar: This combination coffeehouse and wine bar features live classical, jazz, and folk music every night of the week. (*$, 49 West St., Annapolis, (410) 626-9796, 49westcoffeehouse.com*)

Metropolitan: If you've had enough of watermen and local color, drop by this lounge/restaurant for a whiff of snazzy big-city chic. Metropolitan has rooftop dining during warm weather, a martini bar, and a wine bar. If you like creative nouvelle cuisine, pick up a fork and stay awhile. This is one of Annapolis's see-and-be-seen spots. (*$$, 169 West St., Annapolis, (410) 268-7733*)

O'Brien's Oyster Bar: Near the City Dock, O'Brien's has live music every night downstairs, starting at 10:00 p.m. (On Fridays the bands crank it up at 5:30 p.m.) There's also a dance floor that tends to get crowded as the night goes on. (*Menu $$, Entertainment $, 113 Main St., Annapolis, (410) 268-6288, obriensoysterbar.com*)

For more information: To learn about other attractions in Annapolis, log on to *hometownannapolis.com.*

The Ultimate Tailgater's Travel Guide

Boston

There are more than 68,000 seats inside Gillette Stadium, and more than 16,500 parking spaces outside. Both are packed on game days. Winning Super Bowls will do that.

But it wasn't always that way for the New England Patriots.

When they began playing as the AFL's Boston Patriots in 1960, they played at Boston University. They put pretty good teams on the field, but they just didn't always know which field they'd be on. During their first 10 years they'd alternate stadiums between BU, Harvard, and Fenway Park (yep, the home of baseball's Red Sox).

In 1971 the team changed its name to the New England Patriots and changed its address to Foxborough, where they still play. That was about the time of the AFL/NFL merger, and the team found itself mired in a series of losing seasons. That changed in the '80s and the team found its way to Super Bowl XX. It lost. The '90s saw a trip to another Super Bowl. And another loss.

The new millennium brought Tom Brady and better luck. Much better luck. The Patriots won the Super Bowl after the 2001, 2003, and 2004 seasons, and now have plenty of fans who turn out in the Massachusetts cold and snow to tailgate and cheer their Pats.

Tailgating at Gillette Stadium starts 4 hours before kickoff. Like most stadiums, there's tailgate parking for cars and SUVs ($35), buses ($200), and RVs ($125). Unlike most stadiums, there's also an area for limos for those of you tailgating in high style ($125). Getting to your spot is pretty easy; just follow the signs for your type of vehicle. If you're in an RV, they made a change in 2005, and all RVs must now enter at entrance P10.

If you park in an off-site lot and walk to the game, you'll notice colored lines designating the best routes to the stadium. Follow them. Fans will be allowed to cross Route 1 only on these paths.

There aren't any shuttle buses to Pats games, but there is train service from Boston and Providence. It will cost you $10 round trip. For details and train departure times, log onto mbta.com, and click on the train link with the Patriots logo.

Down the road in Chestnut Hill is Boston College (it used to actually be in Boston). BC joined the Atlantic Coast Conference in 2005 in hopes that it will add millions more in revenue to its coffers and further strengthen its football program. It certainly should help the tailgating. The ACC is a bigger tailgating conference than the Big East.

Founded in 1863, the Jesuit University now has about 14,500 students and is well known for its academic achieve-

NEW ENGLAND PATRIOTS
Gillette Stadium
Foxborough, Massachusetts
(508) 543-1776

Parking close; no shuttle needed. RVs have specific area; RV $125, cars $35, buses $200. Arrive early to get good spaces. RVs enter at P10, limos $125 at P2 or P6, buses or disabled at P5 or P6. Check www.gillettestadium.com for prohibited item updates.

Train Info: MBTA commuter trains leave from both Boston's South Station and Providence. Each train makes three stops along the way before arriving at the stadium. Cost is $10 for round-trip ticket and may be bought with cash only. Train times vary for early and late games. For details log onto mbta.com and click on the train link with the Patriots logo.

Patriots Media Partners: 104.1-FM WBCN, WCVB Channel 5 (ABC)

ments. Its biggest football achievement came in 1940, when the Eagles beat Tennessee in the Sugar Bowl to go undefeated and claim part of the national championship (shared with Stanford and Minnesota). The school's most memorable football moment came in 1984, when quarterback Doug Flutie launched the ultimate Hail Mary pass for a winning touchdown in the closing seconds for an upset victory over defending national champion Miami, effectively locking up the Heisman Trophy for Flutie. In both cases, Baldwin was flying high.

Who's Baldwin? Well, he's BC's official mascot. The eagle became the school's mascot in the early 1920s. Today BC has two official mascots: Baldwin and Baldwin Jr. They came up with the mascot's name by blending *bald eagle* with the word *win*. Baldwin is a 6 ½-foot tall mascot, and Baldwin Jr. is a 9 ½-foot tall inflatable mascot.

If Baldwin wanted to tailgate on campus, he probably could. You probably can't.

Only donors are allowed to park on campus, and they and alumni get most of the tailgating spaces near Alumni Stadium, pushing the rest of us off campus. The school wants all single-game ticket holders to park in the Needham Industrial Park satellite lot, near the Sheraton-Needham. There are other satellite lots as well, if Needham gets full. The good news is that parking is free in these university-rented lots. The bad news is they're a bit of a hike and tailgating is prohibited.

The bottom line here is if you want to tailgate at a BC game, find a donor or alumnus with a parking pass, and make fast friends.

About Boston

Beantown (named for its famous baked beans) is one of America's oldest and most intriguing cities.

Its history developed on two shores, and it got its name thanks to a legal loophole and college buddies sticking together. Here's how.

Boston's first resident was a man named William Blaxton, who settled on Beacon Hill in 1617. Five years latter the first settlers joined him.

At about the same time, across the pond, a group of Protestant Puritans were less than thrilled with the Protestant-hostile King Charles I, and they decided to make a break for it (not an easy thing to do at the time). Their first stop was Amsterdam, but that didn't work out so well. Now, the king wasn't going to let them just scamper off to the New World, so they pulled a fast one. They created a trading company, but in the charter left out the requirement that management be in England. The king didn't notice, signed it, and they were off.

The Ultimate Tailgater's Travel Guide

They landed in Salem, but didn't receive much help there, so they headed to the mouth of the Charles River, where one of the group had a college buddy from back home who said it would be a good place to settle. It was. Another old college pal suggested calling the place Boston, in honor of Boston, Lincolnshire, back home. They did.

By then it was the 1630s, and the town of Boston was beginning to thrive. Of course, you know the next part of the story.

In 1773 the only folks to visit Boston were the Redcoats, and the area was in the middle of the Revolutionary War. After the war, the area continued to grow. It became a city in 1822 and over time turned from a homesteading community into the economic and cultural hub of New England. Finance, healthcare, and education are the three largest industries now (if you don't count winning Super Bowls).

Where to Stay

RV PARKS

Canoe River Campground: It offers 245 sites with electric and sewer hookups, and 30 sites for tents. Canoe River offers basic amenities, as well as a snack bar, dumping station, and mobile dumping services. The sites vary in size, and some have WiFi. Rates depend on the amperage used in your electric hookup running from $28 to $30. Weekly rates are $168–$180. The place gets crowded during fall and winter, so call ahead. (*137 Mill St., Mansfield, (508) 339-6462, canoeriver.com*)

Circle CG Farm Adult Campground: No, it's not *that* kind of adult campground—it just means there's no playground or structured activities for children. Located less than 15 miles from Gillette Stadium, Circle CG has 150 sites with standard amenities along with the nonstandard beauty parlor and petting zoo. There's also a basketball court, bocci, horseshoes, fishing, and mini-golf. Rates are $39-$42. Some sites lack sewer, but those are cheaper. (*131 North Main St., Bellingham, (508) 966-1136, campmass.com/pilgrim.html*)

Normandy Farms Family Campground: This is less than 5 miles from Gillette Stadium and loaded with amenities that sound more like a resort than a place to park your RV. There are 400 sites, along with two rental cabins and three 37-foot rentable travel trailers. Those aforementioned amenities: a lodge with a fully equipped gym, video arcade, indoor heated pool, double Jacuzzi and three-way sauna, a snack bar, a common area, and an upstairs lounge for adults. Outside, there are three more swimming pools, one heated and two Olympic-sized. There's also a fishing pond, soccer and softball fields, areas for horseshoes, shuffleboard, a kids' playground, and more.

Reserving a space will cost you about $52 on weekends, $42 during the week, or $283 for a seven-night stay. Rates go down in December. There's a dumpsite, but its use is an extra fee: $20–$25 depending on the day. Be aware that visitors are charged $10 to get in if they stay more than an hour—but they

BOSTON COLLEGE
Alumni Stadium
Boston, Massachusetts
(617) 552-3000

Only donors allowed to park on campus. Visitors park off campus free in university-rented lots. Most are a good distance away—shuttles provided. Tailgating pretty much reserved for donors, alumni. No tailgating in off-campus lots.

Shuttle Info: Free shuttle service is provided, starting 2 ½ hours before the game, and continuing for 2 ½ hours after the game, or until all visitors have been returned to their vehicles. For details call the Boston College Information Hotline at (617) 552-AUTO.

Eagles Media Partner: 850-AM WEEI

Patroits tailgaters fill the lots outside Gillette Stadium. (Photo: New England Patriots)

can use all the facilities. (*72 West St., Foxborough, (508) 543-7600, normandyfarms.com*)

For more information: For additional RV parks and campsites visit campingworld.com/campsearch.

Hotels

The Residence Inn: Again, we're breaking our rule against listing major chains, as this is a part of the Marriott hotel family. But since this place was originally intended for business travelers staying for a week or more, the rooms are larger than average and come as studios, or one- and two-bedroom suites, with full kitchen facilities in all. And it's near Gillette Stadium. Rates range from $109 for a studio or a one-bedroom, to $155 for a two-bedroom suite. (*250 Foxborough Blvd., Foxborough, (508) 698-2800, marriott.com*)

Charlesmark Hotel: Originally built in the late 1800s as a private residence, this 33-room hotel offers beautifully done rooms just steps from **Newbury Street** (see page 48), the **Prudential** and **Copley Place** shopping centers, and other attractions. The atmosphere feels like what you might experience on a yacht, with custom furnishings. While rooms are small, they're designed well enough to hold the basics, plus a comfy chair, and still feel breathable. Breakfast is included, and light refreshments such as bottled water and fruit are always available at no charge. A couple of things to be aware of: self-parking in the nearby garage is $32, and the hotel has only one elevator. Prices range from $99 to $249, and kids under 18 stay free in parents' rooms. Pets allowed with prior approval. (*655 Boylston St., Boston, (617) 247-1212, thecharlesmark.com*)

Harborside Inn: Harborside Inn is a renovated warehouse across the street from **Faneuil Hall Marketplace** and the harbor. Exposed-brick walls and cherry wood accents create an urban feel. Rooms are fairly large and some overlook the skylight-studded central atrium, while others look out onto the harbor. Rates range from $160–$204. Off-site parking is $20, but you can walk to the **New England Aquarium** (see page 46) and other landmark places around town. (*185 State St., Boston, (617) 723-7500, harborsideinnboston.com*)

For more information: To learn about more hotels in the area visit tripadvisor.com for listings and guest reviews.

B&BS

A quick note: while there are more than 200 bed and breakfasts in the Boston area, few serve a hot-cooked breakfast, since serving food cooked on the premises requires owners to have a restaurant license.

A Cambridge House Bed & Breakfast Inn: Despite being located on Cambridge's busy main street, Cambridge House has a country inn feel to it. The three-story building is a restored 1892 Victorian that's listed on the National Register of Historic Places. The 15 guest rooms vary widely in size; they're decorated with Waverly-Schumacher fabrics and period antiques. Most contain working fireplaces. The owners have also adapted one of the rooms to better serve guests with physical challenges. Prices range from $129 to $229 April–November, and drop to $109 to $179 December–March. (*2218 Massachusetts Aven., Cambridge, (800) 232-9989, acambridgehouse.com*)

Charles Street Inn: Often confused with the Charles Hotel, the Charles Street Inn looks like something on an MGM movie set. Built in 1860 as a model home to spur development in the area, this Victorian townhouse showcased the choicest architectural styles and interiors of its time. Today its nine guest rooms have antique furniture, whirlpool tubs, Sub-Zero mini-refrigerators stocked with drinks, and more. Rooms range from $225 to $375, depending on the season and whether you're staying on a weekday or weekend. (*94 Charles St., Boston, (877) 772-8900, charlestreetinn.com*)

Newbury Guest House: This B&B is housed in three former single-family Victorian residences, built in the Queen Anne and Ruskin styles. Renovated in the early 1990s, all three were combined to create a 32-room bed and breakfast in the heart of Boston. The inn still contains many original details and some new ones such as bathrooms, telephone, WiFi, and cable TV. Handicap-accessible rooms are available, and there's an elevator on the premises. Rates run $155–$195. Rates are higher Fridays and Saturdays. (*261 Newbury St., Boston, 800-437-7668, newburyguesthouse.com*)

To learn about more B&Bs in the area visit bedandbreakfast.com for a detailed directory.

Where to Eat

TAILGATER GROCERIES

Stop & Shop: Carries a full selection of produce, meats, and seafood, including some gourmet items—and it's close to Gillette Stadium. (*141 Main St. Foxborough, (508) 543-5791*)

BOSTON BAKED BEANS

Boston is called Beantown because in colonial days beans baked in molasses for several hours was a favorite dish. The city had plenty of molasses, since it was a large rum-producing center and molasses is a by-product of that process. Today there isn't a company in town making baked beans, but they're still a beloved tradition here and they're simple to make. If you have an RV or fancy tailgate kitchen you can make them at the game, but your best bet is to make them a day or two before and heat them up in the parking lot.

1 pound navy beans

1 large onion, chopped

2 tablespoons Dijon mustard

¼ cup dark brown sugar

⅓ cup light brown sugar

¼ cup molasses

1 teaspoon salt

In a large bowl, combine the beans with plenty of cold water and soak overnight for 6 to 8 hours. Drain the beans and combine them in a large pot with enough water to cover them plus 1 inch. Bring to a boil, lower the heat to simmer, and cook for 45 minutes or until they are just tender. Drain the beans, setting aside the cooking liquid.

Preheat the oven to 325°.

In a bean pot or deep casserole with a lid, combine the beans with the onion, mustard, dark and light brown sugar, molasses, and salt. Add enough of the cooking liquid to just cover the beans. Stir to blend them. Bring the bean pot to a boil and transfer it to the oven; bake for 2 hours, checking every 30 to 40 minutes to make sure the beans aren't dry. Add more cooking liquid if necessary. Once the beans are tender, uncover the pot and cook for 20 to 30 minutes more until the top has crusted slightly.

Makes 6 servings

SPORTS BARS

The Sports Grille: 140 TVs (that's not a typo) and 15 satellite channels make this a one-of-a-kind sports fan's hangout. There's even a TV outside so you can watch the game while waiting for a table. Once inside, you'll find a menu full of staples, such as pizza and burgers alongside turkey tips and salads. (*$, 132 Canal St, Boston, (617) 367-9302*)

Stadium Sports Bar & Grill: With more than 30 flat-screen TVs mounted almost every 8 feet throughout the bar, including restrooms, there isn't a bad seat in the house (pun intended). It's a uniquely high-tech sports bar within a glossy upstairs lounge for singles. Stadium offers a choice of draft beers, alongside an impressive martini list. (*$, 232 Old Colony Ave, South Boston, (617) 269-5100, stadiumbars.com*)

The Fours: Originally called The Number Four's in honor of hockey great Bobby Orr (who wore number 4 for the Boston Bruins), the restaurant is so well known that it's shortened its name. All the sports memorabilia on display makes you think the restaurant is a sports museum, too. There's a pretty impressive selection of seafood, sandwiches, and entrées named after Boston sports greats, such as Bobby Orr, Larry Bird, Doug Flutie, and others. *Sports Illustrated* has named The Fours the "Number One Sports Bar in America." (*$, 166 Canal St., Boston, (617) 720-4455, thefours.com*)

RESTAURANTS

Mike's City Diner: This is the real deal as diners go, from black-and-white-checkered tablecloths to waitresses with trays of food, zipping to hungry tables. Elvis music floats over the rumble of customers. A cross section of South Enders and urbanites makes for prime people-watching, and no one seems to mind the cramped quarters. The menu ranges from made-from-scratch Belgian waffles and omelets to Red Bliss home fries and corned beef. (*$, 1714 Washington St, Boston, (617) 267-9393*)

Aquitaine: Aquitaine is part of Boston's newer, hipper South End on "restaurant row." It's a very Parisian little bistro serving dinner and an excellent brunch. The brunch menu includes Brioche French toast with pear and maple syrup, omelets, pan-seared trout, and a pressed duck and Gruyère sandwich. Brunch is served Saturday and Sunday from 10:00 a.m. to 3:00 p.m. (*$$, 569 Tremont St., Boston, (617) 424-8577, aquitaineboston.com*)

Great Bay: Located inside the **Hotel Commonwealth,** this seafood restaurant isn't cheap, but it's good. Its marine-themed dining room hosts dishes such as stuffed lobster with tarragon and baby veggies, and lamb shank with barley risotto, parsnips, and spinach. But the menu changes almost daily. Parking can be tough; it's worth it to pay the $14 for the valet to scrounge for that space for you. (*$$$, 500 Commonwealth Ave., Boston, (617) 532-5300, gbayrestaurant.com*)

Montien Thai Restaurant: When you think of Boston, you usually don't think of Thai food. Think again. You probably don't know that Thailand's King Bhumibol was born across the river in Cambridge. Montien is one of Boston's best Thai places. Authentic dishes dominate the menu (ask for the Thai menu specifically or you might be handed the Americanized version), and they show off the region's sharp flavors: lemongrass, Kaffir lime leaves, galangal, and chile. (*$, 63 Stuart St, Boston, (617) 338-5600, montien-boston.com*)

Silvertone Bar and Grill: The whole effect is a retro vibe inside this tiny but very popular restaurant and bar. It's a modern room of slate-gray and poplar, with concrete floors, sepia-toned vintage family pictures and old liquor posters on the wall, and an old brushed-steel radio (a Silvertone, of course) on the stairway. The menu is stick-to-your-ribs New England comfort food such as meatloaf and mashed potatoes, calamari, tuna melt, and mussels. (*$, 69 Bromfield St, Boston, (617) 338-7887*)

For more information: For a directory of additional places to eat in the area visit opentable.com. You can also book a reservation for many restaurants on the site.

What to Do

DURING THE DAY

5W!TS—TOMB: Down the street from **Fenway Park,** 5W!TS (trust us, that's the way it's spelled, but it's pronounced "five wits") offers one of the most unusual and exciting entertainment experiences you'll find anywhere. What you get is part Disney, part *Indiana Jones,* part classic fun house. Matthew DuPlessie, 5W!TS creator, decided to re-imagine theme park entertainment into a new "pocket theme-park" concept with puzzles, problem-solving, cutting-edge special effects, and environmental settings detailed enough to be mistaken for the real thing.

You'll test your problem-solving skills (and nerve) as you enter the tomb of an Egyptian pharaoh, whose angry spirit has booby-trapped the entire space. Unless you perform a list of tasks, solve puzzles, and find hidden magical objects, you'll be joining him in the underworld.

Due to its popularity, TOMB will stay in Boston through at least 2006. (A new show under development will open at the **Spy Museum** (see page 211) in Washington, DC, in 2007.) (*$$, 186 Brookline Ave., Boston, (617) 375-WITS, 5-wits.com*)

5W!TS—TOMB.
(Photo: Bryan Borgal)

The Blue Man Group: Yep, the guys from those Intel commercials. They give you a performance experience that's . . . well . . . hard to describe. It features the three enigmatic blue-headed guys doing stuff with light, music, homemade percussion, paint, and God-knows-what-else. It's groovy, brainy, squishy, head-scratching, jaw-dropping entertainment that's part rock concert, part vaudeville, and part science experiment. Heck, they call the seats near the stage "poncho seats," so you can guess what happens there. (Put it this way: wear old clothes and bring a raincoat. Seriously.) (*$$$, Charles Playhouse, 74 Warrenton St., Theater ticket phone: (671) 931-2787, BMG Phone (617) 426-6912, blueman.com*)

Boston Children's Museum: Here you'll find good, inexpensive fun for little kids, big kids, and grownups. Founded in 1913 by a group of teachers, the museum offers an interactive environment that covers about every discipline there is—art, science, culture, and physical health. You can scramble up a vertical climbing wall, create artwork, or help put on a play. If you pull into town by Friday, visit the museum Friday evening after 5:00 p.m., when admission is only a dollar. (*$, 300 Congress St., Boston, (617) 426-8855, bostonkids.org*)

Boston Tours: There are several tours designed for you to see Boston's historic sites and modern attractions in just a few hours. Tours range from trolley, to bus, to boat, and many allow you to hop off and explore. You can search "Boston Tours" on the Internet and find many companies offering rides. Three to get you started are:

The New England Aquarium.
(Photo: New England Aquarium)

Boston Tours: (800) 301-3239, bostontours.com

All Boston Tours: (800) 566-5868, allbostontours.com

Historic Tours of America: (800) 868-7482, historictours.com/boston

Freedom Trail: The trail is the perfect introduction to Colonial Revolutionary Boston, taking you to 16 historical sites and covering 2½ centuries of America's past in about 2½ hours. You can take the self-guided tour, or take it with a guide who knows more than you do (even after you read the signs). The trail includes **Boston Common** (one of the oldest public parks in the country), the site of the Boston Massacre, and **Paul Revere's house.** (*$, Call the Boston Convention and Visitors Bureau for details: (888) SEE-BOSTON, cityofboston.gov/freedomtrail*)

The Museum of Bad Art (MOBA): It's exactly what it says it is—a museum dedicated to preserving "art too bad to be ignored." Nor do they accept just any old bad art. First, it can't be created badly on purpose. Second, it's got to be really bad. Like a train wreck, or reality TV, you can't turn away from these works of mad, bad genius. *Lucy in the Field with Flowers,* the museum's founding "masterpiece," is a 24 x 30 inch piece found in the trash. Actually, a lot of the collection was snatched from the trash.

The museum is open during the Dedham Community Theater's hours of operation (the MOBA is in the basement, next to the men's room, appropriately). Since it's a movie theater, hours are usually Monday though Friday 6:00–10:00 p.m.; and Saturday, Sunday, and holidays 1:00–10:00 p.m. (*Free, 580 High St. in Dedham Center, Dedham, MOBA phone: (781) 444-6757, Theater phone: (781) 326-0409, museumofbadart.org*)

New England Aquarium: Located on Boston's Central Wharf, the aquarium offers changing exhibits, seals, penguins, and whale watching. To see the whales, you take a high-speed boat to Stellwagen Bank, which is pretty cool in itself. Whale watching runs from May through October; but during September and October the boat makes only one trip per day, at 10:00 a.m. There are interactive opportunities for kids and adults, and outdoor and indoor cafés. (*$$, Central Wharf, Boston, (617) 973-5200, neaq.org*)

Paul Revere's Home: On the night of April 18, 1775, silversmith Paul Revere left his home and began a journey that made him a legend and helped make America a nation. Tours of the restored house are self-guided and include information about the historic home, Paul Revere's life, and his midnight ride. (*$, 19 North Sq., Boston, (617) 523-2338, paulreverehouse.org*)

The Town of Salem: Salem is only about 15 minutes up the road and has more than just witches. But let's start with those, since that's probably why you have heard of this place.

The witch trials of 1692 are the featured attraction for the **Salem Witch Museum,** the **Witch Dungeon** (where the accused were held in chains) the **Salem Wax Museum,** the **Witch Village** (where you can take a gander at what's happening in witchcraft today), and the **Witch House,** home of Witch Judge Jonathon Corwin and the only home still standing with a direct link to the trial.

Salem is also home to the **New England Pirate Museum,** whale watching tours, and haunted walking tours. Salem's pirate museum includes a half-hour stroll through **Old Salem's Dockside Village,** where you can board a pirate ship and explore an eighty-foot bat-filled pirate cave.

For details and contact information for Salem attractions, log on to www.salem.org and www.salemweb.com.

Faneuil Hall at night.
(Photo: Greater Boston CVB)

AT NIGHT

Mr. Dooley's Boston Tavern: There are several Irish pubs in Boston, as you would expect, but this one is the real deal. Those accents you're hearing are genuine, too—Dooley's is listed on Emigrant.ie, a Web site for the global Irish community. Its dark green walls are covered with portraits of noted Irishmen (including Dooley). The menu includes bangers and mash and shepherd's pie, as well as 13 beers on tap. (*$, 77 Broad St., Boston, (617) 338-5656, somersirishpubs.com*)

Tir na nÓg: This traditional Irish bar is a local hangout and a part of the neighborhood. Guitars, fiddles, and squeezeboxes fill the bar with Irish folk music every night (the music usually starts around 10:00 p.m.) Tir na nÓg means "Land of the Young," and the crowd is fairly true to the name—those in their 20s and 30s mostly. Expect pub food like fish and chips and steak tips. If you drive here, don't park in the lot adjacent to the bar; your car will be towed. (*$, 366A Somerville Ave, Somerville, (617) 628-4300, thenog.com*)

Wally's Café: This club is a local legend for jazz and blues. In addition to local acts, many budding jazz and blues talents at the Berklee College of Music play here. Wally's status as a local jazz institution is disproportionate to its size; expect a crowd and long lines on weekends after 10:00 p.m. And read this sentence carefully: Wally's accepts only cash, so bring enough. (*No cover charge, 1-drink minimum, 427 Massachusetts Ave., Cambridge, (617) 424-1408, wallyscafe.com*)

The Middle East: You have your choice here of three live-music performance rooms, two family-style restaurants with bars, and the upscale bistro, **ZuZu.** Several rooms also serve as art galleries, offering a showcase for local and international artists. You'll hear everything from funk, Latin, and soul to alternative rock here, depending on the night. Wednesday and Sunday nights feature belly-dancing. The feel reflects the owners' Lebanese roots, including the menu. (*Food-$, Music-$–$$, 472 Massachusetts Ave., Cambridge, (617) 864-3278, mideastclub.com*)

The Fenway Park Area/Kenmore Square: Lansdowne and Ipswitch Streets and Brookline Avenue are where you'll find an active club scene with more than a dozen places to drink, dance, and party late into the night. From **Axis** (which is really two clubs in one—80s on one floor, techno on the other)—to **The Big Easy** (where it's always Mardi Gras), to **Dad's Beantown Diner** (one of the most popular college scenes in town) you'll find something to fit your mood. (*Lansdowne and Ipswitch Sts. and Brookline Ave. all border Fenway Park.*)

SHOPPING

The Nostalgia Factory: With more than 41,000 items in inventory, chances are you'll find any movie posters, passes, press books, press kits, and other movie ephemera you're looking for. Items range from current theatrical releases all the way back to the silent era. (*51 N. Margin St., (800) 479-8754, nostalgia.com*)

Fenway Park anchors an active nightclub area. (Photo: Greater Boston CVB)

Lannan Ship Model Gallery: Boston Harbor has seen more than four centuries of ships pass through, and Lannan's has models of a lot of them—antique and contemporary ships. Here you'll find almost every model you can think of, such as tugboats, frigates, runabouts, clipper ships, sailing yachts, and pond yachts ranging from five-inch miniatures to 10-foot ocean liners. There's also marine art and nautical antiques to pore over. Though a sign on the door says it's open by appointment only, a simple knock almost always gets you in—but call ahead just to be sure. (*99 High St., Boston, (617) 461-2650, lannan.com*)

Ars Libri, Ltd.: The largest collection of rare and out-of-print books in America rests within these walls. The shop specializes in books on photography and architecture, out-of-print art books, monographs, and exhibition catalogues. Some books here are extremely rare and will set you back $12,000 or so. Other rare books cost as little as $10, making this a great place to find a really unique gift. (*560 Harrison Ave., Boston, (617) 357-5212, arslibris.com*)

Porter Square: This shopping district has distinctive clothing stores, as well as crafts shops, coffee shops, natural food stores, restaurants, and bars with live music. Parking's not too bad here, either. (*West on Massachusetts Ave. from Harvard Sq., Cambridge*)

Harvard Square: This famous area isn't all Ivy League tweed. While the whole district stretches about 4 miles, Harvard Square itself takes up just a few blocks and holds more than 150 stores selling clothes, books, records, furnishings, and specialty items—along with some national chain stores as famous as their Cambridge address. (*Massachusetts Ave. at Peabody St., Cambridge*)

Downtown Crossing: This outdoor pedestrian mall houses **Filene's Basement,** Boston's famous department store. Other stores in this district run the gamut from clothing to sports gear, jewelry, toys, and more. You also have your choice of several coffee houses and restaurants. (*Intersection of Washington, Winter and Summer Streets*)

Newbury Street: Here is Boston's version of Rodeo Drive, with merchants such as **Armani, Kate Spade,** and **Brooks Brothers** alongside local boutiques and cafés. Some of Boston's architectural gems share the eight-block district, including the Art Deco **Ritz Carlton,** Richard Upjohn's **Church of the Covenant,** and the **Temple for the Working Union of Progressive Spiritualists.** (*Newbury St. between Massachusetts Ave. and Arlington*)

Reruns Antiques: This might look like a salvage store, but don't let the looks deceive you. Poke around and you might come up with a Hiroshige print, a 19th-century Moroccan lamp, or an Asmat ancestral figure. If you're in the mood for a history or an anthropology lesson, owner Tom Armstrong is happy to oblige. Yes, it's all a little eccentric—the store doesn't even have a phone, let alone a Web site—but that's part of the fun. (*125 Charles St., Boston*)

For more information: To learn more about things to do in the area visit cityguide.aol.com/boston.

The Ultimate Tailgater's Travel Guide

Charlotte

The Carolina Panthers joined the NFL in 1995, and in their first year set a league record for first-year franchises by winning seven games. Just a year later they came within one game of making it all the way to the Super Bowl. In 2003 they would make it there, only to lose to the New England Patriots on a late field goal.

The Panthers also did something else unusual—they privately financed their own stadium without having to fight the city council and tax battles as most other teams building new stadiums do. In Charlotte, Jerry Richardson—the former Colts wide receiver-turned-businessman who owns the Panthers—said he'd get it built without a public dime. That'll help your expansion bid.

The result is the 73,000-seat, open-air Bank of America Stadium in Uptown. There are 11 acres of public spaces around the stadium—including walkways, green spaces, and parking. The latter means tailgating.

You can tailgate anywhere except in the parking decks. You will need a pass, though, and there is no overnight parking. (For parking pass information call (704) 358-7000.) There are more than 30,000 parking spaces within a 15-minute walk of the stadium, and for varying fees the folks who own them will let you park there. Not all allow tailgating, so be sure to ask. (In fact, try turning into one without asking, and you will get your yea or nay pretty quickly. Works every time.)

If you do park on-site, you must confine your tailgate to your space. And if you're grilling, you have to keep the flame at least 10 feet from any vehicle. There are ash and coal bins in tailgating lots, which come in handy if you're not cooking with gas.

If you didn't drive, you can get to and from the stadium by taxi (there's a taxi stand two blocks away on Church Street, between First and Stonewall streets, for when you're leaving the game). Fans with disabilities can park in Lot B to catch a shuttle for $20, including parking. To use this service, you must have an accessible-parking placard.

If you're not camped out in your chair, next to the buffet, enjoying your tailgate party (and even if you are), you'll find cheerleaders and mascots, food and drinks, contests and giveaways at the Catwalk and the Panthers Lair. The Catwalk is outside the North Gate; the Panthers Lair is outside the South and East Gates. You can get your face painted at the Panthers Lair, too.

If you go down the road to Lowe's Motor Speedway, you will find that tailgating is different from its Panthers football cousin. It's really camping. But first, a little history.

In 1959 O. Burton Smith (the current track chairman) and the late Curtis Turner (one of NASCAR's first drivers) partnered to

CAROLINA PANTHERS

Bank of America Stadium
Charlotte, North Carolina
(704) 358-7000

All parking is within a half-mile radius of the stadium. Tailgate anywhere but parking decks; no overnight parking. Go to the CatWalk and Panthers Lair for free pregame festivities.

Taxi and Shuttle Info: A taxi stand is located two blocks from the stadium on Church Street, between First and Stonewall Streets, for easy drop-off and pickup. Game-day shuttle for fans with disabilities; park in Lot B to catch the shuttle. It costs $20, including parking, and you must have an accessible-parking placard to use the service.

Panthers Media Partners: 1110-AM and 99.3-FM WBT, WCCB-TV Channel 18 (FOX)

LOWE'S MOTOR SPEEDWAY

Concord, North Carolina
(770) 455-3209
(800) 455-FANS ticket office

RVs choose between general camping $75 per space or track's Fleetwood Campground with electric, water, sewer hookups, up to $530 per week. Keep fires contained; no fire pits; emphasis on safe, considerate behavior. Shuttles, trams available.

Traffic information: 103.7-FM WSOC

fulfill a dream and built this 1.5-mile track on the outskirts of the Queen City. In 1960 the first World 600 was run on the track. In 1961 the Speedway went into Chapter 11.

It would eventually emerge from bankruptcy, but Smith left the Speedway. For a while. By 1975 he was the majority owner again and shepherded a series of improvements. Lowe's Motor Speedway is now one of NASCAR fans' favorite tracks. And the Dirt Track at Lowe's Motor Speedway extends the season for race fans.

If you're one of those fans, and you're there for the paved track, you should get there early. It seats 167,000, and there's a lot of staff here, too—it takes about twice the effort to host a race here than it does to put on the Super Bowl. It gets congested; tune into 103.7-FM WSOC for traffic reports on race day.

There's free parking surrounding the Speedway, and drive-up camping is available on the property for $75 per space during NASCAR race weeks. You have to reserve the camping spots in advance, and it's first-come, first-served. All camping areas are near restroom/shower facilities, or a shuttle stop that will get you there. (For more RV camping at and around the Speedway, see page 51.)

Once you're settled, and your tailgate or campsite is in place, you can take a walk or shuttle to souvenir row for prerace activities and to visit displays, vendor booths, and such. It's a comfortable, friendly atmosphere building up to race time. And if you want to get into a heavy NASCAR conversation, the tailgaters around you are often described as some of the most hard-core fans in America, so you're in the right place.

About Charlotte

In 1775 Thomas Polk (the uncle of President James K. Polk) built a home at the crossroads of an Indian trading path and the Great Wagon Road from Philadelphia. That intersection became the village of Charlotte Town. It was named for King George's wife, Charlotte of Mecklenburg-Strelitz, hence the city's nickname, "the Queen City." It also answers the question why Charlotte is in Mecklenburg County.

The city is a major financial center. Those roots run deep. In about 1800 the first gold mine in the country

The Ultimate Tailgater's Travel Guide

was discovered here. In 1837 the U.S. Mint opened a branch in Charlotte, which remained open until Confederate forces seized it during the Civil War. Within the last 30 years or so, Hugh McColl turned North Carolina National Bank into Bank of America, and local bank First Union grew and merged into Wachovia. Now Charlotte is the second-largest banking center in America, trailing only New York City.

It is also now the largest city between DC and Dallas, and has a regional population of more than 2 million. Those people do more than just work at banks. More than 200 of the Fortune 500 companies do business here, and Charlotte is also home to the Billy Graham ministries.

Panthers pregame tailgating.
(Photo: Pantherfanz.net)

Where to Stay

RV PARKS

Charlotte/Ft. Mill KOA: 40 acres of peaceful wooded country in Ft. Mill (just outside Charlotte) with swimming pool, laundry facilities, restaurant, and lounge on-site. There's a gas station/convenience store on the property (with limited groceries), and if you want to take prepared food to the game, there's also a Hunt Brothers Pizza and Blimpie sub shop. Also offers horseshoes, volleyball, miniature golf, and more. There are more than 200 RV and tent sites, as well as Kamping Kabins (it's a KOA, so they spell it with a "K"). RV rates are $30–$50; Kabins run $35–$85. (*940 Gold Hill Rd., Fort Mill, (888) 562-4430, charlottekoa.com*)

Fieldridge Acres: This is a basic, family owned park, but if you want to be close to downtown (eight miles) and stay cheap ($15), then it's not a bad choice. The park has 94 sites with hookups and basic amenities. You can tent here, and there's onsite groceries for your tailgate. Pets allowed, but there are some restrictions. (*7800 Wilkinson Blvd., Charlotte, (704) 399-3521, fieldridgeacres.com*)

Fleetwood RV Racing Camping Resort: Part of the Lowe's Motor Speedway complex, Fleetwood is located just across the highway from the track. It offers 460 sites with full hookups and the usual amenities. The park also has a pond for fishing, play equipment for kids, and an equipped pavilion. Reserve early, as spots sell out quickly on race weekends. Rates: $530 for a week's worth of camping on race weekends; otherwise $20–$25 per night.(*6600 Speedway Blvd., Concord, (704) 455-4445, lowesmotor speedway.com/tickets/camping*)

McDowell Nature Preserve: It's about 25 miles from the stadium (although only five from **Paramount's Carowinds** theme park), but the RV park is nestled in this beautiful nature preserve. Hiking trails, fishing, boating, and other recreation is available here (see page 55). Each campsite includes a grill, water, and electricity. You can tent here, too. There are 116 sites that run $12. (*15222 York Rd., Charlotte, (704) 583-1284, charmeck.org—click on "Leisure & Recreation," then on "Parks," "Nature Centers and Preserves," and "McDowell"*)

Tailgating at Lowe's Motor Speedway.
(Photo: Laidbackracing.com)

For more information: For additional RV parks and campsites visit campingworld.com/campsearch.

HOTELS

Ballantyne Resort: A golf course, professional golf and tennis lessons, a spa—yep it's a resort. The rooms have 10-foot ceilings, WiFi, and high-speed Internet (for a fee), custom-designed furniture, and the amenities you would expect from a resort-type hotel. Dining ranges from the casual **19th Hole** to the not-so-casual **Grill Room.** Brunch served on Sundays. Rooms run $199 and up. (*10000 Ballantyne Commons Pkwy., Charlotte, (866) 248-4824, ballantyneresort.com*)

Dunhill Hotel: This historic hotel originally opened in 1929, and today it offers luxury of a bygone era. All rooms are furnished in 18th-century European antiques but offer modern amenities, including televisions and refrigerators (stocked with complimentary beverages) housed in armoires. Guests can use the Crown Athletic Club fitness center. The restaurant has been named Charlotte's "Best Hotel Restaurant" the past couple of years. The hotel is close to Bank of America Stadium, and rooms cost $119–$269. (*237 N. Tryon St., Charlotte, (704) 332-4141, dunhillhotel.com*)

The Park Hotel: With a one-to-one guest-to-employee ratio, and located in the SouthPark neighborhood (where **Nordstrom** and **Tiffany's** are just a block or two away), you get the idea that the Park Hotel will treat you well. Rooms come with WiFi, 25-inch TVs with Nintendo, and marble bathroom vanities. Guests can also spend time on a 9-hole putting green, in the sauna, or at the restaurant or bar. ATM on-site. Rooms run $110–$160. (*2200 Rexford Rd., Charlotte, (800) 334-0331, theparkhotel.com*)

For more information: To learn about more hotels in the area visit tripadvisor.com for listings and guest reviews.

The Duke Mansion.
(Photo: Van Miller)

B&BS

The Duke Mansion: Built in 1915, it was tripled in size about four years later by new owner James B. Duke. Heard of Duke Energy or Duke University? That's this Duke. This 20-room bed and breakfast is listed on the National Register of Historic Places. All rooms are exquisitely furnished in period antiques and have private baths. There are porches with rocking chairs scattered around and 4½ acres of gardens. It's a bed and breakfast, but lunch and dinner are available, too. Rooms cost $169–$249. (*400 Hermitage Rd., Charlotte, (888) 202-1009, dukemansion.org*)

Morehead Inn: Built in 1917 by the owner of a successful local Buick dealership (the first one south of the Mason-Dixon Line), this inn is close to the action but secluded. There are 16 guest rooms, all with private baths and period furnishings, along with whirlpool tubs, balconies, or private entrances. Rates run $125–$199. (*1122 E. Morehead St., Charlotte, (704) 376-3357, moreheadinn.com*)

The VanLandingham Estate Inn: Now on the National Register of Historic Places, this California-style bungalow was built in 1913 and recently renovated. There are period furnishings throughout, as well as private baths and high-speed Internet for each room. You can also wander through 5 acres of Mecklenburg County's oldest premier gardens, which are also on the National Register of Historic Places. Rooms cost $125–$199. (*2010 The Plaza, Charlotte, (888) 524-2020, vanlandinghamestate.com*)

For more information: To learn about more B&Bs in the area visit bedandbreakfast.com for a detailed directory.

Where to Eat

TAILGATER GROCERIES

Charlotte Farmers' Market: They say, "If it was any fresher, it would still be in the garden." Fresh produce is available, as are baked goods, jams and jellies, and other items grown and prepared by the farmers who are selling it. (*1801 Yorkmont Rd., Charlotte, (704) 357-1269, agr.state.nc.us/markets/facilit/farmark/charlott/*)

Reid's Uptown Market: A downtown Charlotte tradition since 1928, Reid's award-winning butcher shop is a good place to get food for the grill. You'll find Jeff Gordon Wines over on the wine shelves, too. (*225 E. 6th St., Charlotte, (704) 377-1312, reids.com*)

SPORTS BARS

Fox & Hound: Will three floors of wall-to-wall TVs (even in the restrooms) be enough for you? The Fox & Hound has them, along with pool, checkers, trivia, and nightly live music. The menu is pretty standard pub food, but the kitchen's open until 2:00 a.m. Selected the *AOL City Guide's* "Best Sports Bar" for 2005. (*$, 330 N. Tryon St., Charlotte, (704) 333-4113, www.tentcorp.com*)

Picasso's Sports Café: The atmosphere of Picasso's is set by the wall-sized TV that can be seen from the line at the Blockbuster Video store across the street. Not that you want to watch it from there. Other TVs hang over the bar. Several schools' Charlotte alumni chapters meet here to watch their teams' games, too. Basic American food on the menu includes burgers, pizza, and hot wings. One note: parking can be tough, so keep an eye out for street spots along the way. (*$, 1301 East Blvd., Charlotte, (704) 331-0133*)

Smokey Bones Barbeque and Grill: Yes, it's a chain (and not what you would usually call a sports bar) but with 30 TVs, and individual tabletop sound controls so you can choose what you watch on TV, it's a good place to watch a game. They serve a full menu, but barbecue is their specialty. If you're dropping by for a pregame pit stop on the way to the stadium, they have party packs to go. Located near the UNC-Charlotte campus. (*$, 8760 JM Keynes Dr., Charlotte, NC (704) 549-8282, smokeybones.com*)

Stool Pigeons: Three big screens and 17 TVs show the games, and Bank of America Stadium is just a few blocks away. The bar's wall of windows looks out on the downtown scene. The menu includes burgers and sandwiches, as well as pizza by Charlotte's award-winning Wolfman Pizza. There are also two other Charlotte area locations. (*$, 214 N. Church St., Charlotte, (704) 358-3788, stoolpigeons.biz/uptown.html*)

Tipsey McStumble's: This is an Irish sports bar with 8 satellites and 25 TVs (12 on the big wall). Casual vibe, pool tables, dartboards, pub grub, a dance floor, and nightly drink specials make this a popular university area hangout. Cover charge varies nightly, and Monday is College Night. (*$, 10008 University City Blvd., Charlotte, (704) 503-6300, tipseys.com*)

RESTAURANTS

Blue: Mediterranean cuisine—from Italy and Spain to Greece and Morocco—is offered in an expansive menu. The Jumbo Diver Scallops won as the 2004 Taste of the Nation "Best Appetizer." Entrées run from Lamb Tagine (Morocco), to Buffalo Ricotta & Baby Spinach Ravioli (Italy). The interior is contemporary-meets-Old-World—but it works. (*$$$, 214 N. Tryon St., Charlotte, (704) 927-2583, bluerestaurantandbar.com*)

Brixx Pizza: This casual, family-friendly local pizza chain serves up award-winning wood-fired thin-crust pies. You have the traditional pizzas but also get a taste of the world with their Mexican, Hawaiian, and Greek pizzas. They also serve specialty sandwiches, salads, and pastas. There are several locations in the area; check the Web site for details. (*$, 225 E. Sixth St., Charlotte, (704) 347-2749, brixxpizza.com*)

Coco Osteria: An osteria is the Tuscan version of a neighborhood bistro, and this uptown osteria serves rustic Italian fare in that tradition. The meal moves from cheeses and cold cuts, to pasta, to comfort-food entrées. The menu offers everything from Agnello in Fricassea (Tuscan-style lamb) to the house lasagna. The restaurant is fairly small—about 40 seats or so—so you might want to call ahead, especially on weekend nights. (*$, 214 N. Tryon St., Charlotte, (704) 344-8878, cocoosteria.com*)

Latorre's: It's funky (in a good way) and serves adventurous Nuevo Latino cuisine in a Miami-style atmosphere. Stefan Latorre, the owner, was born in Colombia, South America, grew up in Miami, and traveled extensively in South America. He brought his favorite dishes to Charlotte. Regulars rave about the desserts, and you can get real Cuban coffee. After dinner on Fridays and Saturdays, it's a hot Latin dance club. (*$$, 118 W. 5th St., Charlotte, (704) 377-4448, latorresrestaurant.com*)

Mickey & Mooch: Experience the feel of a classic, upscale steakhouse in the post-war era of the '40s, with big-band music sharing time with live music from the Baby Grand. A regional favorite, you can also get seafood and pasta. If you're a martini drinker, you should try the lobster martini. (*$$$, 9723 Sam Furr Rd., Huntersville, (704) 895-6654, mickeyandmooch.com*)

Quaker Steak & Lube: You just gotta love the name. It's a chain, but the motor sports-themed family restaurant fits in well with the nearby Lowe's Motor Speedway. When Jig and Moe opened the first one in a converted gas station, you had to cook your own food. Good for you the place did well and they can afford to hire cooks now. Their wings are national award winners and popular—across all the Quaker Steaks they serve more than 30 million of them a year. The menu also has items such as burgers, steaks, and chicken. (*$, 7731 Gateway Ln. NW, Concord, (704) 979-5823, quakersteak.com*)

Taqueria Guadalajara: You know it's real Mexican food when menudo is on the menu (no, not the band). Alongside it are other specialties of central Mexico, including quail and fish tacos. Nothing fancy here, but the food is good and authentic. Close to Bank of America Stadium. (*$, 4517 N. Tryon St., Charlotte, (704) 596-2239*)

For more information: For a directory of additional places to eat in the area visit opentable.com. You can also book a reservation for many restaurants on the site.

What to Do

DURING THE DAY

Carolina Raptor Center: Located within the Latta Preserve complex, the Raptor Center focuses on research and rehabilitation, helping injured birds heal and return safely into the wild. Visitors can stroll along the nature trail for a self-guided tour, observe raptors in their aviaries, and, on weekends, watch a presentation of live raptors. These birds—raptor species range from vultures to owls—are being nursed back into the wild, so don't be surprised if you see these birds of prey catch and eat their meals. (*$, 6000 Sample Rd., Huntersville, (704) 875-6521, carolinaraptorcenter.org*)

Charlotte Museum of History and Hezekiah Alexander Homesite: This 1774 stone house is where Hezekiah Alexander and his wife, Mary, reared 10 children. The oldest dwelling in the county, it's on the National Register of Historic Places. It is decorated in period style, which paints a vivid picture of what life was like in the pre-Colonial Piedmont area. Exhibits on-site showcase the region, its people, and their cultural heritage. (*$, 3500 Shamrock Dr., Charlotte, (704) 568-1774, charlottemuseum.org*)

Discovery Place: You could easily spend a day here with a nature museum that exhibits the animals and plants of the Piedmont (including the popular Butterfly Garden), an IMAX theater, aquariums, a three-story rain forest, and a hands-on science museum.. Plus, they have rat basketball. Really tall rats—okay, they're regular rats, but they shoot hoops. Please, no wagering. (*$$, 301 N. Tryon St., Charlotte, (800) 935-0553, discoveryplace.org*)

McDowell Nature Center.
(Photo: McDowell Nature Center
& Preserve)

Fourth Ward Historic District: Built in the late 1800s as a political subsection of town for electoral purposes, this beautiful old neighborhood on the edge of Uptown is made up of tree-lined streets and quaint Victorian homes. Pick up a brochure at the visitors center (330 South Tryon St.) and then take the walking tour of eighteen historic places of interest, including the **Gothic Revival First Presbyterian Church,** the **Old Settlers Cemetery** (with tombstones that date from the 1700s), **Fourth Ward Park,** and others. There are also restaurants and a market. (*The area bordered by Graham, Brevard, Trade, and 11th Sts.*)

James K. Polk Memorial: This state historic site just south of Charlotte is on the 400-acre farm where the 11th U.S. president was born in 1795. It houses period buildings (although not ones Polk lived in) and offers a view of life in the 19th-century South. Guides in period clothing help lead tours. (*Free, US 521, Pineville, (704) 889-7145, www.ah.dcr.state.nc.us/sections/hs/polk/polk.htm*)

McDowell Nature Preserve: This spectacular natural park preserves habitats for 119 species of birds, 21 species of mammals, 21 species of reptiles, and 14 species of amphibians, plus rare and endangered plants. There are water activities, playground, fishing, hiking, picnic areas, camping, and more. (*$, 15222 York Rd., Charlotte, (704) 583-1284, charmeck.org—click on "Leisure & Recreation," then on "Nature Centers & Preserves," and then on "McDowell Parks"*)

Mint Museum of Craft + Design: This modern museum (in a building originally built as Wadsworth Livery Stable) is one of the country's major crafts museums, with permanent collections of ceramics, glass, fiber, jewelry, metal, and wood. Exhibits highlight the area's rich craft tradition, celebrate the art in design, and feature works by well-known artists such as Dale Chihuly, Tom Patti, Stanislav Libenský, and Jaroslava Brychtová, whose architectural commissions in glass are on display. (*$, 220 N. Tryon St., Charlotte, (704) 337-2000, mintmuseum.org; save your receipt—it's good for free admission to the Mint Museum of Art*)

Checker Flag Lightning: So you think you can handle a race car? Do you tell your buddies Jeff Gordon's got nothing on you? Slide in behind the wheel of a real NEXTEL Cup car simulator and prove it. Checker Flag Lightning is in Concord Mills Shopping Mall and has 14 fully equipped, 750-horsepower interactive stock cars to take for a virtual spin. You'll feel like you're at the track—even when you wreck. (*$$, Concord Mills Shopping Mall, 8111 Concord Mills Blvd., Suite 202, Concord, (704) 979-3000*)

AT NIGHT

Boardwalk Billy's Raw Bar & Ribs: A University Place favorite, Boardwalk Billy's menu has everything from wings to steak, fish to pasta, if you're hungry. But at night the features are the drink specials and live music. Local bands play Thursday–Saturday nights. There are also two other area locations. (*$, 9005 J.M. Keynes Dr., Charlotte, (704) 503-7427, boardwalkbillys.com*)

The Comedy Zone: Need a laugh? The Comedy Zone hosts nationally known headliners and local comics. Located in Uptown, the Zone has a full bar as well as pizzas, salads, and sandwiches. Make reservations—these shows (including a smoke-free show on Fridays) fill up fast, especially for touring acts. (*Admission varies, 516 N. College St., Charlotte, (704) 348-4242, thecomedyzone.net*)

Connolly's on Fifth: This dim but cozy Irish pub is the real thing: Harp lager, Guinness stout, and weekly Irish traditional music are offered. After-work drinkers tend to hang out downstairs, and the late-night crowd is upstairs. Don't come hungry; they don't serve food. (*$, 115 E. 5th Street, Charlotte, (704) 358-9070*)

Crush: South Beach meets the Queen City. This Uptown dance club is upscale, and both dance floors get crowded. It's the home of Caliente Thursdays and Martini Party Fridays. The big sound system and a four-projection screen light show keep the two dance floors crowded. (*$, 300 E. Stonewall St., Charlotte, (704) 377-1010*)

House of Jazz: Downstairs you'll find a New Orleans take on the menu (creamy crawfish and sausage dip, Cajun crawfish poppers, jazzy wings). Amble upstairs and you'll find a cheerful bar with local and national jazz acts nightly. They do take reservations. (*Admission varies, 322 S. Church St., Charlotte, (704) 377-0008, thehouseofjazz.net*)

Double Door Inn: This is Charlotte's oldest live-music place, and the music is the blues. For more than 30 years, acts such as Buddy Guy, Koko Taylor, and Gatemouth Brown have entertained at this laid-back, late-night (music doesn't start until 10:00 p.m.) venue. Local acts play here, too. On Tuesday nights the "Americana Showcase" takes the stage. (*Admission varies, 218 E. Independence Blvd., Charlotte, (704) 376-1446, doubledoorinn.com*)

SHOPPING

Antique Shopping: There are antique stores in Charlotte, but locals will tell you that the towns of **Waxhaw, Pineville,** and **Matthews** are where you really want to go for antiques. Thirty-six miles south of downtown and with a population of just 2,600, Waxhaw's antique stores are easy to find in the city's downtown (which is on the National Register of Historic Places). Matthews is a Charlotte suburb just southeast of town; head to Mint Hill Road for the best selection. Twenty-one miles south-west of Charlotte is Pineville. The antique shops are in the city's historic downtown.

Founders Hall: Look for the big building downtown. That's the Bank of America Corporate Center, and Founders Hall is connected to it. This unique shopping destination features boutiques **(Burke & Co., Belle Ville),** a bookstore, apparel stores, and gift shops. **WBTV's Center City Studio** is here (it's Charlotte's CBS station and you can take a tour of the studio) as is the **Blumenthal Performing Arts Center.** (*100 N. Tryon St., Charlotte, (704) 386-0120, foundershall.com*)

NoDa (North Charlotte's Historic Arts District): This was a dynamic community in the North Carolina Textile Industry from 1903 to 1975. Then the last mill closed, and North Charlotte was all but forgotten until the 1980s. That's when young artists moved in and rebuilt the community. Now you'll find galleries, theaters, clubs, restaurants, and shops. Many are trendy, eclectic boutiques like **Everyday Essentials** for nature-based products, **Sunshine Daydreams** for jewelry, gifts, vintage clothes, and **Real Eyes** bookstore. If you're there when the sun goes down, visit **Evening Muse,** a listening room, art gallery, and café featuring live music 5-plus nights a week. (*From downtown, head north on N. Davidson St.; park at 36th St., and explore toward 35th St. and beyond, noda.org*)

For more information: To learn more about things to do in the area visit cityguide.aol.com/charlotte.

Chicago

The Chicago Bears are one of only two charter members of the NFL still playing. Their founder, George Halas, also founded the NFL in 1920.

As was the custom then, a company sponsored the team—the Staley Starch Company. Their first two seasons they were actually the Decatur Staleys; they moved to Chicago in 1922 and became the Bears. Since then they have been in and out as one of the most successful teams in the league, with more players in the Hall of Fame than any other franchise and nine NFL championships, including Super Bowl XX that featured a colorful cast that included Walter Payton, "Refrigerator" Perry, Jim McMahon, Buddy Ryan, and Coach Mike Ditka.

When they moved to the Windy City, the Bears played at Wrigley Field. They moved to the newly built Soldier Field in 1924 (actually it was Municipal Grant Park Stadium in 1924, renamed the next year to honor American soldiers who had died at war). At the turn of the century, the legendary stadium on the lake underwent massive renovations and reconstruction to create New Soldier Field, which hosted its first game in 2003.

Most of the parking around the stadium is "zone" parking, which means you can't park there to tailgate. Instead, you need to park in any of a number of lots in the area, many of which have free shuttles to the stadium.

Parking passes (they call them "coupons") are required to park in the North Garage, Waldron Deck, and South Lot. Season-ticket holders get these via a lottery.

You, on the other hand, should look for the cash lots: the East Monroe lot, the Millennium Park garages, and the 31st Street McCormick Place lots. Free shuttles will take you to the game. You can also park in the Grant Park South garages, but there's no shuttle service. Whichever lot you choose, it's going to cost you $35.

CHICAGO BEARS

New Soldier Field
Chicago, Illinois
(847) 615-BEAR ticket office
(888) 79-BEARS fan services
(312) 583-9153 parking hotline

RVs, bigger vehicles park in Adler Planetarium on first-come, first-served basis. No overnight parking. No alcohol, ad banners, or displays; no political campaigning or protesting, tents, canopies, tethered blimps, balloons, oversized inflatables, weapons, fireworks, disorderly conduct, saving spaces, or in/out privileges; stay inside your space.

Shuttle Info: Free shuttles run from the East Monroe lot, the Millennium Park garages, and the 31st Street McCormick Place lots. You can also get to the stadium area on Chicago's transit system; visit rtachicago.com for details.

Bears Media Partners: 780-AM WBBM, WMAQ-TV Channel 5 (NBC)

Tailgating is allowed on all surface lots and on the top level of the Waldron Deck. You're going to find yourself next to some of the most experienced tailgaters in the country, and if you don't have a good brat recipe, steal one from these people. You have to keep your tailgate party confined to your space, but you'll find several groups will just merge their tailgates into one big one. Alcohol is not allowed in these lots. At least that's what it says on paper.

RVs park at the Adler Planetarium Lot northeast of the stadium. It's first-come, first-served, and there is no overnight parking allowed. Parking here runs $75. Buses park here, too, for the same fee.

If you have questions about parking or tailgating at Bears games, call (312) 583-9153 or visit soldierfieldparking.com.

If you're not driving, the Chicago public transportation system has bus and train routes that can get you to Grant Park and the Soldier Field area. Just log on to rtachicago.com for details and costs.

Evanston is 20 miles up the road from Chicago. Although it's technically a suburb, it's adjacent to the city and is considered by many to be a part of Chicago. Northwestern University is here on a lakefront campus (Lake Michigan).

NU is nationally recognized for its academic programs and achievements. For a long time, that's what alumni talked about—not the football team, which was, well, bad. In the 1970s and '80s the Wildcats had one losing season after another. That continued until Coach Gary Barnett turned the team around and took them to the Rose Bowl in 1995. Since then the Wildcats have alumni (Charlton Heston, among them) and fans talking football.

That nickname, by the way, comes from a *Chicago Tribune* writer who, when describing the team in a 1924 game, wrote "Football players had not come down from Evanston; Wildcats would be a name better suited." From then on Northwestern has been the Wildcats.

The Wildcats play at Ryan Field, which has limited parking. This parking is reserved for season-ticket holders. However, there are a number of free parking lots on, and just off, campus. All of them are near stops for the free shuttle that runs to the stadium beginning 2 hours before kickoff. For a map of lots and shuttle stops, go to nusports.com, click on "Football," and then on "Ryan Field on a Football Game Day."

RVs are required to park on campus at Lot #2/MLS. Parking for RVs costs $30 per day, but overnight parking is permitted.

If you're coming in from Chicago, or don't want to bother with the parking, you can take a bus or a train. Both have stops within a few blocks of Ryan Field. For routes and fares, log on to rtachicago.com.

Once at Ryan Field, you can visit Wildcat Alley for food, drinks, games, and entertainment. NU's pregame party is free and located on the Northwestern baseball field (Rocky Miller Park) next door to Ryan Field.

About Chicago

The nation's third-largest city began as a simple settlement, built in 1779 by a Haitian of African descent named Jean-Baptiste Pionte du Sable. The settlement was where the Michigan Avenue Bridge is today.

Chicago—the name is thought to have come from an Indian word meaning "strong" or "great"—incorporated in 1883 and quickly became one of our nation's most colorful cities.

A defining moment in the city's history was, of course, the Great Chicago Fire in 1871. No one knows how it started in the cow barn behind a house on the west side, but most of the city burned to the ground. Hundreds died, tens of thousands were homeless. But the city rebuilt, and by 1875 there was little evidence left of the tragedy that had occurred.

This rebuilding also sparked a Chicago trademark: the skyscraper. The first skyscraper in the world was built here in 1885. That's a relative term. It was nine stories tall. However, it was built with steel supports—the first time ever—and led the way to taller and taller buildings. The tallest in the city (and for a while the world) is the Sears Tower at 110 stories.

Now, about that "Windy City" nickname. It does not refer to those brisk breezes off Lake Michigan or the whipping wind generated by and through Chicago's tall buildings. It was actually coined by *New York Sun* editor Charles Dana in 1893, when he'd grown tired of hearing long-winded politicians boasting about the World's Columbian Exposition held in Chicago that year. The wind in Windy City is hot air.

NORTHWESTERN UNIVERSITY
Ryan Field
Evanston, Illinois
(847) 491-7887

Good news—overnight RV parking $30. Bad news—all must leave 2 hours after game. No real restrictions; just keep within own tailgate space. Wildcat Alley has fun games for younger kids.

Shuttle Info: Free shuttles run to Ryan Field from several stops on and near campus. You can also ride a Chicago bus or train to Evanston; both have stops within walking distance of the stadium. Log on to rtachicago.com for details and fares.

Wildcats Media Partner: 720-AM WGN

Where to Stay

RV PARKS

Chicago Northwest KOA: You'll find lots of trees, full hookups, a swimming pool, and mini-golf at this park, which is about an hour outside of Chicago and open April–October. Rates are $25–$45. Kamping Kabins are available (it's a KOA, so everything they can spell with a *K* they do). (*8404 S. Union Rd., Union, (800) 562-2827, koakampgrounds.com/where/il/13101/*)

Windy City Beach & Camping Resort: This park is between Chicago and the Chicagoland Speedway. It offers 100 full hookup sites, a small lake with a beach, fishing, paddle boats, and a snack shop. Daily rates run $32–$34. Cabins available. (*18701 S. 80th Ave., Tinley Park, (708) 720-0030, windycitycampground.com*)

Bears fans fire up their grills early on game day.
(Photo: Roy Taylor)

For more information: For additional RV parks and campsites visit campingworld.com/campsearch.

HOTELS

Hotel Allegro: Located in the theater district, this Art Deco–designed hotel has bright colors and a hip, club-like atmosphere. Rooms feature flat-screen TVs, sound systems, fully stocked mini-bars, plus all the usual amenities. Rooms run $129–$229; more for the suites. (*171 W. Randolph St., Chicago, (866) 672 6143, allegrochicago.com*)

The Orrington: Newly reopened after a $34 million renovation, the hotel is near the North Shore and Northwestern. It has all the expected amenities plus a stocked mini-bar, fitness center, and business center. Restaurant and bar on-site. Rooms run $129–$169, based on season. (*1710 Orrington Ave., Evanston, (847) 866-8700, hotelorrington.com*)

Palmer House: This historic Chicago landmark was destroyed in the 1871 fire and rebuilt more opulently than before. The hand-painted ceiling in the lobby is spectacular. It's been renovated since then, too, of course, and the rooms have all the usual amenities. Fitness center is on-site. Pet friendly. It's now owned by Hilton, so we're breaking our no-chain rule a bit, but the architecture and decor is worth breaking it. Rooms run $179–$234. (*17 E. Monroe St., Chicago, (800) 445-8667, hilton.com—search for Chicago, IL*)

For more information: To learn about more hotels in the area visit tripadvisor.com for listings and guest reviews.

B&BS

Flemish House of Chicago: Studio and one-bedroom apartments make up this 1890s greystone row house. Furnished in English Arts and Crafts decor, each of the seven apartments includes a stocked kitchen and individually controlled air conditioning. Located in the Gold Coast neighborhood close to Michigan Avenue and the lakefront. Rooms run $135–$185. (*68 E. Cedar St., Chicago, (312) 664-9981, chicagobandb.com*)

The Wheeler Mansion: This 1870 historical landmark is one of the last of the stately mansions that survived the Great Chicago Fire. It isn't your typical B&B—it's a bit more like a boutique hotel—and has seven rooms, two junior suites, and two suites, all with private baths. Suites have fireplaces. Rooms run $230–$285; suites up to $365. (*2020 S. Calumet Ave., Chicago, (312) 945-2020, wheelermansion.com*)

For more information: To learn about more B&Bs in the area visit bedandbreakfast.com for a detailed directory.

Where to Eat
TAILGATER GROCERIES

Chicago's Green City Market: This nonprofit farmers' market features locally grown, sustainable, and organic foods. The market supports and promotes small, family farms that provide produce, cheeses, and more. Scores of local restaurants support the market, too, so you may just find one of Chicago's top chefs trying to buy the same tomato you are. (*South end of Lincoln Park between 1750 N. Clark and Stockton Dr., Chicago, (312) 649.5806, chicagogreencitymarket.org*)

SPORTS BARS

Joe's Bar: The name is simple, but inside is 20,000 square feet of sports bar. There are more than 120 TVs (including 14 10-foot screens) that show just about any game you'd ever want to see. Joe's is also home to more than a dozen school alumni groups from the Fighting Illini to the Florida Gators. The bar also hosts live music and touring acts. The menu is what you'd expect and includes pizza and sandwiches. (*$, 940 W. Weed St., Chicago, (312) 337-3486, joesbar.com*)

ESPN Zone: A slew of televisions, including a 16-foot HDTV big screen, set the mood. The bar has several games, including Madden NFL Football on a 15-foot screen and an interactive Power Pitcher, where you can try to strike out Bonds, Sosa, and Griffey. The menu is upscale bar food. (*$, 43 E. Ohio St., Chicago, (312) 644-3776, espnzone.com/Chicago*)

Chicago fans are some of the most loyal tailgaters in the country. (Photo: Roy Taylor)

Murphy's Bleachers: Opened in 1930 as Ernie's Bleachers, and renamed Ray's Bleachers in 1965 (remember the Bleacher Bums?), it became Murphy's Bleachers when Jim Murphy bought it in 1980. It sits across the street from Wrigley Field and is truly a Chicago institution. The menu is heavy on sandwiches and burgers. Named by *AOL CityGuide* as "Chicago's Best Bar" in 2005. (*3655 N. Sheffield, Chicago, (773) 281-5356, murphysbleachers.com*)

RESTAURANTS

Chicago Firehouse Restaurant: This popular restaurant is located in a restored turn-of-the-century firehouse. (The courtyard was once the stables, where the horses who pulled the fire wagons lived.) The menu features upscale American cuisine such as the Mango and Chili Barbecued Pork and an extensive American wine list. (*$$, 1401 S. Michigan Ave., Chicago, (312) 786-1401, chicagofirehouse.com*)

Davis Street Fish Market: The flavors of New Orleans are infused in the menu here, from Shrimp and Scallop Stew (they call it Louisiana chili), to etouffee, to po' boys. There's also a 70-seat raw bar with a variety of oysters. (*$, 501 Davis St., Evanston, (847) 869-3474, davisstreetfishmarket.com*)

Gino's East of Chicago: Chicago reinvented the pizza with its deep-dish pies, and Gino's helped make it famous. Open since 1966, Gino's is a Chicago landmark. They serve thin-crust pizza, too, but you can get that almost anywhere. (*$, 633 N. Wells St., Chicago, (312) 943-1124, ginoseast.com*)

Harry Caray's Restaurant: Named for the late Hall of Fame baseball announcer, this restaurant has won awards for its steaks, its wine, and its bar scene. There's memorabilia from the Chicago legend's broadcast career and a gift shop where you can buy a "Holy Cow" hat or shirt. The building is remarkable, too. Built in 1895, it's the last example of 19th-century Dutch Renaissance architecture left in Chicago. (*$$, 33 W. Kinzie St., Chicago, (312) 828-0966, harrycarays.com*)

Mike Ditka's Chicago: Few people are as closely linked to a city as Mike Ditka is to Chicago. The former Bears coach won a Super Bowl here (he also won one in Dallas as a player) and "Da' Coach" is often at the restaurant mingling with diners. The menu covers steaks to chops, fish to pasta. (*100 E. Chestnut, Chicago, (312) 587-8989, mikeditkaschicago.com*)

The Saloon Steakhouse: The house favorite is the 24-ounce Cowboy Cut, but you can get smaller servings of what many call the best steak in the city. The menu also has chicken, ribs, seafood, and pasta. Located in the **Seneca Hotel,** the restaurant isn't as crowded with tourists as many other Chicago steakhouses are, and it is a couple of blocks from both Michigan Avenue and the lake. (*$$, 200 E. Chestnut St., Chicago, (312) 280-5454, saloonsteakhouse.com*)

For more information: For a directory of additional places to eat in the area visit opentable.com. You can also book a reservation for many restaurants on the site.

What to Do
DURING THE DAY

The Art Institute of Chicago. (Photo: The Art Institute of Chicago)

Art Institute of Chicago: The museum is home to one of the best and most diverse art collections in the world, including Grant Wood's *American Gothic,* Edward Hopper's *Nighthawks*, Pablo Picasso's *The Old Guitarist*, and Georges Seurat's *A Sunday Afternoon on La Grande Jatte–1884.* The two lion statues flanking the museum's main entrance have been there since 1893. (You'll probably recognize them.) (*$$, 111 S. Michigan Ave., Grant Park, Chicago, (312) 443-3600, artic.edu*)

Chicago Museum Campus: This scenic, 57-acre lakefront park is a series of public parks and gardens that connect the city's three most prominent museums. There are walkways and a free trolley between the attractions. (*1400 S. Lakeshore Dr., Chicago, (312) 409-9696*)

Adler Planetarium & Astronomy Museum: This was the first public planetarium in the western hemisphere (opened in 1930). In addition to Sky Theater, there are a number of exhibits and interactive activities, including a space-flight simulator. (*$$, (312) 922-STAR, adlerplanetarium.org*)

Field Museum of Natural History: The museum, named for bene-factor Marshall Field (yep, the department store guy), has exhibits illustrating art, archaeology, science, and history from around the world. Exhibits include everything from the world's largest Tyrannosaurus rex to King Tut. (*$$, (312) 922-9410, fieldmuseum.org*)

John G. Shedd Aquarium: Built in 1930 and still the world's largest indoor aquarium, the Shedd has exhibits featuring fish and animals from around the world. Some are in pools that appear to blend into Lake Michigan. (*$$, (312) 939-2426, sheddaquarium.org*)

Navy Pier: Built in 1916 as a commercial shipping pier, it's been transformed into an entertainment destination that draws more than eight million visitors a year. Attractions include an IMAX theater, miniature golf, the **Children's Museum,** a carousel, shopping, and restaurants. The pier's most famous attraction is its 150-foot-high Ferris wheel, which was built in 1893 for the city's World Columbian Exposition and moved here. *($, 600 E. Grand Ave., Chicago, (312) 595-7437, navypier.com)*

Sears Tower Skydeck: Recently renovated, the Skydeck in this 110-story building (once the world's tallest) has exhibits, interactive kiosks, and telescopes. And then there's the view. You can see for about 50 miles on a clear day—which means you can see Illinois, Indiana, Michigan and Wisconsin. *($–$$, 233 S. Wacker Dr., Chicago, (312) 875-9696, the-sky-deck.com)*

The Ferris wheel at Navy Pier. (Photo: NAVY PIER®)

AT NIGHT

Buddy Guy's Legends: He's a Chicago legend, a blues legend (and in the Rock and Roll Hall of Fame) and his bar Legends is one of the nation's top blues clubs. Memorabilia is on the walls, and artists such as Eric Clapton, Stevie Ray Vaughn, and ZZ Top have graced the stage. Of course, most nights feature local, regional, and touring acts. *($–$$, 754 S. Wabash Ave., Chicago, (312) 427-0333, buddyguys.com)*

Celtic Crossings: It's not big, but it's been called the most authentic Irish pub in Chicago (and there're a bunch of them here). Designed and owned by Irishmen, there are more than a dozen beers on tap, traditional Irish pub food, and live traditional Irish music on weekends. *($, 751 N. Clark St., Chicago, IL, (312) 337-1005)*

The Cotton Club: Recreating the Harlem original, this popular spot for live music offers the Cab Calloway room with contemporary jazz and blues combos, and DJs spinning hip-hop and urban contemporary in the rear Gray Room. And if you're wondering, its name comes from a unique definition of "cotton," meaning "to make friends." *($, 1710 S. Michigan Ave., Chicago, (312) 341-9787)*

The Keg of Evanston: This hangout close to Northwestern is part pub, part restaurant. There is a full menu, with everything from a salad bar, to steaks, to seafood, but it's the two bars, game room, and general party atmosphere that fills up the place. After-work and dinner crowds are a bit older, but as the sun sets the college kids take over. *($, 810 Grove St., Evanston, (847) 869-9987)*

Sound-Bar: Upscale and hip, this 20,000-square-foot, multilevel dance club (the dance floor by itself is 4,000 square feet) has several bars and lounges, and it features international DJs spinning a wide variety of music. *($–$$, 226 W. Ontario St., Chicago, (312) 787-4480, sound-bar.com)*

SHOPPING

Chicago Music Mart: A diverse collection of music retailers all housed under one roof. You can shop for musical instruments, CDs, sheet music, and music-themed gifts and souvenirs. Free concerts at lunchtime, too. *(333 S. State St., Chicago, (312) 362-6700)*

The Magnificent Mile: This legendary shopping and entertainment district runs down Michigan Avenue, bounded by Oak Street on the north and the Chicago River to the south. There are more than 450 retail stores, including big boys such as **Neiman Marcus, Saks Fifth Avenue,** and **Bloomingdale's.** There are also scores of smaller shops and boutiques, restaurants, and clubs. *(themagnificentmile.com)*

Cars park for free. Park on west side of Chicagoland Speedway; use shuttle. Several RV tailgater packages—from $350 for RV Land campground to $1,000 for parking on the field. Overnight parking at RV campgrounds only. No open fires, unauthorized vehicles, or tent camping; one space per vehicle. Miller Lite sponsors free concert Friday evening of NASCAR Pole Day. Free shuttle from Joliet Union Station and back.

For more information: To learn more about things to do in the area visit cityguide.aol.com/chicago.

JOLIET

The Chicagoland Speedway is on several hundred acres in Joliet, a suburb of Chicago about an hour from downtown. Joliet has had its economic troubles, and most who visit spend their time in Chicago. On NASCAR and IRL race weekends, though, tens of thousands descend on the town.

Chicago's racing history began in 1895, when the first gasoline-powered race was held up and down the Chicago lakefront. Today, sellout crowds of 75,000 come to the Speedway to watch cars race much faster.

There are 700 acres of free parking at the track. That will hold 50,000 vehicles. There is no overnight stay in these lots. For overnights, RVs can park in the infield, on Speedway Ridge, or in the new RV Land campsite between turns two and three. Infield lots run $800–$1,000 (the higher cost is if you have electric hookup) and Speedway Ridge costs $550–$750. Camping in RV Land is $350, and that includes electric hookups. Trams run from the parking areas to the track. For more information and to reserve spots, call (815) 727-RACE.

When not watching the race, you can visit Expo Village by the main gate, which has activities and entertainment.

Where to Stay

RV PARKS

Martin Campground: Located about 10 minutes from the Speedway, this campground has 110 sites with all the basic amenities. LP by meter and weight, and play equipment is available. The sites can accommodate big rigs. (*2303 New Lenox Rd., Joliet, (815) 726-3173*)

For more information: For additional RV parks and campsites visit campingworld.com/campsearch.

HOTELS

Empress Hotel: Part of the Empress Casino complex, the hotel has all the usual amenities, along with satellite TV, indoor pool, and whirlpool. Rooms run $59–$89, based on what night of the week you stay. (*2200 Empress Dr., Joliet, (815) 744-9400, argosy.com/chicago*)

Harrah's: On-site with the casino, rooms have all the basic hotel amenities. Each room includes a TV web browser. Rates run $59 and up, based on the day of the week. (*151 N. Joliet St., Joliet, (815) 740-7800, harrahs.com/our-casinos/jol*)

For more information: To learn about more hotels in the area visit tripadvisor.com for listings and guest reviews.

Where to Eat

SPORTS BARS

City of Champions Sports Bar and Grill: This spacious bar has 30 TVs and a game room. The menu ranges from sandwiches to burgers (one-pounders), wraps to wings. DJs and dancing Thursday–Saturday. (*$, 2727 W. Jefferson St., Joliet, (815) 730-4755, cityofjoliet.com/BUSINESS/cityofchampions.htm*)

Down From The Tracks Sports Bar & Grill: Located in Joliet's historic Union Station, this is your basic sports bar with plenty of TVs, games, a pool table, darts, and a full menu—theirs features sandwiches. Friday night is dancing and a DJ. (*$, 50 E. Jefferson St., #103, Joliet, (815) 724-1190, downfromthetracks.com*)

RESTAURANTS

Barolo Ristorante: The chef/owner is from Bari, Italy, and trained at the Italian Culinary School in Rome. But the menu doesn't stick with Italy as an influence—you get flavors from all around the Mediterranean. Fresh fish is flown in daily. There's also a children's menu that changes daily. (*$, 158 N. Chicago St., Joliet, (815) 722-1744, barolofinedining.com*)

Public Landing Restaurant: Originally the construction depot for the digging of the Illinois & Michigan canal, this 1838 limestone building is now home to modern American cuisine. The menu goes from Potato Encrusted Tilapia to Rack of Lamb, with several stops in between. All the dressings are handmade, too. (*$–$$, 200 W. Eighth St., Joliet, (815) 838-6500, publiclandingrestaurant.com*)

For more information: For a directory of additional places to eat in the area visit opentable.com. You can also book a reservation for many restaurants on the site.

What to Do

DURING THE DAY

Splash Station: This water theme park has pools, water slides, tubing "rivers," and concessions. Open May–September. (*$–$$, 2780 US Route 6, Joliet, (815) 741-7250, jolietsplashstation.com*)

DAY AND NIGHT

Argosy Empress Casino: This casino complex has gaming, dining, and entertainment, along with a hotel and RV park (see page 64). (*2300 Empress Dr., Joliet, (888) 436-7737, argosy.com/chicago*)

Harrah's: This casino complex includes gaming, dining, entertainment, and shopping. There's also a hotel (see page 64). (*151 N. Joliet St., Joliet, (815) 740-7800, harrahs.com/our-casinos/jol/index.html*)

For more information: To learn more about things to do in the area visit cityofjoliet.info

DEKALB

About an hour west of Chicago, and on the border of our 60-mile rule, is Northern Illinois University in DeKalb. "Barb City" (barbed wire was invented here) is a small college town with about 40,000 residents. A little more than half that many attend NIU, which opened its doors in 1895.

NIU was founded as a teacher's college, and its teams were called the Profs. That gave way to Cardinals (they wore red jerseys) and a couple of other nicknames before coming full circle and being called the Teachers. In 1940 a committee looked for a better name and the winner was Huskies.

Huskie Stadium seats 30,000 and has plenty of parking within a few blocks of the stadium. General parking is $5 and RVs park for $10. There is no overnight parking allowed, and tailgating must be within your parking spot. There's also the Tent-A-Gate area next to Huskie Stadium for tailgating, although you'll need to get a permit for your tent. Call (815) 753-1923 to do that.

Where to Stay
RV PARKS

Sycamore RV Resort: This campground sits on a picturesque lake in the middle of farmland and has a swimming beach as well as fishing and boating. It also has 86 sites, the usual amenities, and LP by meter and weight. Daily rates are $25–$28 for four people. (*375 E. North Ave., Sycamore, (815) 895-5590, sycamorervresort.com*)

For more information: For additional RV parks and campsites visit campingworld.com/campsearch.

HOTELS

Stratford Inn: A historic inn housed in buildings built in 1882 and 1926, the Stratford has been renovated and includes modern hotel amenities such as DSL lines and whirlpool suites. There's a restaurant on site. Rooms run $68–$80; suites are $110–$139. (*355 W. State St., Sycamore, (800) 937-8106, stratfordinnhotel.com*)

For more information: To learn about more hotels in the area visit tripadvisor.com for listings and guest reviews.

Where to Eat
SPORTS BARS

Fatty's Pub & Grille: Located just off campus, this is a popular place to watch a game or play pool or arcade games. Basic pub menu. (*$, 1312 W. Lincoln Hwy., DeKalb, (815) 758-7737*)

RESTAURANTS

Hillside Restaurant: Family owned since 1955, it specializes in home-cooked favorites. Part of the menu rotates, based on seasonal ingredients; there are also vegetarian selections. (*$, 121 N. 2nd St., DeKalb, (815) 756-4749, hillsiderestaurant.com*)

Lincoln Inn Family Restaurant: A downtown fixture for more than 30 years. The restaurant is open for breakfast, lunch, and dinner. Fresh-baked breads are a house specialty. (*$, 240 E. Lincoln Hwy., DeKalb, (815) 756-2345*)

For more information: For a directory of additional places to eat in the area visit opentable.com. You can also book a reservation for many restaurants on the site.

NIU fans tailgating outside Huskie Stadium. (Photo: Scott Walstrom, NIU Media Services)

What to Do
AT NIGHT

O'Leary's Irish Pub & Grill: Relatively new to the downtown area, O'Leary's is a popular Irish Pub and hangout with dark beers on tap and traditional dishes such as corned beef and cabbage on the menu. (*$, 260 E. Lincoln Hwy., DeKalb, (815) 748-0000*)

For more information: To learn more about things to do in the area visit dekalbareacvb.com

SOUTH BEND, IN

South Bend is about 90 miles from Chicago, and, yes, outside our 60-mile rule, but come on, this is Notre Dame. We're not leaving out *this* road trip.

The Fighting Irish are about as rich in tradition and lore as a team can be. Knute Rockne. The Four Horsemen. Win One for the Gipper. Seven Heisman Trophy winners. Joe Montana. Rudy. "Touchdown Jesus."

That last one is, of course, a reference to the now famous mosaic on the outside wall of the Hesburgh Library, depicting Jesus with outstretched arms as if signaling a touchdown. The Irish have scored a lot of touchdowns at Notre Dame Stadium.

The stadium seats 80,795, officially. More have been known to squeeze in for big games. Games are sold out and the tailgating is as legendary as the team. These are loyal fans. (By the way, no one really knows where that "Fighting Irish" nickname came from, but most think the media coined it at some point. One thing we do know is that the university officially adopted the nickname in 1927.)

All general parking is in the White Field North near the intersection of Pendle and Juniper Roads. Cars are $20; RVs run $60. There are free shuttles that run from the parking lot to Library Circle just north of the stadium. Lots open at 7:30 a.m. on game day.

While tailgating is a long tradition at Notre Dame, the school has recently put some restrictions on it. There is now no tailgating allowed during the game. Before and after is fine, but if you're tailgating while the game is in progress, security will remove you. The school is trying to crack down on people who, as they put it, use the game as an excuse for an all-day drinking party.

In addition, you cannot use a charcoal grill for your tailgate—gas grills only. Kegs are also prohibited. While the rules say you must use only one parking space, you may use the aisles for your parking-lot party.

About South Bend

South Bend is in northern Indiana and was incorporated in 1865. About 20 years later Henry and Clem Studebaker opened the Studebaker Manufacturing Company, where they made wagons. Around the turn

UNIVERSITY OF NOTRE DAME
Notre Dame Stadium
South Bend, Indiana
(574) 631-7356

Cars park for $20; RVs park for $60. All parking is in the White Field North. No overnight parking available; RVs restricted to one lot. No tailgating during game; no tents, charcoal grills, or kegs; stay within your space.

Shuttle Info: Shuttles run from the White Field North parking lot to the stadium. The shuttle is free.

Fighting Irish Media Partners: 93-FM WNDU, 1490-AM WNDU, 640-AM WVFI

of the century, they were one of the few who successfully converted their business into making cars, and for several years the Studebaker often outsold Ford in terms of number of cars sold. The plant shut down in 1963.

Where to Stay
RV PARKS
South Bend East KOA: This is the closest RV park to Notre Dame. It has 80 sites in a tall pine forest, with a nature trail, bike rentals, mini-golf, and a swimming pool. All the usual amenities, LP gas (by weight and meter), and a grocery store to pick up last-minute tailgating items. Rates run $29–$48. Kamping Kabins available. (*50707 Princess Way, Granger, (574) 277-1335, koa.com/where/in/14153*)

For more information: For additional RV parks and campsites visit campingworld.com/campsearch.

HOTELS
The Inn at Saint Mary's: This quietly upscale hotel is nestled on the campus of Saint Mary's College, adjacent to the University of Notre Dame. It has all the basic amenities plus free high-speed Internet and a fitness center. Rooms cost $109–$119. (*53993 US Hwy. 933, South Bend, (800) 947-8627, innatsaintmarys.com*)

For more information: To learn about more hotels in the area visit tripadvisor.com for listings and guest reviews.

B&BS
Cushing Manor Inn: This 1872 French Victorian mansion is filled with period antiques and located in South Bend's historic district. Each of six guest rooms has a private bath. Common areas have fireplaces, and there's a large, covered porch. Rooms run $95–$155. (*508 W. Washington St., South Bend, (866) 268-7790, cushingmanorinn.com*)

The Oliver Inn: This Queen Anne home on a shaded lot, with tall maple trees, is a local historical landmark and was home to the Oliver family for more than 100 years. It offers nine guest rooms, some with built-in fireplaces or double Jacuzzis. There's also a Carriage House Retreat. Rooms run $95–$195; the Carriage House costs $249–$329 and has a two-night minimum. (*630 W. Washington St., South Bend, (888) 697-4466, oliverinn.com*)

For more information: To learn about more B&Bs in the area visit bedandbreakfast.com for a detailed directory.

The Ultimate Tailgater's Travel Guide

Where to Eat

SPORTS BARS

Between the Buns: This locally owned neighborhood sports bar has been named "Best Sports Bar" and "Best Bar & Grill" by the *South Bend Tribune*. TVs are scattered around for you to watch while eating. The menu is typical pub food, but with atypical names—care for The Four Horseman Platter or the Ryne Sandburger? (*$, 1803 South Bend Ave., South Bend, (574) 247-9293, betweentheburs.com*)

Notre Dame Stadium seats 80,795.
(Photo: University of Notre Dame)

Linebacker Inn: Founded by a former ND player (but since sold), this 50-year-old pub is a Notre Dame game-day tradition. Lots of TVs and memorabilia; burgers and sandwiches on the menu. Across the street from campus, or as they put it, "a touch-down pass away." (*$, 1631 South Bend Ave., South Bend, (574) 289-0186, backernd.com*)

RESTAURANTS

East Bank Emporium: This restaurant is in a historic, early 1900s saloon. On the east bank of the St. Joseph River, hence the name, the restaurant serves casual American cuisine, with plenty of beef and seafood selections. Outdoor seating during good weather. (*$, 121 S. Niles Ave., South Bend, (574) 234-9000, eastbankemporium.com/Emp/ebmain.html*)

LaSalle Grill: Housed in a post-Civil War hotel, the LaSalle is an award-winning restaurant serving casual fine dining. The menu has contemporary American dishes such as Horseradish Crusted Sea Scallops and Roasted Vegetable Frittata. Beef and fish are also on the menu. You'll need to dress a bit to dine here; coats and ties are preferred for men, but not required. (*$$, 115 W. Colfax Ave., South Bend, (800) 382-9323, lasallegrill.com*)

For more information: For a directory of additional places to eat in the area visit opentable.com. You can also book a reservation for many restaurants on the site.

What to Do

DURING THE DAY

College Football Hall of Fame: From "Slingin'" Sammy Baugh to Ronnie Lott, the Hall of Fame celebrates the history and heroes of college football. The Hall contains memorabilia, exhibits and special events, and interactive activities, where you can test your own punting, passing and blocking skills, as well as speed and agility. (*$$, 111 S. Saint Joseph St., South Bend, (800) 440-3263, collegefootball.org*)

Studebaker National Museum: The Studebaker family built their carriages and cars in South Bend, and this museum chronicles that history as well as that of the industry. Exhibits have also included President Lincoln's carriage and other historic examples of the development of transportation. (*$, 201 S. Chaplin St., South Bend, (888) 391-5600, studebakermuseum.org*)

The College Football Hall of Fame.
(Photo: College Football Hall of Fame)

AT NIGHT

Fiddler's Hearth Public House: Not far from campus, this Irish pub's menus—food and beer—hold to Celtic tradition. Okay, they do have some American dishes for those who don't want to try Welsh Rarebit or Corned Beef and Cabbage. Traditional Irish music most nights, but sometimes they slip into bluegrass. (*$, 127 N. Main St., South Bend, (574) 232-2853, fiddlershearth.com*)

Legends of Notre Dame: Here you're surrounded by moments and figures from ND's past, as well as 24 taps and a college crowd. Legends is close to campus and is also a popular place to watch ball games. There are nightly themed drink specials, and, in case you're hungry, the pub has a restaurant in the same building. (*54801 Juniper Rd., Notre Dame, (574) 631-2582, legendsofnotredame.org*)

SHOPPING

Downtown South Bend: There are more than 50 shops in the downtown area selling everything from fashion to flowers, books to gifts. There are also art galleries. The downtown has restaurants and other attractions, too, including a manmade whitewater course.

For more information: To learn more about things to do in the area visit cityguide.aol.com/southbend.

Dallas

Tom Landry. Roger Staubach. Jimmy Johnson. Troy Aikman. Emmitt Smith. Five Super Bowl rings (an NFL record shared with the Pittsburgh Steelers). The Dallas Cowboys Cheerleaders. And that famous hole in the roof. This is America's Team.

The Dallas Cowboys joined the NFL as an expansion team in 1960. They had five losing seasons and then began their record run of 20 winning seasons in a row. In 1971 they moved into Texas Stadium and won Super Bowl VI. There's no conclusive proof of a relationship, but the stadium is one of the most unique ever built.

The partially domed stadium was designed to keep fans covered but leave the field open to the elements. It was also said the hole in the roof was so Tom Landry could talk directly with God. Either way, the 65,000-seat stadium never really worked as planned—rain doesn't usually fall straight down—but many fans are sad to see it go. The Cowboys will move into a new stadium in 2009.

You can tailgate in all of the parking lots around Texas Stadium; of course, many of those lots are reserved for season-pass holders, but you can buy game-day passes. One parking pass means you can take up only one space; if you have a grill on a trailer, you'll have to pay for a second pass. The Blue Lots circle the stadium; the Red and Green Lots are on the other side of Highway 114. The Green Lot is a hike. RVs park on the other side of the stadium and across Loop 12 (there's a walkway across the highway). You can buy passes from the Cowboys or from one of several brokers in town that sell them—just do an Internet search for Dallas Cowboys Parking. Since many of the brokers buy up passes to resell them, they may be your best bet on short notice; they'll charge you from around $35 for the outer lots to $120 for the VIP parking area in the Blue Lots.

If you'd rather let someone else do the driving, the Dallas Area Rapid Transit system runs trains and busses from 13 Metroplex cities. Log on to dart.org for routes, schedules, and fares.

The Cowboys' pregame party is called the Corral Club. The Corral is a tent outside Gate 8. It opens 3 hours before the game, and costs $3 and a game ticket. Without the game ticket, no amount will get you in. The Corral has big-screen TVs, live music, entertainment, food, and drinks. If you want to let the traffic clear out after the game, the Corral stays open for 2 hours after the final whistle.

Dallas is also home to the SMU Mustangs, the college home of greats like Don Meredith and Eric Dickerson. The Mustangs were a good football team,

DALLAS COWBOYS

Texas Stadium
Dallas, Texas
(972) 785-4000

Tailgating allowed in all Texas Stadium parking lots. Occupy as many spaces as you've got parking passes for. If bringing grill on trailer, buy additional spot for trailer. Ash cans and trash cans located throughout parking lots. Buses, shuttles available. Pre- and postgame party at the Corral tent, outside Gate 8. Fee is $3 with game ticket.

Shuttle Info: The Dallas Area Rapid Transit system runs trains and buses from 13 Metroplex cities. Log on to dart.org for routes, schedules, and fares.

Cowboys Media Partner: 98.7-FM KLUV

regularly challenging for conference titles. In 1982 they went 10-1-1 and were ranked No. 2 in the nation. A few years later the sky fell when the school's legacy of cheating finally came back to haunt it, although in those days about half of the Southwest Conference membership was on one sort of NCAA probation or another.

In 1985 SMU was put on probation for the fourth time in 11 years. In 1986 they were caught in the middle of a recruiting-violation scandal. And in 1987 they were given the NCAA's "death penalty"—the program was shut down. That remains the only time in NCAA history a Division I school has received the death penalty. Two years later 74 freshmen took the field to try and rebuild the program. They've been a losing team ever since.

The team that once played to crowds in the Cotton Bowl and Texas Stadium now plays in the 32,000-seat Gerald J. Ford Stadium (no, not the president, an alumni donor). It's a new stadium, opened in 2000.

You can tailgate in the parking lots, but few do. All the tailgating action is along the campus's Bishop Boulevard, simply known as the Boulevard. Just west of the stadium, this is where you find tents and grills, music and games, vendors and fans.

If you didn't bring a tent, you can rent umbrella tents; groups can rent larger tents. Call (214) 768-2582. But you can also stroll up and down the median visiting with friends and making new ones. Tailgating along the Boulevard has a real community event feel to it, so don't be surprised to have people stick a drink in your hand or offer you a plate.

Oh, about the mascot you'll see running on the sidelines. No, that's not a mustang. That's a miniature horse named Peruna, which was a popular medicinal tonic with a kick in 1933, when a miniature horse became the team's mascot. Guess it's easier to handle than a wild mustang.

About Dallas

The first settlers in this part of the world were French explorers. But it was a man named John Neely Bryan who founded the city in 1841. It's believed he named his city after George M. Dallas, who was vice president at the time (for James K. Polk), although that's not 100 percent certain. Historians say Bryan's exact words were just that he named the city "after my friend Dallas."

It was after the Civil War that Dallas came into its own. The railroads helped make it a trading center. The turn of the twentieth century saw Dallas become a center for banking, insurance, and other businesses. In the 1930s oil was discovered nearby and Dallas became a financial center for the oil industry. In the '50s and '60s the city was a technology center that included hometown companies LTV Corporation and Texas Instruments. The building boom came in the '70s and '80s, which

The Ultimate Tailgater's Travel Guide

gave Dallas its distinctive skyline. Then there was the television show of the same name, which many in town had wished was just a bad dream.

Where to Stay

RV PARKS

Dallas West Mobile Home–RV Park: This is a very basic park with 90 sites, laundry and cable, but not much else. All sites are full hookups. The park is in the middle of town and within an easy drive to several attractions. (*400 W. Commerce St., Dallas, (214) 748-1538*)

Sandy Lake RV Park: This park is in suburban Dallas and is an easy drive to Texas Stadium. There are 260 full hookup sites that accommodate big rigs. Besides the usual amenities, there's a grocery market to pick up tailgate supplies. A night here costs $25. (*1915 Sandy Lake Rd., Carrollton, (972) 242-6808, sandylakervpark.com*)

Traders Village RV Park: This is more than just an RV park. The Traders Village complex has a flea market every weekend with more than 2,500 vendors (see page 76). The park has 212 sites, a grocery store, recreational activities, and all the usual amenities. Rates run $25–$28. (*2602 Mayfield Rd., Grand Prairie, (972) 647-2331, tradersvillage.com/hnrv.html*)

For more information: For additional RV parks and campsites visit campingworld.com/campsearch.

HOTELS

Four Seasons Resort and Club Dallas at Las Colinas: Four hundred rolling acres of north Texas hills, a TPC golf course, a sports club and spa—all less than 15 minutes from Texas Stadium. The resort's landscaping is beautiful, and the rooms have all the amenities you'd expect from a luxury resort. A stay costs $220–$350, more for packages. (*4150 N. MacArthur Blvd., Irving, (972) 717-0700, fourseasons.com/dallas*)

The Melrose Hotel: This historic hotel (built circa 1924) has large rooms with European marble baths and dramatic views of the city skyline. Rooms come with Web TV and Nintendo. Close to downtown and to shopping. Rooms run $149–$345. (*3015 Oak Lawn Ave., Dallas, (214) 521-5151, melrosehoteldallas.com*)

Stoneleigh: This historic, uptown hotel was built in 1923 and at the time was the tallest building in Dallas, as well as the tallest hotel west of the Mississippi River. It was also built with trap doors, sliding mirrors, and secret passageways that are still there. All the usual amenities and there's a fitness center. Rooms run $119–$259. (*2927 Maple Ave., Dallas, (214) 871-7111, stoneleighhotel.com*)

SOUTHERN METHODIST UNIVERSITY
Gerald J. Ford Stadium
Dallas, Texas
(214) 768-2582

Campus lots reserved for season ticket holders; few spaces left for visitors. Most visitors park in nearby lots and walk or use DART. Most tailgating done in grassy picnic area called the Boulevard. Limited space, but maybe you'll get lucky. No gas grills allowed.

Shuttle Info: The Dallas Area Rapid Transit system runs trains and buses from 13 Metroplex cities. Log on to dart.org for routes, schedules, and fares.

Mustangs Media Partner: 1310-AM KCTK

Texas Stadium's famous hole in the roof makes it one of the NFL's most unique stadiums. (Photo: Irving CVB)

For more information: To learn about more hotels in the area visit tripadvisor.com for listings and guest reviews.

B&BS

The Sanford House and Spa: Featured on *Best Romantic Inns,* this mock Victorian (actually built in 1996) offers well-appointed rooms—four in the main house and three in the Carriage House—that have a two-person Jacuzzi and fireplace. A French chef is on staff, and the Sanford Spa and Salon is on-site. Rooms cost $125–$200. (*506 N. Center St., Arlington, (817) 861-2129, thesanfordhouse.com*)

The Corinthian Bed and Breakfast: Built in 1905, this historic home was originally a boarding house for young ladies. Five suites are all furnished with antiques. The Carriage House Mayor's Suite includes a kitchen. Rates run $95–$245, based on room and season. (*4125 Junius St., Dallas, (866) 598.9988, corinthianbandb.com*)

Bailey's Uptown Inn: A modern home with three guest rooms in the heart of Dallas. Each room has a private bath, sitting area and desk, and satellite TV. Rooms run $125–$240. (*2505 Worthington St., Dallas, (214) 720-2258, baileysuptowninn.com*)

For more information: To learn about more B&Bs in the area visit bedandbreakfast.com for a detailed directory.

Where to Eat

TAILGATER GROCERIES

Eatzi's: Here you can pick up much of the stuff you need for your tailgate, or just pick up your entire meal already prepared by a chef. Individual and family-sized portions are available, and you can get anything from sushi, to casseroles, to pasta, to grilled meat and fish. (*3403 Oak Lawn Ave., Dallas, (214) 526-1515, eatzis.com*)

SPORTS BARS

Ben's Half Yard House: Several college alumni groups consider this home on game day, and there's always a crowd when local teams play. During many football games, you can play Football Bingo. Several TVs, 30 beers on tap, basic sports bar food. (*$, 7102 Greenville Ave., Dallas, (214) 363-1114, benshalfyard.com*)

Cowboys Sports Cafe: This sports bar is owned by several former Cowboys players and is located in a shopping center in Valley Ranch, near the team's training facility. There's memorabilia here, and now and then you'll find a current or former player here. The menu features wings, burgers, and the like. (*$, 9454 N. MacArthur Blvd., Irving (972) 506-8088, cowboyscafe.com*)

Milo Butterfingers: Located just down the street from SMU, this hangout is consistently on the city's "Best of" lists. TVs are scattered around the bar, and you can also play pool, darts, and other games. A basic bar menu. College alumni groups meet here to watch their teams a lot, too. (*5645 Yale Blvd., Dallas, (214) 368-9212*)

The Ultimate Tailgater's Travel Guide

RESTAURANTS

Abacus Restaurant: *Bon Appetit* calls the chef's tasting menu here a "top pick." Mobil has given it four stars. It's good. The decor is hip with dramatic lighting. Ask about sitting at the chef's table, which has a view of the European-style theater kitchen that sends out dishes like Black Truffle Crusted Dover Sole and Merlot Braised Kobe Beef Cheeks. *Food and Wine* rated the wine list as one of the nation's best. (*$$, 4511 McKinney Ave., Dallas, (214) 559-3111, abacus-restaurant.com*)

The Butcher Shop Steakhouse: You can pick your own steak from their display and, if you'd like, cook it yourself on a large charcoal grill. They'll cook it for you, too, of course. Located in West End, this is a casual steakhouse that also serves dishes that don't come from a cow. (*$$, 808 Munger Ave., Dallas, (214) 720-1032, thebutchershop.com/html/dallas.html*)

Big Tex welcomes you to the State Fair of Texas.
(Photo: State Fair of Texas)

Campisi's Egyptian: In 1946 Joe Campisi bought the Egyptian Lounge from a Greek family that had to get out of town fast. He dropped the "Lounge" because he thought it would keep families away and added his name to the restaurant. Campisi's Egyptian then became part of Dallas's history. The first pizza in Big D was served here. Jack Ruby (a regular) dined here the night before the Kennedy Assassination. Campisi's serves traditional Italian food, but those pizzas are the specialty. They've opened other locations in Dallas, but this is the original, near SMU. (*$, 5610 E. Mockingbird Ln., Dallas, (214) 827-0355, campisis.us*)

Dickey's Barbeque Pit: In 1941 Travis Dickey sold barbecue beef brisket, ham, and ribs from a one-room building near downtown Dallas. By 1994 Travis's sons had grown the business to 14 stores. Now, thanks to franchising, Dickey's has taken its Texas barbecue to a dozen states. The menu is bigger than it was in 1941, but the taste is still pure Texas. There are several locations in the Metroplex. (*Near Texas Stadium: 5330 N. MacArthur Blvd., Suite 168, Irving, (972) 580-1917; near SMU: 4610 Central Expwy., Dallas, (214) 370-4550; dickeys.com*)

El Ranchito: The *Dallas Observer* newspaper calls this the best Mexican restaurant in the city. You can get Tex-Mex standards here, but it's the more authentic Mexican food that you'll want to try, such as the grilled goat—a dish the owner enjoyed growing up in Monterrey, Mexico. Be ready for strolling mariachis. (*$, 610 W. Jefferson Blvd., Dallas, (214) 946-4238*)

For more information: For a directory of additional places to eat in the area visit opentable.com. You can also book a reservation for many restaurants on the site.

What to Do

DURING THE DAY

Fair Park: The Fair Grounds first opened in 1886, but Fair Park really began to grow for the Texas Centennial Exposition in 1936. It is home to the Cotton Bowl, which hosts the Texas/OU game as well as the post-season bowl game of the same name each year, the **Texas State Fair** (September–October), and to a number of museums and activities. The Fair Park Passport is your most cost-effective way to see attractions at Fair Park. It cost $23.99 for adults, $13.99 for children, and gets you into eight attractions, including the **Dallas Aquarium,** the **Dallas Museum of Natural History,** and the **Science Place** (a hands-on, interactive museum for children). (*Admission varies by attraction, 1300 Robert B. Cullum Blvd. at Grand, Dallas, (214) 421-9600, da lascityhall.com/dallas/eng/html/fair_park_information.html*)

Lone Star Park: This racetrack just outside of Dallas has live horse racing and simulcasting of races around the country for wagering. The track also has dining and a gift shop. (*1000 Lone Star Pkwy., Grand Prairie, (800) 795-7223, lonestarpark.com*)

Nasher Sculpture Center: Ray Nasher acquired his first sculpture in 1954. During the next half-century the collection grew in size and stature, to include works by Rodin, Picasso, Matisse, Moore, and scores of others. In 2003 the Nasher Sculpture Center opened to showcase the collector's pieces. Hundreds of works are on display in the galleries and sculpture garden. (*$, 2001 Flora St., Dallas, (214) 242-5100, nashersculpturecenter.org*)

The Texas School Book Depository includes the Sixth Floor Museum. (Photo: Bret St. Clair/The Sixth Floor Museum at Dealey Plaza)

Sixth Floor Museum at Dealey Plaza: The sixth floor of the Texas School Book Depository is where the Warren Commission said Lee Harvey Oswald fired the shots that assassinated President John F. Kennedy in 1963. The corner window is as it looked on November 22 when Kennedy's motorcade passed. You can see Dealey Plaza as Oswald saw it, view exhibits about the event, the investigators, and even the conspiracy theories. (*$, 411 Elm St., Downtown, Dallas, (214) 747-6660, jfk.org*)

Traders Village: This famous Texas flea market is spread over 120 acres and includes more than 2,500 dealers and frequent special events, such as rodeos, chili cook-offs, and more. Hours: 8:00 a.m. to dusk every Saturday and Sunday, year-round. (*Admission free, Parking $, 2602 Mayfield Rd., Grand Prairie, (972) 647-2331, tradersvillage.com/gp1.html*)

AT NIGHT

Barley House: Just a few blocks from SMU, this casual bar has a basic menu and more than a dozen beers on tap (more in bottles). Live music showcases local bands. (*$, 5612 Yale Blvd., Dallas, (214) 824-0306, barleyhouse.com*)

Cowboys Dancehall: This is Texas, so you'll find a number of country bars. This one is a big one that has music and two-steppin', as well as concerts, special events, and mechanical bull riding. Dance lessons Wednesdays and Fridays. (*$, although admission can vary by event, 10310 Technology Blvd., Dallas, (214) 352-1796, cowboysdancehall.com/Dallas*)

Deep Ellum: This area originally housed factories (Henry Ford built a plant here in 1913), but in the '20s the neighborhood was born and was a mecca for jazz and blues artists. As suburbs grew, the area declined, but it's now revitalized as one of the hippest arts and entertainment districts in the Southwest. It's just three blocks from downtown, and you'll find scores of clubs from dance, to country, to **Coyote Ugly.** (*deepellumtx.com*)

The Ultimate Tailgater's Travel Guide

Lower Greenville: This is one of the oldest entertainment districts in Dallas. While the names on the shops and bars might have changed some over the years, this has been a destination area for generations. Along Greenville Avenue, between Mockingbird Lane and Ross Avenue, you'll find a slew of clubs from hip to hole-in-the-wall.

Vain: They ask: "How vain are you?" They answer: "As vain as you want to be." Lots of people want to be. This crowded, hip dance club in downtown Dallas features hit DJs and special events. Celebrity sightings are common. (*$—$$, 2026 Commerce St., Dallas, (214) 747-1122, vainlounge.com*)

SHOPPING

Highland Park Shopping Village: It's been called the Beverly Hills of Dallas. The shopping area is a National Historic Landmark and features more than two dozen mostly upscale shops, including **Jimmy Choo** and **Hermes.** There are also home and specialty stores, along with restaurants. (*Mockingbird Ln. at Preston Rd., Dallas, (214) 559-2740, hpvillage.com*)

The Shops at West End Marketplace: Located in the West End Historic District, the Marketplace has several stores, including **The Official Dallas Cowboys Pro Shop.** You'll find everything from fashion to food here.(*603 Munger Ave., Dallas, (214) 748-4801, westendmarketplacedallas.com*)

Galleria Dallas: This is a mall, but it's not your usual mall. Anchored by stores such as **Nordstrom** and **Saks,** you'll find high-end shops like **Tiffany & Co,** and **Louis Vuitton** alongside local boutiques and other stores. You can also spend some time on the ice—there's an indoor ice rink. (*I-635 (LBJ Freeway) at Dallas North Tollway, (972) 702-7100, galleriadallas.com*)

For more information: To learn more about things to do in the area visit cityguide.aol.com/dallas.

FORT WORTH

TCU's first football game was played in 1896, although they weren't actually known as TCU then. They weren't even in Fort Worth, for that matter.

But, nonetheless, the forbearer of TCU, AddRan Christian University (brothers Addison and Randolph Clark owned it) beat Toby's Business College of Waco, 8–6. The school was located in Waco then. It changed its name to Texas Christian University in 1902, and moved to Fort Worth in 1911 following a fire that gutted the school's Waco building.

The Horned Frog mascot comes from those Waco days at AddRan, too. The Horned Frog—which is actually a lizard—lived around the AddRan campus. A lot of them did. In 1897 four students decided that since the Horned Frog population was so large in the area, it should be the school mascot. In 1992 it became the state reptile, too.

Today, the Horned Frogs around campus are embroidered on shirts and stuff. You can find a lot of them in the

TEXAS CHRISTIAN UNIVERSITY
Amon G. Carter Stadium
Fort Worth, Texas
(817) 257-5658

RVs park night before game (Friday) on campus RV lot; $50 for weekend. Parking, tailgating spots vary in distance; shuttles provided for distant lots. No open fires; alcohol must be concealed.

Shuttle Info: Shuttle buses run from Paschal High School to the stadium. The buses are free, as is the parking.

Horned Frogs Media Partners: 103.3-FM KESN, KTXA-TV Channel 21

TEXAS MOTOR SPEEDWAY
Fort Worth, Texas
(817) 215-8500

Millions of dollars were recently spent on parking and camping improvements. Huge selection of reserved and general spaces for RVs, tent camping, cars, but it still sells out quickly. Prices range from $50 to $2,000. Best bet—call or go to www.texasmotorspeedway.com and click on Visitor Info. No open fires or ATVs; respect quiet-time rule.

Shuttle Info: The Victory Lane Express runs buses from Forth Worth to the Speedway. Call (817) 215-8600 for routes, schedules, and fares.

Texas Motor Speedway Media Partners: 92.5-FM KZPS, 96.3-FM KSCS, 105.3-FM KLLI, the *Dallas Morning News*.

parking lots around Amon G. Carter Stadium. But you'll need season tickets to see them in the lots adjacent to the stadium—those spaces are reserved. There is limited parking nearby; if you can find any it costs $10. (If you end up in Lot 5, keep the beer packed away—no alcohol is allowed.) The better bet is to park at the TCU Baseball Stadium ($5) or on the east side of campus, which is free. Parking at Paschal High School is also free (3001 Forest Park Blvd., off Barry St.) and they run free shuttles to the stadium.

Other than in the parking lots, the biggest pregame party is Frog Alley, on the northeast side of the stadium between Lots 5 and 6. This is where the pregame radio broadcasts originate; there's live music, face painting, clowns and jugglers, and the like. It's free; just look for all the tents.

About 20 minutes north of downtown Fort Worth, up I-35, is the Texas Motor Speedway. The track is built along the historic Chisholm Trail, where millions of cattle were driven north to market. A whole other kind of driving goes on here now.

Unreserved event-day parking is free at the Speedway. Or you can purchase Express Parking for $10–$40 (based on the race), and Daily VIP parking for $25–$75. To reserve a spot, call (817) 215-8500.

There are five camp areas at the Speedway. Reserved camping will cost you $50–$200, depending on the race. Unreserved camping is $50, but only for select races, and not on the east side of the track, so make sure to call ahead (817) 215-8500) to see what's available.

You can also camp in the infield. These are reserved spots, and you'll need to have an infield pass, which you can either purchase at the gate or buy in advance for $65. If you park in the interior infield, it will cost you $700. The infield wall runs $1,400. If you camp in the Paddock, passes cost $1,750–$2,000. You can use your grill in the infield, but all fires must be out during practice sessions and during the race.

There's also a tent city on the property that costs $50–$75. No generators are allowed in the tent areas.

To get from the camping areas to the racetrack, just hop on the shuttle trams that continually loop around Lone Star Circle. They're free, and there are several drop-off points.

About Fort Worth

In 1849 Maj. Ripley Arnold established a fort near the spot where the forks of the Trinity River merged. The idea was to protect settlers from Indian attacks. He named the settlement after Gen. William J. Worth, who had most recently been commander of the Texas army and who died that same year. Later it became a stop on the Chisholm Trail, where millions of cattle were driven north to market. Fort Worth became a center of cattle drives and ranching, and it was a colorful town with gambling, saloons, and

The Ultimate Tailgater's Travel Guide

dance halls. In the 1870s the railroad came to town, and the Fort Worth Stockyards became a premier livestock center. That's how Fort Worth got the name "Cowtown."

In 1919 oil was discovered to the west. Refineries and related installations were built in the area as the oil industry grew in the state. But Fort Worth was never dependent on the oil industry and has had a diversified economy. Clothing, food products, and electronics equipment manufacturing have been important industries, as has aerospace. Bell Helicopter and American Airlines are headquartered here.

Where to Stay

RV PARKS

Fort Worth Midtown RV Park: Located west of downtown, this is a small park (just 18 sites) but centrally located. This is as basic as parks come, but it does have WiFi and a small store for supplies. Pets are welcome. Daily rate is $29. (*2906 W. 6th St., Fort Worth, (817) 335-9330, midtownrvpark.com*)

White Settlement RV Park: Just 10 minutes from downtown, and an easy drive to the Texas Motor Speedway, this park has 98 full hookup spaces and can accommodate big rigs. It's a basic site with limited other amenities, but is convenient to a number of Fort Worth attractions. (*410 N. Cherry Ln., Fort Worth, (877) 646-7008*)

For more information: For additional RV parks and campsites visit campingworld.com/campsearch.

HOTELS

The Ashton Hotel: Located downtown in two historic buildings—one built in 1890, the other in 1915 (they were connected in 1937)—the hotel has some rooms with two-person Jacuzzi tubs. All rooms have a mini-bar and DSL access. There's a restaurant in the building, and the hotel is decorated with art from the Fort Worth Circle, a group of artists who worked in Fort Worth from the 1930s to 1960s. Rooms cost $250–$330. (*610 Main St., Fort Worth, (866) 327-4866, theashtonhotel.com*)

Green Oaks Hotel: In suburban west Fort Worth, this hotel has rooms and suites with all the usual amenities, including high-speed Internet. There are two pools, two tennis courts, a restaurant, and a golf course across the street. Rooms run $89–$129, more for the suites. (*6901 West Fwy., Fort Worth, (817) 738-7311, greenoakshotel.com*)

Stockyards Hotel: Staying here is like stepping back into the Old West, but with better amenities. Built in 1907, the hotel hosted cattle barons, cowboys, and visiting dignitaries. Renovated in 1984 into the 52-room floor plan it has today, it keeps its historic look by decorating the rooms in one of four period styles: Victorian, Native American, Mountain Man, and Old West. Nightly rates run $125–$200. (*109 E. Exchange Ave., Stockyards, Fort Worth, (800) 423-8471, stockyardshotel.com*)

For more information: To learn about more hotels in the area visit tripadvisor.com for listings and guest reviews.

B&BS

Bed and Breakfast at the Ranch: This former working ranch is just a few minutes from the Raceway. In addition to the five rooms (all with private baths), the Ranch has an in-ground spa, pinball and darts, a three-hole putting green, mountain bikes and trails, and a tennis court. Room rates are

Flowers brighten up the tailgate buffet.
(Photo: Bruce Newman)

$95–$159. (*8275 Wagley Robertson Rd., Fort Worth, (817) 232-5522, bandbattheranch.com*)

Etta's Place Bed & Breakfast: Butch Cassidy and the Sundance Kid lived here. Really. In fact the B&B is named for Etta Place, who was the Kid's girlfriend. Etta's Place is in downtown Fort Worth and has seven rooms and three suites, named for the members of Butch Cassidy's Hole in the Wall Gang. All have private baths, and the three suites have kitchens. Rooms run $125–$165. (*200 W. Third St., Fort Worth, (866) 255-5760, ettas-place.com*)

The Texas White House Bed and Breakfast: It is, indeed, a white house, built in 1910, and with three guest rooms and two suites, all with private baths. The rooms have claw-foot tubs; the suites have jetted tubs. Located about 5 minutes from the TCU campus. Rooms here run $125–$205. (*1417 Eighth Ave., Fort Worth, (800) 279-6491, texaswhitehouse.com*)

For more information: To learn about more B&Bs in the area visit bedandbreakfast.com for a detailed directory.

Where to Eat

TAILGATER GROCERIES

Fort Worth Rail Market: The market is located in the historic **Santa Fe Warehouse** and is a mix between a farmers' market and shopping district. You can get fresh produce and other items sold by the farmers who produced them. The market also has shops and restaurants, as well as live entertainment. Open May–October. (*1401 Jones St., Fort Worth, (817) 335-6758, fortworthrailmarket.com*)

SPORTS BARS

Bobby V's Sports Gallery Cafe: Bobby V is Bobby Valentine, who used to manage the Texas Rangers. His bar has memorabilia all over the walls and shellacked onto the tables. The menu ranges from burgers, to fish, to Tex-Mex. Plenty of TVs. Located between Dallas and Fort Worth, not far from Ameriquest Field, where the Rangers play ball. (*$, 4301 S. Bowen Rd., Arlington, (817) 467-9922, bobbyvsports.com*)

Bronx Zoo Sports Cafe: With 18 TVs, including four big-screens, and all the satellite packages, you can catch just about any game here. There's also a game room with pool tables and live bands on Saturdays. The menu is basic sports bar, but you can get a wings plate with 100 of them on it. (*$, 700 Carroll St., Fort Worth, (817) 870-0008, bronxzoobar.com*)

Tumbleweed's Sports Bar: Located on the north side of town on Loop 820, Tumbleweed's is an easy drive to the Speedway or TCU. While you're there, you'll be able to watch games and play games (darts and pool). The menu is what you'd expect, and they have fenced-in patio seating. (*$, 1008 NE Loop 820, Fort Worth, (817) 626-5225, tumbleweedssportsbar.com*)

RESTAURANTS

Blue Mesa Grill: This popular contemporary Southwestern restaurant has won city awards for everything from "Best Margarita" to "Best Healthy Dining." The menu ranges from traditional Tex-Mex, to creative Tex-Mex, to more healthy options such as the Spa Chicken & Spinach Enchiladas. Blue Mesa Grill is just a few minutes north of TCU's campus. (*$, 1600 S University Dr., Suite 609E, Fort Worth, (817) 332-6372, bluemesagrill.com*)

Cattlemen's Steak House: If you see a big cow, you've found Cattlemen's. Oh, and look on the roof. Don't be afraid, it's not a real cow, but it's a good indicator of what you're going to find inside. Located in the Stockyards District, this Fort Worth landmark has been serving thick-cut steaks for almost 60 years. They serve other things, too, but it is a steakhouse, and this is Texas. (*$$, 2458 N. Main St., Fort Worth, (817) 624-3945, cattlemenssteakhouse.com*)

Joe T. Garcia's Mexican Restaurant: When they opened this place on the Fourth of July in 1935, Joe and Jessie Garcia could seat 16 people in their tiny restaurant. But Jessie's enchiladas and hand-made tortillas became popular and lines would form of people trying to get in. And the lines got only longer. Now, after several renovations, Joe T.'s seats more than 1,000, takes up a city block, and includes a pool, fountains, and flowered patios. Bring cash, because they don't take credit cards. (*$, 2201 N. Commerce St., Fort Worth, (817) 626-4356, joets.com*)

J. Christen's Grill and Bar: Almost across the street from the Texas Motor Speedway, it's fittingly decorated with racing pictures, racing-car doors, checkered flags, and framed fire suits. The menu is more "grill" than "bar," with more upscale steak, chicken, and fish dishes than you would normally find in a place with racing stuff on the walls. You can get Tex-Mex here, too. (*$, 6480 I-35 West, Fort Worth, (817) 847-9802*)

For more information: For a directory of additional places to eat in the area visit opentable.com. You can also book a reservation for many restaurants on the site.

What to Do
DURING THE DAY

Cultural District: This area west of downtown is home to several museums. Two are nationally known and critically acclaimed:

> **Amon Carter Museum:** This is one of the foremost museums of American and Western art. Includes works by Homer, O'Keeffe, Stieglitz, and others. It also houses the collections of the two greatest artists of the American West: Frederic Remington and Charles Russell. (*Free, 3501 Camp Bowie Blvd., Fort Worth, (817) 738-1933, cartermuseum.org*)

> **Kimbell Art Museum:** This is architect Louis Kahn's most famous American building. Inside are collections of both early 20th-century European art and old masters, including Goya, Monet, Rembrandt, and others. It also has a substantial collection of Asian art. (*Free, 3333 Camp Bowie Blvd., Fort Worth, (817) 332-8451, kimbellart.org*)

Fort Worth Zoo: The zoo is the oldest continuous zoo site in Texas. When it opened in 1909, it had one lion, two bear cubs, an alligator, a coyote, a peacock, and a few rabbits. Now the zoo has more than

Elephants are some of the 6,000 animals at the Fort Worth Zoo. (Photo: Fort Worth CVB)

6,000 exotic and native animals from more than 350 species, including a rare white tiger. There are dining areas and shops, too. (*$, 1989 Colonial Pkwy., Fort Worth, (817) 759-7555, fortworthzoo.com*)

Grapevine Steam Railroad: From 1896–1959, Steam Engine #2248, affectionately known as "Puffy," ran the rails of the Southern Pacific Railroad. Now you can ride it. Fully restored, this historic train runs the historic Cotton Belt and Trinity River Routes that are a part of Cowtown's history. During your trip, train robbers ride up on horseback to attack the train. Okay, they're actors, but it adds adventure to the ride. The train runs Saturday and Sunday; no service in January. (*$–$$, Train boards at either the Stockyards Station, 140 E. Exchange Ave., Fort Worth, or the Cotton Belt Depot, 707 S. Main St., Grapevine, (817) 410-3123, grapevinesteamrailroad.com*)

AT NIGHT

White Elephant Saloon: With a history dating back to the 1880s, this saloon in the Stockyards District is more than just a Fort Worth institution. High-stakes gamblers used to play poker upstairs (it's now a private party room). The real cowboys and cowgirls have been replaced with our modern-day equivalent, although some on the dance floor sure look like the real thing. Live music is featured on the weekends. (*$, 106 E. Exchange Ave., #110, Fort Worth, (817) 624-8273, whiteelephantsaloon.com*)

Billy Bob's Texas: It's one of the most famous honky-tonks in the world. It's certainly the largest. When this building was built in 1910, it housed livestock. It still does. Sort of. They don't have a mechanical bull here; they have real ones—although only professionals ride them. Billy Bob's also has concerts by some of country's name acts, a huge dance floor, games, and a gift shop. (*$, 2520 Rodeo Plaza, Fort Worth, (817) 624-7117, billybobstexas.com*)

The Aardvark: This has been a popular live music venue for years. Students and others in the TCU area enjoy the Aardvark for the diversity of live music and the cheap prices. The club books both local and nationally touring acts. (*$, 2905 W. Berry St., Fort Worth, (817) 926-7814, the-aardvark.com*)

SHOPPING

Camp Bowie Blvd: For generations the 30 or so blocks along Camp Bowie have been a Fort Worth shopping destination. You'll find shops with stuff to wear, stuff to display, stuff to use, and stuff to give. There are also galleries and restaurants along the Boulevard.

Sundance Square: This historic marketplace is bounded by Houston, Commerce, 2nd, and 3rd Streets downtown. Revitalized with brick-laid, flower-lined sidewalks, the area boasts unique specialty shops, clothiers, art galleries, museums, restaurants, and more. There're also two movie theaters, and the **Bass Performance Hall** is here.

For more information: To learn more about things to do in the area visit cityguide.aol.com/fortworth.

DENTON

The University of North Texas Mean Green play at 30,000-seat Fouts Field, named for Theron Fouts, who came to what was then North Texas State Normal College as the head coach for all Mean Green sports. Except they weren't called that yet.

The Mean Green moniker came in the late 1960s. Fans spontaneously cheered the defense with chants of "Mean Green"—they did wear green, after all. The athletic department then referred to the "Mean Green Defensive Unit" in a press release and it stuck.

Game-day parking is in the (not Mean) Green, Orange, and Blue Lots around the stadium. However, the Green and Orange Lots are reserved for Mean Green Club members, so forget they're even there. Look for the Blue Lot off North Texas Boulevard on the east side of Fouts Field. It's first-come, first-served here and will cost you $10, unless you're in an RV—then it will cost you $50.

UNT, like most schools, throws its own tailgate-style party. Theirs is called Mean Green Village, where there are tents, food and drinks, live music, and children's activities.

UNIVERSITY OF NORTH TEXAS

Fouts Field
Denton, Texas
(940) 565-2527
(940) 369-7643

Visiting RVs park early if you call ahead. Tailgaters stay until midnight. No glass containers; don't drive stakes into ground for tents; please clean up afterward. Practice field has music, fun, kid stuff—just don't park there.

Mean Green Media Partners: 100.7-FM KWRD, 88.1-FM KNTU

About Denton

Denton is about 35 miles north of the Dallas/Fort Worth Metroplex and is one of those towns founded for a simple purpose: Denton County needed a county seat. Presto, Denton was born in 1856. It became an incorporated city 10 years later. John Denton gave his name to the city. He was a lawyer, preacher, and soldier.

Education is a major industry in this town of about 100,000. It is home not only to UNT but also Texas Woman's University. Combined, about 40,000 students are in Denton each year. Music is also a part of the fabric here; the Grammy Award–winning Brave Combo is from Denton, as is the UNT jazz ensemble 1 O'Clock Lab Band (also Grammy winners). Grammy winner Don Henley is also from Denton, but he was in a different band.

Where to Stay

RV PARKS

Post Oak Place: The park gets it name from the 100-year-old trees that shade many of the 95 sites, which will accommodate any sized RV. The park has the basic amenities, plus an exercise room and recreational facilities. The rate is $23. (*109 Massey St., Denton, (940) 387-8584, postoakplace.com*)

Destiny Dallas: Lots of amenities can be found in this park, in addition to the 177 full hookup sites. The park has a playground, sports fields and courts, fitness center, car/RV wash, and more. A stay

*Scrapy tailgates with
North Texas fans.
(Photo: UNT URCM Staff)*

here costs $31–$39. *(7100 S. I-35 E., Denton, (888) 238-1532, destinyrv.com/dallasrvresort.htm)*

For more information: For additional RV parks and campsites visit campingworld.com/campsearch.

HOTELS

Note: The hotels in Denton are major chains and by now you know our rule about that in this book. If you would like a listing of these hotels visit discoverdenton.com/stay.shtml#motels.

B&BS

Wildwood Inn: Surrounded by 4 acres of woodlands, this secluded European-style bed and breakfast offers Old World elegance in new construction. The 13 rooms include whirlpool tubs, fireplaces, WiFi, and more. You can also eat at an award-winning restaurant on-site. Rooms run $125–$250. (*2602 Lillian Miller Pkwy., Denton, (940) 243-4919, denton-wildwoodinn.com*)

Heritage Inns Bed and Breakfast Cluster: Three historic landmark homes—the Redbud House (1912), the Magnolia House (1902), and the Pecan House (1916)—near the courthouse square offer accommodations with character. The homes' six rooms and six suites all have private baths and **Giuseppe's Italian Restaurant** is located on the first floor of the Magnolia House. (*812-829 N. Locust, Denton, (940) 565-6414, theheritageinns.com*)

For more information: To learn about more B&Bs in the area visit bedandbreakfast.com for a detailed directory.

Where to Eat

SPORTS BARS

JT's Dugout: Centrally located off the square, JT's has TVs placed around the bar, good bar food on the menu, and video games. The bar is popular with UNT students. (*$, 104 N. Locust St., Denton, (940) 566-3614*)

Fry Street Tavern: A popular hang-out with Dallas's teams on the TVs—other games, too. They also have eight ball, darts, foosball, and Golden Tee. The menu is pretty basic bar food. Note that they are technically a private club, which means you'll pay a nominal membership fee to be able to drink; after 9:00 p.m. no one under 21 is admitted. (*$, 121 Ave. A, Denton, (940) 383-2337, frystreettavern.com*)

RESTAURANTS

Ruby's Diner on the Square: Obviously on the square, and not far from UNT, Ruby's is a 1940s-style diner that serves home-cooked comfort food. But don't be surprised to see wild game on the menu, such as breaded quail. The diner is open for breakfast, lunch, and dinner. (*111 N. Elm St., Denton, (940) 387-7706*)

El Matador Restaurant: They work to create an authentic atmosphere and menu here. They have Mexican painted pots and pictures (which you can buy in their little shop) decorating the place and your basic Mexican favorites on the menu. Margaritas come in several flavors (is that authentic?). The restaurant is located on University Drive, which is close to the other university here—Texas Woman's University. (*$, 720 W. University Dr., Denton, (940) 387-1137*)

For more information: For a directory of additional places to eat in the area visit opentable.com. You can also book a reservation for many restaurants on the site.

What to Do

DURING THE DAY

Sky Theater: This is one of only 20 planetaria in the world that feature the Digistar II projection system. Sure, that sounds fancy; but what does it mean? It means this 100-seat, domed theater can reproduce that night's sky with digital detail, so you feel like you're traveling in space. Only without that whole no-gravity thing. (*$, Science and Technology Building, Hickory St. and Avenue C, UNT Campus, (940) 369-8213, skytheater.unt.edu*)

UNT Art Galleries: The University of North Texas School for the Visual arts operates two galleries on campus: **The University of North Texas Art Gallery** and the **Cora Stafford Gallery.** Exhibits rotate, so you'll want to call or visit the Web site for details. (*Art Gallery: (940) 565-4316; Cora Stafford Gallery: (940) 565-8798, art.unt.edu/gallery/index.html*)

AT NIGHT

Cool Bean's: If it's nice outside, head straight upstairs to the rooftop. If not, stay indoors in the bar area, where they have pool tables and darts. This is a popular hangout that has live music many nights. (*1210 W. Hickory St., Denton, (940) 382-7025*)

Downtown Denton: The downtown square has several nightspots and restaurants, and draws a crowd many nights. Walking around the area, you'll likely find a place to hang out for a while.

Rubber Gloves Rehearsal Studio: What was once a cement factory is now one of Denton's top music venues. Only beer and wine are served, but the acoustics are good. During the day they rent rehearsal rooms to local bands. (*411 E. Sycamore St., Denton, (940) 387-7781, rubberglovesdentontx.com*)

SHOPPING

Antiques: North Austin and North Locust Streets are the city's antiques district—although they don't call it that. Here you'll find a half-dozen antique shops to visit.

For more information: To learn more about things to do in the area visit cityofdenton.com.

Denver

Denver is a tailgater's town. The Broncos not only encourage tailgating—they promote it.

Some quick history. The Broncos at one time were a pretty lousy AFL team. They were a poorly funded team, too. In its inaugural season in 1959 players wore discarded uniforms from the defunct Copper Bowl in Tucson—they were cheaper than buying new uniforms.

Fast forward to 1970, and the AFL merges with the NFL. Three years later the Broncos have their first winning season, and today the Mile High City boasts one of the NFL's biggest winners—the Broncos have won six AFC championships and back-to-back Super Bowls—XXXII and XXXIII. Since the merger they've hosted sellout crowds every year (shy of the strike-replacement games, but no one counts those anyway). INVESCO Field at Mile High seats 76,125, and if you have a ticket, the team wants you out in the parking lot having fun before the game.

If your road trip brought you to the stadium by car, you may want to drive up to Lots C and M. While tailgating is encouraged at all stadium parking lots, Lots C and M are where some of the ultimate tail-gaters park. It costs $30 per space to get in, but you'll be with some of the most loyal tailgaters in the league. Tickets for these lots go on sale the day before games; check the team's Web site for details (denverbroncos.com—click on "Stadium" and then on "Tailgating").

No matter which lot you land in, you're eligible to be the team's "Most Valuable Tailgater." The Broncos' big helmet car cruises the concrete looking for tailgate parties that best show off Broncos Country.

But, hey, you're traveling. You flew to town. A shuttle got you to the stadium. You don't have all your tail-gating gear. You know, someone should set up a tailgate party for you. And they should bring the Broncos' cheerleaders, too.

They do.

Welcome to the Broncos Barn, a huge tent erected on the Sports Legends Mall on the south end of the stadium, with the Denver skyline as its backdrop. Five bucks gets you in (food and drink cost extra, but they have two-dollar beer and barbecue for the first hour of the party) and the festivities include a live band, big screen TVs, raffles and prizes, special guests, and who knows how many Bronco fans who left it to someone else to set up the party. And the cheerleaders show up, too.

About Denver

The Mile High City started as a mining town, founded by a party of prospectors in 1858, after discovering gold at Cherry Creek and the South Platte River. More gold discoveries sparked a mass migration of some 100,000 in 1859–60, leading to the establishment of the Colorado Territory in 1861.

Denver has since weathered several boom and bust economies, from gold mining, cattle, and oil and gas, to establish a more diversified economy that includes tourism, electronics, computers, aviation, and the nation's largest telecommunications center.

Where to Stay
RV PARKS

Dakota Ridge RV Park: Located 10 miles to the west of Denver, in Golden, this campground offers some nice touches, from landscaped pads to WiFi. The cost is $36. Many services are a la carte, such as electric hookups, but most prices are only a dollar or two. If you're caravanning with other fans, Dakota Ridge offers discounts to RV groups of 10 or more. (*17800 West Colfax Ave., Golden, (800) 398-1625, dakotaridgerv.com*)

Denver Meadows: Located in the Denver suburb of Aurora, Denver Meadows is only minutes from INVESCO Field at Mile High and Denver's downtown attractions. Denver Meadows also has an on-site security guard and offers the standard amenities. Rates, which include electric hookups, are $33. (*2075 Potomac St., Aurora, (800) 364-9487, denvermeadows.com*)

Delux RV Park: Delux is rather small (just 50 sites), but it's the only RV campground actually within the Denver city limits, so it's a convenient location. The park can accommodate tent or travel trailers as well as motor homes and RVs. Delux sticks with the basics, but it does have a sewage dumpsite. Day rates are $31. The dump station costs $10. (*5520 Federal Blvd., Denver, (303) 433-0452, deluxrvpark.com*)

For more information: For additional RV parks and campsites visit campingworld.com/campsearch.

HOTELS

Brown Palace Hotel: Opened in 1892, this wedge-shaped sandstone and granite building has hosted presidents and kings, Hollywood actors and rock stars. One of the few 19th-century hotels left in the city, the Palace has been completely modernized over time without losing its sense of history. The hotel has 237 rooms, each with the amenities you'd expect from a luxury hotel. Every afternoon, English tea is served in the atrium lobby, and every Sunday is the Dom Perignon brunch. Dogs are welcome and provided with doggie beds, bowls, and special Bone-Apetit treats. Weekend rates for a double start at $169; weekdays are $279–$339 for doubles and $359–$1,159 for suites. (*321 17th St., Denver, (800) 321-2599, brownpalace.com*)

DENVER BRONCOS
INVESCO Field at Mile High
Denver, Colorado
(720) 258-3000 parking information

Single game parking in southwest corner of stadium; $30 per space, first-come, first-served. RVs will likely use two spaces. Stadium has shuttles for elderly, disabled. No glass bottles, kegs, open fires, saving spaces, unauthorized vehicles, or blocking pedestrian access. Broncos host tailgating contests with themes for different games.

Shuttle Info: The Broncos Ride shuttle leaves from 28 Park & Ride locations around Denver and costs $8 round trip. There's also a shuttle from Federal and Market Streets for $3. (For details log on to rtf-denver.com and click on "Special Rides" to find the Broncos Ride link.)

Broncos Media Partners: 850-AM, KOA; 1280-AM, KBNO (Spanish); KCNC-TV, Channel 4 (CBS).

A Denver tailgater checks his grill.
(Photo: orangeforceone.com)

Hotel Teatro: One of Denver's newest hotels, the Teatro is also one of the most dramatic. The Denver Center for the Performing Arts (across the street) inspired the decor, which features elaborately framed costumes from past productions. This historic landmark, constructed in 1911 as the Denver Tramway Building, now boasts 21st-century perks. Every room has a view—some of the Rocky Mountains, others of downtown Denver. Rooms run from $195 to $325; suites $345–$1,400. (*1100 Fourteenth Street, Denver, (888) 727-1200, hotelteatro.com*)

Burnsley All Suite Hotel: It's just what it sounds like—every room is actually a 700-square-foot suite (or a 520-square-foot studio suite, but most are the larger size). That's what happens when you take a 1963 apartment building and turn it into a hotel. All the suites come with private balconies and separate living area, bedroom, dining area, and fully stocked kitchen. Pricewise, the Burnsley is a relatively good value. Heck, for between $109 and $209 a night, you'll be staying in what's basically a one-bedroom apartment that comes with covered parking and free shuttle service. (*1000 Grant Street, Denver, (800) 231-3915, burnsley.com*)

For more information: To learn about more hotels in the area visit tripadvisor.com for listings and guest reviews.

B&BS:

Queen Anne Bed & Breakfast Inn: The Queen Anne is actually two homes side-by-side with a shared backyard garden/patio area and 14 rooms. Each room is decorated after an American artist or with something of Colorado's environment or history in mind. Prices range from $75 to $175, depending on the room and the season. (*2147-51 Tremont Pl., Denver, (800) 432-4667, queenannebnb.com*)

Adagio Bed and Breakfast: A beautiful inn with nine rooms, all named for a composer, so you can book the Holst Room or the Copland Suite, for example. Rates range from $85 to $175. (*1430 Race St., Denver, (800) 533-4640, adagiobb.com*)

The Gregory Inn: This inn offers nine rooms with homey features and LCD TVs. All rooms but one have working gas fireplaces; most have whirlpool tubs. Prices run $119–$189 during the week, with a $10 jump in price for weekend nights. The carriage house, with full kitchen, dining area, living room with entertainment media and bedroom can be yours for $249/$259. (*2500 Arapahoe St., Denver, (800) 925-6570, gregoryinn.com*)

For more information: Visit denver.org and click on "Lodging" for a complete directory of hotels and other lodging in the Denver area.

Where to Eat

TAILGATER GROCERIES

Marczyk Fine Foods: If you need to pick up a couple of unique items for your tailgate party, head over to Marczyk's and browse through fresh organic vegetables, exotic olives, fresh seafood and meats, exquisite wines, and specialty desserts. Box lunches are available to go, but give the store 24 hours' notice if you're ordering more than six. (*770 E. 17th Ave., Denver, (303) 894-9499; www.marczykfinefoods.com*)

SPORTS BARS

The Giggling Grizzly: Located near Coors Field and the heart of LoDo, the Grizzly is one of the few constants in one of Denver's fastest-changing areas. It's definitely got a college vibe, and it opens 2 hours before all Colorado Rockies home games and 1 hour before all Michigan State University football games. Really. (*$; 1320 20th St., Denver, (303) 297-8300, giggling-grizzly.com*)

Charlie Brown's Bar and Grill: By far the coolest guy at the bar is Paulie, an elderly, almost blind pianist whose personality is as bright as the neon sign out front. Sales are rung up on a '50s-era cash register, and their menu ranges from burritos to lobster tails. (*$$; 980 Grant St., Denver, (303) 860-1655*)

Jackson's All-American Sports Grill: Some of the best burgers in Colorado, along with all the big- and small-screen TVs you could want, can be found here. It's a two-tiered bar, with all the sports fans cheering on the first floor and everybody else grooving to the dance music on the second floor. It's a young crowd, and a fun crowd. (*$; 4948 South Yosemite, Englewood, (303) 220-0222, jacksonsallamerican.com*)

ESPN Zone: Denver's got one—just like you've seen on TV. They have lots of TVs, too, along with games, crowd noise, and food, including a couple of entrées such as the plank salmon that rise above the usual pub fare. (*$$; 1187 16th Street, Denver, (303) 595-3776, espnzone.com/denver*)

RESTAURANTS

The Buckhorn Exchange: For more than 100 years the Buckhorn Exchange has been serving food to railroad adventurers, trappers, traders, travelers, and bigwig potentates. Tailgaters, too. The frontier-style decor probably looks about the same as when it first opened in 1893. Rumor has it Buffalo Bill was to the Buckhorn what Norm Peterson was to Cheers. Appetizers include fried alligator tail and rattlesnake; dinner offers succulent buffalo prime rib, dry-aged, prime-grade Colorado steaks, elk, pheasant and more. (*$$$; 1000 Osage St., Denver, (303) 534-9505, buckhorn.com*)

Bump and Grind: This wacky coffee house offers great java all the time and a simplified breakfast menu during the week. But come Sunday, it's party time and the Petticoat Bruncheon, with a full menu, and servers in campy drag. If you've never experienced being served by a 6-foot, 5-inch guy with a goatee and feather boa, now's your chance. Try their Mexican Benedict, banana waffles, or the egg-, sausage-, and veggie-filled empanada. Bump and Grind is also very kid-friendly. (*$; 439 E. 17th Ave., Denver, (303) 861-4841*)

Elway's: Yep, that Elway. This upscale restaurant draws crowds of sports fans hoping to catch a glimpse of legendary Broncos quarterback John Elway—or any other famous folks for that matter—while enjoying prime cuts of steak. The menu also offers seafood and chicken dishes and lots of side items. He might have been a Pro Bowl athlete, but Elway's isn't a sports bar. Instead, think loud, clubby, dark-wooded restaurant atmosphere. (*$$$; 2500 East First Av., Unit 101, Denver, (303) 399-5353, elways.com*)

Jay's Patio Café: The reason why the food is so good here is its owner, Jay Solomon. A chef for more than 20 years, Jay has authored 14 cookbooks exploring various cuisines. Now he's turned his attention to daytime fare. Try the roast beef with wasabi mayo and Swiss on sourdough, or the turkey with red ancho chile mayo, Jack cheese, and yellow peppers on whole grain, or . . . you get the idea. Jay's also does a healthy box lunch business, and with a little advance notice, can prepare however many you might need. (*$; 2563 Upper 15th St., Denver, (303) 455-9275*)

JJ Chinese Restaurant: If you've ever suspected the Chinese don't actually eat General Tzo's chicken themselves—by the way, you'd be right—and want to experience the real thing yourself, JJ Chinese Restaurant is the place for you. This place serves authentic dishes from China's Guangdong Province, with no compromising for Western palates. Here you'll find chicken feet, jellyfish strips, snake soup, and duck chin, among other dishes. (*$; 1048 S. Federal Blvd., Denver, (303) 934-8888*)

Pete's Kitchen: This is the café for good, diner-style breakfasts served any time of the day or night. And for weary tailgaters driving into Denver at 4:00 a.m., that can be a good thing. No matter what time you're there, you'll find everything from a steak and egg breakfast to sandwiches featuring pitas and gyros on the menu. (The "Pete" of Pete's Kitchen is Pete Contos, and the whole menu is sprinkled with basic Greek items.) (*$; 1962 E. Colfax Ave, Denver, (303) 321-3139, petesrestaurantstoo.com*)

For more information: For a directory of additional places to eat in the area visit opentable.com. You can also book a reservation for many restaurants on the site.

What to Do
DURING THE DAY

Beer Tours: Both the **Coors Brewery** in Golden, about 15 miles down the road, and the **Anheuser-Busch Brewery** in Fort Collins, about an hour away, offer free tours of their facilities. Yes, you get some beer, but the tastings aren't all-you-can-drink. Both tours are free and family-friendly. While the Anheuser-Busch brewery is more of a drive, their tour includes a chance to visit the Clydesdales stables and see these grand horses up close. (*Free, 13th and Ford Sts., Golden, (866) 812-BEER, coors.com*) (*Free, 2351 Busch Dr., Fort Collins, (970) 490-4691, budweisertours.com*)

Black American West Museum & Heritage Center: A third of the men and women who tamed the Wild West were black, and their stories come to life here. Founded in 1971, the museum is housed in the former home of Dr. Justina Ford, Denver's first African-American doctor, who delivered more than 7,000 babies in her career. The collection contains 35,000-plus personal artifacts, memorabilia, newspapers, legal documents, clothing, letters, photographs, and oral histories. (*$, 3091 California St., Denver, (303) 292-2566, blackamericanwest.org*)

Buffalo Bill's Grave and Museum: Located in Golden, this venue has on display original photographs, weapons, and beaded costumes from Bill Cody's various careers as Pony Express rider, buffalo hunter, and world's greatest showman. His gravesite is simple, with his wife beside him, and it commands a spectacular view of Denver from Lookout Mountain. Youngsters can check out the Kids' Cowboy Corral, too.

The Black American West Museum & Heritage Center. (Photo: David Falconer/Denver Metro CVB)

The museum is best approached from the Lariat Trail from Highway 6. The trail is a winding scenic highway with a dozen pull-offs offering panoramic views. (*$, 987½ Lookout Mountain Rd, Golden, (303) 526-0747, buffalobill.org*)

Butterfly Pavilion & Insect Center: Just a few minutes up Highway 36, in Westminster, this is the nation's only stand-alone insect zoo, a 16,000-square-foot facility covering 5 acres. The 7,200-square-foot conservatory houses a tropical forest, a babbling brook, and more than 1,200 butterflies representing more than 50 species

The Ultimate Tailgater's Travel Guide

from around the world. Plus, if you wear white or bright colors, butterflies will land on you, which is really cool and makes for great pictures. (*$; 6252 W. 104th Ave., Westminster, (303) 469-5441, butterflies.org*)

Celestial Seasonings Tour: Celestial Seasoning takes visitors on a tour of how tea is turned from leaves on a bush to the drink in your cup. The tour includes the herb garden and a stop in the hair-raising mint room. (*Free, 4600 Sleepytime Dr., Boulder, (800) 434-4246, celestialseasonings.com*)

The Garden of the Gods: This 1,380-acre park features spectacular sandstone formations that make up the garden. There are 13 miles of trails to explore in this park, which has an unearthly feel, like you're on Mars surrounded by giant-sized alien toys. (*$; 1805 N. 30th St. (at Gateway Rd.) Colorado Springs, (719) 634-6666, gardenofgods.com*)

There are several ski resorts near Denver. (Photo: Jack Affleck)

Pikes Peak: At an altitude of 14,110 feet above sea level, it's the most-visited mountain in North America, and the second-most-visited mountain in the world (behind Japan's Mount Fuji). There's a reason why all those people visit Pikes Peak—the view is incredible. If you're driving to the summit, pay attention to the tips given to avoid overheating your engine on the way up, and your brakes on the way down. Ignore them and "Pike's Peak or Bust" will mean something different to you than it did to all those pioneers. (*$; Pikes Peak Highway, Hours: September: 7:00 a.m. to 5:00 p.m., October to end of April: 9:00 a.m. to 3:00 p.m., May to August 7:00 a.m. to 7:00 p.m., (800) 318-9505, pikespeakcolorado.com or pikes-peak.com*)

Skiing: You're in Colorado. If it's winter, you're going skiing. It may be a state law. With several skiing Meccas within a couple hours drive, there're enough ski slopes available to fit every interest and skill level (skicentral.com.colorado.html has a complete directory of slopes throughout the state). Veterans often recommend **Winter Park Ski Resort** for closeness, and great snow. **Arapahoe Basin Ski Resort** is the highest ski area in North America (13,050 feet at the summit). Then, of course, there's the largest resort in the U.S.: **Vail Ski Resort.** Vail offers guests 193 trails on 5,289 acres of terrain within three different mountain experiences.

Wings Over the Rockies Air & Space Museum: This is every tech-head's dream come true. Housed in a former Air Force hangar, the museum has 30 historic air and space vehicles, including a B-1 Stealth Bomber, model planes, uniforms and other aircraft exhibits. You can even see Luke Skywalker's X-Wing Fighter from *Star Wars*. (*$; Hangar No. 1, Bldg. 401 of Old Lowery Air Force Base, 711 E. Academy Blvd., Denver, (303) 360-5360, wingsmuseum.org*)

AT NIGHT

El Chapultepec: All the greats have played here since the jazz club opened in 1951. Sinatra. Bennett. Fitzgerald. Rock and rollers, including McCartney, Jagger, and Richards have played here, too. Bring cash; they don't accept checks or credit cards. (*No cover charge; 1962 Market St., Denver, (303) 295-9126*)

Herman's Hideaway: This local favorite plays every kind of danceable music, with a dance floor big enough for everybody. The music is live, and the drinks are reasonably priced. The crowd is mostly your basic 20- and 30-somethings out to bust a move and have fun. There's a lively singles scene here, so if you lack a date for your tailgate party . . . *($; 1578 S. Broadway, Denver, (303) 777-5840, hermanshideaway.com)*

Rise Nightclub: You'll find all the madness and music you could want here. Downstairs, scantily clad go-go dancers with KISS-style makeup gyrate wildly on blocks while suburbanites try to keep up. Platinum-haired waitresses in skintight silver deliver cocktails against a background of trippy kaleidoscope images. Funk-tastic DJs set the mood here. Different nights feature different music. *($; 1909 Blake (19th and Blake), Denver, (303) 298-1515, rise-nightclub.com)*

Ziggie's Saloon: This rough 'n' tumble dive features live, working-class blues, blues-rock, and draft beer. On game days, Ziggie's rocks twice as hard, as hometown football fans pack the joint for cheap drinks and game spirit. What they don't pack the place for is food, because Ziggie's doesn't serve any. *($; 4923 West 38th Ave. Denver, (303) 455-9930, ziggiessaloon.com)*

SHOPPING

American Vogue Vintage Clothing: It's considered one of the city's best vintage shops for its consistent supply of thrifty yet nifty apparel for both guys and girls. Knowledgeable fashionistas will appreciate Ace's attention to detail, with accessories such as Zippo lighters, cuff links, hankies, hats, and shoes. *(10 S. Broadway, Denver, (303) 733-4140)*

Mile High Flea Market: Ten minutes northeast of downtown Denver, in Henderson, this market attracts more than 1.5 million shoppers a year to its 80 paved acres that offer close-outs, garage sales, and seasonal merchandise. But it also has more than a dozen places to eat and snack, plus family rides. It's open year-round on Wednesday, Saturday, and Sunday from 7:00 a.m. to 5:00 p.m. *(7007 E. 88th Ave, Henderson, (303) 289-4656)*

The Native American Trading Company: Just around the corner from the State Capitol, you'll find serious art and craft works by some of the west's best American Indian artists and artisans including pottery, jewelry, and weavings. You'll also find original photogravures by 19th-century photographer and chronicler Edward Sherrif Curtis. *(231 W. 13th Ave., Denver, (303) 534-0771, nativeamericantradingco.com)*

For more information: To learn more about things to do in the area visit cityguide.aol.com/denver.

BOULDER

The Colorado Buffaloes play at Folsom Field. But they weren't always the Buffaloes. In fact, until 1934 the team was called everything from the Silver Helmets, to the Yellow Jackets, to the Arapahoes and Grizzlies. But a student newspaper contest put an end to the revolving mascot, and since then Colorado has been the Buffaloes, or Buffs for short.

The first live mascot appeared that same year. It was a rented calf that cost a group of students $25—including a real cowboy to handle it. Later Ralphie became the official mascot, and today Ralphie IV roams the sidelines. The current Ralphie was donated by media, sports, and restaurant entrepreneur Ted Turner, who sent this buffalo to Boulder instead of Ted's Montana Grill. Lucky buff.

Like most Big 12 schools, tailgating is serious at CU. There are several fields and lots to park in, and the farthest is just about a half-mile from the stadium. Take your gas grill, though, because they don't allow charcoal or oversized cookers in the fields. Spaces will cost you $20–$80 depending on how much space you need.

Also, be aware they shut down the Route 209 loop through campus 2 hours before the game and don't reopen it until 1 hour after the game, so make sure you plan for that detour.

About Boulder

To live in Boulder is to be passionate about the outdoors, and to live with everyone from enviro-hippies, artists, musicians, and Buddhist monks to bankers, lawyers, and executives—some of whom are also enviro-hippies, artists, musicians, and Buddhists (if not monks.) In many ways Boulder is the stereotypical college town.

In the summer Boulder is a haven for all kinds of outdoor sports—rock climbing, kayaking, hiking, biking, and on and on. With cooler weather comes snow and skiing or snowboarding. If nature is your thing, be sure to take in the view from Flagstaff Mountain and try a Chautauqua hike.

UNIVERSITY OF COLORADO
Folsom Field
Boulder, Colorado
(303) 492-1411 parking ext.

Tailgaters park in fields or lots; farthest is ½ mile from stadium. Parking is $20 for cars, up to $80 for oversized vehicles. No overnight parking, oversized cookers in fields, charcoal grills, or open containers of alcohol.

Shuttle Info: The BuffRide will get you to the game for $6 round-trip and picks up at several Park & Ride locations in the greater Denver area. The Boulder Buff Shuttle is $3 and runs from the Boulder Park & Ride and Folsom Street/Colorado Ave. (For details, visit rtf-denver.com and click on "Special Rides" to find the BuffRide link).

Buffaloes Media Partner: 850-AM KOA

Where to Stay

RV PARKS

If you're looking for a good RV campground the closest you'll find are in the Denver area—there really isn't much right around Boulder. (See the RV Parks entries for Denver, page 87.)

For more information: For additional RV parks and campsites visit campingworld.com/campsearch.

HOTELS

Boulder Outlook Hotel & Suites: You can't beat the location; it's across the street from campus. This two-story motor lodge offers pleasant, colorful surroundings and a uniquely Boulder-esque feel, with chlorine-free indoor pools, climbing rocks, and even an enclosed pet park. The Adventure Concierge Service can help orchestrate outdoor adventure activities geared toward proficiency levels. You also get some unique amenities such as a dog-walking service. Rooms run $75. (*800 28th St., Boulder, (800) 542-0304, boulderoutlook.com*)

Hotel Boulderado: This historic hotel is one block away from the **Pearl Street Pedestrian Mall** (see page 95), and it offers a slice of history with a four-star rating and a great downtown location. This hotel's ornate decorations include original pieces from its 1909 opening. Rooms are luxurious, although not large by modern standards. Since it's an old hotel, there's no pool or workout room. The hotel's restaurant, **Q,** is one

of the city's best. Rooms run from $195 to $365, but a wide variety of rate discounts can drop the price of a room by as much as $90. (*2115 13th St., Boulder, (800) 433-4344, boulderado.com*)

To learn about more hotels in the area visit tripadvisor.com for listings and guest reviews.

Colorado tailgaters outside Folsom Field.
(Photo: Jamie Spittler)

B&BS

The Alps: Seven minutes west of Boulder, you'll find this historic lodge, formerly a stagecoach stop in the late 1800s. Now it's a B&B with arts and crafts and mission furnishings, sitting on a mountainside. Of the inn's twelve rooms, most have two-person Jacuzzi or antique claw-footed tubs, and private balconies or French doors opening to patios. Each room is different and named after a Colorado mining town; all have working fireplaces, queen beds, and individual thermostats. Rooms run from $99 to $274, depending on the season. (*38619 Boulder Canyon Dr., Boulder, (800) 414-2577, alpsinn.com*)

The Briar Rose: This is a perfect example of Boulder's spin on life: filled with antiques and feather comforters, it's as homey as Grandma's house—and one of its owners is a Zen Buddhist monk. Go figure. There are 10 guest rooms, several with business amenities such as modem hookups, large worktables, and bright lighting. Two rooms have fireplaces. Four of the carriage house rooms have either a patio or a balcony. Rates are $129–$159, depending when you stay here. (*2151 Arapahoe Ave. Boulder, (888) 786-8440, briarrosebb.com*)

For more information: To learn about more B&Bs in the area visit bedandbreakfast.com for a detailed directory.

TAILGATER GROCERIES

Boulder County Farmers' Market: This is the largest farmers' market in Colorado and features everything from fruits and vegetable, to wine and cheese—all produced by the people who sell it to you. Many of the products are organically grown. The market is open from April to November but times vary, so call ahead. Located beside Central Park, there's free parking in lots along Canyon Boulevard. (*1900 13th St., Boulder, (303) 910-2236, boulderfarmers.org*)

SPORTS BARS

Barrel House: Consistently voted the number-one sports bar in Boulder by local newspaper readers, the Barrel House offers twenty-five beers on tap, mostly Colorado microbrews. There are close to 40 TVs, including 4 big-screens. The bar is a traditional pregame meeting place for CU football fans. (*$; 2860 Arapahoe Rd., Boulder, (303) 444-9464, thebarrelhouse.com*)

Lazy Dog Sports Bar and Grill: With televisions covering every angle you can see, it's easy to get distracted from your meal. Normally that's no big deal, but the Dog offers everything from portabella mushrooms to salmon steaks, so you might actually feel a little conflicted. Okay, probably not. But the food is good and definitely a step up from normal pub grub. (*$$; 1346 Pearl St. (inside the mall), Boulder, (303) 440-3355, thelazydog.com*)

RESTAURANTS

Casa Alvarez: This place serves some very different Mexican food. Instead of cheese-covered combo plates, you'll get brilliantly flavored seafood, lamb, and pork dishes and a quartet of award-wining chile sauces. (*$; 3161 Walnut St., Boulder, (303) 546-0630*)

Frasca Food and Wine: It's new, it serves Northern Italian cuisine, and it has everyone in Boulder excited. Why all the love? Because Frasca's staff includes chefs from the famed French Laundry in California. (*$$$; 1738 Pearl St., Boulder, (303) 442-6966, frascafoodandwine.com*)

Glacier Homemade Ice Cream: So what if it's November? This is the best spot for incredible home-made ice cream in Boulder, with flavors you have to sample to believe. (*$; 3133 28th St., Boulder, (303) 440-6542, glacierhomemadeicecream.com*)

The Kitchen: A simply decorated, lively café that boasts upscale versions of French and Italian peasant fare. It also serves breakfast. Dig in to organic poached eggs with a side of sautéed wild mushrooms, crepes, pastries, homemade granola, and more. (*$$; 1039 Pearl St., Boulder, (303) 544-5973, thekitchencafe.com*)

L'Atelier: A smallish restaurant that serves up a large menu of French-inspired choices. All are excellently prepared and consistently delicious. The owner-chef, Radek Cerny, is noted for preparing dishes with lots of edible eye appeal; everything looks like a work of art, while still looking like food. (*$$; 1739 Pearl St., Boulder, (303) 442-7233, latelierboulder.com*)

What to Do

Fox Theatre: Enjoy everything from alt-rock bands to blues, folk, jazz, and jam-grass artists. Major-label acts and rising local stars alike call the Fox home. (*Admission varies; 1135 13th St., Boulder, (303) 443-3399, foxtheatre.com*)

Pearl St. Pub & Cellar: This is Boulder's closest thing to a dive bar. It's three bars in one: the upstairs pub, the music-filled back room, and the grungy basement pool and foosball room. (*$; 1108 Pearl St., Boulder, (303) 939-9900*)

Soma: Cool electronica served in a surprisingly warm manner—you don't need to be cool to get on the dance floor, you just need to dance. (*$; 1915 Broadway, Boulder, (303) 938-8600, or (303) 402-1690 after 7:00 p.m., somalounge.com*)

SHOPPING

Pearl Street Pedestrian Mall: This four-block area of Pearl Street, between 11th and 15th Streets, is lined with trees and filled with flowers, wooden benches, and sculptures. It's also chock-full of shops along with galleries, cafés, bookstores, and more. You'll also find street musicians, palm readers, jugglers, magicians, and others earning their tips in front of the county courthouse.

For more information: To learn more about things to do in the area visit bouldercoloradousa.com.

Houston

Outside Reliant Stadium there's a group of tailgaters who call themselves the Bulls and Babes Tailgate Team. Their tailgate party includes lobster, a live band, and a cigar roller. They didn't tailgate like this for the Houston Oilers.

But then again, this town is making sure the Houston Texans know they're welcome here. It helps that the owner isn't Bud Adams, who wore out his welcome and turned the Oilers into the Titans. (Nashville, on the other hand, was, for the most part, thrilled to welcome him—you can read about that on page 127.)

The Texans took the field in 2002 after owner Bob McNair failed to bring an NHL team to Houston, only to be more successful with the NFL. Tailgaters spread out all over Reliant Park, which is made up of four Reliant-branded buildings: the stadium, the Astrodome, the arena, and a convention/meeting facility called Reliant Center. You can tailgate only in your space and behind your vehicle, but you can also buy a pass that gives you an extra parking space in which to spread out. That extra room might be what you need to win the team's "Tailgater of the Game" contest. (You will have to get parking passes before the game, and they go fast; call (832) 667-2000 for details.)

If you're pulling a full-sized barbecue behind you, you're required to buy two spaces. You'll see a lot of these here. Barbecue is a Texas specialty, and there are rows and rows of grills and smokers. They make more than they can eat, so if you ask nicely, you might get a plate or two.

RVs also have to purchase two spaces and park in designated RV sections of the lot.

If you didn't bring a tailgate party of your own, the Budweiser Plaza is the team's tailgate party. You'll find it at the south end of the stadium and enjoy food, drinks, games, bands, and visits from the cheerleaders and mascot.

A quick note if you're not parking at the stadium: the Texans do not run shuttle buses to Reliant Park, but the city's rail service will drop you off there. It runs from downtown Houston to the Fannin South Lot just past the stadium (but it is the closest lot to it).

A seven-mile drive east of Reliant Stadium is Robertson Stadium, which is home to the University of Houston Cougars. The stadium was built in 1941 as a joint project of the Houston Independent School District and FDR's WPA. (Until 1945 the University was part of the city school system.) The stadium has been renovated since, of course, and seats 32,000.

Now, there's a tradition at most of the schools that were in the old Southwest Conference. Each school has

a hand sign. Texas has its Hook 'em Horns, Texas A&M has its Gig 'em Aggies, and Houston has its Cougar Hand Sign. Okay, it's not as catchy a name, but it has a colorful history.

The hand sign you'll see fans sporting has the thumb bent over the ring finger, pressing it against the palm. The other fingers are straight. If this doesn't look like a good cougar paw to you, it shouldn't. It actually was a sign University of Texas students created in 1953 to mock Houston students when their live cougar mascot, Shasta, had a finger on her paw accidentally severed when a cage door closed on it. The next time the teams played (albeit 15 years later), the Cougars tied the favored Longhorns; students thought maybe there was some luck in that sign, so they kept it.

Now Shasta walks the crowd along Tailgate Alley before games. Don't worry—it's the one with the guy in a costume. Tailgate Alley is a grassy, shaded area on the west side of the stadium that also has live performances, games, and other fan activities. If you can grab a spot here, you should. You have to reserve these spots ahead of time; call (713) 743-9450 to do that.

Otherwise, you can park in the Blue Lot on campus for $5. RVs have a separate area for overnight parking ($100–$200); call (713) 743-4684 for details. The tailgating in the lots is modest by most college standards, but they have fun.

Another former SWC school in town is Rice University. The Owls play in Rice Stadium, a football-only stadium (if you don't count concerts and such) that seats 70,000. It's the 32nd-largest college stadium in America.

Did we mention enrollment at Rice is just over 4,000?

In 1949 the Owls won the Southwest Conference championship, and civic leaders felt the old Rice Stadium, which held fewer than 37,000, wasn't big enough for a championship team and a growing city. The next year, they had a stadium nearly as big as the Orange Bowl. Fans did fill it up for some games in the '50s and early '60s, but since then there have been a lot of empty seats. For good reason.

Rice fans haven't had much to cheer about for a while. The Owls have been fighting for winning seasons, but usually losing. The tailgating seems to follow suit. That's why when you talk with Rice fans, they'll often talk about the apathetic attitude toward home games. But that doesn't mean there isn't any tailgating.

You will find diehard fans in the Stadium Lot before the game. You won't mistake it for an Auburn tailgate party, and there's a good chance you'll see more opponents' shirts and flags than Rice shirts and flags, but the tailgaters are having fun, and that's what it's all about.

There isn't any charge to park in the Stadium Lot, but you can't park overnight, and if you have a keg you have to register it with the police. Really.

HOUSTON TEXANS
Reliant Stadium
Houston, Texas
(832) 667-2000

Stadium parking for season ticket holders. City parking within walking distance; cost varies; no parking overnight. Put away all tailgating items before entering game. No oversized balloons allowed; no alcohol before 10 a.m. Sunday.

Train Info: Houston's METRORail takes fans from downtown to Reliant Stadium, with several stops along the way. You can park at one of several lots to catch the train; the closest to the stadium is the Fannin South Lot ($8 to park). Trains stop at each station about every 10 minutes. Cost is $1 each way. For more information visit ridemetro.org.

Texans Media Partners: 610-AM and 103.3-FM KLIT, KTRK-TV Channel 13 (ABC)

UNIVERSITY OF HOUSTON
Robertson Stadium
Houston, Texas
(713) 743-GOUH

Visitors park in Blue Lot on campus, $5 for cars. RVs park overnight in separate area, must get special parking pass $100–$200. Be prepared for hot weather; bring sunscreen.

Cougars Media Partner: 790-AM KBME

RICE UNIVERSITY
Rice Stadium
Houston, Texas
(713) 348-6930

Tailgaters park in Stadium Lot next to stadium, no charge. No overnight parking; come at 9:00 a.m. game day instead. No glass bottles; kegs okay, but must be registered with police. At afternoon games stay all day; evening games leave by 11:00 p.m.

Owls Media Partner: 790-AM KBME

About Houston

Houston is big and spread out. It's the nation's fourth-largest city, and covers more than 615 square miles. But it almost didn't happen.

Houston was founded by two brothers—Augustus and John Allen—in 1836, when they bought about 6,000 acres at the headwaters of the Buffalo Bayou. (It was named for Sam Houston, the first president of Texas.) Their town was growing. It was the nation's capital (Texas was a country then, not a state). Things looked good. Then the capital was moved to Austin.

To save the town, the residents who stayed decided to build a port from which to ship livestock and crops. They finished digging and building the Houston Ship Channel in 1914—just in time to benefit from the war. Houston is now one of the world's busiest ports.

But it was in 1901 that Houston hit it big, at a place called Spindletop, east of town, in Beaumont. That's when they discovered "black gold," the Texas tea you remember from the *Beverly Hillbillies* theme song. By the time of the Great Depression, there were 40 oil companies in Houston. By the '70s people were moving to Bayou City in droves—1,000 a week. But when oil went bust in the '80s, so did Houston. Since then it has worked its way back, diversifying its economy into technology, health care, and other fields.

The other industry here, of course, is space. The kind where astronauts go. In 1961 what's now called the **Johnson Space Center** (see page 104) was established to handle America's manned space flight program. Since then, Houston's other nickname has been "Space City."

Where to Stay
RV PARKS
Houston Central KOA: You'll like the lawns and trees in this city-center park that feels more like you're in the country. In addition to the usual amenities, there's an air-conditioned social hall, covered patio garden, swimming pool, and playground. The park is secure and gated. If you want to explore a bit, you can rent bicycles here, too. Rates run $26–$32. It is a KOA, so you can also rent Kamping Kabins (that's really how they spell that here). *(1620 Peach Leaf St., Houston, (800) 562-2132, koa.com/where/tx/43194/index.htm)*

Lake View RV Resort: About six miles south of Reliant Stadium, Lake View has 150 sites and all the usual amenities, along with several recreational options including picnic areas with grills, a swimming pool, Jacuzzi, and fitness/recreation and computer rooms. It also does have a view of a lake—a 4-acre one on the property for fishing or just enjoying. All this will run you $27–$38. There are also cabins for rent. (*11991 S. Main St., Houston, (800) 385-9122, lakeviewrvresort.com*)

South Main RV Park: Less than three miles from Reliant Stadium, this park has 107 sites and offers large shaded lots, paved streets, and concrete patios. South Main has the usual amenities, and there's WiFi for many of the sites. The park is also a secure site that is fenced, gated, and requires codes to access. Rates run $34–$36. (*10100 S. Main, Houston, (800) 626-PARK, smrvpark.com*)

The DIM Fiefelmann Cookers man the grill in Reliant's Yellow Lot. (Photo: DIMcookers.com)

Traders Village: This is a big RV park (287 sites) that sits next to a permanent swap-meet/flea market (also called **Traders Village;** see page 106 for more about that). They allow any length vehicle here, have a good number of pull-through spaces and paved roads, and they offer the usual amenities. There's also a mini-mart on-site to pick up tailgating supplies and an ATM. The Traders Village complex holds a number of special events throughout the year; football season brings an art car show and a chili cook-off, among others. (*7979 N. Eldridge Rd., Houston, (281) 890-5500, tradersvillage.com/hnrv.html*)

For more information: For additional RV parks and campsites visit campingworld.com/campsearch.

HOTELS

Hotel Derek: This boutique hotel close to the **Galleria** (see page 106) is named after a fictitious aging rock star—and it's easily one of the coolest hotels in Houston. Retro-modern furnishings create a casual but functional atmosphere, and amenities run from personal comfort such as rain showers and a spa treatment suite, to business function like WiFi and FedEx supplies in your room. The on-site restaurant serves fusion Chinese and Cuban cooking and also hosts a popular bar. The stretch SUV Derek Mobile offers a free shuttle around town. Rooms run $125–$269, depending on when you stay. (*2525 W. Loop South, Houston, (713) 961-3000, hotelderek.com*)

Hotel Icon: If you want to stay downtown, Hotel Icon is a neat place to do it. It used to be the Union National Bank building, but it's been renovated into a luxury hotel with fine dining, fine wines, a spa, and amenities you'd expect to go with it. The rooms average 400 square feet. If you want to splurge, try the two-level Presidential Suite, or the three-level Penthouse with its own 600-foot rooftop terrace. A METRORail station is nearby and will take you to Rice or Reliant Stadium. Rates average about $189; packages are available. (*220 Main, Houston, (713) 224-ICON, hotelicon.com*)

Houston Grand Plaza: Walk out the door, look across the street, and you can see Reliant Stadium. Bought and renovated in 2005 (it used to be a Park Plaza hotel), the hotel has garden suites available in addition to its standard rooms. The hotel's top floor is the Celestial Suite, once the most expensive hotel room (the *Guinness Book of World Records* said so); it was designed by the same guy who designed the sets for *20,000 Leagues Under the Sea*. The hotel also boasts Houston's largest hotel ballroom, but

Tailgating outside Reliant Stadium.
(Photo: DIMCookers.com)

don't expect to be able to use it for your tailgate. Rooms run $109–$139. (*8686 Kirby Dr., Houston, (713) 748-3221, houstongrandplaza.com*)

Inn at the Ballpark: The ballpark is Minute Maid Park downtown (where the Astros play), but it's not too bad of a drive to any of the football stadiums. You can also take the METRORail trains. The rooms are well outfitted, and there's a fitness center and restaurant. You'd expect there to be a restaurant since the place is owned by Houston-based Landry's Restaurants, which owns a couple dozen restaurant chains including Joe's Crab Shack, Brenner's Steakhouse, and the Rainforest Café. Rates at the Inn run $109 and up. (*1520 Texas Ave., Houston, (866) 406-1520, innattheballpark.com*)

La Colombe d'Or: This exclusive, European-style hotel was built in 1923 and exudes warmth and charm. Located in the Montrose area, and furnished with genuine antiques, it also houses an award-winning restaurant and a small, but cozy bar. Suites have kitchens, balconies, and Jacuzzi tubs. This beautiful mansion is also a Texas historical landmark. It's not cheap; rooms cost $200 and up. (*3410 Montrose Blvd., (713) 524-7999, lacolombedorhouston.com*)

Sofitel Houston: The French flag once flew over Texas, and while we're sure there's no tie to that, the Sofitel Houston is appointed with French Country furnishings, and the restaurant serves up French/American cuisine. Located near Bush International Airport, the hotel offers basic amenities plus a fitness center, piano lounge, currency exchange, and dry-cleaning services. It's also pet friendly. Rooms are $89–$245. (*425 N. Sam Houston Pkwy. E. [Kennedy Blvd.], Houston, (281) 445-9000, sofitel.com [type "Houston, TX" into the Quick Search box]*)

For more information: To learn about more hotels in the area visit tripadvisor.com for listings and guest reviews.

B&BS

Lovett Inn: Built in 1923 by former Houston mayor Joseph Hutcheson, this historic home is wonderfully preserved and located in the Montrose-Museum District. Most of the rooms overlook the Inn's landscaped grounds and pool. The home also offers a sunroom and Jacuzzi. Rooms offer amenities such as whirlpool tubs and private balconies and will run from $95 to $250. (*501 Lovett Blvd., Houston, (800) 779-5224, lovettinn.com*)

Patrician Bed and Breakfast Inn: This large three-story, Colonial revival-style mansion built in 1919 offers cozy accommodations in the heart of the Museum District. The home is within walking distance of the Rice campus—as well as **Hermann Park** and the **Zoological Gardens.** If you want some surprises with your dinner, try Pat's Murder Mystery Dinners. Pat is the owner, who requires at least 14 people for the mystery dinners. Most rooms have private baths with whirlpool tubs. Rates are $85–$150. (*1200 Southmore Blvd., Houston, (800) 553-5797, texasbnb.com*)

Robin's Nest Bed and Breakfast: This 1898 Victorian home is decorated in a funky, eclectic style suitable for the Montrose arts district it sits in. Although downtown skyscrapers are just about a mile away, the house was the personal protest of the Kaufholds, who built it in what was then way out in the country to protest Houston's rising taxes. A huge wrap-around porch is perfect for watching the activity of this popular neighborhood. Whirlpool baths and small refrigerators are in every room. It's pet friendly, too. Rates range from $95 to $175. (*4104 Greeley St., Houston, (713) 528-5821, therobin.com*)

Sara's Bed and Breakfast Inn: A large Texas Victorian house with wrap-around porch, plenty of gingerbread trim, and even a turret, Sara's offers period decor in each of the 12 rooms, all named for various Texas locations. All rooms offer private baths and cable TV with VCR (and plenty of movies to borrow). The house sits on a spacious lot in Historic Heights with maintained gardens. One note: this B&B is just a B on Mondays (no breakfast). Rates are $90–$145. (*941 Heights Blvd., Houston, (800) 593-1130, saras.com*)

Sara's Bed and Breakfast Inn. (Photo: Easton Photography)

For more information: To learn about more B&Bs in the area visit bedandbreakfast.com for a detailed directory.

Where to Eat
TAILGATER GROCERIES

Central Market: From prep-less produce to chef-prepared meals and everything in between, you'll find plenty for your tailgate party here—including handmade sausages and marinated meats ready for grilling. Oh, if you like cheese, you'll love this place; they have more than 600 kinds of cheese. (*3815 Westheimer Rd., Houston, (713) 386-1700, centralmarket.com*)

Eatzi's: For a traveling tailgater, the great thing about this place is that it has a huge selection of prepared dishes for takeout. From chicken to sushi, salad bar to dessert, you name it, there's a good chance you'll find it. Eatzi's is the brainchild of the guy who created the burger chain Fuddrucker's. It gets crowded after work as folks pick up dinner to take home. (*1702 Post Oak Blvd., Houston, (713) 629-6003, eatzis.com*)

SPORTS BARS

Brian O'Neill's Restaurant and Irish Pub: Okay, this is more of an Irish Pub than a traditional sports bar, but it is a five-time *Houston Press* "Best of Houston" winner and shows games on big-screen TVs. Close to the Rice campus, Brian O'Neill's has Irish and American dishes on the menu, along with tapas. A large beer selection (15 draft and 30 bottled) and live music Wednesday through Saturday nights keeps the place active after the game's over, too. (*$, 5555 Morningside Dr., Houston, (713) 522-2603, brianoneills.com*)

Ernie's on Banks: Named for famed Chicago Cubs shortstop Ernie Banks, this two-story bar in the Museum District is the game-day home for serious and casual fans. The decor includes a gallery of vintage baseball caps (including a rare, 25-year-old ESPN hat), and you can play darts, pool, video games, and shuffleboard. Don't expect to find banks of televisions, but do expect to find a mix of college students and neighborhood locals. (*$, 1010 Banks St., Houston, (713) 526-4566*)

Griff's: Billed as Houston's oldest surviving sports bar (since 1965), Griff's shows NFL and college football games via satellite on 15 TVs, including three big-screens. When Griff opened the place, he wanted to mix his love of sports and "a wee bit of the Irish," so expect a pub feel. Fire-grilled steaks and the Double Trouble Burger come from the kitchen, and a Jaegermeister machine and 25 varieties of cold beer pour from the bar. The bar is also home to Griff's Army—a group of fans who turn out to watch the games and often

DIM'S PORK RIBS

If you take a look in the Yellow Lot outside Reliant Stadium on a Texans game day, you'll find the Dimozine. Inside you'll find The DIM Fiefelmann Cookers working on some barbecued ribs. If you're wondering what a Dimozine (rhymes with limousine) is, they'll tell you it's a big smoker with a trailer wrapped around it. You'll recognize it by the logo on the side and the flags on top. Barbecue is a specialty in Houston and this is one of DIM Cookers' most popular recipes.

Lawry's Seasoned Salt

Freshly ground black pepper

Paprika

3 racks of pork ribs, with knuckles on

Barbecue sauce

Preheat the smoker to 225° to 250°.

In a bowl combine generous amounts, to taste, of the salt, pepper, and paprika to create a rub. Work the rub into the meat thoroughly. Place the meat in the smoker, bone side up. Be sure to avoid having the meat in direct flames, using a shield if necessary.

Cook for 2 to 3 hours or until the meat pulls back ½ to ¾ inch from the bone tips.

Remove the meat from the smoker and place it on aluminum foil (with the edges folded up to create a "boat") and apply your favorite barbecue sauce—but avoid really sweet sauces since they tend to gum up when cooked for a long period. Wrap the foil "boat" shut to seal in the sauce and place it in the cooker for 1 hour more.

Note: If you're cooking with a gas grill, buy some Liquid Smoke and pour it on several times during cooking to get the flavor a charcoal or wood fire would naturally give the meat.

Makes 9 to 12 servings.

take bus trips to away games. (*$, 3416 Roseland, Houston, (713) 528-9912, griffshouston.com*)

SRO Sports Bar & Cafe: It stands for Standing Room Only, and it can get crowded here. Their goal is to show every game and sports event they possibly can, so they've plugged in more than 200 TVs of various sizes to pull it off. In addition to Houston teams, SRO hosts alumni-watching parties for schools ranging from Penn State to Washington State, and a bunch of colleges in between. The game room has pool tables, darts, and video games. Full menu and a raw oyster bar. (*444 Northwest Mall, Houston, (713) 683-5025, srosportsbar.com; Second location: 6982 FM 1960 W., Houston, (281) 537-0691*)

RESTAURANTS

Américas Restaurant: A dramatic interior that echoes Incan artifacts and mythology compliments the New World Cuisine that draws from the foods and cooking techniques of North, Central, and South America—hence the name. Try the signature dishes Tirtas (potato-crusted filets of calamari), Pargo "Américas" (pan-roasted filet of Gulf snapper crusted with fresh corn), and Torta de Queso y Maix (native-style cheesecake, bound with fresh sweet corn). Reservations are recommended. (*$$, 1800 Post Oak Blvd., Houston, (713) 961-1492, cordua.com/Americas_hm.htm*)

Backstreet Café: Located in a '30s-era two-story home, Backstreet offers a beautiful interior—but it's the legendary backyard deck where you'll want to sit in nice weather. Serving a menu of chef-prepared New American cuisine, you'll find new twists on old favorites (try the meatloaf tower: a hearty slab of meatloaf atop a tower of garlic mashed potatoes and sautéed spinach), an excellent wine list, and, on Saturdays and Sundays, a brunch accompanied by a popular jazz trio. Parking is problematic, so let the valet do it. (*$$, 1103 S. Shepherd Dr., Houston, (713) 521-2239, backstreetcafe.net*)

Bocados: By day a subdued lunch spot, by night a lively hot spot. Serving traditional Tex-Mex as well as Southwestern-style seafood in a cozy bungalow in the Montrose area, Bocados turns from restaurant into club after 8:00 p.m. You'll want to try the Bocados sampler (for many it's enough for their entrée). You'll also find some Cuban dishes on the menu, hand-me-downs from a sister restaurant that closed a couple of years ago. (*$, 1312 W. Alabama, Houston, (713) 523-5230*)

Backstreet Café.
(Photo: Backstree Café)

D'wine Restaurant & Bar: Featuring an exotic fusion menu—European, Asian, South American, and American—this hip restaurant also features the **Papparazzi Lounge.** Try the Lobster Ravioli, Bombay Chicken, or Curry Lamb Stew. D'wine takes its cocktails as seriously as its food (the specialty: Bellinis). There are two dining patios, and after your meal you can head to the lounge for cigars and cordials. (*$$, 4304 Westheimer Rd., Houston, (713) 626-9463, dwinerestaurant.com*)

Green's Barbeque: Located near the University of Houston, this casual old-time barbecue joint has been in business for more than 25 years, and it is known for its tender ribs and homemade sausage. It's a family run business—not the Green family, but the family the Green's sold to in the '90s. But the new family didn't change much, and locals are happy about that. Make sure to take cash or a checkbook, because Green's doesn't accept credit cards. (*$, 5404 Almeda Rd., Houston, (713) 528-5501*)

Grotto Ristorante: Serving up a hearty Neopolitan-influenced Italian menu, Grotto's is one of Houston's enduring favorites. Although seafood and pasta lovers will find a lot to choose from, the wood-fired pizzas are also a house specialty. Colorful murals, a full bar, and a chatty ambience make this locale a fun and relaxing place to eat. You'll want reservations on weekend nights. (*$$, 4715 Westheimer Rd., Houston, (713) 622-3663, www.grottohouston.com; there's also a second location in The Woodlands*)

Otto's Barbeque: Their slogan is "Where the president eats beef." Yep, they mean that president, and the President Bush before him. A Houston landmark for more than 50 years, Otto's has been serving up barbecue and hamburgers—both specialties and served on different sides of the restaurant. They have two new locations, but this is the original. (*$, 5502 Memorial Dr., Houston, (713) 864-2573, ottosbarbecue.com*)

Pappas Brothers Steakhouse: This Houston landmark hasn't changed in 60 years—and that's a good thing. The clubby dining room is always packed (you'll want reservations); the dry-aged steaks keep bringing them in. Okay, the homemade desserts probably bring in a few folks, too. The wine list is extensive—more than 2,300 bottles extensive. When you're finished, you can head to the cigar room or the snug lounge for a cognac. (*$$$, 5839 Westheimer Rd., Houston, (713) 780-7352, pappasbros.com*)

Pappasito's Cantina: Considered to have the best fajitas in Houston—and routinely on Houston "Best of" lists—Pappasito's has three locations, and they all stay busy. Decked out with the look of a border-town cantina (complete with strolling mariachis), the menu is filled with Tex-Mex favorites. Portions are plentiful. (*6445 Richmond Ave., Houston, (713) 784-5253; 2536 Richmond Ave., Houston, (713) 520-5066; and 2515 South Loop West, Houston, (713) 668-5756; pappasitos.com*)

Ruggles Grill: This popular restaurant serves up an extensive, eclectic menu that leans toward Southwestern. The portions are generous, part of the owners' philosophy of take-home food, meaning take some home for tomorrow. You'll want to try dessert, like the white chocolate bread pudding. Live jazz is also featured in this renovated old house. Reservations are a good idea here. Closed Mondays. (*$, 903 Westheimer Rd., (713) 524-3839, rugglesgrill.com*)

For more information: For a directory of additional places to eat in the area visit opentable.com. You can also book a reservation for many restaurants on the site.

What to Do

DURING THE DAY

Armand Bayou Nature Center: This wildlife and nature preserve is in the middle of a relatively populated suburban area and is one of only four Texas State Coastal Preserves. Located right on Central Flyway, a North American migratory bird route, it offers walking trails, tours, wildlife exhibits, and a look at some of the region's original ecosystems. A visit to the Center's Martyn Farm will take you back to Texas farm life in the late 1800s. (*$, 8500 Bay Area Blvd., Pasadena, (281) 474-2551, abnc.org*)

Downtown Aquarium Houston: More than just an aquarium, this family-friendly park features rides and amusements in addition to a bunch of fish. With 500,000 gallons of visible underwater tanks exhibiting more than 200 species of marine life, there's plenty of educational fun. For an incredible view of the city, hop on the 100-foot Diving Bell Ferris wheel. You can also travel by train into an acrylic tunnel with live sharks swimming overhead, experience the petting tanks, or visit the rare white tiger exhibit. There's a seafood restaurant on-site, too. Ironic, but the place is a division of Landry's Restaurants. Everything is priced separately, or you can get a day pass for everything. (*$$, 410 Bagby St., Houston, (713) 223-3474, downtownaquariumhouston.com*)

Hermann Park: Like the outdoors? Well, you're going to love this place: 545 acres of trees, lawns, duck-filled reflecting pools, paddleboats, picnic areas, and an 18-hole golf course. Oh, did we mention the **Houston Zoo, Japanese Garden, Zoological Garden,** and **Baker Planetarium?** It can fill up a day. (*The park is free; admission varies by attraction, Hermann Dr. at Fannin & Montrose, Houston, (713) 526-0077, hermannpark.org*)

The Houston Museum of Natural Science: Established in 1909 and located in Hermann Park, this excellent Museum of Natural Science includes the **Baker Planetarium, Cockrell Butterfly Center,** and **Wortham IMAX Theater,** among its many permanent and traveling exhibitions. Check out the Foucault pendulum, and you'll want to see the rainforest environment at the Butterfly Center (which also has an insect zoo). Each venue has its own admission charge. (*$, 1 Hermann Circle Dr., Houston, (713) 639-4600, hmns.org*)

Kemah Boardwalk: Twenty miles from downtown Houston toward Galveston is Kemah, Texas, and the Kemah Boardwalk. What began as a waterfront dining development has turned into a day—if not week-

end—getaway destination. Along the boardwalk are 10 restaurants, a hotel, rides and games, shopping, and **Joe's Boardwalk Beast.** The Beast is a 70-foot long, 18-foot-wide, customized, open-deck speedboat that holds 140 passengers; you can be one of them. All rides and attractions have separate ticket fees, but you can buy various passes and packages. (*$–$$, Bradford & Second Streets, Kemah, kemahboardwalk.com*)

Lyndon B. Johnson Space Center/Space Center Houston: Remember when Neil Armstrong said from the moon, "Houston, the Eagle has landed?" Or in Apollo 13 when Tom Hanks's character says "Houston, we have a problem?" This is where they were talking to. Originally the Manned Spacecraft Center, it was renamed in honor of president, and Texan, Lyndon B. Johnson and is responsi-

The Houston Aquarium.
(Photo: David Wang)

The Ultimate Tailgater's Travel Guide

ble for the design, development, and operation of human space flight. It's also a cool place to visit. A tram tour gives you a look behind the scenes. There's an IMAX theater, interactive Kids' Space Place, exhibits about the history of manned spaceflight, Astronaut Gallery, and Mission Status Center. (*$$, 1601 NASA Rd. 1, Houston, (713) 224-2100, spacecenter.org*)

*The Kemah Boardwalk.
(Photo: Landry's Restaurants, Inc.)*

Museum of Fine Arts: Founded in 1900 as the first art museum in Texas and located in the Museum District, the original 1920s-era building has bold, modern additions by famed architect Mies van der Rohe. The MFA is a cultural complex consisting of two museum buildings, two art schools, two decorative arts centers, and a sculpture garden. It displays fine art from ancient to modern and offers large traveling exhibits. (*$, 1001 Bissonnet St., Houston, (713) 639-7300, mfah.org*)

San Jacinto Battleground State Historic Site: This is the spot where Sam Houston defeated Santa Anna's army and gained independence from Mexico in 1836. A National Historic Landmark, the 1,200-acre park consists of the battleground, monument, museum, and the *Battleship Texas*. (*$, One Monument Circle, La Porte, Houston, (281) 479-2431, tpwd.state.tx.us/spdest/findadest/parks/san_jacinto_battleground*)

AT NIGHT

Bayou Place: Located in the heart of the downtown theater district, this venue offers more than 100,000 square feet of dining and entertainment establishments to please virtually every taste—movie and cultural event theaters, nightclubs, cafés, concert stages, and restaurants are all conveniently located and make for easy entertainment and bar-hopping. You'll find Houston's **Hard Rock Cafe** and **Slick Willie's** here. (*500 Texas Ave., corner of Louisiana and Texas Avenues, Houston*)

Blanco's: Put on your boots if you're headed to Blanco's, an authentic country joint, where you'll hear some of the best country music in Houston from local and traveling acts (while you're eating some of the best fried catfish anywhere). There's live music most nights; when there's not, there's the jukebox. You can dance the two-step, or just enjoy it all while sipping a Pearl beer—Blanco's is one of the few places in Houston that still serves the old Texas brew. Open for lunch, too. (*Cover charge varies, 3406 W. Alabama St., Houston, (713) 439-0072*)

The Davenport: This trendy place defines Rat Pack swank, with its intimate, '50s-style decor, including couches and chairs, and a TV screen showing a faux crackling fireplace. Martinis are the house specialty, but the bar also boasts more than 42 different single-malt scotches and 35 vodka varieties. The club also features live DJs every Wednesday from 9:00 p.m. until close. (*$, 2117 Richmond Ave., Houston, (713) 520-1140, thedavenport.com*)

The Ginger Man: Named after J.P. Donleavy's best-selling book (and there are copies on hand, if you want to read up), this casual, unpretentious Rice Village-area pub is a good one. Located in an old brick house, you can watch the sun set from the wrap-around porch while you enjoy one of 60 draft beers or 110 bottled varieties—indeed, you can tour the world through beer, with ambers, stouts, and ales hailing everywhere from the Czech Republic and Netherlands to Japan and South America, plus your favorites. There's also an outdoor beer garden. But there's no real food—just snack-type stuff. (*$, 5607 ½ Morningside Dr., Houston, (713) 526-2770, gingermanpub.com*)

HOUSTON

The gallery at the Johnson Space Center Museum. (Photo: Another Off the Wall Production, Inc.)

Maxwell's Club: The dance floor at this south Houston hot spot is packed from 6:00 p.m. on by upscale, mature, (mostly) singles grooving to retro funk. Plenty of tables and couches, but it's not about sitting here. Depending on the day, Maxwell's offers buffets, drink specials, ladies nights, contests with cash prizes, pool tournaments, and more. Know that if you're under 25, you're not getting in. (*$, 9255 Main St., Houston, (713) 661-1915*)

McGonigel's Mucky Duck: Rustic Irish in theme, this live-music pub, a Houston landmark, has featured well-known local and regional acts, including Lyle Lovett, and it offers traditional Irish music on Wednesdays with no cover charge. *Billboard Magazine* has listed the Mucky Duck as one of the nation's top 20 acoustic venues. The menu is basic bar food, and it has a good beer selection. If you want to try your hand at stardom, Monday is open mic night. (*$, 2425 Norfolk, Houston, (713) 528-5999, mcgonigels.com*)

Scott Gertner's SkyBar and Grille: This sexy penthouse nightclub—offering a stunning nighttime view of downtown Houston—is all about cool, from the array of champagnes, wines, and martinis, to the hand-picked cigars. It's a jazz bar that lands on Houston's "Best of" lists. Two terraces and an oversized, U-shaped bar are perfect for people watching. (*$, 3400 Montrose Blvd., Houston, (713) 520-9688, scottgertner.com*)

SHOPPING

The Galleria: With spectacular architecture and all the upscale shops you could want, including **Fendi, Sephora, Gucci, Armani Exchange,** and **Versace** (plus a **Cheesecake Factory**), this is one of the crown jewels of Houston's shopping scene. Heck, there's even an indoor ice rink. There are also several other restaurants and shopping areas in the immediate area. (*5085 Westheimer Rd., Suite 4850, Houston, (713) 622-0663 simon.com/mall/default.aspx?ID=805*)

Rice Village: This shopping district has been a Houston destination since the 1930s. Located next to Rice University and amidst an upscale residential neighborhood, the area is known for its wide variety of restaurants, nightlife venues, and shopping, which has both national names **(Chico's, Structure, Häagen Dazs)** and a multitude of small and eclectic shops and boutiques. From Japanese animation at **Planet Anime** and art at **The Goldstein Collection,** to gifts at **Europe in the Village** and **Artisans Designs,** you can spend a day wandering around the 14-plus blocks that make up Rice Village. (*University Blvd. and Kirby Dr., Houston, ricevillageonline.com*)

Traders Village Flea Market: This isn't just any flea market. It's 60 acres and an average of 1,000 merchants, and it's open every Saturday and Sunday. Browse, buy, and trade collectibles, crafts, army surplus, furniture, clothing, jewelry, and much more. With on-site restaurants and kiddie rides to go with the shopping, you can make a day of it. (*7979 N. Eldridge Rd., Houston, (281) 890-5500, tradersvillage.com/hn1.html*)

Uptown Park: This European-style shopping village is lined with boutiques, fountains, and lavish landscaping, and it features restaurants, spas, and other unique shops. Stock up at the **Cigar Vault,** explore the **Children's Art Project Boutique,** and grab a bite at **Uptown Sushi**. There are more than 45 shops in all. (*1131 Uptown Park Blvd. (Post Oak Blvd. and Loop 610), Houston, uptownparkhouston.com*)

For more information: To learn more about things to do in the area visit cityguide.aol.com/houston.

The Ultimate Tailgater's Travel Guide

Kansas City

Lamar Hunt was frustrated. He'd been trying to get an NFL team for years, but he had failed. So in 1959 he took a different route, cofounding the American Football League, the idea being that if you start a league yourself, you get to have a team. Fair enough. Hunt put one of his own in his hometown and named it the Dallas Texans. The league began play in 1960.

That was also the year the NFL put an expansion team in Dallas—the Cowboys. Although the Texans were successful, winning the AFL title in 1962, Hunt felt it would be best for the AFL if he moved his team.

So in 1963 he moved the team to Kansas City and renamed it the Chiefs. The Chiefs continued winning, including an AFL championship in 1966, making them the first team to represent the AFL in the Super Bowl. And in 1969 they went on to win Super Bowl IV.

During those early years in Kansas City, the Chiefs shared a stadium with baseball's Kansas City Royals. Now they share a parking lot. The Chiefs' Arrowhead Stadium and the Royals' Kauffman Stadium make up the Harry S. Truman Sports Complex. Built in 1972, it was the first complex in the nation to have sport-specific parks share infrastructure such as roads and parking.

For tailgaters, that was great. It meant more parking spaces. That helps make for better tailgating. And perhaps nowhere in America is NFL tailgating better than in Kansas City.

When you're here on game day, it is a sea of red. And many of the boats on that "sea" are grills and smokers cooking barbecue, a Kansas City specialty. Fans here are loyal, spirited, and friendly. They also have many of the parking spaces reserved.

But not all of them. Lots A, L, and N are nonreserved cash lots that cost $20. They open up 3½ hours before kickoff. If you're pulling a trailer of any kind, you'll be charged for two parking spaces and must park in the grass.

If you're not parking your car and hosting your own tailgate, you can get to Arrowhead on the Chiefs Express shuttle buses. There are routes from downtown and the Country Club Plaza, as well as from more than a dozen Park & Ride locations in the area. The shuttles cost $10 round trip, but you can save $2 if you buy them in advance. Log on to kcata.org/chiefs.html for shuttle details.

Racing came to Kansas City in 2001 when the Kansas Speedway opened. This state-of-the-art track has a flexible capacity of 81,000–150,000 seats and holds several events, including the NEXTEL Cup Series' Banquet 400.

KANSAS CITY CHIEFS
Arrowhead Stadium
Kansas City, Missouri
(816) 920-4382

Parking is close to stadium; shuttles available but unnecessary. Can't buy extra spaces, but there are grass areas for use. Tailgate in front of or behind vehicle; parking passes for vehicles, not trailers or tables.

Shuttle Info: Chiefs Express shuttle buses serve three routes and 14 Park & Ride locations in the KC area. Tickets are $10 round trip, $8 if purchased in advance. Visit kcata.org/chiefs.html for details.

Chiefs Media Partner: 101.1-FM KCFX

KANSAS SPEEDWAY
Kansas City, Kansas
(913) 328-7223

Kansas Speedway's Reserved Infield, Motor Home Terrace, and Kansas Campground allow overnight stays. Season pass only. Tailgating starts early in the morning; no open fires; don't bring food, drink, or large bags into stadium. No parking in pit.

If you want to come the day of the race, parking lots open at 6:00 a.m., and all lots are free. Keep in mind, there is no overnight parking in the parking lots. To do that, you need a campsite—and an RV.

There are three camping areas on the property: Motor Home Terrace, Reserved Infield, and Kansas Campground. Only self-driven, self-contained RVs are allowed in the lots; although campers can stay in the Infield and Campground. You can pull in the Thursday evening before the race. None of the spaces have hookups or dumping stations. Camping costs vary between sites, so call (866) 460-RACE for details.

To help fans get around the Speedway property, shuttles, trams and trolleys are provided to run on race days between several locations, including the Sprint Fan Walk.

The Sprint Fan Walk is an interactive area in the infield, where you can take a look behind the scenes. You can watch crew chiefs and teams work on cars, observe race-day press conferences, and hang out in Autograph Alley to catch your favorite driver. There are also concession stands.

Another popular pre-race area is the Souvenir and Display Midway located on either side of the main entrance.

About Kansas City

Kansas City was built on trade by some enterprising settlers in the early 1800s.

In 1821, the same year Missouri was admitted into the Union, a Frenchman from St. Louis opened a trading post on the Missouri River. That was the beginning. During the next several years, others opened up shop along the Santa Fe Trail (the first was Westport, now an entertainment district; see page 114) and at other points on the river. These men fought to wrest control of trading ports and routes from neighboring communities, first the waterways and later the railways. They succeeded.

The railroads helped make possible Kansas City's first major industry: cattle. Not long after the Civil War, Kansas City became one of the world's largest cattle markets. The city's famous stockyard was founded in 1870, and the Kansas City Livestock Exchange there was, in its heyday, the largest building in the world dedicated exclusively to livestock interests. That's why it's known as "Cowtown."

Trade is still an important part of the city. Kansas City's foreign trade zone is well known, and it is still the second largest

The Ultimate Tailgater's Travel Guide

railroad hub in the country, behind Chicago. It is also headquarters for Hallmark Cards.

Where to Stay
RV PARKS

Worlds of Fun Village: It's not the RV park that's Worlds of Fun, but it's part of the **Worlds of Fun** theme park complex, which also includes **Oceans of Fun.** In fact, you can walk to the theme parks. The RV park has 82 sites, each with a grill and picnic table. You can also rent cabins and cottages. The park is fully landscaped and includes a grocery market. RV sites run $37 for up to six people. Open April–October. (*4545 NE Worlds of Fun Dr., Kansas City, MO, (800) 877-4FUN, worldsoffun.com/trip_planning/village/index.cfm*)

Setting up early at Arrowhead Stadium. (Photo: Chiefstailgaters.com)

Stadium RV Park: This isn't a big park (just 25 sites), but it's as close as you'll get to Arrowhead Stadium. It's also a very basic site, with hookups, laundry, and patios—but not much else. Rates are $22–$25. (*10021 E. US Hwy. 40, Independence, MO, (816) 353-0242*)

Cottonwood Camping: Open since 1998, it's the newest RV park in the KC area, and it's just 5 minutes from the Speedway. Cottonwood has 100 sites (most of them pull-through), LP, and a dump station—as well as the usual amenities. Daily rates are $19–$23. (*115 S. 130th St., Bonner Springs, KS, (913) 422-8038, cottonwoodcamping.com*)

For more information: For additional RV parks and campsites visit campingworld.com/campsearch.

HOTELS

Hotel Phillips: This art-deco hotel is a Kansas City landmark. Built in 1931 for what seemed like a fortune at the time ($1.6 million), it was KC's tallest hotel at 20 stories. In 2001 a renovation that cost more than 10 times what it cost to build the hotel brought it up to modern standards with modern amenities, while keeping its European flavor. Rooms run $139 and up. (*106 W. 12th Street, Kansas City, MO, (800) 433-1426, hotelphillips.com*)

Chateau Avalon: Known as an experience hotel, the exterior has a cobbled courtyard and ornate fountains and statuary. Inside each suite there is offered a different theme and decor with names such as Pirate's Cove, Venetian, and Mayan Rainforest. Some of the rooms are smallish, others extravagant. Rooms include flat-screen TV/DVD players (27"–60") and spa tubs with Chroma Therapy. Most rooms run $179–$399, although some get up to more than $600. (*701 Village West Pkwy., Kansas City, KS, (877) 522-8256, chateauavalon.net*)

Great Wolf Lodge: This isn't just a hotel—it's a self-contained theme park. More resort than hotel, this four-story log-sided building houses 281 suites, as well as restaurants, spa, and entertainment. Oh, did we mention the 49,000-square-foot, indoor water park? Suites hold from 6 to 8 people and run $279–$399. A two-night stay is required for certain times of the year. (*10401 Cabela Drive, Kansas City, KS, (913) 299-7001, kc.greatwolflodge.com*)

KANSAS CITY **109**

Toasting the Chiefs in Kansas City. (Photo: Chiefstailgaters.com)

The Raphael Hotel: They bill themselves as "Kansas City's Original Boutique Hotel" and were voted one of the "World's Best Places to Stay" by *Condé Nast Traveler*. Built in 1927 as the Villa Serena Apartments, the building was transformed into the Raphael Hotel in 1975. Rooms feature high-speed Internet access and refrigerators. But one of the best features is the location—on the **Country Club Plaza** (see pages 113 and 114). Rooms run $130–$199. (*325 Ward Pkwy [on the Country Club Plaza], Kansas City, MO, (816) 756-3800, raphaelkc.com*)

For more information: To learn about more hotels in the area visit tripadvisor.com for listings and guest reviews.

B&BS

Back In Thyme Guest House & Herb Garden: This Queen Anne–style guest home has been featured in national magazines and is nestled on 10 wooded acres with herb gardens and a fishing pond (they provide the tackle and bait). There are four rooms with features varying from room to room, but all include a fireplace, Jacuzzi tub, and screened porch. Rooms run $100–$195. (*1100 S. 130th St., Bonner Springs, KS, (913) 422-5207, backnthyme.com*)

Southmoreland on the Plaza: This B&B is in the heart of KC, just two blocks from shopping and dining at the **Country Club Plaza** (see pages 113 and 114). It's a 1913 colonial inn with 12 rooms and a luxury suite in the Carriage House. Most rooms have a private bath, and many have private balconies, whirlpool tubs, and fireplaces. Rooms run $135–$215; $250 for the Carriage House. (*116 E. 46th St., Kansas City, MO, (816) 531-7979, southmoreland.com*)

Woodstock Inn Bed and Breakfast: Built in 1900 as a doll and quilt factory, this historic, award-winning inn has 11 guest rooms with private baths (many with spa tubs). The rooms are tiered as Standard Guest Rooms ($87–$96), Superior Guest Rooms ($98–$108), and Luxury Suites ($164–$219). The rooms are decorated with antiques and—based on the level of room—have amenities that range from what you'd expect at a hotel, to stuff you probably have at home. (*1212 W. Lexington, Independence, MO, (800) 276-5202, independence-missouri.com*)

For more information: To learn about more B&Bs in the area visit bedandbreakfast.com for a detailed directory.

Where to Eat

TAILGATER GROCERIES

City Market: In the River Market area, just north of downtown, City Market is a collection of markets—including the city's largest farmers' market—offering all sorts of meats, produce, baked goods, ethnic and specialty foods, and even live animals (not that you're looking for any). (*20 E. 5th St., Kansas City, MO, (816) 842-1271, kc-citymarket.com*)

KANSAS CITY STRIP PIZZA

The Kansas City strip steak is one of the tenderest cuts of beef. You have a few choices when cooking it. You can just toss a couple of them on the grill—which will taste great—or you can do something a bit more creative with it. The creative option will impress your friends more. (Before you get started, make sure the pizza pan will fit on your grill. If not, you can use a smaller pan and make two pizzas.)

1 (14-inch) pizza crust (store-bought dough is fine)

¾ cup barbecue sauce

5 ounces Kansas City strip steak, cut into 1-inch pieces

½ red onion, thinly sliced

7 ounces Mozzarella cheese, shredded

3 ounces provolone cheese, shredded (you can use Parmesan or a similar cheese, too)

1 tablespoon oregano (fresh chopped or dried will work)

Preheat the grill to high (if you have a grill with a thermometer, heat it until 400° inside).

Place the crust on a 14-inch pizza pan. Spread the barbecue sauce evenly over the crust, and top it with the steak and onions. In a bowl mix the cheeses, and sprinkle them evenly on the pizza. Top the pizza with the oregano and place it on the grill. Close the lid and cook the pizza for 10 to 15 minutes, until the crust is crisp.

Makes 4 to 8 servings.

SPORTS BARS

Coach's Bar & Grill: They say they're KC's oldest sports bar (they opened in 1983). They have 4 HDTV big-screens, 12 other 32-inch TVs, and subscribe to all the various game packages. They have a private room they call the Green Bay Packer Room that you can reserve if you have a group—unless the Pack are playing that day. The menu is typical sports bar food, but they do have a wide salad selection. (*$, 414 W. 103rd St, Kansas City, MO, (816) 941-2286, coach-s.com*)

The Granfalloon: Right on the **Country Club Plaza,** the Granfalloon has 18 large TVs and seats 234. It's not uncommon for professional athletes and celebrities to sit in some of those seats. The menu is a step or two up from most sports bars, with items such as Herb Crusted Salmon and Filet Mignon. They also have game packages for the Chiefs that include bus transportation from the bar, drinks on the bus, and a lower-level game ticket. (*$, 608 Ward Parkway, Kansas City, MO, (816) 753-7850, thegranfalloon.com/default_plaza.htm*)

Tizers Sports Bar & Grill: This place serves 50-some-odd appetizers. Hence, Tizers. They serve other food, too. They also have a place that's great to watch a game. With nearly 40 TVs hanging from the ceiling, there really isn't a bad view. You can also play pool, darts, or Golden Tee video golf. (*$, 4050 Pennsylvania Ave., Kansas City, MO, (816) 931-8585*)

RESTAURANTS

Barbecue: Kansas City is known for its barbecue. There are several places in town to get good barbecue, but there are two joints that have a national reputation. Heck, the Food Network's Bobby Flay even came to town to profile them.

L.C.'s Bar-B-Q: Here, the spare ribs take center stage. It's on the east side of the city, but once you get there you'll find a roadside diner with hunting trophies and slow-cooked meat with authentic Kansas City sauce that keeps the place packed. (*$, 5800 Blue Pkwy., Kansas City, MO, (816) 923-4484*)

Arthur Bryant's: They call Arthur Bryant the "King of Ribs," but it's the sauces he perfected that have presidents and celebrities coming by—not to mention thousands of everyday folks. They've been written about in magazines from *Playboy* to *Fortune*, and the burnt ends are what had Bobby Flay talking. There are three locations; Brooklyn Avenue is the original. (*$, 1727 Brooklyn Ave., Kansas City, MO, (816) 231-1123, arthurbryantsbbq.com*)

Bluestem: Chef-owners Colby and Megan Garrelts trained with some of America's best chefs, then brought their Progressive American cuisine to KC. *Food & Wine Magazine* included them in the "Best Chefs of 2005" issue. The menu includes entrées like La Belle Duck, Wagyu Flatiron, and Tasmanian King Salmon. The decor is simple with a glimpse into the kitchen. (*$$, 900 Westport Rd., Kansas City, MO, (816) 561-1101, kansascitymenus.com/bluestem*)

George Brett's: Yep, this is the K.C. Royals and Hall of Famer George Brett's place. It has plasma TVs on the wall, sports memorabilia everywhere, and wings on the menu, but this isn't a sports bar. The restaurant is located on the **Country Club Plaza** and has a menu that also includes everything from pizza, to ribs, to steak. (*$, 210 W. 47th St., Kansas City, MO, (816) 561-6565, georgebretts.com*)

Plaza III Steakhouse: You know Kansas City is a steak town. Heck, there's even a cut of beef named after it. Plaza III, located in the **Country Club Plaza** area, is noted by *Zagat* as one of the 10 best steakhouses in the country. Live music on the weekends. (*$$–$$$, 4749 Pennsylvania Ave, Kansas City, MO, (816) 753-0000, plazaiiisteakhouse.com*)

Stephenson's Old Apple Farm: Also known as the Apple Farm, Stephenson's opened in 1946. It still is family owned and serves you in an old red barn. This is food like Mom used to make: brisket, chicken and ham, served with vegetables, apple fritters, and dessert. Don't know if your mom served escargot, but they do here. (*$, 16401 E. Hwy 40, Independence, MO, (816) 373-5400, stephensons.bigstep.com*)

For more information: For a directory of additional places to eat in the area visit opentable.com. You can also book a reservation for many restaurants on the site.

What to Do

DURING THE DAY

American Jazz Museum: In the historic 18th and Vine District, this is where jazz greats such as Charlie Parker, Count Basie, and Big Joe Turner defined the sounds of the 1920s–40s. The museum tells their stories, as well as hundreds of others, as it walks you through the history of this truly American music genre. There's also the **Blue Room,** a working jazz club. (*$, 1616 E. 18th St., Kansas City, MO, (816) 474-8463, americanjazzmuseum.com*)

Harry S. Truman Presidential Library Museum. One of 10 presidential libraries in the country,

The Ultimate Tailgater's Travel Guide

the museum chronicles the life of Harry Truman, the nation's 33rd president and the man who ordered atomic bombs dropped on Hiroshima and Nagasaki, effectively ending World War II. Displays include photos, personal artifacts, and traveling exhibits. (*$, 500 W. U.S. Hwy 24, Independence, MO, (816) 833-1400, trumanlibrary.org*)

Negro Leagues Baseball Museum: African-Americans began playing baseball in the late 1800s, in time playing with white players on professional teams. But racism and "Jim Crow" laws forced them from these teams and they formed their own leagues. This museum uses film, memorabilia, and other exhibits to tell their stories. (*$, 1616 E. 18th St., Kansas City, MO, (816) 221-1920, nlbm.com*)

Nelson-Atkins Museum of Art: Just look for the huge badminton birdies. Okay, it's actually an exhibit called *Shuttlecocks*, and is part of the museum's sculpture garden (which also has the largest collection of monumental bronze pieces by Henry Moore). Inside you will find one of America's premier art institutions, renowned for its outstanding Asian-art collection, including Chinese works from 1200 B.C.–500 B.C. (no, that's not "Before Chiefs"). (*Free, 4525 Oak, Kansas City, MO, (816) 751-1227, nelson-atkins.org*)

The Shuttlecocks at Nelson-Atkins Museum of Art. (Photo: Kansas City CVA)

Swope Park: In 1896 Colonel Thomas Swope donated to the city land that now comprises a park named for him. It was one of Kansas City's first parks and is one of the area's largest. It is also filled with stuff to do besides walking, exercising, or relaxing. It is home to the **Starlight Theatre,** a golf course, a nature center, and the **Kansas City Zoo.** The recently renovated zoo includes a 5,000-acre African-plains exhibit and is home to more than 1500 animals. (*Park: 4701 E. Gregory Blvd., Kansas City, MO, (816) 513-7500; Zoo: $, 6700 Zoo Dr., Swope Park, Kansas City, MO, (816) 871-5701, kansascityzoo.org*)

AT NIGHT

Country Club Plaza: It's the oldest shopping district in the country and still one of the best known. It has Spanish style buildings, European charm, and American flair, and it offers a day full of shopping (see below) and a night full of fun. There's **Fred P. Ott's,** a neighborhood pub, and **O'Dowd's Little Dublin,** an Irish pub. **Re: Verse** is a hip lounge, **Mi Cocina** is a Mexican restaurant with a Latin lounge. And there are several places with themes in between. (*47th and Main Sts., Kansas City, MO, (816) 753-0100, countryclubplaza.com*)

Kabal: One of Kansas City's most popular dance clubs. The music ranges from hip-hop to reggae, jazz to Top 40, depending on the night and which floor you're on. Upstairs is also a restaurant with a full menu, and it is open for lunch and dinner. There's a VIP room off the dance floor, but that will cost you extra. (*$, 503 Walnut St., Kansas City, MO, (816) 471-0017, kabalkc.com*)

Phoenix Piano Bar & Grill: The Phoenix is in KC's Garment District in a building built in 1888 and thought to house a brothel. A hundred years later the Phoenix opened here and is one of the last ties modern Kansas City has to the city's legendary jazz era.

The Phoenix Piano Bar & Grill. (Photo: Kansas City CVA)

KANSAS CITY

The grill part of the place has a full menu with entrées beyond your normal bar food. The place is packed on Friday and Saturdays, but closed most Sundays and every Monday. (*$–$$, 302 W. 8th St., Kansas City, MO, (816) 472-0001, phoenixjazz.com*)

Velvet Dog: They claim to be KC's original Martini Lounge. Along with the funky retro decor are pool tables and bocce ball. The first Thursday of every month is their Wear Haus Trunk Show & Happy Hour, featuring original designs from Kansas City designers. (*$, 400 E. 31st St., Kansas City, MO, (816) 753.9990, velvetdog.com*)

Westport Historic District: Once a thriving trading town, Westport was the gateway to the western frontier. Now it's a thriving entertainment district with shops, restaurants, and plenty of nightspots. If you're looking for music, you have several choices here, such as **The Hurricane** and **Blayney's. The Beaumont Club** offers line dancing and a mechanical bull. There's **Tizers** sports bar (see page 111) and **Kelly's Westport Inn,** an Irish pub. *AOL's Cityguides'* pick for KC's best cheap drinks, **Harpo's,** is here, too. Harpo's is also KC's HQ for Mizzou fans—the original is in Columbia, home of the University of Missouri. (*40th St. to 43rd St., between Main St. and SW Trafficway, Kansas City, MO*)

UNIVERSITY OF KANSAS
Memorial Stadium
Lawrence, Kansas
(785) 864-3946

Parking begins morning of game, tailgating 3 hours before game. Call for updated parking prices. Shuttles available for distant lots. No tailgating once game begins. No set departure time, but those tailgating after game can be ticketed.

Shuttle Info: Park in the garage north of Allen Fieldhouse, at the Burge Union in Lot 72 next to the Fieldhouse, or in Lot 90 south of Robinson Center to catch the shuttle to Memorial Stadium. Parking is free, but the shuttle is $2 one way, $3 round trip.

Jayhawks Media Partners: 1320-AM KLWN, 105.9-FM KLZR

SHOPPING

Country Club Plaza: Built in 1922 and fashioned after the Moorish architecture of Seville, Spain, this is America's oldest shopping district. There are more than 180 shops, along with some of the city's best hotels, restaurants, and clubs (see page 113). You'll find famous names such as **Armani, Harold's,** and **Adrienne Vittadini** here, as well as local boutiques like **Hemline, Hudson & Jane,** and **Pinstripes.** (*47th and Main Sts., Kansas City, MO, (816) 753-0100, countryclubplaza.com*)

Crown Center: Joyce Hall and his son Donald built Crown Center as a redevelopment project for a decaying area near downtown. Now their company, Hallmark Cards, is headquartered here, and the Center boasts hotels, specialty shops, dining, theater, and a multiplex cinema. It's also home to the only public outdoor skating rink in Kansas City, which is open from November to March. (*2450 Grand Blvd., Kansas City, MO, (816) 274-8444, crowncenter.com*)

For more information: To learn more about things to do in the area visit cityguide.aol.com/kansascity.

LAWRENCE, KS

Okay, first topic: what the heck is a Jayhawk?

Well, the origin of the word isn't certain, but the first time it was used in present-day Kansas was about

1858. It wasn't really a good word. It was associated with robbery and other forms of general lawlessness. But during the Civil War it took on a different, more respectable meaning.

In 1861 a colonel charged with raising a regiment of cavalry called his men the Independent Mounted Kansas Jayhawkers, even though the official name was the First Kansas Cavalry. During the war the word *Jayhawk* became associated with courageous fighting and comradeship. Five years later the University of Kansas adopted the mythical bird as part of a yell, and it developed into the mascot.

Athletically, Kansas has had a strong basketball history. The basketball program is the only one founded by Dr. James Naismith, the guy who invented the game. Oddly enough, he's also the only KU basketball coach in history to own a losing record.

Eight years prior to that, the Jayhawks football team played its first game. That was in 1890, and they played in old Central Park on Massachusetts Street. In 1892 the school built McCook Field, and in 1921 Memorial Stadium opened on the same site. It could seat 22,000 then. It seats 50,000 today, and it still carries a rich history. Only six Division I-A schools play in older stadiums.

There are several lots surrounding the stadium; many of the tailgating lots are grass lots, so keep that in mind if it's raining. Call (785) 864-3946 to check availability and pricing.

If you're not tailgating at your own space outside Memorial Stadium, you can park in the garage north of Allen Fieldhouse, at the Burge Union in Lot 72 next to the Fieldhouse, or in Lot 90 south of Robinson Center and take a shuttle bus to the game. Parking in these lots is free, but the shuttle runs $2 for a one-way ticket, $3 round-trip.

Once the game kicks off all tailgating must stop. They do not allow tailgating during the games, and while there's no set time to leave after the game, if you hang around and tailgate too long, they'll ask you to leave. Ignore their requests to leave, and they'll cite you.

About Lawrence

Lawrence is one of the few cities founded purely for political reasons. It's named for Amos Lawrence, a New Englander who financed a group of abolitionists that came to Kansas shortly after the territory was opened up in 1854. They came to try and keep the state from becoming proslavery. When the Civil War broke out, Kansas chose to be a free state, and Lawrence became an important stop on the Underground Railroad.

The city's antislavery stance also brought violent proslavery forces to town. The first group came in 1856; they burned down the Free State Hotel (see page 116). The second group rode into town in 1863. They burned the hotel and the rest of the city, and they massacred its citizens. Their goal was "to burn every house and kill every man." They almost succeeded.

But the city rebuilt again and has become a thriving community and home to three universities, including the Haskell Indian Nations University.

Where to Stay
RV PARKS

Clinton State Park: Located just four miles west of Lawrence, the park has 404 sites, 240 of them with hookups. As you would expect, the park is loaded with outdoor recreational activities such as hiking, fishing, and boating. The park has basic amenities, along with fire rings. You can't beat the

Shrimp's on the menu in Lawrence.
(Photo: Bruce Newman)

rates: $7–$8. (*798 N. 1415 Rd., Lawrence, (785) 842-8562, kdwp.state.ks.us/news/state_parks/locations/clinton/camping*)

Lawrence/Kansas City KOA: Close to lakes for fishing and boating, and the Kansas River for canoeing, this park is in a country setting and has 100 sites. The campground has the basic amenities, including LP gas (by weight and by meter) and a dump station. Plenty of recreational activities are on-site or at least close by. Rates run $27–$35. Tents and cabins are also available. (*1473 Hwy. 40, Lawrence, (800) KOA-3708, koakampgrounds.com/where/ks/16104*)

For more information: For additional RV parks and campsites visit campingworld.com/campsearch.

HOTELS

Eldridge Hotel: This is more than a hotel; it's an American history lesson. The Free State Hotel was built on this site in 1855, but it was burned to the ground—twice—by proslavery forces. Colonel Eldridge rebuilt the hotel each time, the last time giving his name to the place, but time took its toll on the hotel. In 1925 a group of business leaders tore down the original Eldridge and built the current one. In 2005 it was renovated and is now an all-suite, full-service hotel with restaurant and bar on-site. Rooms run $119–$179. (*701 Massachusetts St., Lawrence, (785) 749-5011, eldridgehotel.com*)

For more information: To learn about more hotels in the area visit tripadvisor.com for listings and guest reviews.

B&BS

Circle S Guest Ranch & Country Inn: This 1,200-acre ranch, homesteaded in the 1860s, has been in the innkeeper's family for five generations. The home and its 12 rooms feature many authentic prairie-life touches, while being thoroughly modern. Many of the rooms have whirlpool tubs, fireplaces, and private baths. They also offer spa services. Rooms run $155–$245. (*3325 Circle S Ln., Lawrence, (800) 625-2839, circlesranch.com*)

Halcyon House Bed & Breakfast: The Victorian house, built in 1885, is located three blocks from downtown Lawrence and on the northeast edge of the KU campus. There are nine guest rooms with European-inn flair. Rooms run $49–$149. There is also a Carriage House with a private bath, whirlpool-style tub, and kitchenette. Daily rates for the Carriage House are $129–$149, depending on the days you stay. (*1000 Ohio St., Lawrence, (888) 441-0314, thehalcyonhouse.com*)

For more information: To learn about more B&Bs in the area visit bedandbreakfast.com for a detailed directory.

Where to Eat
TAILGATER GROCERIES

Community Mercantile: The consumer-owned co-op—also known as "the Merc"—offers natural and organic foods produced locally. They cut steaks, chops, and chicken every day and grind hamburger almost daily. They also sell cooking utensils, in case you forget your tongs. (*901 Iowa St., Lawrence, (785) 843-8544, communitymercantile.com*)

SPORTS BARS

J. B. Stouts: J.B. Stouts is an upscale sports bar with a menu that includes seafood, pasta, and steaks. If you like beer, you're going to like this place—they have more than 60 types. For watching the game you have 27 TVs to choose from. (*721 Wakarusa Dr., Lawrence, (785) 843-0704*)

Johnny's Tavern: Charles Robinson, the founder of Lawrence and the first governor of Kansas, owned the land where this bar sits. But it was in 1953 when John Wilson bought it and opened Johnny's Tavern, the city's original sports bar. Pizza, burgers, and sandwiches fill the menu. Tailgating is allowed in the parking lot on game days. There are five locations in the greater KC area, but this is the original. (*$, 401 N. 2nd St., Lawrence, (785) 842-0377, johnnystavern.com*)

RESTAURANTS

Bigg's Barbeque: We probably could have put this in the sports bar section, considering that Bigg's theme is "sports, ribs, and rock 'n' roll"—but since they have a complete barbecue menu we put it here. (But they do have 16 TVs.) The specialty is slow-smoked ribs—and brisket, pork, chicken, and sausage—served without sauce to highlight the hickory-smoked flavor of the meat. Don't worry, you can get sauce on the side. (*$, 2429 Iowa St., Ste. H, Lawrence, (785) 856-2550, biggsribs.com*)

Hereford House: A Kansas City tradition, the Hereford House opened in Lawrence in 2000 and was quickly named the city's "Best New Restaurant and Best Steakhouse" by local publications. The atmosphere is western, with an American cowboy decor and a stone fireplace. This is a steakhouse, but they do serve fish and lobster. (*$$, 4931 W. 6th St., Lawrence, (785) 842-2333, herefordhouse.com/hhlawrence.htm*)

Paisanos Ristorante: Traditional Italian countryside dishes such as veal, seafood, and pastas served in generous portions highlight the fare. Paisanos has an extensive wine list and offers some outdoor seating. You can also sit in the lounge/martini bar. (*$, 2112 W. 25th St., Lawrence, (785) 838-3500*)

For more information: For a directory of additional places to eat in the area visit opentable.com. You can also book a reservation for many restaurants on the site.

What to Do

DURING THE DAY

Atchison: The historic town of Atchison is about 50 miles from Lawrence, and it makes for a nice day trip. It is probably best known as the birthplace of Amelia Earhart. Her grandparents' Victorian home is now the **Amelia Earhart Birthplace Museum** run by the Ninety-Nines, an organization of women pilots the aviator formed in 1929. The **International Forest of Friendship** is here, which is a living memorial to those involved in aviation and space exploration. There's a park and trees representing the 50 states and 35 countries. A good way to see Atchison is to ride the **Atchison Trolley,** which has narrated tours—and Haunted Tours. They say Atchison is "the Most Haunted Town in Kansas."

KU Natural History Museum: Established in 1866, the museum is nationally recognized for its exhibits and collections as well as research and graduate education. Popular exhibits include Comanche, the horse that was the only U.S. Army survivor of the Battle at the Little Bighorn, and Annabelle, an impressive 50-

The Atchison Trolley. (Photo: Atchison Area Chamber of Commerce)

foot-long, 140-million-year-old camarasaurus dinosaur. (*$, Dyche Hall, 14th St. and Jayhawk Blvd., Lawrence, (785) 864-4173, nhm.ku.edu*)

Midland Railway: Take a ride on an excursion train on this line, built in 1867. The trip takes you on a 20-mile ride through Eastern Kansas farmland using vintage railway equipment. If you're traveling with a group, they offer discounts for charter trips. Train runs June–October. (*$–$$, 1515 High St. (adjacent to the grain elevator), Baldwin City, (800) 651-0388, midland-ry.org*)

The Spencer Museum of Art: Considered one of the nation's top university art collections, the museum's 11 galleries feature something for everyone, from the photography of Ansel Adams, to the glass work of Dale Chihuly, to the art of Claude Monet. There are interactive programs for children on Saturdays. (*Free, 1301 Mississippi St., Lawrence, (785) 864-4710, spencerart.ku.edu*)

AT NIGHT

Massachusetts Street: This street lights up when the sun goes down. It's also where most every nightspot in the city is located. There's live music at places such as **Bottleneck** and **Granada.** Granada is also a popular dance place, along with **Abe & Jake's.** Restaurants include the **Free State Brewing Co.,** which, when it opened in 1989, was the first legal brewery in Kansas in more than 100 years.

SHOPPING

Massachusetts Street: This street isn't just for nightlife, it's for shopping during the day. There are blocks and blocks of antique shops, boutiques, quirky coffee houses and cafés, street musicians, and more. **The Lawrence Antique Mall** features more than 75 dealers. And **Jayhawk Spirit** features anything with a KU Jayhawk on it—but you probably guessed that.

For more information: To learn more about things to do in the area visit visitlawrence.com.

Miami

No pro football team has gone from nothing to champion faster than the Miami Dolphins.

The team joined the AFL in 1966 and went 4-10 in its first year. Six years, and a merger with the NFL later, the Dolphins, under Hall of Fame coach Don Shula, ran the table for a perfect 17-0 season. No other team has done that. Shula is the winningest coach in pro football history, and his Dolphins won two Super Bowls.

Shula's Dolphins of that era played in the Orange Bowl; today's Dolphins play in Dolphin Stadium, which seats 75,000. Baseball's Florida Marlins play here, too. On game day early parking gates—Gates 2 and 5— open 4 hours before the game; all other parking gates open 3 hours before kickoff. If you plan to tailgate with friends, be sure to get there early; parking is first-come, first-served and no saving of spaces is allowed. Car parking is $20; RVs, buses, and limos are $50.

You also cannot set up tents on the grass at Dolphins Stadium. Small tents can be erected behind your vehicle on the cement, which is also where they allow you to set up small grills.

If you'd rather not hassle with the traffic, Park & Rides run from both Broward and Dade Counties to Dolphin Stadium from several pickup spots. For details and fares in Broward County, call (954) 357-8400; in Dade County the number is (305) 770-3131.

Once at the stadium you can visit the team's tailgate party—T.D.'s Tailgate Zone. The party begins 2 hours before kickoff in the Gate B Helix on the northwest side of the stadium. Your Zone ticket gets you all you can eat and drink (it's an open bar), along with appearances by T.D. (the Dolphins' mascot), the cheerleaders, and former players who will sign autographs. They also have TVs set up in the area. The downside for traveling tailgaters is they sell tickets in three-, five-, and eight-game packages. For a three-game package, the cost is $150, $105 for children.

The Dolphins' former stadium, the Orange Bowl, is the home of the University of Miami Hurricanes. The Hurricanes are one of the nation's most successful college programs of the last 25 years, and the stadium fills up on Saturdays. The parking lots fill up, too, mostly with people who have season parking passes.

If you don't have such a pass, your option is to park in Lot 18 just across the Miami River, and then ride the free shuttle to the stadium. Parking here runs $7. This is also a Park & Ride shuttle drop-off.

If you can't park here, there are parking lots—and in some cases yards—along the streets surrounding the

MIAMI DOLPHINS
Dolphin Stadium
Miami, Florida
(305) 623-6000

Visitor parking is close to the stadium; attendants will help you park. RVs have designated spots. No tents in the grass, saving spaces, kegs, or glass. Parking is first-come, first-served. The weather is usually great; visit South Beach and enjoy Miami nightlife, too.

Shuttle Info: Park & Rides run from both Broward and Dade Counties to Dolphin Stadium. For details and fares in Broward County, call (954) 357-8400; in Dade County the number is (305) 770-3131.

Dolphins Media Partner: 790-AM WAXY

stadium. What you pay to park here will vary based on how much the guy who owns the lot or building wants to charge you.

Your other option, of course, is public transportation. Park & Ride shuttles are available from the Golden Glades exchange, the Culmer station, and the Tamiami station. The Metrorail will get you to the Culmer station, where you can hop on the shuttle. For fare and schedule information, call (305) 770-3131 in Dade County and (954) 357-8400 in Broward County. The number for the Tri-Rail is (800) 874-7245.

Oh, and once you're at the game, if you're wondering exactly what Miami's mascot is, it's an Ibis named Sebastian. The tie to the Hurricanes is that folklore says the Ibis—a symbol of knowledge found in the Everglades—is the last wildlife to take shelter before a hurricane and the first to emerge once the storm has passed. Now you know.

A little farther south is Homestead, FL, and the Homestead-Miami Speedway. The Speedway opened in 1995 with the Busch Series Jiffy Lube Miami 300 (trivia answer number one: Dale Jarrett won); its first NASCAR Cup Race was held in 1999 (trivia answer number two: Tony Stewart won).

The Speedway is on 600 acres near the coast. There are 30,000 parking spaces that are free. There are 1,300 parking spaces for RV's that are not. Those spots are in the Palm Drive RV Lot at the track. You have to have at least two race tickets to snag a spot here, and they'll direct you to a spot when you get there—no reserving a particular space. RV lot fees and availability vary for races; call (305) 230-RACE for details.

About Miami

When Miami was incorporated in 1896, it had 300 residents. Today, Miami is a "world city" with a metro area population of more than 5 million, although the city itself has fewer than 400,000.

Miami grew in the 1920s in part because the city allowed gambling and didn't do much to enforce prohibition laws; that's what motivated northerners to go south. But the big population boom began around 1960, when Fidel Castro took over in Cuba and many exiles immigrated to the area. Today the Miami area is a melting pot of residents from Cuba, Latin America, the Caribbean, and other areas.

All this has made Miami culturally diverse and the "Gateway to the Americas." The Latin-American headquarters for dozens of major companies including American Airlines, FedEx, and Microsoft are here. Tourism, of course, is a major industry in the area, as is commerce and manufacturing.

Where to Stay
RV PARKS
The Boardwalk: Here you'll find 160 full hookup sites, some as wide as 40 feet. The park has a pool, clubhouse, and fitness center. It's just five miles from the Speedway and also convenient to shopping and

The Ultimate Tailgater's Travel Guide

golf. Rates here range from $35 to $65, depending on the season and the site. (*100 NE Sixth Ave., Homestead, (305) 248-2487, boardwalkcommunity.com*)

C.B. Smith Park: This 320-acre county-run park, about 20 miles northwest of Miami, offers 60 full hookup sites, 24-hour security, shower facilities, picnic tables, and grills. No cable or telephone hookups are available here. Staying here will cost you $19 for non-residents during the off-season, $23 in-season. (Note: Before heading here for the 2006 football or racing season, call ahead to check availability. The park's sites were used to host victims of Hurricane Katrina, although they expect sites to be available by fall). (*900 N. Flamingo Rd, Pembroke Pines, (954) 437-2650, broward.org/parks/*)

Larry & Penny Thompson Park & Campground: This 240-site campground is county owned and operated, part of the 270-acre park. All sites have full hookups, although you won't get cable or telephone hookups here. The park also has 24-hour security with regularly scheduled patrols. The sites are large, and it's nice and quiet at night. The daily rate is $22 for four people. (*12451 SW 184 St., Miami, (305) 232-1049, co.miami-dade.fl.us/parks/parks/larry_penny.asp*)

For more information: For additional RV parks and campsites visit campingworld.com/campsearch.

UNIVERSITY OF MIAMI
Miami Orange Bowl
Coral Gables, Florida
(305) 284-6699

Parking around stadium is for donors; depending on location, prices range from $5 to $450. Game-day parking in lot 18 across the river for $7. Shuttles available. Visit beach and tour Miami's Art Deco District.

Shuttle Info: Park & Ride shuttles are available from the Golden Glades exchange, the Culmer station, and the Tamiami station. The Metrorail will get you to the Culmer station, where you can hop on the shuttle. For fare and schedule information, call (305) 770-3131 in Dade County and (954) 357-8400 in Broward County. The number for the Tri-Rail is (800) 874-7245.

Hurricanes Media Partners: 560-AM WQAM, 1210-AM WNMA (Spanish), 90.5-FM WVUM (student station)

HOTELS

Biltmore Hotel: This place isn't cheap (actually it's expensive), but it's pretty darned amazing. Built in 1926, it's the oldest Coral Gables hotel and a National Historic Landmark. It also looks like something out of a (good) movie. Guest rooms are big; the suites are bigger and have furniture you'd want in your own house. The grounds are manicured and include a golf course, tennis courts, spa, and fitness center. A night here runs $259–$609, depending on the room and season. Suites run $609–$2,500. Al Capone used to stay in the $2,500 one. (*1200 Anastasia Ave., Coral Gables, (800) 727-1926, biltmorehotel.com*)

Circa39 Hotel: This is a hip Miami hotel, but just outside the chaos that the hip Miami scene can create. The decor is Miami white-on-white with touches of blue; furnishings are modern and sleek. If you want to hit the beach, just walk across the street (be careful, it's a big street, with four lanes). And if you want to step into Miami's party scene, South Beach is just minutes away. Rooms run $123–$193, depending on the season. (*3900 Collins Ave., Miami Beach, (877) 824-7223, circa39.com*)

Don Shula's Hotel & Golf Club: The hotel is part of the Main Street shopping and entertainment complex in Miami Lakes. There's an emphasis on fitness here (hey, the guy was a football coach), with lighter breakfasts served and a 44,000-square-foot fitness center (although there's a charge to use it). On the other

HOMESTEAD-MIAMI SPEEDWAY
Homestead, Florida
(305) 230-7223

RV parking for two- or three-day weekend is $195 in designated parks. Free day parking. Only RVs park overnight. No gas grills or bonfires. Speedway is updating fan guidelines; call for updated information.

end the hotel has two restaurants, which serve steak and other less-than-light items. Of course, there's a golf course, too. Rooms run $179–$254, depending on when you're here. (*6842 Main St., Miami Lakes, (800) 24-SHULA, donshulahotel.com*)

El Palacio Sports Hotel: This hotel is located just a half-mile from Dolphin Stadium. Rooms have all the usual amenities plus microwaves and refrigerators. **Legend's Sports Grill** is on the ninth floor, with great views of the South Florida skyline and the bar's 10-foot HDTV screens. A room here will cost you $100–$165, depending on when you stay. (*21485 NW 27th Ave., Miami, (305) 621-5801, miamielpalaciosportshotel.com*)

The Hotel: This art-deco hotel is in the heart of South Beach. The rooms, although on the smallish side, have Miami touches such as lavish use of color, hand-cut mirrors, tie-dyed bathrobes, and rain-head shower heads. The rooms have been sound-proofed; there's a roof-top pool, fitness center, and restaurant. Rates here run $295–$345. (*801 Collins Ave., Miami Beach, (877) 843-4683, thehotelofsouthbeach.com*)

For more information: To learn about more hotels in the area visit tripadvisor.com for listings and guest reviews.

B&BS

Miami River Inn: With 40 rooms, this little-known inn is actually four cottages tucked inside a gated compound, just outside Miami's Little Havana. Every room has hardwood floors and is furnished with a variety of antiques dating from 1908. Of the guest rooms, all but two have private baths, and they overlook either the garden, the Miami River, or the city skyline. There's also a small café and grocery store at the NeoLofts apartments next door. Rooms run $69 to $199, based upon season. (*118 SW South River Dr., Miami, (800) 468-3589, miamiriverinn.com*)

Villa Paradiso: Located in South Beach, this guesthouse offers 17 apartments, all facing an interior garden courtyard. The apartments have hardwood floors, French doors, wrought-iron furniture, and marble tile in the bathrooms. All have full kitchens. Rates range from $69 to $199, based on apartment size and time of year. One-bedroom apartments require a minimum stay of six days. (*1415 Collins Ave., Miami Beach, (305) 532-0616, villaparadisohotel.com*)

For more information: To learn about more B&Bs in the area visit bedandbreakfast.com for a detailed directory.

Where to Eat
TAILGATER GROCERIES

Coconut Grove Farmers' Market: On the south end of Miami, in Coconut Grove, lies South Florida's oldest farmers' market. In addition to its selection of organic fruits and vegetables, this open-air market features a unique raw-foods deli, selling everything from salads to nori rolls. You'll also find an assortment of

The Ultimate Tailgater's Travel Guide

Vietnamese cooking, homemade baked goods, handicrafts, crystals, and live music. Open Saturdays. (*Grand Ave. and Margaret St., Miami, (305) 238-7747*)

SPORTS BARS

Dan Marino Fine Food & Spirits: The Hall of Fame QB built a hip sports bar with brick walls full of sports photos and jerseys. The menu offers ribs, pasta, fish, and steak, and there are two 52-inch plasma TVs in the bar—and another one in one of the dining rooms—to watch the game while you eat. Dan does show up now and then. There are also locations in St. Petersburg and Coral Springs. (*$, 5701 Sunset Dr., Miami, (305) 665-1315, danmarinosrestaurant.com*)

Tailgating gets tropical in Miami. (Photo: Yvonne Thompson)

Hooligan's Pub and Oyster Bar: This neighborhood sports bar has 41 TVs, four of which are HDTV. The kitchen churns out wings, crab, and other Florida bar food. Aside from watching the game, you can shoot pool and listen to live music. (*$, 9555 S. Dixie Hwy, Miami, (305) 667-9673, hooliganspub.com*)

Shula's2: Located inside **Don Shula's Hotel** (see page 121), it's a hybrid between a casual sports bar and the upscale **Shula's Steak House.** You won't find the 48-ounce porterhouse here, but you will find walls covered with banks of video screens and sports memorabilia. It has a more casual dress code than the coat-and-tie Steak House. But, it's still upscale—heck, the tabletops are granite. (*$$–$$$, 6842 Main St., Miami Lakes, (800) 24-SHULA, donshulahotel.com*)

RESTAURANTS

Big Pink: It's a family-friendly diner in South Beach serving "real food for real people." The menu is pretty much comfort food, assuming your mom was a master of Asian-fusion cuisine. All the food here is served in huge portions; the restaurant expects you to take some home with you. The decor is sleek and almost industrial, but with long rows of pink-topped tables, and pink stools at the bar. (*$, 157 Collins Ave., Miami Beach, (305) 532-4700, bigpinkrestaurant.com*)

Casa Juancho: This Spanish restaurant, located in Little Havana, looks like a Spanish villa straight from the Old World. But, the food is the real star here. Scores of tapas, seafood, four kinds of paella, and, of course, Sangria. They serve an extensive Spanish wine list along with bottles from other parts of the world. They must be doing something right; the Spanish Ministry of Tourism gave them an achievement award. (*$$, 2436 SW 8th St. (Calle Ocho), Miami, (305) 642-2452, casajuancho.com*)

Talula: Run by two innovative chefs (one of whom is a former *Food and Wine* "Ten Best Chefs" recipient), Talula serves what they call Creative American Cuisine. That means taking dishes that sound familiar, like salmon, and putting a twist on it to become grilled Atlantic salmon with potato-smoked bacon hash, asparagus, and a Dijon garlic vinaigrette. You can also eat on the garden patio. (*$$, 210 23rd St., Miami Beach, (305) 672-0778, talulaonline.com*)

Tap Tap: This South Beach Haitian restaurant is filled with brilliantly colored murals by artist Wilfrid Daleus. The menu is authentic Haitian, like you'd get in Port-au-Prince—dishes such as shrimp in Creole sauce and grilled goat or tender conch fritters. (*$, 819 5th St., Miami Beach, (305) 672-2898, taptaprestaurant.com*)

FINTIKIS "WHISKEY BARREL SALMON"

Finchef and Huligirl (also known as Tommy and Yvonne Thompson) set up their FinTiki tailgate party each week in Section 12 of the Dolphins Stadium parking lot (see photo on page 123). Tommy's a real, live chef, as well as a tailgate chef, and he prepares a complete menu for every tailgate party.

8 tablespoons light brown sugar

2 teaspoons ground cumin

1 teaspoon ground coriander

1 teaspoon kosher salt

1 teaspoon chili powder

1 teaspoon cayenne pepper (or 1 scotch bonnet pepper)

½ teaspoon freshly ground black pepper

Zest of one small orange

Zest of one lemon

Zest of two limes

About 10 tablespoons honey mustard

6 salmon fillets (about 6 ounces each) with skin on

Enough cedar planks to hold all of the fish

Maker's Mark

At home before the game: Combine the sugar, cumin, coriander, salt, chili powder, cayenne pepper, black pepper, orange zest, lemon zest, and lime zest in a small bowl. Brush honey mustard on each fillet and place in a glass baking dish. Sprinkle the fillets evenly with the sugar and spice mixture and pat lightly to make the mixture adhere. Allow the fish to marinate at least 2 to 6 hours in the refrigerator.

In a separate container soak the cedar planks in Maker's Mark overnight.

At the game: Preheat the grill on high for approximately 10 minutes. Place the cedar planks on the grill and allow them to get hot and start smoking. Brush the top side of the planks liberally with olive oil and place the fillets skin side down on the planks. Turn the heat on one side of the grill down to medium and move the cedar plank to that side of the grill, keeping the other side of the grill on high heat.

Close the lid and cook 15 to 20 minutes or until the fillets are cooked through and flake easily. While the fillets are cooking, peek under the lid occasionally to be sure the planks have not caught on fire. If they have, put out the flames with a squirt bottle of water and reduce the heat if necessary to avoid flare-ups.

While it is quite the show to serve the salmon on the plank, it is not really practical at a tailgate party, so serve it on a plate instead.

Makes 6 servings.

Versailles: Located in Little Havana, this diner-cum-French Chateau (no, really, we're serious) is the place to go for real-deal homemade Cuban food. The menu includes dishes like *boliche* (a Cuban version of pot roast, stuffed with chorizo and onions or peppers) and *masas de puerco* (fried pork chunks seasoned with mojito sauce). Versailles is a neighborhood institution and a favorite meeting place for Cuban-American power brokers. (*$, 3555 SW 8th St. (Calle Ocho), Miami, (305) 444-0240*)

For more information: For a directory of additional places to eat in the area visit opentable.com. You can also book a reservation for many restaurants on the site.

What to Do
DURING THE DAY

Biscayne National Park: Only 5 percent of this park is above water. The rest is a marine world, perfect for snorkeling, scuba dives, kayaking, or boating. Daily guided snorkeling trips come with a mask, snorkel, fins, snorkeling vest, and instruction (good of them to throw in that last one). Licensed scuba divers can sign up for a dive with two air tanks and weights included. (*Free–$$$, 9700 SW 328th St., South Miami-Dade County, (305) 230-1144, nps.gov/bisc*)

Snorkeling at Biscayne National Park. (Photo: John Brooks/NPS)

Deep-Sea Fishing: Just think of the bragging rights when you take home the marlin or sailfish you caught. There are several companies that offer deep-sea fishing excursions, but here are a couple that can get you out on the water:

Kelly Fishing Fleet: Full-, half-day, and night trips. Rods, tackle, and bait are provided (*(305) 945-3801, miamibeachfishing.com*)

Reward Fishing Fleet: Trips include bait, rod, reel, and tackle. (*(305) 372-9470, fishingmiami.com*)

Eco-Adventure Tours: Miami-Dade Parks and Recreation Department offers guided nature, adventure, and historic tours involving biking, canoeing, snorkeling, hiking, and bird-watching. Usually, you're provided with everything you'll need—a bike, scuba mask and snorkel, kayaks, or canoes. Tours are geared toward a variety of fitness levels. Some are free, some cost money. (*Free–$$$, (305) 365-3018, miami-dade.gov/parks*)

Ft. Lauderdale: Ft. Lauderdale isn't just for drunken college kids on spring break anymore. With the deepest harbor in Florida, it's a great place to watch the boats or hop on one for a river tour, some with dinner and entertainment. There are wildlife safari tours, historic homes, dining, clubs, and, of course, shopping. (*sunny.org*)

Mystery and Mayhem Crime Coach Tour: Learn where all the bodies are buried, and who did what to whom, on this entertaining tour of Miami's shady past, from Al Capone to Gianni Versace. Tours happen only once every few months, so call before you head to town and find out when the next one is scheduled. (*$$$, 101 W. Flagler St., Miami, (305) 375-1492, historical-museum.org*)

Canoeing at Biscayne National Park (Photo: Gary Bremen/NPS)

South Beach is shopping during the day and partying at night. (Photo: VISIT FLORIDA)

At Night

Abbey Brewing Company: In the midst of all the South Beach glitz lies this small, dark, cozy, and relatively quiet hole-in-the-wall bar. Abbey serves its own beer, of course, and a large selection of imported brews. (*$, 1115 16th St., Miami Beach, (305) 538-8110*)

The Rose Bar: Inside the **Delano Hotel,** this chic little spot pours one of the best martinis in town. Lounge in overstuffed armchairs, and enjoy the glamour and glitz of Miami night life—but without having to sweat on the dance floor. (*$$, 1685 Collins Ave., Miami Beach, (305) 672-2000, ianschragerhotels.com*)

Amika: This hip dance club features some of the city's top DJs, and a pulsing light show that revs things up. Three rooms, four bars, and a sound system that will help you feel the music make things exciting. Dress like you're going out and you'll be okay here—it is South Beach, after all. (*$$, 1532 Washington Ave., Miami Beach, (305) 534-1499, amikamiami.com*)

Space: This club has more than 30,000 square feet of dance space, and it still gets crowded—but at least you'll have *some* room to move. This is one of those clubs that doesn't get cranking until 3:00 a.m., and some weekends it doesn't end until 10:00 a.m. They have no set schedule so call before you go to find out what's happening. (*$$, 34 NE 11th St., Miami, (305) 372-9378, clubspace.com*)

The District: This is a neighborhood bar and grill, with a DJ spinning tunes by the glass bar, or at other times there's a live band on stage. Theme nights during the week include Winedown Wednesdays, Latin Fridays, and Posh Saturdays. (*$–$$, 35 NE 40th St., Miami, (305) 576-7242, thedistrictmiami.com*)

Tobacco Road: Over the years, this blues house's two stages have featured legends such as B.B. King, Koko Taylor, and Albert Collins. It's also one of the few places around where local bands regularly perform. You'll find your usual bar fare, plus what's probably the cheapest porterhouse steak in town. (*$, 626 S. Miami Ave., Miami, (305) 374-1198, tobacco-road.com*)

SHOPPING

Coconut Grove: Originally this neighborhood was a bohemian village; now it's one of the best areas for strolling and browsing through shops. There are gift shops along the open-air promenade called **Streets of Mayfair,** and there are upscale boutiques along **CocoWalk.**

Coral Gables: Called the City Beautiful, this was one of the country's first planned communities. The village of **Merrick Park,** a very upscale, and very large, outdoor shopping complex hosts the city's **Miracle Mile** including shops such as **Giorgio's European Clothing, Books & Books,** and **Modernism Gallery.**

Little Havana: Go to Calle Ocho (8th Street) between SW 27th Avenue and SW 12th Avenue to find shops selling cigars, baked goods, shoes, furniture, and record stores specializing in Latin music. Visit **El Credito Cigars,** where workers at wooden benches turn tobacco leaves into cigars by hand.

South Beach: This 10-mile area packs in the shops—names such as **Kenneth Cole, Sephora,** and **Armani Exchange,** along with lesser-known names selling everything from fashion to attitude.

To learn more about things to do in the area visit cityguide.aol.com/miami.

Nashville

Tailgating is relatively new to Nashville. Really, parking-lot parties didn't start here until the Houston Oilers moved to town in 1998. (If you're wondering how that gibes with your NFL trivia book, remember that the Oilers played in Memphis in 1997, moved to Vanderbilt's stadium in Nashville in 1998, changed their name from the Tennessee Oilers to the Tennessee Titans and moved into the Coliseum in 1999. It was a busy few years.)

Until the NFL came to Music City, the biggest tailgates were those of another Tennessee team—the visiting Volunteers from Knoxville—who came to town every other year and usually beat up on Vanderbilt (they still do most of the time).

The Oilers left Houston on bad terms with fans, playing their final games before sparse crowds of mostly family and friends. Rolling into Tennessee, they found themselves welcomed by a football-loving state whose pro-football prayers had been answered. A trip to Super Bowl XXXIV helped their popularity even more.

That Super Bowl year was the team's first year in their new home: the Coliseum. This open-air stadium seats nearly 69,000 fans, and every game has been a sellout, even if not all the tickets have been used the past couple of years.

For season-ticket holders with a parking pass, Titans tailgating starts the morning of the game at lots surrounding the stadium, all within walking distance. Tailgating is allowed only behind your vehicle, but the team does provide coal bins for disposing of charcoal ash. (For stadium and tailgating rules, go to titansonline.com—click on "Stadium" and then "Policies.") Tailgaters in these lots also have a shot at being chosen as the "Titans' Most Valuable Tailgater"—which gets you prizes and on the scoreboard.

If you don't have a parking-lot pass, you can park across the Cumberland River, in downtown Nashville, and walk across the pedestrian bridge that empties on the south side of the stadium, just a few steps from the gates—and from the team's pregame party featuring the NFL Experience, games, music, and more.

About a 15-minute drive from the Coliseum is Vanderbilt University. It may be a Southeastern Conference school, but you probably wouldn't realize it from the tailgating. Vandy is the smallest school in the conference (just 6,200 undergraduates) and has a history of poor football teams. Okay, bad football teams.

The Commodores (aka the 'Dores), and the school, get their names from Commodore Cornelius Vanderbilt, whose $1 million gift founded the school in 1873. The school sits in what is

TENNESSEE TITANS
The Coliseum
Nashville, Tennessee
(615) 565-4000

Tailgating takes place in stadium lots, within walking distance. RV parking for season ticket holders; no overnight parking. No saving spaces, rowdy behavior, running, or jogging. Tailgate in front of or behind vehicle only. Stay inside your space; need permit for tents or canopies. Dispose of charcoal in coal bins.

Shuttle Info: The End-Zone Express bus service includes a $6 (round-trip) shuttle bus from one of four downtown locations, or a $10 express bus from one of five outlying locations. For details and pick-up locations log on to nashvillemta.org and click on "End-Zone Express" and then on either "Shuttle Locations" or "Express Locations."

Titans Media Partners: 103.3 WKDF-FM, WKRN Channel 2 (ABC), WZTV Channel 17 (FOX)

VANDERBILT UNIVERSITY
Vanderbilt Stadium
Nashville, Tennessee
(615) 342-8525

All parking is very close to stadium. Visiting RVs and buses park off campus in Harris-Hillman School parking lot on Blakemore (Lots 106, 107, 108) beginning 5 p.m. Friday, leaving Sunday. No glass bottles, kegs, or open fires. Keep tents inside space; charcoal bins are provided. Nashville offers clubs, dining, music, museums within walking distance.

Commodores Media Partner: 104.5-FM WGFX

now the middle of Nashville and is considered one of the nation's top universities and medical centers. It is also considered a pushover on most Saturdays.

But the program has been improving as of late, and with that comes more fans and more tailgating. If you don't drive a vehicle to the game or bring your tailgating gear, you can hang out in Vandyville, the school's "Pregame Pigskin Party" with the Spirit of Gold Band, big-screen TVs, activities for kids, giveaways, and more. There are some tailgating tents and spots for vehicles in Vandyville, but they're limited and reserved for season-ticket holders. (Visit vucommodores.com/vandyville for details.)

If you drove to Nashville and are ready to set up your tailgate party, you'll be glad to know all parking is very close to the stadium. That's one of the benefits of being a smaller school in the heart of the city. Several lots are reserved for season-pass holders and National Commodore Club members, but there are public lots that cost $10. You can also find parking at Centennial Park across West End Avenue. But don't park in the neighborhoods around the university, or you'll be winding up your tailgating experience at a tow lot.

About Nashville

In 1779 a band of pioneers built a settlement along the Cumberland River and called it Fort Nashborough, named in honor of General Francis Nash, who had won acclaim in the Revolutionary War. In 1784 the name was changed to Nashville.

Nashville grew into a prosperous city and then was hit hard by the Civil War and was occupied for several years by Union forces. The Battle of Nashville in 1864 was the Confederacy's last aggressive front. It failed, of course.

In the years after that, Nashville became prosperous again—and also became Music City, home to bluegrass and country, the Grand Ole Opry and Music Row. You'll also find rock, jazz, and other music here. Nashville's also one of the country's largest centers for printing and publishing, finance, medical research, insurance, and technology.

The Ultimate Tailgater's Travel Guide

Oh, and wear a cowboy hat and everyone will know you're a tourist. Remember, this is the South, not a dude ranch.

Ribs are on the menu outside the Coliseum. (Photo: Ed Rode)

Where to Stay
RV PARKS
Countryside Resort: Located east of Nashville, just outside of Lebanon, this park is roughly equidistant from both Murfreesboro and Nashville, with quick interstate access to each. The park is open all year and has 100 sites. Individual sites are large, and rates are $25 for full-water, electric, and sewer hookups. Expected amenities include WiFi, tent sites, and dumping stations. Unexpected amenities include a stocked fishing pond (catch and release) and a nine-hole "target green" golf course. Countryside is also pet-friendly, with 30 acres of mowed fields for pets to stretch their legs. (*2100 Safari Camp Rd., Lebanon, (615) 449-5527, countrysideresort.com*)

Music Valley Drive: Located near the **Gaylord Opryland Resort** (see below) and **Opry Mills Mall,** this stretch of road offers three parks just a short drive from I-40.

Two Rivers Campground: Open year-round, this campground has 104 sites. Fall and winter prices range from $28 to $33, but they offer discounts. The roads are wide enough for larger motor homes to maneuver, but it's an older property, so the sites might seem a little smallish. Amenities include WiFi, dump site, a playground, and rec hall. (*2616 Music Valley Dr., Nashville, (615) 883-8559, www.tworiverscampground.com*)

Nashville KOA: This is a site that caters to big rigs; however, if your RV has slideouts or awnings, you might find yourself a bit pressed for space. There's WiFi and the standard amenities, but no cable television. Prices for full hookups range from $45 to $57. (*2626 Music Valley Dr., Nashville, (800) 562-7789, koa.com/where/tn/42148*)

Yogi Bear's Jellystone Camp Resort: There are 238 sites in this park, all of them 60-by-30-foot pull-throughs. Be aware that the sites aren't paved, which can create some muddy conditions after a heavy rain. During their peak months of May–October, rates are $38 and $44. Prices drop November–April to $31 and $35. (*572 Music Valley Dr., Nashville, (800) 547-4480, nashvillejellystone.com*)

Nashville/I-24 Campground: You'll find this campground in Smyrna, almost exactly halfway between Nashville and Murfreesboro, just a couple of miles off I-24. There are 140 sites that can handle up to 40-foot RVs, and they're open year-round. This campground has standard amenities and a dump station. A bonus for tailgaters is the on-site convenience store, where you can pickup ice, groceries, and propane. Sites run $21–$23. (*1130 Rocky Fork Rd., Smyrna, (615) 459-5818*)

For more information: For additional RV parks and campsites visit campingworld.com/campsearch.

HOTELS
Gaylord Opryland Resort: To say this is just a hotel is like saying Mount Rushmore is just a big rock. Okay, not exactly, but you get the idea. Opryland has thousands of rooms, 9 acres of indoor gardens as well

The Gaylord Opryland Resort.
(Photo: Gaylord Opryland Resort &
Convention Center)

as waterfalls and a river (yes, an indoor river on which you can take a boat ride). It also has 15 restaurants and cafés, and 5 bar/lounges—including **Rusty's Sports Bar & Grill.** Rooms with an atrium garden view run from $199 to $264. Self-parking is $10 a day. *(2800 Opryland Dr., Nashville, (615) 889-1000, gaylordhotels.com/gaylordopryland)*

The Hermitage Hotel: This historic, five-star hotel in downtown Nashville features spacious, 475-square-foot rooms. You'll find plenty of luxuries and special services, including 24-hour room service, custom beds, and grooming for pets, even a chef-prepared pet menu. For children there's a special room-service menu, and chef-prepared-to-order baby foods. As you would expect, the Hermitage Hotel is pricey, with room rates north of $200. (*231 Sixth Ave. N., Nashville, (615) 244-3121, thehermitagehotel.com*)

Loews Vanderbilt Plaza: When celebrities visit Nashville, they often stay here. This upscale hotel is across the street from Vanderbilt University and offers plush rooms. It is pet friendly but does not have a pool. There's a beauty salon and clothing boutique within its walls, and a **Ruth's Chris Steak House** is connected to the hotel. Rooms run anywhere from $170 for a standard room to $655 for the executive suite. (*2100 West End Ave., Nashville, (615) 320-1700, loewshotels.com*)

The Ramada Limited at the Stadium: Okay, we're breaking our chain hotel rule, but this place backs up to the Coliseum. The hotel serves as a tailgate lot for Titans games and parking is free with your room if you stay Saturday. They also have a guitar-shaped pool for Music City flavor. Rooms run from $125 to $165. (*103 Interstate Dr., Nashville, (615) 244-6690, www.ramada.com*)

For more information: To learn about more hotels in the area visit tripadvisor.com for listings and guest reviews.

B&BS

The Big Bungalow: This large, Craftsman-style cottage offers three guest rooms and some unexpected B&B amenities such as in-house massages and music nights. Yep, four or five local songwriters sit in the round performing their original songs in the living room. Well, it is Music City. Rooms range from $90 to $150; children over 10 years are welcome. (*618 Fatherland Street, Nashville, (615) 256-8375, thebigbungalow.com*)

The Timothy Demonbreun House: This is a 22-room mansion, restored to the hilt and looking very luxurious and grand. Due to local laws, just three of those rooms are rented to guests. The rooms include gas fireplaces, hardwood floors, attractive furnishings, and private bathrooms for $175. (*746 Benton Avenue, Nashville, (615) 383-0426, tdhouse.com*)

Top O'Woodland Bed & Breakfast Inn: This is a huge, meticulously restored Queen Ann brick home with the original wallpaper and furnished with many period antiques. The main house has three guest rooms, with connecting doors—perfect for a group of friends. There's also a separate cottage capable of housing another six people. Price for the Master Two-Room Suite is $145 for one or two people. Since the suite can be expanded to accommodate five people, guests three through five pay only $35 each. The cottage goes for $160. Minimum stay is usually two nights. If you're bringing kids, you need to let them know ahead of time and there's a $15-per-child charge. *(1603 Woodland St., Nashville, (888) 228-3868, topofwoodland.com)*

The Ultimate Tailgater's Travel Guide

For more information: To learn about more B&Bs in the area visit bedandbreakfast.com for a detailed directory.

Where to Eat
TAILGATER GROCERIES
Nashville Farmers' Market: Bordering the Bicentennial Mall (which is a park commemorating the state's 200th anniversary, not a shopping mall), the Farmers' Market is just north of downtown and convenient to both the Coliseum and Vanderbilt. In addition to booths filled with produce, meats, and fish, you'll find several restaurants (mostly ethnic) and a flea market. In 2006 the market was preparing for a complete renovation. Open every day from 9:00 a.m. to 6:00 p.m. during the summer; fall hours are 9:00 a.m. to 5:00 p.m. (*900 8th Ave N., Nashville, (615) 880-2001, nashvillefarmersmarket.org*)

SPORTS BARS
Sam's Place Sports Bar & Grill: This **Hillsboro Village** (see page 134) bar is what you expect a college neighborhood sports bar to be. It has several TVs, a good, basic menu, and a healthy selection of beers. Sam's attracts a lively, enthusiastic crowd on game days. (*$, 1803 21st Ave. S., Nashville, (615) 383-3601*)

Bailey's Pub & Grill: This downtown bar features big-screen TVs and pool tables, and is walking distance from the Coliseum. (*$, 408 Broadway, Nashville, (615) 254-5452, totent.com/locations.php*)

The Sportsgrille: Located beneath the **Hilton Suites Nashville** at street level, the Grill has an "upscale pub" feel to it, with lots of brick, tile, and wood, along with sports memorabilia, and 25 plasma TVs (ranging from 40 to 60 inches in size). It's across the street from the **Gaylord Entertainment Center** (where the NHL's Nashville Predators and AFL's Nashville Kats play) and walking distance to the Coliseum. (*$$, 121 4th Ave. S., Nashville, (615) 620-1000, nashvillehilton.com*)

Two Doors Down Sports Bar & Grill: Just off Music Row, along lively Demonbreun, Two Doors Down sports five 65-inch HDTVs, nineteen 27-inch flat-screen TVs, and a 46-inch plasma screen in the VIP room. (*$, 1524 Demonbreun St., Nashville, (615) 780-0020, twodoorsdown.net*)

RESTAURANTS
Bosco's Nashville Brewing Company: Bosco's straddles the line between restaurant and brewpub. The interior is large, with tall ceilings and an open kitchen. The food is good, but the real stars are the microbrews. Pair these liquid jewels with one of Bosco's excellent small-size pizzas or their duck rolls. The Flaming Stone and the Bombay IPA beers are award winners. Sunday brunch offers live jazz music. (*$$, 1805 21st Ave S., Nashville, (615) 385-0050, boscosbeer.com*)

Margot Café and Bar: Chef Margo McCormack offers French and Italian cuisine that's simple with robust flavors true to what you'd find in a neighborhood café in France or Italy's countryside. The menu features dishes such as braised lamb shank with polenta and escarole and tomato rosemary broth. The menu changes both seasonally and daily. (*$$, 1017 Woodland St., Nashville, (615) 227-4668 margotcafe.com*)

Nick & Rudy's: Nashville has several high-end, chain steakhouses, but Nick & Rudy's is 100 percent local. The retro menu starts with classics like oysters Rockefeller, and moves to steaks that come with generous sides. The menu also features fish and fowl. (*$$, 204 21st Ave. S., Nashville, (615) 329-8994, nickandrudys.com*)

Noshville: Their slogan is: Make your mother happy . . . eat and enjoy! And you will. Noshville is an authentic New York-style delicatessen with food you'd expect to see on New York's Broadway, rather than Nashville's. Dishes use authentic ingredients, including some flown in from New York. The Broadway location is the original, but there's a second Noshville in suburban Green Hills. (*$, 918 Broadway, Nashville, (615) 329-NOSH, noshville.com*)

Restaurant Zola: Spanish, Italian, and French cuisine are the main influences on chef-owner Deb Paquette's menu, with Greek, North African, and Turkish influences chiming in. Recent offerings included paella, Moroccan shrimp, venison with Marsala foie gras butter, and Mediterranean duck filo burrito. Plenty of vegetarian dishes are on the menu, too. This is a high-end and popular place; reservations are a good idea. (*$$, 3001 West End Ave., Nashville, (615) 320-7778, restaurantzola.com*)

For more information: For a directory of additional places to eat in the area visit opentable.com. You can also book a reservation for many restaurants on the site.

What to Do
DURING THE DAY

The Carter House: This rather modest brick house served as the Battle of Franklin's ground zero— Union and Confederate soldiers fought hand-to-hand on the front lawn and the steps of the house. Today, you can tour the house and 8 acres of preserved battlefield. The house is lovely inside, despite the many bullet holes still peppering the walls. (*$, 1140 Columbia Avenue, Franklin, (615) 791-1861, carter-house.org*)

Country Music Hall of Fame and Museum: From Hank Williams and Minnie Pearl, to Elvis and Alabama, the Country Music Hall of Fame and Museum celebrates the history that made Nashville Music City. Located downtown, the Hall of Fame has exhibits for both "traditional" country fans and those who might know of Kenny Chesney, but not Porter Wagoner. (*$$, 222 5th Ave. S., Nashville, (615) 416-2001, countrymusichalloffame.com*)

The Frist Center for Visual Arts: Housed in an impressive art-deco building are continually changing exhibits of modern and classic masterworks. There are four art galleries, a children's discovery gallery, a 250-seat auditorium, gift shop, café, art workshops, and an art resource center. (*$, 919 Broadway, Nashville, (615) 244-3340, fristcenter.org*)

Country Music Hall of Fame and Museum. (Photo: Tim Hursley)

The Grand Ole Opry: First on the air in 1925 (just five years after commercial radio was born) this is America's longest continuously running radio show, and it airs live before an audience from the Opry House. The lineup changes from show to show and includes acts from Opry legends such as Little Jimmy Dickens to current stars such as Martina McBride. (*$$$, 2401 Music Valley Dr., Nashville, (615) 889-9490, opry.com*)

The Hermitage: This historic home was the estate of Andrew Jackson (aka Old Hickory), Tennessee's first U.S. president. Since it became a museum in 1889, more than 14 million people have toured this well-preserved home—some rooms still have their original wallpaper. Tours also address slave life during

The Ultimate Tailgater's Travel Guide

the 18th and 19th centuries. (*$$, 4580 Rachel's Lane, Hermitage, (615) 889-2941, hermitage.org*)

The Parthenon: It was built as a temporary building for the state's Centennial celebration, but Nashville fell in love with this exact replica of the Parthenon in Athens, Greece (as it looked before time and war left it in ruins). Recently renovated—including the gilding of the 42-foot statue of Athena—the Parthenon also houses the city's municipal art museum. (*$, Centennial Park, West End and 25th Ave. N., Nashville, (615) 862-8431, nashville.gov/parthenon*)

The Parthenon at Centennial Park. (Photo: Ed Rode)

The Ryman Auditorium: Built in 1892 as a tabernacle, it became the Mother Church of Country Music and is one of the nation's most famous venues, and one of the most revered by artists. The Grand Ole Opry used to perform here, and it's been host to most of country's greats. The stage has also welcomed acts from Charlie Chaplin to Bruce Springsteen. There are tours daily, and check the schedule to see who's playing at night. (*Ticket prices vary, 116 Fifth Ave. N., Nashville, (615) 458-8700, ryman.com*)

AT NIGHT

Club615: This extra-large nightspot combines the best of sports bar and urban music club, with lively game-day tailgate parties. When it's not tailgating, it's live music or DJs, with a diverse rap and hip-hop flavor. This is a big place, with two lounge areas and seating for 450 people, so don't be afraid to bring a crowd. (*Admission varies, 201 Woodland St., Nashville, (615) 248-3100, club615.com*)

Bar Twenty3: Step into this hip nightclub and you won't think you're in Nashville anymore. Maybe New York. This club has been named one of the top 100 nightclubs in the country and has the crowd and celebrity sightings to back it up. (*$, 503 12th Ave. S., Nashville, (615) 963-9998, bartwenty3.com*)

The Bluebird Café: The Bluebird is legendary, both for the performances and as a listening room that requires quiet. You will be scolded for talking. Keep it up and you'll be asked to leave. Every night you hear Nashville's best songwriters, most often accompanied by just a guitar or keyboard. They don't sing "covers" and they don't jam here. Often you'll hear a famous song, but from the mouth of the person who wrote it. (*Admission varies, 4104 Hillsboro Rd., Nashville, (615) 383-1461, bluebirdcafe.com*)

Bourbon Street Blues and Boogie Bar: Nashville's best, rowdiest blues joint. The house band, Stacey Mitchhart and Blues U Can Use, plays Wednesdays through Saturdays, and they've attracted a big following. National level blues and R&B acts play here frequently. (*$, 220 Printers Alley, Nashville, (615) 242-5837, bourbonstreetblues.com*)

Exit/In: It's a landmark night club featured in Robert Altman's film *Nashville* and has hosted everyone from Linda Ronstadt, to Jimmy Buffett, to Steve Martin. These days, Exit/In showcases cutting-edge blues, indie, country, and rock bands. (*Admission varies, 2208 Elliston Place, Nashville, (615) 321-4400, exit-in.com*)

Lower Broad: These few blocks in downtown Nashville near the Ryman are where for generations folks have come to town with a guitar in hand and played, hoping to be discovered. Some were. Others are still trying. **Tootsie's Orchid Lounge** is where country music icons like Roger Miller, Kris Kristofferson, and Willie Nelson started their careers. Today, bands play nightly on one stage downstairs and another upstairs. **Legend's Corner** is one of the best of Nashville's gritty, downtown honky-tonks. **Robert's Western World** features some of Nashville's best rockabilly and country artists seven nights a week. And **The Stage** is one of the few honky-tonks big enough for you to show up with a bunch of buddies on Saturday night and find seats for everyone.

SHOPPING

Abbie & Jesse's: Want to dress like a supermodel? Well, now you can see what a supermodel likes at this Cool Springs store owned and run by '90s supermodel Niki Taylor. It's kind of high-end, but not like shopping Dior or anything. Chances are you'll find the perfect outfit for clubbing or just looking cool—if you're a girl. If you're a guy, you can find some nice jeans. (*420 Cool Springs Blvd., Franklin, (615) 771-5054*)

The Factory: A 20–30 minute drive from either Nashville or Murfreesboro, this restored historic landmark houses numerous one-of-a-kind shops, galleries, studios, offices, and restaurants. You'll even find a greenhouse and a seasonal farmers' market. There are a total of fifteen buildings, each offering something you'll want to see. (*230 Franklin Rd., Franklin, (615) 791-1777, factoryatfranklin.com*)

Hillsboro Village: This stretch of about three blocks along 21st Ave. South, between Magnolia Boulevard and Wedgewood Avenue (just off Vanderbilt's campus), is a great place for funky window shopping, browsing, and hanging out. It's a nice neighborhood shopping area with a coffee shop, restaurants (including **Sunset Grill** and the **Pancake Pantry,** where celebrities stop in now and then), clothing stores, a bookstore, trinkets, antiques, and a couple of art galleries.

For more information: To learn more about things to do in the area visit cityguide.aol.com/nashville .

MURFREESBORO

Middle Tennessee State is one of the bigger universities you might not know much about. There are 22,500 students—just 3,000 fewer than the University of Tennessee, about whom you've heard more. But then again, Middle Tennessee (also still colloquially known by its old moniker, MTSU) hasn't had national-championship teams. It's still trying to have winning teams.

Located in Murfreesboro, about a half-hour's drive southeast of Nashville, the Blue Raiders have a core group of fans who turn out to tailgate in the fields and parking lots around "Red" Floyd Stadium. While some of the lots are reserved, you can drive up and find plenty of places to park close to the stadium.

On campus, both the Blue Zone (the area between Cope Building and Peck Hall) and the White Zone (the Greenland Drive area) have tailgate parking, face painting, and other activities. The Raider Walk, when the football team heads to the stadium, is in the Blue Zone 3 hours before kickoff.

Some of the more serious tailgaters fire up their grills at the "Hillbilly Hilton" and are happy to fill the plates of anyone who visits. It's a good option and a ready-made tailgate party for you, if you didn't bring your own gear. (For more information on tailgating and campus-area attractions, log onto goblueraiders.com.)

And if you're wondering about the name Blue Raiders, it was the winner of a 1934 contest, "borrowed" from the Colgate Red Raiders by its entrant. He won five dollars for it. The nicknames it succeeded included the Normalites and the Pedagogues. Change is good.

About Murfreesboro

Murfreesboro exists because in 1811 a committee appointed by the state legislature picked 60 acres of land to be the new Rutherford County seat. It was the state capital briefly, but Nashville took the title back.

Murfreesboro was mainly an agricultural community, but it had become an educational center complete with three colleges and several academies by 1853. The Civil War and military occupation hit the area hard. It wasn't until after World War II the area matured from an agricultural economy into an industrial and manufacturing one. The stronger economy brought more people, and it is now the state's sixth largest city.

Where to Stay

RV PARKS

There aren't any RV Parks in Murfreesboro, but the **Nashville/I-24 Campground** isn't too far (see page 129). For additional information visit camping-world.com, click on "Resources" and then on "Campground Search."

MIDDLE TENNESSEE STATE UNIVERSITY

Johnny "Red" Floyd Stadium
Murfreesboro, Tennessee

(615) 898-2210

RVs park the night before. There are parking lots, grass lots, parking on local streets, all within walking distance. No alcohol on campus; leave by Sunday night. Visit Hillbilly Hilton—serious tailgaters with huge grills feeding anyone within reach. Activities for kids.

Blue Raiders Media Partner: 1450-AM WGNS

B&BS

Byrn-Roberts Inn: Housed in a scrupulously maintained Queen Anne mansion, the Inn has five large, comfortable guest rooms furnished with antique furniture, working fireplaces, and private baths, and most have special features such as a whirlpool tub or a shower for two. There's free WiFi and a fitness center with a beverage and snack bar. Pets are not allowed. Children must be 12 or older. Rooms range in price from $140 to $225. (*346 East Main St., Murfreesboro, (615) 877-4919, byrn-roberts-inn.com*)

Carriage Lane Inn Bed & Breakfast: There are four rooms in the main building, plus a separate three-bedroom cottage. Rooms here are a little frilly, but not overwhelmingly so, and they offer private baths; some come with whirlpool tubs. No pets, and no children, unless your group reserves the cottage or the whole inn. Prices range from $100 to $155. If you decline breakfast, you'll receive a 15-percent discount on your room (except for the $100 room). The owners specialize in events, and often rent out the inn's rooms to groups. Doing so can net you a substantial savings—four couples could rent out the main building, or cottage, for $350 (or $87.50 each.) (*411 N. Maney Ave., Murfreesboro, (800) 357-2827, carriagelaneinn.com*)

For more information: To learn about more B&Bs in the area visit bedandbreakfast.com for a detailed directory.

Where to Eat

SPORTS BARS

Fanatic's Fun Eatery: Located inside the **Murfreesboro Doubletree Hotel**, this sports-themed bar offers 24 TVs, including a 56-inch big screen. There are areas for pool tables, darts, and there's plenty of sports memorabilia on tables and walls. (*$, 1850 Old Fort Pkwy., Murfreesboro, (615) 494-3995, doubletreemurfreesboro.com*)

Fat Willie's Billiards Sports Bar & Grill: Six 32-inch TVs and Gold Crown 3 pool tables make

Tailgating outside "Red" Floyd Stadium.
(Photo: MTSU Photo)

Willie's exactly what you'd expect a billiards/sports bar to be. (*$, 244 River Rock Blvd., Murfreesboro, (615) 848-1801*)

RESTAURANTS

Sushin: You'll find fresh, authentic sushi, along with tasty soba and udon dishes at this Japanese restaurant. (*$, 528 N. Thompson Ln., Murfreesboro, (615) 895-7585*)

Puleo's Grille: Southern meat-and-three meets Italian, making for one super-big menu. Get fried green tomatoes or calamari, country-fried chicken, lasagna or filet Oscar. (*$, 730 Northwest Broad St., Murfreesboro, (615) 867-3312, puleosgrille.com*)

Toots: Imagine Hooter's reinvented as a family-friendly restaurant. Really. And they serve really good fried pickle chips. (*$, 860 NW Broad St., Murfreesboro, (615) 898-1301, toots.com*)

Marina's: Located on the city's charming town square, this local favorite serves up pasta with warm Southern hospitality. (*$, 25 N. Maple St., Murfreesboro, (615) 849-8881*)

For more information: For a directory of additional places to eat in the area visit opentable.com. You can also book a reservation for many restaurants on the site.

What to Do

AT NIGHT

The Boro Bar and Grille: A favorite local hangout, you'll find good, live music any night of the week. (*Admission varies, 1211 Greenland Dr., Murfreesboro, (615) 895-4800*)

Bunganut Pig: The Pig is an English-themed restaurant and club, with a full calendar of local bands and songwriters. (*$, 1602 W. Northfield Blvd, Murfreesboro, (615) 893-7860, bunganutpig.com*)

Wall Street: Rockers will love Wall Street, since it often features some of the best alt, grunge, and pop rock outside of Nashville. Oddly, they serve breakfast and lunch, but no dinner. (*$, 121 N. Maple St., Murfreesboro, (615) 867-9090, wallstreetbar.biz*)

Bluesboro Rythm & Blues Co.: Night owls will love this club, as it only starts to rev up after 9:00 p.m. If you get here earlier, you'll enjoy Happy Hour specials, though. (*$, 114 N. Church St., Murfreesboro, (615) 907-1115, bluesborolive.com*)

For more information: To learn more about things to do in the area visit rutherfordchamber.org.

New York City

Tim Mara bought the New York Giants franchise in 1925. Cost: $500. Before the first season was over, he had pumped another $25,000 into the team to keep it afloat. That assured New York of a team and, many argue, assured the NFL of success. The league needed a team in New York for the media attention, for the fan base, and for it to survive.

The fan base came quickly. That first season saw 70,000 at the Polo Grounds to see the Giants take on Red Grange and the Chicago Bears. Today that many fans, and more, turn out for every Giants home game at Giants Stadium, which is actually across the river in East Rutherford, New Jersey. It might seem odd that New York's team plays in New Jersey, but by 1973 the Giants had outgrown Yankee Stadium, where they had played since 1956. Real estate isn't as tight in New Jersey as it is in New York City. It also isn't really farther away from the city. Yankee Stadium is 6.6 miles from Times Square. Giants Stadium is 6.9 miles from Times Square, just in the other direction. (This proximity is also why we've combined New York and New Jersey attractions in this chapter.)

Another benefit to building the 75,000-seat stadium in East Rutherford: lots of parking. Giants Stadium is in the Meadowlands Sports Complex, which is also home to Continental Airlines Arena and a race track. Parking Lots 4, 15, and 18 are reserved for pass holders. Other lots are for general parking. Those on the stadium side of the Sports Complex cost $15, and those on the Arena side cost $10. Buses pay $20 to park, and Lot 14 is reserved for them. There's no overnight parking allowed in the lots, but tailgaters show up early here and have some of the best spreads in the league.

The New York Jets share the stadium with their cross-town rivals, although they call it the Meadowlands.

The Jets began playing in New York in 1960, but they were called the New York Titans then. The team played pretty well, despite the controversial ownership tactics of Harry Wismer. In 1963, a group led by "Sonny" Werblin bought the bankrupt Titans for $1 million, changed the name to the Jets, and moved the team from the Polo Grounds to Shea Stadium. Five years later, with "Broadway" Joe Namath at quarterback and guaranteeing victory, the Jets upset the favored Baltimore Colts to win Super Bowl III.

The team moved to the Meadowlands in 1984 and has sold out every game since. If you're tailgating with those fans, you can park in Lots 20–24 for $10, and in all but three other lots for $15. Those other three lots—Lots 4, 15, and 18—are for reserved

NEW YORK CITY   **137**

NEW YORK GIANTS
NEW YORK JETS

Giants Stadium/The Meadowlands
East Rutherford, NJ
(201) 460-4187

Both teams use the same stadium. Parking surrounds stadium. If full, buses available on game day. No grilling on sidewalks or next to buildings; no open fires, ball playing, or Frisbee tossing. No overnight parking; dispose of charcoal safely. Giants don't host any parties; Jets have four Oasis stations with different themes, alumni, gear, and more. Each has beer garden, seats 250, sells food. Check out the deluxe portable bathrooms. Very swank!

Shuttle Info: Buses run to the stadium from the Port Authority Bus Terminal in Manhattan (8th Ave. at 41st St.). $6.50 round trip.

Giants Media Partners: 660-AM WFAN, WNYW-TV Channel 5 (FOX)

Jets Media Partners: 770-AM WABC, 1050-AM WEPN, 1280-AM WADO (Spanish), WCBS-TV Channel 2 (CBS)

parking, which costs $25. Buses must park in Lot 14.

If you're not driving to the stadium—to see either the Jets or the Giants—there are shuttles running from the Port Authority Bus Terminal in Manhattan (8th Ave. at 41st St.). The ride is about 20 minutes, and it will cost you $3.25 each way if you buy tickets at the Port Authority. If you buy your return ticket on the bus at the Meadowlands, it will cost you $4.

About New York City

Before it was New York, it was known as New Amsterdam. That's what the Dutch called it when they settled here in 1613. After some back and forth with the British, the Dutch finally gave the city to the British, and it was renamed New York.

New York has been a number of things, among them a battlefield in the Revolutionary War, our nation's capital (1788–1790), the entry point for countless immigrants (see page 143), and the nation's crime capital of the 1970s. It has now become a model for revitalizing major cities. There is amazing history here. There are also an amazing number of people living here.

The city has grown to more than 8 million. The metro area has 22 million. It's the 15th-largest city in the world. It's crowded here. But, there are more entertainment and cultural activities here than most anywhere. There is a spirit and culture here that is unmatched. It's just the Big Apple.

Where to Stay

RV PARKS

Note: Guess what? New York City doesn't have any RV parks. Okay, not a surprise. These are fairly close and convenient to the Meadowlands.

Liberty Harbor Marina & RV Park: The park is about 12 miles from the Meadowlands and across the Hudson River from New York. It has 24-hour security, and views of the **Statue of Liberty** (see page 143) and New York's skyline. Basic amenities are offered on what's basically a gravel lot. There's a restaurant and bar on-site. Rates are $60 per family, and there are winter discounts. (*11 Luis Munoz Marin Blvd., Jersey City, NJ, (800) 646-2066, libertyharborrv.com*)

Pine Cone Resort: Pine Cone is roughly an hour outside of East Rutherford. There are 124 sites that are 40 feet wide; but only 35 sites have full hookups. The park has the usual features along with recreational facilities. It's also close to Freehold Raceway, a harness racetrack. Rates here run $35–$38. (*340 Georgia Rd., Freehold, NJ, (732) 462-2230, pineconenj.com*)

Pleasant Acres Farm Campground: This was once a large, working farm and, to an extent, it still is. There are 297 full-hookup sites, but most are taken on a season-al basis, so call ahead. It's about an hour outside NYC, and you'll pay $40, but almost everything (including Sunday breakfast) is included. (*61 DeWitt Rd., Sussex, NJ, (800) 722-4166, pleasantacres.com*)

For more information: For additional RV parks and campsites visit campingworld.com/campsearch.

HOTELS

Note: The only hotels near the Meadowlands Sports Complex are basic chains. You know our rule about listing those in the book. But if you want to stay close to the stadium, the **Fairfield Inn East Rutherford Meadowlands, Homestead Meadowlands-East Rutherford,** and **Extended Stay America Rutherford-Meadowlands** are within a half-mile.

The Giant Nuts Project's tailgate setup. (Photo: giantnutsproject.com)

Cosmopolitan Hotel-Tribeca: The 105 rooms are small, with double beds and private bathrooms. You can also stay in a mini-loft: the bed is in a built-in alcove above, giving you more room. The hotel is just off Times Square, and there's a subway station right outside. Rooms will cost you $149 to $199. (*95 W. Broadway, New York, (888) 895-9400, cosmohotel.com*)

The Muse: Located in the theater district, and not far from **Central Park,** (see page 142) the Muse has large rooms and bathrooms, and classic-meets-contemporary decor. The hotel has standard rooms and suites, some with terraces and wide-screen TVs, and a 24-hour fitness center on-site. Rooms run $269 and up. (*130 W. 46th St., New York, (877) 692-6873, themusehotel.com*)

Radio City Suites: Formerly apartments, these 85 guest rooms all have full kitchens and nice pri-vate baths. You have your choice of studio, one-bedroom, and two-bedroom units, with various combi-nations of twin or double beds, but they're on the smallish side. Prices start at $130 for a studio, topping out at $250 for a two-bedroom unit with a sofa bed. Near **Rockefeller Center.** (*142 W. 49th St., New York, (866) LUXE-411, luxehotels.com*)

Trump International Hotel & Tower: You might not be his apprentice, but you can live like the Donald for a couple of nights. Here, you'll find 37 rooms and 130 suites that resemble mini-apartments. All have fully equipped kitchens with black-granite countertops, entertainment centers with stereo/CD players, and mini-telescopes for gazing through the floor-to-ceiling windows at **Central Park** across the street. Complimentary cellular phones are provided. The hotel's restaurant, **Jean-Georges,** is one of the city's finest. All this ain't cheap—prices start at $665 and stop at $2,250. (*1 Central Park W, New York, (888) 448-7867, trumpintl.com*)

The Waldorf-Astoria Hotel: Welcome to the grand old dame of all New York hotels. This massive building takes up an entire city block, with 1,176 rooms, 276 suites, four restaurants, three bars, sever-al shops, one health club, and a partridge in a pear tree. Okay, no partridge. And no pear tree. The hotel is an art-deco masterpiece, with a gigantic lobby that's worth a visit all on its own. Prices vary greatly, depending on when you're there. For example, August's room rates are $299–$489. September's rates are $629–$1,399 for the same rooms. (*301 Park Ave., New York, (800) 925-3673, waldorfastoria.com*)

For more information: To learn about more hotels in the area visit tripadvisor.com for listings and guest reviews.

B&BS

East Village Bed & Coffee: There are nine guest rooms in this three-story brownstone. Each floor has a kitchen, living room, and full bathroom for guests to share. Rooms are decorated according to their themes, with decorative accents painted on the walls. A room for one runs $85–$110, for two it's $100–$120, rooms for three or four run $130–$140. (*110 Ave. C, New York, (917) 816-0071, bedandcoffee.com*)

The Inn on 23rd: This five-story townhouse offers 14 large guest rooms with private baths, double-glazed windows, and white-noise machines (it's loud in NYC, even at night). The rooms are decorated in a variety of styles. The New School uses the inn's kitchen for their cooking and baking classes—watch for leftovers. Rooms run $249–$289, sometimes higher during holiday weekends. One note: there is a shelter next door, but residents don't approach guests. (*131 W. 23rd St., New York City, (877) 387-2323, innon23rd.com*)

Plainfield Pillars: The inn offers five guest rooms and two suites, ranging from $114 to $250. Rooms are decorated in a turn-of-the-century Americana style and have names like the John Philip Sousa Suite (his first concert was in Plainfield more than 100 years ago), the Clementine Yates, and the Captain's Quarters. Breakfast can start as early as 4:30 a.m., if you need it to. (*922 Central Ave., Plainfield, NJ, (888) PILLARS, pillars2.com*)

Whistling Swan Inn: This inn is a restored Victorian mansion on the main street of Stanhope, near Hopatcong State Park. There are seven guest rooms and two suites, decorated with elements of Victorian, art deco, and 1940s era furnishings. All rooms have private baths and queen-sized beds. The inn has a 24-hour complimentary hospitality bar, and it is walking distance to antique shops. Rooms here will cost you $105–$219. (*110 Main St., Stanhope, NJ, (973) 347-6369, whistlingswaninn.com*)

For more information: To learn about more B&Bs in the area visit bedandbreakfast.com for a detailed directory.

Where to Eat

TAILGATER GROCERIES

Rutherford Farmers' Market: This open-air market is pretty close to the Meadowlands, and you can stock up on a variety of fresh, locally grown fruits and veggies. It also has homemade breads, frozen meats & seafood, cheeses, and even frozen fruit bars. Open Wednesdays, July–October. (*176 Park Ave., Rutherford, NJ,(201) 460-3000, ext. 3156*)

Chelsea Market: Located in a converted Nabisco factory, this famous market is a shopping mall for food. You can get everything from coffee beans to lobsters. Shops have imported oils, cheeses, and specialty preserved meats, as well as fresh produce and regular meat for your tailgate grill. **Bowery Kitchen Supply** has cookware if you forgot something. (*75 9th Ave., New York, (212) 242-7360, chelseamarket.com*)

SPORTS BARS

The 40/40 Club: It's a swank lounge. No wait, it's a sports bar. In fact, it's both. It's the brainchild of rapper Jay-Z. Chairs are covered in vanilla leather. The floors are Italian marble. A collection of flat-screen televisions (including three 60-inch plasmas) display the games. A cigar lounge and three VIP rooms are on the second level. The menu features appetizers and snacks. Dress to be seen. (*$, 6 W. 25th St., New York, (212) 989-0040, the4040club.com*)

ESPN Zone: The Big Apple location offers HD on 33 of the flat-screen TVs in their Studio Grill and on two of the 14-foot projection screens in their Screening Room. You can also call ahead for free tickets to ESPN's sports talk show, *Quite Frankly*. The menu is the same as in other locations, with a rotating selection of specials. (*$$, 1472 Broadway, New York, (212) 921-3776, espnzone.com/newyork*)

The Lighthouse Tavern: The owners wanted their neighborhood sports bar to feel like an extension of their living room, and they pretty much succeeded. It's a comfortable place to get together and watch the game, play pool, darts, or Golden Tee, or just to chat. They show up to six different games on their flat-screen TVs. Weather permitting, you can sit in the heated garden-patio and watch the game on an 8-by-10-foot projection screen. The menu is a mix of American and Costa Rican sandwiches, burgers, and snack foods. (*$, 243 5th Ave., Brooklyn, (718) 788-8070, lighthousetavern.net*)

Manny's Restaurant & Sports Bar: On game days this friendly Italian place is jammed with people watching 15 TV screens. On the walls of the dining room, there are large paintings of the New York Giants in action. Near the bar, there are framed photos of Lawrence Taylor, Phil Simms, and other Giants heroes. Manny's provides a pregame brunch, then shuttles patrons over to the game. (*$, 110 Moonachie Ave., Moonachie, NJ, (201) 939-1244*)

Waterfront Café Steak and Clam House: This isn't your typical sports bar by any means. This marina café and bar, located just down the road from the Meadowlands, lets patrons whack balls from a 35-stall driving range, putt along a 17-hole mini-golf course, or play a round of pool or darts. The menu is a mix of seafood, chicken, and steak. (*$, 1 Paterson Plank Rd., Carlstadt, NJ, (201) 507-5656, waterfrontcafe.net*)

RESTAURANTS

Note: Okay, this is New York. If you want to find a good place to eat, walk outside, turn right, walk a couple of blocks, and you're there. There are more than 30,000 places to eat in the New York/New Jersey area, but here are a few to get you started.

Bar Americain: The guy in the kitchen? Yeah, that's Bobby Flay. Well, he might be there, if he's not at another of his eateries or busy being an Iron Chef. The food is regional American fare as reinterpreted by Flay. Look for entrées of duck, lamb, pork, and fresh fish. Steaks, too. The space, decorated in shades of buckskin, copper, and black, is large, airy, and hip. (*$$, 152 W. 52nd St., New York, (212) 265-9700, baramericain.com*)

Café Matisse: From the outside, you'll think, "So what?" But step inside this former firehouse, and you'll find yourself somewhere along the sun-baked Mediterranean coast. Small chandeliers are festooned with jewel-colored crystals and the colorful walls highlight copies of Matisse's works. The menu offers Mediterranean dishes, with subtle Asian accents added to many entrées. If the weather is nice, consider eating in the restaurant's garden. (*$$, 167 Park Ave., Rutherford, NJ, (201) 935-2995, cafematisse.com*)

Gramercy Tavern: A landmark New York dining spot, the Gramercy offers two options. You can reserve a table in the dining room and enjoy classic American food such as salt-baked King Salmon, braised lamb, even rabbit. Or you can eat in their casual, no-reservation Tavern Room and eat similar dishes, but made more simply. The second option costs less. (*$$–$$$, 42 E. 20th St., New York, NY, (212) 477-0777, gramercytavern.com*)

iCi: If the owner, Laurent Saillard, looks familiar it might be because you saw him briefly as the maitre d' of Rocco's on *The Restaurant* (it was canceled before the first season ended). Now he and his wife have a place in Brooklyn that serves French bistro food in a low-key atmosphere. The menu features braised short ribs, fish, and roasted chicken. Open for breakfast, lunch, and dinner. (*$, 246 DeKalb Ave., Brooklyn, (718) 789-2778, icirestaurant.com*)

Lombardi's: This is where it all began. In 1905 Gennaro Lombardi opened the first pizzeria in the United States. One hundred years later it still gets write-ups in publications such as *ZAGAT* and *Bon Appetit*. The decor isn't fancy, but you wouldn't expect it to be. Lombardi's recently expanded, almost doubling its space and halving the once formidable wait. They've also added a bar. (*$, 32 Spring St., New York, (212) 941-7994 lombardisoriginalpizza.com*)

Medieval Times Dinner & Tournament: It's dinner and a show, circa A.D. 1100. Created in Spain in 1973, this dinner theater with horses and swords has become popular enough to support several locations in the United States and Europe. Basically, you get a decent four-course meal of bread, soup, meats, potatoes, and a dessert, plus an elaborate performance that includes jousting, sword fights, and trick riding, with stage-lighting and a plot. The meal is served "Medieval style": no silverware, but lots of napkins. (*$$$, 149 Polito Ave., Lyndhurst, NJ, (888) WE-JOUST, medievaltimes.com*)

Park & Orchard Restaurant: Inside this huge space near the Meadowlands, you'll find an equally huge menu, offering Chinese, French, Mexican, Cajun, and Italian cuisines. The real theme here isn't a national cuisine, it's good health. Many dishes can be adapted to specialized diets; all are free of refined sugar, bleached white flour, preservatives, colorings, or artificial ingredients. (*$, 240 Hackensack St., East Rutherford, NJ, (201) 939-9292, parkandorchard.com*)

Tom's Restaurant: This is the diner where Jerry, Elaine, George, and Kramer hung out. Okay, that was actually a set, but the exterior of Tom's Restaurant was used for the diner on *Seinfeld*. This is your classic New York diner. Inside you'll find *Seinfeld* memorabilia on the walls; eggs, burgers, and fries on the menu; and waitresses who make you say, "Yep, I'm in New York." (*$, 2880 Broadway, New York, (212) 864-6137*)

For more information: For a directory of additional places to eat in the area visit opentable.com. You can also book a reservation for many restaurants on the site.

What to Do
DURING THE DAY

Bronx Zoo: It's one of the largest zoos in the world, spread out on 265 acres and housing 4,500 animals representing over 600 species. It's also one of the finest zoos in the world, with important breeding programs, conservation efforts and educational outreach. The zoo has habitats, exhibits, restaurants, and shops. (*$–$$, 2300 Southern Blvd., Bronx, New York, (718) 220-5100, bronxzoo.org*)

Central Park: The Park was the first artificially landscaped park in the United States, taking 16 years to complete. It was commissioned so New York would have public grounds comparable to London and Paris. Its 843 acres of meandering wooded paths, ponds, and open meadows draw people to exercise, relax, and people-watch. There's also a small, kid-friendly zoo. (*Between 5th and 8th Aves. and 59th and 106th Sts., New York, (212) 360-3444, centralpark.org*)

Tom's Restaurant.
(Photo: Laurent Linn)

Landmark Buildings: New York has some of the largest, tallest, longest, and most famous buildings in the world. In addition to their size, the architecture tells the history of the city. Here are a few you should try to see:

The Chrysler Building: This art-deco skyscraper is one of New York's most striking. Built in 1930, it was briefly the tallest building in the world. The ground floor sports a ceiling mural of airplanes and other innovations of the first half of the 20th century. (*405 Lexington Ave., New York*)

The Empire State Building: For quite a while it was the tallest building in the world. King Kong climbed it, and comic book heroes lived on its top floor. Kids will enjoy the New York Skyride on the second floor (you will, too). (*$–$$, 350 5th Ave., New York, (212) 736-3100, esbnyc.com, skyride.com*)

The Sheep Meadow in Central Park. (Photo: Sara Cedar Miller/ Central Park Conservancy)

The Flatiron Building: This was the first wedge-shaped building ever built. Its shape generated strong winds, resulting in male gawkers waiting on 23rd Avenue to see a few up-blown skirts. Policemen kept shooing them away, hence the phrase "23 skiddoo." (*175 5th Ave., New York*)

The United Nations Headquarters: The headquarters are actually three buildings: the Secretariat Building; the smaller, domed General Assembly Building; and the Dag Hammarskjöld Library. Take the 45-minute tour, which leads you through some of the main meeting rooms and includes displays on modern events and several notable works of art. (*$$, 1st Ave. and E. 46th St., New York, (212) 963-8687, un.org, un.org/tours/*)

The Woolworth Building: In 1913, this was the tallest building in the world. It was a big-enough deal that, for its grand opening, President Woodrow Wilson pressed a button from the White House illuminating the building's 80,000 electric light bulbs. (*233 Broadway, New York*)

Statue of Liberty and Ellis Island: Two of our greatest historical treasures lie on neighboring small islands in Upper New York Bay. **The Statue of Liberty** stands on **Liberty Island,** a 241-foot tall monument to freedom and opportunity given to America by the French in 1886 as a symbol of friendship. Lady Liberty was reopened to visitors in 1990 after extensive renovation. (*Free, (866) 782-8834, nps.gov/stli*). **Ellis Island** processed and admitted the ancestors of more than 40 percent of present-day America, some 12 million people in all. This is a very moving place, full of photos, records, and items of clothing, jewelry, and other objects donated by the descendants of those immigrants. The museum offers an audio tour for $6. (*$, (212) 363-3200, ellisisland.org*). To get here you need to ride the ferry. (*$, (212) 269-5755, statueoflibertyferry.com*)

Times Square: Once a raw and seedy place, it's now a safe, popular, busy place. MTV has its studio here, the **Hard Rock Cafe** is here, and of course the big ball drops here every New Year's. Most Broadway theaters are centered around Times Square, too. (*W. 42nd to W. 47th Sts., at Broadway and 7th Ave., New York*)

MoMA & the Met: Okay, there are entire books written about the museums of New York. This isn't one of those books. You're here for just a few days, and one of those days is going to be at the stadium. So we're highlighting a couple of New York's most famous museums. **The Museum of Modern Art** (MoMA) recently expanded to 630,000–square feet. You'll find Van Gogh's *Starry Night,* Rodin's *Monument to Balzac,* and works by Picasso, De Kooning, and many others. (*$–$$, 11 W. 53rd St., New*

York, (212) 535-7710, moma.org) **The Metropolitan Museum of Art** (the Met) is the largest art museum in the western hemisphere, spanning four blocks and almost 2 million square feet. It's home to art masterpieces, Egyptian mummies, ancient Greek statuary, Islamic carvings, and more. (*$–$$, 1000 5th Ave., New York, (212) 879-5500, metmuseum.org*)

Times Square.
(Photo: TimesSquare.com)

AT NIGHT

Bridge Café: This restaurant and bar has been a restaurant or bar, or both (and sometimes a brothel), continuously since 1794. It's the oldest bar in NYC. Inside is a mix of old and modern fixtures that makes it feel like a good, ol' 212-year-old neighborhood joint. It's largely free of tourists. The food ranges from burgers to lobster rolls. (*$$, 279 Water St., New York, (212) 227-3344, eatgoodinny.com*)

Crobar: It's hip, has a dance floor the size of a hockey rink, and can hold 2,500 people. Top DJs draw hordes of their faithful followers. The club also has rotating art exhibits, but don't mistake it for anything but a loud party. (*$$$, 530 W. 28th St., New York, (212) 629-9000, crobar.com*)

The Duplex: Outside it looks like a quiet townhouse. Inside, this cabaret (which has been running shows since the 1950s) has two floors—the first has a piano bar, the second floor has a game room with a mirrored disco ball; the small cabaret theater lies in back. The theater usually hosts one or two shows per night. Performers stage original acts, as well as popular continuing shows and revivals. (*$–$$, 61 Christopher St., New York, 212) 255-5438, theduplex.com*)

Joe's Pub: There are a million places to listen to every kind of music in New York. And that's not much of an exaggeration. You can hear a little of it all at Joe's Pub. Their acts include everyone from Broadway stars to world-music stars who perform in an intimate setting that encourages them to cut loose. The food is Italian and the setting is plush. (*$$–$$$, 425 Lafayette St., New York, (212) 539-8778, joespub.com*)

Off the Wagon: This Greenwich Village bar is a college hangout, loved by NYU students and others. The beer here is cheap and the music loud. There's always a game on the TVs, plus foosball, darts, and a pool table. The menu is typical bar food. (*$, 109 MacDougal St., New York, (212) 533-4487, nycbestbars.com/OTW.htm*)

Theater: New York could fairly be called the world capital of theater. But it wasn't always. While European settlement here began in 1613, theater had to wait until the Netherlands sold their settlement to the British, turning New Amsterdam into New York. The first professional acting performance was recorded in 1732, with the first real performance space following later in 1750. It held 280 people. Today, of course, there's Broadway, off-Broadway, off-off-Broadway, and performance spaces so far from Broadway in theme, content, distance (and sometimes quality) that there aren't enough "offs" for it. To help you find the best, newest, or nuttiest theater around, log on to nytheatre.com. It not only lists every performance in the city, it also breaks them down by neighborhood, venue, genre, and star, and offers reviews and news.

To buy tickets to a show at discounted prices, go to **TKTS.** They have two booths, one on Times Square and another at the South Street Seaport. Lines can get long, but it's worth it to get good seats for less money. TKTS sells tickets only for shows that have been running a while, since new shows usually sell out at full price. The TKTS Web site is tdf.org/tkts.

Webster Hall: This popular dance club and lounge has four huge dance floors, each playing a different style of music, everything from salsa to trance. Depending on the night, you'll find DJs, live music, events, or concerts. You can get discounted tickets on Webster's Web site. (*$$$, 125 E. 11th St., New York, (212) 353-1600, websterhall.com*)

SHOPPING

Bloomingdale's: In the 1860s Joseph and Lyman Bloomingdale opened the first department store in the country. Since then, Bloomingdale's has been synonymous with New York. Bloomie's takes up an entire city block and offers everything from designer fashion, to furniture, to kitchenware. (*1000 Third Ave., New York, 212) 705-2000, bloomingdales.com*)

Chinatown: It's the largest Chinatown in America and has the largest concentration of Chinese in the Western hemisphere. It also has a lot of great restaurants, fish and fruit markets, and shops. Chinatown is loosely defined as the area bordered by Kenmore and Delancey Streets on the north, Allen Street on the east, East and Worth Streets on the south, and Broadway on the west.

The East Village: This trendy neighborhood has everything from vintage record shops, to boutiques, to high-end gadgets. For quintessential New York funkiness, go to St. Marks Place, running east from Third Avenue to Avenue A. There's a permanent street market here, with vendors selling bohemian jewelry, T-shirts, and all manner of other stuff.

F.A.O. Schwarz: This famous toy store makes kids out of adults, and it is heaven for real kids. Whatever you want, it's here—stuffed animals, dolls, games, pinball machines, things that spin, and whirr, and blink, and more. There are also interactive areas that let kids design their own dolls or stuffed animals. (*767 5th Ave., (212) 644-9400, fao.com*)

Fifth Avenue: Although it's no longer the exclusive domain of the mega-rich, you'll still find upscale stores such as **Cartier, Tiffany & Co., Versace,** and department stores such as **Bergdorf Goodman, Henri Bendel,** and, of course, **Saks Fifth Avenue.**

Greenwich Village: For a century this has been the neighborhood for the bohemian, creative, and rebellious. Now they probably couldn't afford to live here, but the spirit remains. This neighborhood is great for gift shopping and browsing among specialty bookstores, antique and craft stores, and gourmet food markets. The park has a carnival atmosphere with the diversity of musicians, skateboarders, and even chess players.

For more information: To learn more about things to do in the area visit cityguide.aol.com/newyork.

WEST POINT/TOWN OF HIGHLANDS

About an hour north of New York City is West Point. The United States Military Academy is here. On the field you know them simply as Army.

Gen. George Washington moved his headquarters to West Point during the Revolutionary War to take advantage of the commanding plateau on the west bank of the Hudson River. In 1802 President Thomas Jefferson established the U.S Military Academy. And in 1890 football officially came to West Point—thanks to the navy. A group of midshipmen challenged the army to a football game. A challenge from the navy was never to be turned down, so the army fielded a team and one of the

U.S. MILITARY ACADEMY AT WESTPOINT (ARMY)

Michie Stadium
West Point, New York
(845) 446-0538

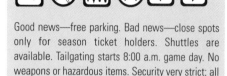

Good news—free parking. Bad news—close spots only for season ticket holders. Shuttles are available. Tailgating starts 8:00 a.m. game day. No weapons or hazardous items. Security very strict; all vehicles searched. Hey, at least you're safe.

Black Knights Media Partners: 1050-AM WEPN, 1380-AM WKDM (Spanish)

most important sporting rivalries in history was born.

Army plays at Michie Stadium. The good news is that it has a beautiful view of the countryside. The bad news is that parking is a hike. The closest lots are reserved, but parking is free, and there are shuttles to the stadium.

Tailgating here is more refined than down the road at the Meadowlands. Here you'll find tablecloths and cloth napkins, real plates, and silverware. You'll also find a spirit and pride that's unmatched almost anywhere, since it's not just a football team they're rooting for—it's the United States Army.

About West Point/Town of Highlands

West Point is in the Town of Highlands in Orange County. The military academy dominates this small town of about 12,000. The region was first explored by Henry Hudson in 1609. The first town here was the Town of Cornwall (founded in 1788), which later became the Town of Highlands in 1872.

Where to Stay

RV PARKS

Black Bear Campground: This is one of the few RV parks close to West Point that offers all the modern conveniences, including cable TV and WiFi. Plus, they're open all year long. Daily rates for the 160 sites run from $30 to $38, depending on your choice of hookups and time of year. Some weekends require multiple-night stays, so call ahead. (*197 Wheeler Rd., Florida, NY, (845) 651-7717, blackbearcampground.com*)

Croton Point Park: Part of the Westchester County park system, Croton offers 71 sites; 48 are specifically reserved for weekend visitors (but they get full; call ahead). All sites are back-in only. The park is patrolled, and there's a security gate. The season runs until the weather turns, usually the first of November. Rates run $18–$30. Cabins are available. (*Croton Point Ave., Croton-On-Hudson, (914) 862-5290, westchestergov.com/parks/ParksLocations02/CrotonPointPark.htm*)

Winding Hills Park/Orange County Park: About 5 miles west of Newburgh, this county-run park offers 51 pull-through sites. It's a small park and can accommodate rigs only up to 29 feet. There are two "comfort stations" with electricity and showers. Rates are $16–$20. The park closes for the season at the end of October. (*Off 17K on old Rte. 17K, Montgomery, (914) 457-4900, orangecountygov.entrexp.com/orgMain.asp?orgid=104&sID=&storyID=974*)

For more information: For additional RV parks and campsites visit campingworld.com/campsearch.

HOTELS

Thayer Hotel: Set on a hilltop overlooking the Hudson River, this national historic landmark sits on the U.S. Military Academy grounds at West Point and is the only full-service hotel on the Hudson River from the George Washington Bridge to Albany. Rooms are done in an understated colonial style. Rates for weekend stays run about $305; midweek rates are $215–$282. (*674 Thayer Rd., West Point, (800) 247-5047, thethayerhotel.com*)

For more information: To learn about more hotels in the area visit tripadvisor.com for listings and guest reviews.

B&BS

Cromwell Manor: It's consistently named one of the "Top 10 Inns of New York State," and has been featured on YES Network's *Ultimate Road Trip*. All nine guest rooms have original working marble fireplaces, private bathrooms, canopy or sleigh beds, and impressive architectural details. A separate cottage, built in 1764, offers four large guestrooms, also with private baths. Rooms are $165–$370. (*174 Angola Rd., Cornwall, (845) 534-7136, cromwellmanor.com*)

Victorian River View: Only a couple of miles south of Michie Stadium, this large country Victorian house offers five guest rooms, with two shared baths. The house has a simple, relaxed country feel to it, with hardwood floors, high ceilings and large windows. Rooms cost $100–$150. (*30 Scott's Cir., Fort Montgomery, (845) 446-5479, visiontownofhighlands.com/Merchants/victorian_river_view.htm*)

For more information: To learn about more B&Bs in the area visit bedandbreakfast.com for a detailed directory.

What to Eat
TAILGATER GROCERIES

Town of Highlands/West Point Farmers' Market: This seasonal market runs through the end of October and offers a range of produce and other items. It's located at the Highland Falls Municipal Parking Lot, across from the West Point Visitors Center. They're open on Sundays, 9:00 a.m.–3:00 p.m. (*(845) 446-2459*)

SPORTS BARS

Stadium: Across the river in the town of Garrison, Stadium is so packed with sports memorabilia it could be a museum. Actually, it is a museum, with more than 1,000 items, ranging from Larry Kelley's 1936 Heisman Trophy, to Babe Ruth's 1934 Yankees contract, to Coach Weeb Ewbank's Super Bowl III trophy. The collection really is amazing. The bar has more than a dozen TVs, plus a big-screen TV. The menu ranges from pub fare to classic American and Italian entrées. (*$–$$, 1308 Rte. 9, Garrison, (914) 734-4000, stadiumbarrest.com*)

RESTAURANTS

Park Restaurant: Just three blocks from West Point, this place is a perfect example of the bar-diner-restaurants you find in small northeastern towns. There's a heavy, polished bar at the front door, dark vinyl banquets, and tables for four set with paper placemats and napkins. The menu is massive, offering wraps to steaks, pasta to seafood. (*$, 451 Main St., Highland Falls, (845) 446-8709, parkrest.com*)

Thayer Hotel Main Dining Room: The dining room has large Gothic-style windows, high ceilings, and stone walls. The menu has classics such as grilled sirloin, rack of lamb, roast duck, broiled pork chops, and Chilean sea bass. Just off the main dining room, the Thayer Lounge hosts a live radio show, *Inside Army Football*, with Coach Bobby Ross every Thursday night during football season. (*$$, 674 Thayer Rd., West Point, (800) 247-5047, thethayerhotel.com*)

For more information: For a directory of additional places to eat in the area visit opentable.com. You can also book a reservation for many restaurants on the site.

What to Do
DURING THE DAY
Kaaterskill Falls: This well-hidden hollow has an impressive 260-foot waterfall, with a short but challenging hiking trail (don't worry, the trail has several resting points). It's also the location of Rip Van Winkle's legendary nap. Yep, right here. The falls are located just off Route 23A and can be a little hard to find, so log on to the Web site for directions. *(Free, angelfire.com/ny4/waterfalls/kaaterskillfalls2.html for directions.)*

Brotherhood Winery: This is America's oldest winery, producing its first commercial vintage in 1839. Brotherhood even managed to stay open during Prohibition by supplying sacramental wine. Today, you can tour the oldest, largest underground cellars in America, where the wine ages in oak casks and barrels, just like it did 200 years ago. And yes, you can have a taste. (*$, 100 Brotherhood Plaza Dr., Washingtonville, (845) 496-3661, brotherhoodwinery.net*)

Knox Headquarters State Historic Site: Built in 1754 for prosperous miller John Ellison, this Georgian-style fieldstone mansion housed Generals Henry Knox, Nathanael Greene, and Horatio Gates during the Revolutionary War. Today, it's one of the best, most historically accurate examples of life during that wartime period. (*$, 289 Forge Hill Rd., New Windsor, (845) 561-5498, nysparks.state.ny.us/sites/info.asp?siteID=16*)

SHOPPING
DUSA Gift Shop: Here's where you go for all things Army, right in the **West Point Museum.** You can get Army logo clothing, souvenirs, knickknacks, and books here. All proceeds from DUSA shops (there are two in town) go to West Point as scholarships or to support one of West Point's community activities. (*West Point Museum, West Point, (800) 890-8253, dusagiftshop.com*)

Woodbury Common Factory Outlets: This 220-store outlet has stores from high fashion to outdoor gear. Some of the shops include **North Face, Gucci,** and **Coach.** (*498 Red Apple Ct., Central Valley, (845) 928-4000, premiumoutlets.com*)

For more information: To learn more about things to do in the area visit visiontownofhighlands.com.

Philadelphia

The Philadelphia Eagles' early years were, if nothing else, interesting.

A group of men, led by Burt Bell, bought a team called the Frankford Yellowjackets for $2,500, moved it to Philadelphia, and renamed it the Eagles, in honor of the New Deal's National Recovery Act. For the NFL, this was a good thing, since the young league needed teams in big cities for the media and fan base.

Then, in 1941, there was a trade. But not just one player. All of them. Pay attention, this gets complicated.

At the time the Eagles were co-owned by Bell and Art Rooney—who had sold the Pittsburgh Steelers to steel heir Alexis Thompson. But in 1941 Bell and Rooney traded franchises with Thompson. Now Bell and Rooney owned the Pittsburgh Steelers, and Thompson owned the Philadelphia Eagles. But that wasn't the end of this unique relationship.

In 1943, due to World War II, there was a player shortage. So the teams merged, calling themselves the Steagles. Greasy Neale of the Eagles and Walt Kiesling of the Steelers co-coached, and the Steagles went 5-4-1. The next year the merger dissolved, and the Eagles went back to being just the Eagles, and the Steelers the Steelers, again. Whew.

Today, the Eagles are a successful team playing at Lincoln Financial Field, the 2003 replacement for Veterans Stadium. The Linc, as it's also known, seats 68,532 and is a part of the Philadelphia Sports Complex, which is also home to Wachovia Spectrum, Wachovia Center, and Citizens Bank Park.

The parking lots around Lincoln Financial Field are reserved, and those around the other three venues at the complex are where the rest of us park for $10 per space (if you use more than one space, you'll pay for more than one space). The good news is there's plenty of room for tailgating. The bad news is some of the lots are a bit of a walk.

If you didn't drive, you can take the SEPTA Broad Street Line train to the stadium. You'll want to get off on the last southbound stop, which is Pattison Avenue You can get schedule information at septa.org/news/bsl_express.html. There is also bus service from south Philadelphia; hop on the southbound Route C bus and take it to Broad Street. Subways and buses cost $2 one-way, but can be more based upon where you board and the transfers you'll have to make. That $2 becomes $1.30 if you buy tokens in advance.

While the Eagles claim Lincoln Financial Field

PHILADELPHIA EAGLES

Lincoln Financial Field
Philadelphia, Pennsylvania
(215) 339-6757

All parking within three-block radius around stadium. No shuttles, but subway is close by, if you come from downtown. RVs pay for number of spots used; no parking overnight; stay within space. No tailgating north of Pattison Ave. Visit Eagles Ultimate Tailgate Party; you'll need a ticket.

Train and Bus Info: The SEPTA Broad Street Sports Express Service runs trains to the Pattison Avenue stop at the stadium. Bus Route C from south Philadelphia will take you to Broad Street near the stadium. Cost is $2 and up ($1.30 if purchase tokens in advance).

Eagles Media Partner: 94.1-FM WYSP

on Sundays, the Temple Owls have it on Saturdays (and all the parking and mass transit rules are the same on Saturdays). Game-day parking is in the lots closest to the stadium and cost $10.

Temple's football past includes several years with the legendary "Pop" Warner at the helm. It was during these years in the 1930s that the school began to play the powerhouse programs at the time—Penn State, Tennessee, Army, and others. This elevated the program, and the Owls won a good number of these games.

Temple is the Owls, by the way, because the Owl is a nocturnal hunter, and the school was founded as a night school for ambitious students of limited means. As Temple's founder put it: "The owl of the night makes the eagle of the day." The metaphor became the mascot.

Tailgating before an Owls game includes the school's parking lot party called the Owls Nest. It's located in Lot E in the Wachovia Center parking lot, across the street from the stadium. There's music, food, face painting, giveaways, and inflatable games.

About Philadelphia

William Penn was a Quaker who founded a colony based on principles of freedom and religious tolerance. He named the capital of his colony Philadelphia, which in Greek means "city of brotherly love."

In time, Philadelphia would play pivotal roles in the birth and development of America. A major center of independence during the Revolutionary War, Philadelphia was where the Declaration of Independence was written, as well as the U.S. Constitution. The city hosted the Constitutional Convention and was briefly the nation's capital. The U.S. Marine Corps began here in 1775 when men were solicited from Tun Tavern to join. It was the home of Ben Franklin who, in addition to his roles in creating America, was the city's first postmaster, started the Union Fire Company to protect the city, organized a Night Watch & Militia to help keep peace, and set up America's first fire insurance company. Oh yeah, there was that whole discovering-electricity thing, too.

Eagles fans line up in the parking lot. (Photo: Mark Matthews)

Today Philadelphia's economy is driven largely by manufacturing, food, and financial services. It is also home to several major companies such as Comcast, CIGNA, and Pep Boys.

And while you might not think of it as a college town, it is the nation's largest. More than 120,000 students attend universities in the city, and more than twice that study in the entire metro area.

Where to Stay
RV PARKS

Beechwood Campground: This park has about 200 RV sites with full hookups available. Individual sites are large, and most are shaded and offer some privacy. Daily rates for full hookups are $32, but an RV club membership cuts that price to $24. (*105 Beechwood Dr., Coatesville, (800) 226-7248, beechwoodcampground.com*)

Old Cedar Campgrounds: Just 18 miles outside of Philly, this campground provides 200 sites, many of them wooded. They also have a mini-zoo, with domestic and wild animals, and mini-golf. The park has the basic amenities, and the daily rate here is $29. (*274 Richwood Rd., Monroeville, NJ, (800) 58-CEDAR, oldcedarcampground.com*)

Timberlane Campground: Located just minutes outside of Philadelphia, Timberlane is a smaller park with 96 spaces. Sites can be narrow, but are level, with paved roads throughout. There's also a pond that provides some good fishing (bring your own pole). Prices range from $35 to $39. (*117 Timberlane Rd., Clarksboro, NJ, 856-423-6677, timberlanecampground.com*)

For more information: For additional RV parks and campsites visit campingworld.com/campsearch.

HOTELS

Alexander Inn: This small-scale hotel offers 48 guest rooms and has the feel of a B&B, with a 1930s art deco/cruise-boat style to the furnishings. Guest rooms also have DirecTV with eight all-movie channels. There's a 24-hour fitness center and a business center for your use, too. (*12th and Spruce Sts., Philadelphia, (877) ALEX-INN, alexanderinn.com*)

Korman Communities–Rittenhouse: If you're planning on staying a few days, this might be your best choice. All of the rooms are actually furnished apartments, from studios to two-bedrooms, with enclosed kitchens. What makes this something other than just another extended-stay hotel are the mahogany furnishings, marble kitchens with upgraded appliances, and bathrooms stocked with Aveda products. Rooms will cost you from $155 to $315. (*222 West Rittenhouse Sq., Philadelphia, (877) KORMAN-2, korman1.com*)

Penn's View Hotel: This small hotel with 51 guest rooms is owned by a local Italian restaurateur and his family. The hotel's interior and guest rooms are done in bold, rich colors; the furniture is Chippendale-style, and some rooms have exposed brick walls. Rooms have all the usual amenities and run $180–$225. Its Center City location is convenient, but since it's close to Market Street's ramp to I-95

TEMPLE UNIVERSITY
Lincoln Financial Field
Philadelphia, Pennsylvania
(215) 204-6267

University and stadium are in downtown Philadelphia, so parking is decentralized. Most parking within walking distance. If parked across town, public transportation available. Visit Owls Nest in Lot E.

Train and Bus Info: The SEPTA Broad Street Sports Express Service runs trains to the Pattison Avenue stop at the stadium. Bus Route C from south Philadelphia will take you to Broad Street near the stadium. Cost is $2 and up ($1.30 if purchase tokens in advance).

Owls Media Partner: 1210-AM WPHT

some rooms can be noisy. Just ask for a room on the other side of the building. (*Front & Market Sts., Philadelphia, (800) 331-7634, pennsviewhotel.com*)

Rittenhouse Hotel: Inside this glass and concrete high-rise sits a five-star hotel. The rooms are actually suites and they're big, even the basic ones. Every suite has a great view, and there's a day spa in the building. The hotel's restaurant, **Lacroix,** is one of the best in Philly. It's a nice enough place that actors such as Bruce Willis and Mel Gibson have stayed here for months at a time when filming movies in the area. Not sure if they paid $245–$750 per night, but you will. (*210 W. Rittenhouse Sq., Philadelphia, (800) 635-1042, rittenhousehotel.com*)

For more information: To learn about more hotels in the area visit tripadvisor.com for listings and guest reviews.

B&BS

The Gables: One of the city's first mansions, this West Philadelphia Victorian B&B offers 10 rooms, all but 2 with private baths. The whole place is filled with antiques, and guest rooms have interesting details such as tiled fireplaces and inlaid wood floors. Three rooms have corner turrets. Free off-street parking is available, but the lot holds about eight cars, so parking is first-come, first-served. Rooms range from $85 to $145, depending on the room and number of people. (*4520 Chester Ave., Philadelphia, (215) 662-1918, gablesbb.com*)

Rittenhouse Square Bed & Breakfast: With 10 guest rooms and suites, this upscale B&B befits its neighborhood. It's all haute-British in style, with marble bathrooms with personal and bath amenities by Penhaligon's of London. The house is equipped with DSL workstations and is equipped for wireless use throughout. The cost for rooms is $239–$499 (the higher price is for their Presidential Suite). If you're staying only Saturday night, add $50 to the price. They also have 24-hour concierge service and don't allow children under 12. (*715 Rittenhouse Sq., Philadelphia, (877) 791-6500, rittenhousebb.com*)

Thomas Bond House: This B&B is located inside Philadelphia's Independence National Historic Park and is actually owned by the National Park Service (though the B&B is run by another entity). The house and its 12 guest rooms are carefully restored and outfitted in Colonial-era furnishings and have private baths. If you're a history buff, this is a great spot—walk out the front door and you'll find **Independence Hall, the Liberty Bell,** and several other historic sites. No children under 10. (*129 S. 2nd St., Philadelphia, (800) 845-2663, winston-salem-inn.com/Philadelphia*)

For more information: To learn about more B&Bs in the area visit bedandbreakfast.com for a detailed directory.

Where to Eat
TAILGATER GROCERIES

The Italian Market: This is the oldest, largest working outdoor market in the United States. It's still predominantly Italian but offers a wide range of foodstuffs representing the region's many ethnic and religious groups. The Market has more than 100 merchants and more than 40 curbside produce vendors offering pretty much anything you need. The market is open Tuesday through Sunday. (*9th St., between Wharton and Fitzwater Sts., Philadelphia, 215) 922-5557, phillyitalianmarket.com*)

Reading Terminal: This is the second-largest market in the city. There are more than 80 mer-

The Ultimate Tailgater's Travel Guide

chants here, offering fresh produce, meats, fish, groceries, flowers, baked goods, crafts, books, and clothing, as well as hard-to-find specialties and ethnic foods. It's open Monday through Saturday. (*12th & Arch Sts., Philadelphia, (215) 922-2317, readingterminalmarket.org*)

SPORTS BARS

The Bayou: Located in Philly's Manayunk neighborhood, this bar & grill has been named "Philadelphia's Best Sports Bar" by ESPN.com. With two floors, three bars, and 16 TVs, plus hard-shell crabs and half-pound burgers, you'll like it, too. (*$, 4245 Main St., Philadelphia, (215) 482-2560, bayoubar.com*)

Chickie's & Pete's: Last year this was named the third-best sports bar in the country by ESPN. There are three locations in Philly and one in New Jersey (they're not a franchise, just successful). The biggest, on Packer Avenue, is walking distance from Lincoln Financial Field. This 24,000-square-foot pub has three bars, with 10- and 14-foot flat-screen TVs. The original location is the one on Robbins Avenue, near Wissinoming. Crabs hold a prominent spot on their menu, and their crab fries are the specialty of the house. (*$, Philadelphia locations: 1526 Packer Ave., (215) 218-0500; 11000 Roosevelt Blvd., (215) 856-9890; 4010 Robbins Ave., (215) 338-1190; chickieandpetes.com*)

McFaddens: They're equipped with state-of-the-art technology, such as digital surround sound, a 110-inch projector screen, a plasma TV, and 18 regular TVs. Yeah, you'll be able to see the game. It's an attractive place, too, with lots of honey-red wood on the walls and floor, and a better-than-average menu for a bar. (*$, 461 North 3rd St., Philadelphia, (215) 928-0630, mcfaddensphilly.com*)

RESTAURANTS

Dalessandro's Steaks: We're not talking T-bones. We're talking Philly cheesesteaks. This is one of the best Philly cheesesteak sandwiches in

PHILLY CHEESESTEAK

There's debate in the City of Brotherly Love about who created the Philly cheesesteak sandwich—and we won't resolve it in this book—but the sandwich is a Philadelphia tradition and one of the city's biggest exports. Bring along a couple of frying pans and your tailgate party can enjoy this Philly favorite.

6 tablespoons oil, divided

1 large Spanish onion, sliced

1 sweet green or red pepper, sliced (optional)

Mushrooms, sliced (optional)

24 ounces thinly sliced rib eye steak

1 can Cheez Whiz (if you don't like the canned stuff, you can use American or provolone cheese)

4 hoagie rolls

Preheat the grill to medium heat. Once hot, heat an iron skillet or a nonstick pan on the grill. Add 3 tablespoons of the oil to the pan and sauté the onions until done. Remove the onions and set aside. Sauté the peppers and mushrooms (if using) in the oil, adding a bit more oil if needed. Remove the peppers and mushrooms and set aside. Add the remaining oil and sauté the meat on both sides until cooked (this won't take long).

Melt the Cheez Whiz (or cheese) in a double boiler or similar setup.

Divide the meat and place it into the four rolls. Add onions to each and pour the cheese on top. Then, if you wish, add the peppers and/or mushrooms, and serve.

Makes 4 servings.

the city. This is not a fancy place; just a few tables, with a short counter and no "atmosphere." Nor is it anywhere near Center City or South Philly, traditional homes of the cheesesteak. But the line of customers here often stretches out the door. *($, 600 Wendover St., Philadelphia, (215) 482-5407)*

Morimoto: *"Allez Cuisine!"* Iron Chef Morimoto has taken his knives from Kitchen Stadium to Morimoto, a contemporary space that includes bamboo ceilings, pale wood walls, and subtle pastel lighting. From the kitchen comes the innovation you've seen the Iron Chef use on TV. Sure, there's sushi, but it is dishes such as king yellowtail prepared at your table in a hot river stone bowl that stand out. Order *omakase*, or chef's choice, and you'll get a multicourse-tasting menu like none other. *($$–$$$, 723 Chestnut St., Philadelphia, (215) 413-9070, morimotorestaurant.com)*

Old Original Bookbinder's: Located in historic Old City, Bookbinder's opened in 1865. For more than a century, it's been considered Philadelphia's prime dining spot and social mecca. The main dining room is visually appealing, and care's been taken to preserve the building's historical elements. Try the snapper soup—the chefs have painstakingly recreated this Bookbinder's recipe from the original. *($$–$$$, 125 Walnut St., Philadelphia, (215) 925-7027, bookbinders.biz)*

Shula's Steak House: Okay, it's a chain. But it's Don Shula's chain. Inside the legendary coach's shrine to football and steak, you'll find more memorabilia than at the Pro Football Hall of Fame. Okay, that's a stretch, but the menu is actually painted on the side of a football the waiter brings you. Their biggest steak is a 48-ounce porterhouse. Finish the whole thing and you'll get mentioned on their Web site. The restaurant's bar, the **No-Name Lounge,** is full of widescreen TVs. *($$–$$$, 17th & Race Sts., Philadelphia, (215) 448-2700, donshula.com/steakhouse/philadelphia)*

Tacconelli's: This is where you go for pizza. Way up in the north end of Philly, this pizza joint makes what some call the best pies in the world. In fact, to make sure you get one, you have to call ahead and reserve your pizza. The pies are baked in a 20-by-20-foot brick oven, which creates a crisp, chewy crust. The owner sticks with the classics: tomato, regular, or white pizza pies are all you'll find in this no-frills, pizza-only establishment. They serve only soft drinks, but you can bring your own alcohol. Tacconelli's stays open until they run out of crusts, which is usually by 9:00 p.m. or so. *($, 2604 E. Somerset St., Philadelphia, (215) 425-4983)*

For more information: For a directory of additional places to eat in the area visit opentable.com. You can also book a reservation for many restaurants on the site.

What to Do
DURING THE DAY

Adventure Aquarium: Here you can swim with sharks. Yes, real sharks. The Aquarium, located across the river in Camden, NJ, has recreated several aquatic environments, including a saltwater tank holding 760,000 gallons of water (and loads of turtles, fish, and other inhabitants). Aside from fish, you'll also be getting up close and personal with seals, penguins, and hippos. And in their interactive area you can touch and play with several sea animals. *($$–$$$, 1 Aquarium Dr., Camden, NJ, (856) 365-3300, adventureaquarium.com)*

Historic Tours: Few cities in America have as much history as Philadelphia. Not many places basically gave birth to a nation, after all. The city has a number of motorized and walking tours available to see all of this history, many geared toward particular topics. Here are a few of them:

Philadelphia Trolley Works and 76 Carriage Company: (215) 925-TOUR, phillytour.com

Big Bus Tours: These are in double-decker, British-style buses. (866) 324-4287, bigbustours.com

Quest for Freedom: The Underground Railroad Walking Tour: (800) 537-7676, independencevisitorscenter.com

Constitutional Walking Tour of Philadelphia: (800) 537-7676, independencevisitorscenter.com

AudioWalk and Tour: Self-guided tour. (800) 537-7676, independence visitorscenter.com.

Independence National Historic Park: The park has 40 buildings on 45 acres of Center City real estate. After seeing the **Liberty Bell** in its new pavilion, and touring **Independence Hall's** rooms (especially the **Pennsylvania Assembly Room** and **Great Essentials Exhibit**), visit the other buildings in the park, such as the **Todd House** or **Philosophical Hall.** Your first stop, however, needs to be the **Independence Visitor Center;** it's where you get tickets for everything at the park. (*Free–$, One North Independence Mall West, 6th and Market Sts., Philadelphia, (800) 537-7676, nps.org, or independencevisitorscenter.com*)

The Liberty Bell and Independence Hall. (Photo: Independence NHP)

Philadelphia Museum of Art: America's third largest art museum is a huge Greco-Roman temple on a hill. To get there, you ascend the same stairs Rocky Balboa did—but you don't have to run. Established in 1870, its collections are eclectic, encompassing almost a quarter of a million works of art ranging from French Impressionists to a Hindu temple. Check out the museum's Art After 5, a popular blend of cocktails, jazz, and international entertainment starting at 5:00 p.m. every Friday in the Great Stair Hall. (*$–$$, Benjamin Franklin Pkwy. and 26th St., Philadelphia, (215) 763-8100, philamuseum.org*)

Philadelphia Zoo: This is the nation's oldest zoo, established in 1874. After some lean times in the '70s, the zoo today has nearly 1,800 animals. Two popular exhibits are the PECO Primate Center, a pavilion that blurs the line between visitors and its 11 resident species, and the Jungle Bird Walk, where you walk among free-flying birds. The white lions, over at Carnivore Kingdom, are pretty popular, too. There are a few things that aren't covered by your admission ticket, such as the Channel 6 Zoo Balloon ($12) or the Treehouse ($1), so bring some extra cash. (*$–$$, 34th St. and Girard Ave., Philadelphia, (215) 243-1100, philadelphiazoo.org*)

AT NIGHT

32 Degrees: The interior is sleek and chic with white ottomans pushed up to tables and a glowing red bar. There's some attitude here—their Web site says, "only the most stylish" can hang out in the VIP lounge or mingle around its two bars. This dance club has European-style service; if you happened to have come from there, they accept Euros and dollars. (*16 S. 2nd St., Philadelphia, (215) 627-3132, 32lounge.com*)

Brasil's: During the week, this Old City restaurant and bar is an imaginative Brazilian restaurant with good food, cascading waterfalls and two large aquariums in the dining room. On weekends, the upstairs turns into a hot Latin club, full of salsa dancing. Not up on your Latin steps? Brasil's offers salsa lessons on Wednesdays. (*$, 112 Chestnut St., Philadelphia, (215) 413-1700, brasils.com*)

Ortlieb's Jazzhaus: Six nights a week, music fans crowd into this narrow bar-restaurant's dining room to listen to greats such as Bootsie Barnes, Sid Simmons, and Mickey Roker. Even though Ortlieb's

The Philadelphia Museum of Art.
(Photo: Philadelphia Museum of Art)

is one of Philly's most respected places for jazz music, it still has an underground feel to it. If you get here a little early, order dinner from the Southern-Cajun style menu. You can park in the small strip mall across the street for free. (*$, 847 N. 3rd St., Philadelphia, (215) 922-1035, ortliebsjazzhaus.com*)

Monk's Café: This cozy pub/bistro takes the love of beer (specifically, Belgian beer) to a whole new stage of expression. Monk's has more than 200 artisanal beers, and its frequent "beer dinners" allow guest chefs (like former Le Bec-Fin chef Daniel Stern) to expand the boundaries of beer cuisine. The menu includes dishes such as rabbit stew braised in Cantillion Gueze, and lamb with a glaze of Gale's Prize Old Ale. (*$, 16th & Spruce Sts., Philadelphia, (215) 545-7005, monkscafe.com*)

Smokey Joes: For 60 years, this has been a college hangout, mostly for students from Penn (they call the place a "Pennstitution"). Smokey's is a friendly place, with a dark-wood interior, low lighting, and brass railings everywhere. It was also voted one of "America's Top 100 College Bars" by *Playboy* magazine, but there're no bunnies here. (*$, 210 S. 40th St., Philadelphia, PA, (215) 222-0770, smokeyjoesbar.com*)

Avenue of the Arts: This is Philadelphia's cultural district, where you'll find more than 37 cultural organizations & venues (and Temple University). On the north half of the Avenue, you'll find places like the **Pennsylvania Academy of the Fine Arts,** the **New Freedom Theatre,** the legendary **Blue Horizon** (one of the top boxing venues in the world), the **Uptown Theater,** and the **Metropolitan Opera House.** On the south side there's the **Academy of Music,** the **University of the Arts,** the **Merriam Theater,** the **Philadelphia Clef Club of Jazz and Performing Arts,** and the **Kimmel Center for the Performing Arts.** There are also numerous restaurants, clubs, and shops along the Avenue. (*York St. to Washington Ave., avenueofthearts.com*)

SHOPPING

Old City: In the shadow of the Benjamin Franklin Bridge, just above Independence Park, you'll find an eclectic blend of 18th-century row houses, 19th-century warehouses, and 20th-century rehabs. You'll also find an eclectic blend of shops and galleries. You'll find **Jewelers Row** centered on Sansom Street between 7th and 8th Streets, one of the world's oldest and largest markets of precious stones, with more than 350 retailers, wholesalers, and craftspeople.

Rittenhouse Square: Bordered by Broad and 21st Streets to the east and west, and Spruce and Market Streets to the south and north, shoppers know it as Rittenhouse Row. The section of Walnut Street, between Rittenhouse Square and Broad Street has **Tiffany & Co.** and **Ralph Lauren** (among other high-end stores) tucked into the **Park Hyatt/Bellevue Hotel.** There are also dozens of shops and art and antique galleries.

For more information: To learn more about things to do in the area visit cityguide.aol/philadelphia.

Phoenix

The Arizona Cardinals are the oldest professional football team still in existence. They've been in continuous operation since 1898, when they were founded as the Morgan Athletic Club. They wore used jerseys from the University of Chicago. The shirts were faded and, in the eye of the team owner, looked more Cardinal red than maroon. That's where the name comes from.

Skip forward to 1920 and the team becomes known as the Chicago Cardinals, which over the years included Hall of Famers like Ernie Nevers and Dick "Night Train" Lane, and two NFL championships (1925 and 1947).

A move in 1960 takes the team to St. Louis where greats Dan Dierdorf and Jackie Smith made their careers. Another move in 1988 makes the team the Phoenix Cardinals. And a name change in 1994 makes them the Arizona Cardinals. In 2006 they move again. But just across town.

The Cardinals will kick off the 2006 season in a new stadium in the Phoenix suburb of Glendale. The 65,000-seat Cardinals Stadium will have a retractable roof and a retractable field. Yep, the field gets to spend game days inside the stadium and then is rolled outside for the rest of the year, so the natural grass can get sun and water. It's the first completely retractable field in North America. As is usually the deal with new stadiums like this, it will play host to Super Bowl XLII on February 3, 2008.

As we sent this book to the printer, the Cardinals had not announced any details of their parking plan, costs, or tailgating rules. They don't have any shuttle information yet, either. We do know the parking lots surrounding the stadium will hold 14,000 vehicles, with adjacent land holding another 11,000. The parking lots are part of Sportsman's Park, which will also include open spaces for activities and the Great Lawn.

While we don't have details, we suspect the tailgating rules for Cardinals Stadium will be similar to the rules the team had for Sun Devil Stadium. That's why we've included them in the stadium guide in this chapter. As soon as details are announced we'll update the venue guide at theultimatetailgater.com

Arizona State University plays at Sun Devil Stadium, which seats more than 73,000 and is nestled between two mountain buttes. The Tostito's Fiesta Bowl is played here. The stadium has also hosted Super Bowl XXX and the Pope. They had to cover up all the Sun Devil logos when the Pope was here. More about the mascot in a bit.

Tailgating's Southwestern flair here is seen not just with the setups, but in the menus. Regional and Mexican-

ARIZONA CARDINALS

Cardinals Stadium
Glendale, Arizona
(602) 379-0102

As of our print deadline, the Cardinals had not announced any new tailgating rules or costs for the new Cardinals Stadium. As soon as they are announced, we'll post an updated venue guide at theultimatetailgater.com.

Cardinals Media Partners: 860-AM KMVP, 620-AM KTAR, 710-AM KMIA (Spanish), KNXV-TV Channel 15 (ABC)

style foods make ASU tailgate a type of fiesta every week. Plus there's the *cerveza* and margaritas.

Parking next to the stadium is reserved for donors and season-ticket holders. Surprise, surprise. There are several general parking lots nearby, but some are a bit of a walk. If you can get a spot in the one on Rio Salado Parkway, take it. Otherwise, your best bet is going to be the lots off of Apache Boulevard. It will cost you $5–$10 to tailgate in these lots—based on the lot—and you have to stay in your space. And don't save spaces for friends—it's first-come, first-served here, and the attendants enforce it. RVs park in Lot 4 on Rio Salado Parkway. Spaces will cost you $20.

If you'd rather have someone else drive you to the game, Tempe in Motion has shuttle buses that run from the Pyle Center (Southern Ave. and Rural Rd.) to the stadium, and to/from downtown Tempe. It costs $2 round trip, $5 for groups of three or more. Kids under 12 ride free. Check tempe.gov/tim or call (480) 350-2775 for details.

Now, about the ASU mascot. No one really knows where it came from. In 1946 someone said "Let's call them Sun Devils," but no one knows who said it. The Sun Devils replaced the Bulldogs as the school's mascot (it was the Owls before that). We do know the student body voted 819-196 to make the change. The mascot logo—Sparky—was drawn by Bert Anthony, who was an artist for Walt Disney and who also created the Stanford Indian logo that's no longer used.

On the other side of Phoenix, in Avondale, there's a race track that in 1964 was carved out of the foothills of the Estrella Mountains. The Phoenix International Raceway was a draw in the early days, but nothing like what it became in 1988, when NASCAR came to town. The track also hosts Indy cars, Busch races, Craftsman Trucks and other races. The Checker Auto Parts 500 is said to be the biggest one-day sports event in Arizona.

General parking is free at PIR, and you can park overnight in the Estrella 3 parking lot. Don't confuse that with camping. You can't camp in this lot, but there are plenty of camping sites on the property.

If you reserve your RV camping spot (go to phoenixraceway.com or call (866) 408-7223), you'll get one tow vehicle pass, too ($150). If you have a reserved space, you must enter through Gate 1.

An illustration of the new Cardinals Stadium.
(Photo: Arizona Cardinals)

If you want to get an unreserved spot once you're here, enter at Sun Lane, and you can park in one of the general parking lots. These are farther out from the track and cost $40 per vehicle. No tow vehicle pass in these lots allowed, though; it will cost you another $40 to park those.

Free trams run between the parking areas and Oasis Drive on the southwest side of the raceway. In the reserved parking area, you'll also find a Bashas' Supermarket, where you can get the groceries and supplies you'll need to tailgate while you're here.

The Ultimate Tailgater's Travel Guide

No matter which venue you're tailgating at, remember that it gets darned hot in Phoenix—it's the desert—and you won't sweat like you're used to (part of that whole "it's a dry heat" thing). Be sure to dress appropriately, drink lots of water (yes, water—beer won't help you), and eat small, light meals. Dishes like kababs are great for hot weather because they become light, bite-sized dishes. And stay in the shade, too.

About Phoenix

The first settlers here were the Hohokam Indians, who lived here as early as 300 B.C. They built an extensive network of irrigation ditches that delivered water from the Salt River to their farmlands. The canal system grew to 135 miles, and their civilization flourished. Then they disappeared about 1450. No one knows why.

In the 1860s the next group of settlers came and named the area Phoenix, since their town would rise from the ashes of the Hohokam's, like a phoenix.

Phoenix is now America's sixth largest city—the result of the Sun Belt boom that began in the early 1950s. That's when low-cost air-conditioning made the desert heat bearable, quadrupling the city's population in just 40 years.

ARIZONA STATE UNIVERSITY
Sun Devil Stadium
Tempe, Arizona
(480) 965-2381

Visiting RVs park in Lot 4 across the street. Tailgating is done alongside vehicles. Tailgaters must stay within parking space. No tailgating within closed areas; no glass bottles. Don't save spaces; it's first-come, first-served.

Shuttle Info: Tempe in Motion shuttles run from downtown and Pyle Center (Southern Ave. and Rural Rd.) to the stadium. The cost is $2 round trip, $5 for groups of three or more. Kids under 12 ride free. Visit tempe.gov/tim or call (480) 350-2775 for details. Confirm rates and locations.

Sun Devils Media Partners: 620-AM KTAR, 860-AM KMVP

Of course, the warm weather draws people to the Valley of the Sun. Many businesses have relocated here, as have many northerners—at least for the winter. "Snowbirds" swell the population in winter months as they flee the cold and snow of their wintry hometowns.

Where to Stay

RV PARKS

Apache Palms RV Park: It's a pretty basic park with 80 sites (all full hookup), but it's just down the street from ASU. It has the usual amenities, along with a heated spa and pool, and free WiFi. Rates run $25–$32. (*1836 E. Apache Blvd., Tempe, (480) 966-7399, apachepalmsrvpark.com*)

Cotton Lane RV Park: A brand new facility near the race track, with 300 sites, indoor heated pool and Jacuzzi, and Internet connections, as well as social and recreational activities. There's also a free golf course—but only four holes are finished. Guess that's why it's free. It will cost you $26 to stay here. (*17506 W. Van Buren, Goodyear, (888) 907-7223, arizonarvresorts.com/cotton_index.htm*)

Phoenix-Metro RV Park: Close to Loop 101, making it easy to get to Tempe or Glendale. The park has 310 sites, but many are

Tailgating outside Sun Devil Stadium. (Photo: ASU/Tom Story)

PHOENIX INTERNATIONAL RACEWAY

Avondale, Arizona

(602) 252-2227

Reserved RV spaces with tow pass, $150. Reserved RV infield parking from $1,545 to $3,315 limited, call eight or nine months ahead to get space. General RV spaces $40 first-come, first-served. No roping off or saving spaces. Keep fires self-contained; weather may prohibit fires; no motorized carts. Child ID bracelets available.

extended stay. Some age restrictions may apply, so call ahead. The park offers basic amenities, a pool, and a rec room. The daily rate is $28. (*22701 N. Black Canyon Hwy., Phoenix, (877) 582-0390*)

Pleasant Harbor RV Resort: Along the shores of Lake Pleasant, the park offers everything from boating, to fishing, to hiking. The park has 294 sites with the usual amenities, as well as recreational facilities, a convenience store, and the **Marina Bar & Grill.** Rates run $30–$35. (*8708 W. Harbor Blvd., Peoria, (800) 475-3272, pleasantharbor.com*)

For more information: For additional RV parks and campsites visit campingworld.com/campsearch.

HOTELS

Hotel San Carlos: Located in Copper Square, this Italian Renaissance-inspired building was constructed in 1928 and is now on the National Register of Historic Hotels. Furnishings preserve a vintage, Old World elegance. Best feature: the rooftop pool, with views of the downtown skyline and surrounding mountains. There are three on-site restaurants. Rooms run $166–$210. (*202 N. Central Ave., Phoenix, (866) 253-4121, hotelsancarlos.com*)

Phoenix Inn Suites: This is a pretty basic hotel, but it has good-sized rooms, some with hot tubs, and standard suite amenities like microwaves and refrigerators. The hotel offers free high-speed Internet and laundry facilities. Rates here are $99–$189. (*2310 E. Highland Ave., Phoenix, (800) 956-5221, phoenixinnsuites.com*)

Twin Palms Hotel: You're not going to find a room closer to ASU unless you register for classes. Across the street from campus, this 1960s-era hotel has been updated to have modern amenities. The ASU Recreation Complex—the largest fitness facility in Arizona—is next door and free for hotel guests. Rooms will set you back $119–$249. (*225 E. Apache Blvd., Tempe, (800) 367-0835, twinpalmshotel.com*)

For more information: To learn about more hotels in the area visit tripadvisor.com for listings and guest reviews.

RESORTS

Arizona Biltmore Resort and Spa: They call it the "Jewel of the Desert." On 39 acres at the foot of the Phoenix Mountain Preserve, the resort has guest rooms, villas, eight swimming pools, seven tennis courts, an 18-hole putting course, and a spa. The resort's architecture was inspired by Frank Lloyd Wright. For nearly half a century, William Wrigley Jr. owned the resort—you've seen his name on gum. Rooms run $159–$300, more if you add golf and spa packages. (*2400 E. Missouri; Phoenix, (800) 950-0086, arizonabiltmore.com*)

The Boulders Resort & Golden Door Spa: Over 160 adobe "casitas" are set among the dramatic

The Ultimate Tailgater's Travel Guide

rock formations at this unique location 33 miles north of Phoenix. Guests can golf on two championship courses, visit the spa, swim, hike, rock-climb, or mountain bike. Each casita features a fireplace, patio, and a tub for two. A stay averages about $300, but specials can lower that. (*34631 N. Tom Darlington Dr., Carefree, (480) 488-9009, theboulders.com*)

The Phoenician: Known for its lavish decor (including an $8 million art collection) and breathtaking views, it ranks among the top resorts anywhere. It boasts 9 swimming pools, 27 holes of golf, 2 tennis courts, on-site spa, 3 award-winning restaurants, and special activities for kids. A stay here costs $295 and up. (*6000 E. Camelback Rd., Scottsdale, (480) 941-8200, thephoenician.com*)

For more information: To learn about more resorts in the area visit tripadvisor.com for listings and guest reviews.

B&BS

Casita Sonora Bed and Breakfast: This traditional hacienda-style guesthouse is located in the heart of downtown Tempe. There are two rooms with private baths in the main house, and a guest house with a bedroom, den (with sofa-bed), bathroom, and kitchen. The backyard has a waterfall, fish pond, and pool. Rooms cost $89–$119. (*599 W. 5th St., Tempe, (480) 966-4240, casitasonora.com*)

Glendale Gaslight Inn: This quaint 10-room inn is in downtown Glendale. Each room has its own theme, and all but one has a private bath. The inn also has a piano wine-bar and lounge with live jazz every weekend. Rooms here run $145–$245. (*5747 W. Glendale Ave., Glendale, (602) 505-1399, glendalegaslightinn.com*)

Maricopa Manor: Built in 1928, this secluded Spanish-style home is in the heart of north-central Phoenix and just minutes from Uptown Plaza's shopping and restaurants. Seven rooms with private baths. Amenities include a swimming pool, saunas, a library, and garden. Rooms run $109–$219. (*15 W. Pasadena Ave., Phoenix, (800) 292-6403, maricopamanor.com*)

The Boulders Resort & Golden Door Spa. (Photo: The Boulders Resort, Carefree, AZ)

To learn about more B&Bs in the area visit bedandbreakfast.com for a detailed directory.

Where to Eat
TAILGATER GROCERIES

Farmers' Markets: There are a slew of farmers' markets in the Phoenix area with fresh, seasonal foods. You'll find them near ASU, Cardinals Stadium, and the Phoenix International Raceway. Just about any of them will have what you need to round out your tailgate menu. For a listing, visit phoenix.about.com/cs/shop/a/farmers01_2.htm.

SPORTS BARS

Alice Cooper'stown: Yep, that Alice Cooper. He lives here and has created a place "where jocks & rock meet." There is a state-of-the-art sound system (they have live music here, too, of course), a huge video wall indoors, and a scoreboard with a big-screen TV outdoors. Jocks and rock meet on the menu, too, with theme-named fare like the Tony LaRussa's St. Louis Rib and the Stevie Nicks Garden Burger. Autographed sports and music memorabilia line the walls. (*101 E. Jackson St., Phoenix, (602) 253-7337, alicecooperstown.com*)

Max's Restaurant & Sports Bar: Named one of the "Top Five Sports Bars in the Country" by *USA Today*, Max's has one of the largest collections of football helmets in the nation, as well as simulcast wagering, 85 televisions, and a steakhouse-style restaurant serving everything from steaks, to pasta, to appetizers. (*$, 6727 N. 47th Ave., Glendale, (623) 937-1671*)

McDuffy's: They ranked fifth on SI.com's list of the "25 Best Sports Bars in America." Guess that's what 12 big screens, more than 70 other TVs, all the satellite packages, and Off Track betting get you. The menu is typical sports bar, with a large beer selection. **The Bash on Ash** music venue is also here. (*$, 230 W. 5th St., Tempe, (480) 966-5600, mcduffys.com/tempe*)

Drivers Sports Grill: It's near the Raceway, but this is a racing- and golf-themed bar, so you have two drivers at play. Lots of memorabilia from both sports are here, including bashed-in car hoods and race cars. The menu ranges from wings, to sandwiches, to meatloaf. It's a popular place in the West Valley to watch football and basketball, too. (*$, 14175 W. Indian School Rd., Goodyear, (623) 536-8571*)

RESTAURANTS

Ajo Al's: Voted *AOL CityGuide's* "Best Mexican Fare with Flair," the Southwestern interior reflects the dishes—Mexico meets Arizona fusion. Mexican standards such as tacos and burritos share the spotlight with seafood-stuffed enchiladas and pollo con queso. Don't forget the margaritas. (*$, 7458 W. Bell Rd., Glendale, (623) 334-9899, ajoals.com*)

Big City BBQ: Atop a number of Phoenix "Best of" lists, the food here is a mix of barbecue, soul food, and Cajun cuisine they call "BBQ with Soul." Where else do you find a menu where a po' boy sits next to Southern fried catfish, which sits next to smoked beef brisket? There's also a Mesa location, but this is the original. (*5118 S. Rural Rd., Tempe, (480) 756-5702, bigcitybbq.com*)

Donovan's Steak & Chop House: The rich mahogany, leather, and white tablecloths say high-end steakhouse, and they're right. Relatively new to Phoenix (the original is in La Jolla, CA), Donovan's has received awards from *Wine Spectator* and *DiRoNA*. The menu is exactly what you'd expect, but unlike many similar steakhouses, the sides are not all extra; vegetable and potato dishes come with the meal. (*$$–$$$, 3101 E. Camelback Rd., Phoenix, (602) 955-3666, donovanssteakhouse.com*)

Eddie V's Edgewater Grille: The menu is inspired by the classic seafood restaurants of Boston, San Francisco, and New Orleans. Look for dishes such as Roasted Chilean Sea Bass in Almond Crust and Broiled George's Bank Sea Scallops. They also serve steaks. This place was named "Phoenix's Best Seafood Restaurant" by both *Phoenix Magazine* and *Scottsdale Magazine*. You can also enjoy live music in the V Lounge. (*$$, 20715 N. Pima Rd., Scottsdale, (480) 538-8468, eddiev.com*)

Kiss the Cook: Tucked in next to car dealerships, this country-style and antique-decorated restaurant has been serving breakfast and lunch for more than 20 years (they don't serve dinner). The homey decor matches the down-home cooking in the kitchen. The menu has favorites such as biscuits and gravy, French toast, and corned beef hash. For lunch, try the Cajun Chicken Caesar Salad or one of several sandwiches. (*$, 4915 W. Glendale Ave., Glendale, (623) 939-4663*)

Oregano's: A Phoenix original, Oregano's has pastas, soups, even wings (do they have those in

Italy?) But it's the pizza that's part of the Gibbilini family lore—they're the ones who own the place. Try one of their originals, or make your own from a long list of ingredients. There are five locations in the Phoenix area. (*$, 523 W. University Dr., Tempe, (480) 858-0501; 1130 S. Dobson Rd., Mesa, (480) 962-0036; 3622 N. Scottsdale, Scottsdale, (480) 970-1860; 7215 E. Shea Blvd., Scottsdale, (480) 348-0500; 1008 E. Camelback Rd., Phoenix, (602) 241-0707; oreganos.com*)

Raul and Theresa's Restaurant: This not a fancy place, but you'll find authentic Mexican food with a few house specialties, such as the Theresa's Special—a spicy dish of diced beef, tomatoes, onions, and four types of hot peppers. (*$, 519 W. Main St., Avondale, (623) 932-1120*)

For a directory of additional places to eat in the area visit opentable.com. You can also book a reservation for many restaurants on the site.

What to Do

DURING THE DAY

Desert Botanical Garden: Opened in 1939 to conserve the ecology of the desert, the Garden is home to thousands of cacti, succulents, trees, and flowers. There are 139 rare, threatened, and endangered plant species from around the world. Kids can play the self-guiding game "Desert Detective." (*$, 1201 N. Galvin Pkwy., Phoenix, (480) 941-1225, dbg.org*)

Heard Museum: The foremost showcase of Native-American art and culture in the U.S., the Heard offers 10 galleries and outdoor courtyards featuring traditional and contemporary Native-American art. The gift shop has authentic, high-quality goods purchased directly from native artists. (*$, 2301 N. Central Ave., Phoenix, (602) 252-8848, heard.org*)

Hot-Air Balloon Rides: There are few places better suited than Arizona for hot air balloons. Look up on most any day, and the skies will be dotted with them. The peaceful ride over the city and desert allows for a special perspective of the Sonoran landscape. There are several companies that offer hot-air balloon rides, but here are a few to get you started:

A Great American Balloon Company: (877) 933-6359, wedoflyphoenix.com

The Hot Air Balloon Company: (800) 843-5987, arizonaballooning.com

Hot Air Expeditions: (800) 831-7610, hotairexpeoditions.com

Phoenix Greyhound Park: More than 1 million people come to the PGP each year to wager on the races. There is pari-mutuel betting on live races and simulcast races from across the nation. Dining is available in the Clubhouse. (*3801 E. Washington St., Phoenix, (602) 273-7181, phoenixgreyhoundpark.com*)

Phoenix Zoo: Voted one of the nation's "Top Five Zoos for Kids," this private, nonprofit zoo is home to 1,200 animals on exhibit. Take the Safari Train for a narrated tour of most major attractions. There are several places to eat on-site. (*$–Child, $$–Adult 13+; 455 N. Galvin Pkwy., Phoenix, (602) 273-1341, phoenixzoo.org*)

Pueblo Grande Museum and Cultural Park: The Hohokam were the first people to settle this part of the world before they disappeared (see page 159). The Park is located at a 1,500-year-old Hohokam village ruins. Here you can wander 102 acres of park grounds that contain the excavated ruins of homes, a ball court, and an 800-year-old platform mound that might have been used for ceremonies. Museum exhibits explore and celebrate the Hohokam culture. (*$, 4619 E. Washington St., Phoenix, (602) 495-0901, pueblogrande.com*)

AT NIGHT

e4: Four rooms under one roof make up one of the hippest spots in the Valley. The environments, as they call them, can work together or apart. Each has its own memorable decor and personality: the Earth Room, Liquid Room, Air Patio, and Fire Room feature dancing, videos, and special events. A full menu and inventive drinks are offered. (*$, 4282 N. Drinkwater, Scottsdale, (480) 970-3325, e4-az.com*)

Dos Gringos Trailer Park: Walking distance from ASU, this place is a popular college hangout. Mexican food's on the menu, but let's be honest, it's the bar that gets the most attention. Dos Gringos is the nation's number-one purchaser of Corona (if you're wondering, that's more than 3 million bottles—hey, they say it's true). Multilevel courtyard, four bars, and a couple dozen TVs keep this place busy. There's also a Scottsdale location. (*$, 1001 E. 8th St., Tempe, (480) 968-7879, dosgringosaz.com*)

Jack's Place: In "old town" Avondale, Jack's is a big club that's been the neighborhood bar since 1935. House DJ Ray has more than 1,800 CDs, so you can imagine how varied the music is. You'll find a full menu and bar. (*$, 613 E. Western Ave., Avondale, (623) 932-0190*)

The Rhythm Room: This Phoenix legend plays the blues, roots music, jazz, and swing, and it has a great house band. The bar sits on one side of the club, the stage on the other, and every night of the week the people in the middle hear live music. The bar on the patio usually has a shorter line. They serve food, and barbecue is on the menu. (*$–$$, 1019 E. Indian School Rd., Phoenix, (602) 265-4842, rhythmroom.com*)

Rockin' Rodeo: Often named "Best Country Bar" by local publications, this club offers several contests to help draw you in, and line dancing lessons on Thursdays and Saturdays. The crowd gets younger on weekends—more of the Kenny Chesney, Gretchen Wilson crowd. The club offers bar food and a full bar. (*$, 7850 S. Priest, Tempe, (480) 496-0799*)

Rúla Búla Irish Pub and Restaurant: Consistently voted "Best Irish Pub" by several area newspapers, this place has lots of authentic Irish touches, from the decorative tiles and flooring, to the bar that was designed and built in Ireland before being dismantled and shipped to Tempe. The menu is heavy on traditional Irish foods, but it also has pub grub and new Irish cuisine. (*$, 401 S. Mill Ave., Tempe, (480) 929-9500, rulabula.com*)

SHOPPING

Antiques: Glendale's historic downtown offers specialty and antique shops nestled around a quaint town square. But it's the antiques that grab national attention. *USA Today* and *Sunset* magazine have named Glendale as one of the nation's top 10 spots for antiquing. (*59th and Glendale Aves., Glendale*)

Biltmore Fashion Park: This is the Southwest's original luxury lifestyle shopping center. The open-air center has more than 70 boutiques and restaurants, anchored by **Saks** and **Macy's.** It was undergoing a renovation in 2006. (*2502 E. Camelback Rd., Phoenix, www.shopbiltmore.com*)

Mill Avenue District: Adjacent to ASU, Mill Avenue has entertainment, restaurants, and shopping. You'll find clothing stores ranging from hip to Harley, lifestyle stores, and a handful of shops that have just about everything the Sun Devils logo has ever been put on.

Scottsdale Fashion Square: If you're looking for high-end, exclusive retailers such as **Neiman-Marcus, Kate Spade, Gucci, Louis Vuitton, Tiffany & Co.,** and the like, this is the place. It's a mall, but a notch up from other malls. (*7014 E. Camelback Rd., Scottsdale, www.fashionsquare.com*)

To learn more about things to do in the area visit cityguide.aol.com/phoenix.

San Diego

The Los Angeles Chargers—charter members of the AFL—played their first season in 1960. They did well, winning the AFL Western Division championship. But they didn't do well with fans, so owner Barron Hilton, of the hotel Hiltons (and yes, they're related—he's Paris's grandfather), moved the team to San Diego at the urging of sports editor Jack Murphy.

For 17 years the Chargers played at San Diego Jack Murphy Stadium. The name was changed to Qualcomm Stadium in 1997, when the San Diego–based telecommunications company bought the naming rights for $18 million.

The Q, as it's also known, seats 71,000, but it has just 18,500 parking spaces. They fill up fast, and the team suggests getting to the stadium 2 to 3 hours before kickoff to get a space. Tailgating is the natural way to fill that time, and with good weather all season long, fans have the grills out early.

There are two parking "rings" at Qualcomm. The Inner Ring has reserved parking spots for $30. Motorcycles are $17, and RVs (or any other vehicle longer than 20 feet) costs $60 to park. The Outer Ring has reserved parking in Lots C2 and N5 for $25. General parking costs $17 for cars, $34 for RVs. This is the only area buses and limos can park; $50 gets them a space.

If you are planning to have a keg or any catering at your tailgate, you must have a permit. You can call (619) 641-3100 to get that process going. You can also reserve space for large parties by calling (619) 281-6316.

If you get to the stadium and the lots are full and locked up, you'll need to turn around and head toward one of the off-site lots down Friars Road. There are four of them. In order, from closest to farthest from the stadium, there's the Pacific Bell Building ($10), the Marriott Mission Valley ($5), Hazard Center (Free), and Town and Country Hotel ($5). You'll be walking to the game from Pac Bell, but it's adjacent to Qualcomm Stadium. The San Diego Trolley will take you from the other lots. The Trolley costs $3–$6, depending on where you hop on. The Trolley runs three routes with stops all over the city. For a map, log on to chargers.com/stadium/trolley_map.cfm.

Another option, if you're not driving, or have someone else setting up your tailgate party, is to take a shuttle bus. There are two of them. The Chargers Express Bus has five pickup locations. You can learn more and buy a ticket ($5 one-way, $8 round trip) at sdcommute.com (click on "eStore"). The North County Express BREEZE Bus runs along the I-5 and I-15 corridors. It costs $5 one-way, $10 round trip (children's tickets are $1 and $2, respectively). Go to gonctd.com for details.

If you're in Solana Beach or farther up the coast, Amtrak runs Chargers Trains on game day.

SAN DIEGO CHARGERS

Qualcomm Stadium
San Diego, California
(619) 641-3100
(619) 281-6316

Parking lot surrounds stadium; first-come, first-served; opens 6:00 a.m. game day. Other parking is close by. Large parties can reserve space in certain lots. No overnight parking, throwing balls, scooters, or rollerblades; stay in your space; get a keg permit; get there before noon.

Shuttle Info: The San Diego Trolley runs three routes to Qualcomm Stadium; tickets are $3–$6. For a map log on to chargers.com/stadium/trolley_map.cfm. The Chargers Express Bus boards at five locations and costs $5 one-way/$8 round trip. You can buy tickets and see pickup locations at sdcommute.com (click on "eStore"). The North County Express BREEZE Bus runs along the I-5 and I-15 corridors; tickets are $5 one-way, $10 round trip ($1 and $2 for children). Go to gonctd.com for details.

Chargers Media Partners: 105.3-FM KIOZ, 1420-AM XEXX (Spanish), KFMB-TV Channel 8 (ABC)

The San Diego State University Aztecs also play at Qualcomm Stadium. Parking isn't as much of a problem since there aren't as many fans. It's also free until 1:00 p.m. on game day; then it's $7.

Tailgating is more family oriented for Aztec games. There's no alcohol allowed and there's a Fun Zone with children's activities. The Fun Zone also has live music and the pregame radio show is broadcast from here.

SDSU was founded as San Diego Normal School to train teachers. It had 91 students. Today the school has 34,000 students and is one of the largest universities in California.

The school's athletic program began in 1921. At the time the media called the teams the Staters or the Professors. For one year, 1923, the school newspaper tried to get the nickname Wampus Cats to catch on. It didn't (not that you're surprised, right?). Eventually, the school selected Aztecs to represent the area's Southwestern image.

On the field the all-black uniforms give the team a certain image, too. When coach Don Coryell came up with the idea in 1961, it was to give his team a threatening, ominous image to opponents since they played at night. The team did well, and players have worn them ever since.

About San Diego

San Diego is considered the birthplace of California. The original town, settled in 1769, was the first of a series of missions established by Father Junipero Serra up and down what is now the west coast of Mexico and the United States. The contemporary city still reflects its Spanish origins in its architecture and culture.

Once a thriving commercial fishing port, modern San Diego has become a popular tourist destination thanks to its pleasant, sunny climate; beautiful scenery; and its beaches.

The military has also played a significant role in the city's economy. The United States Naval Station is here. Biotech is also an important industry, as is communications. Qualcomm calls San Diego home. In turn, the Chargers and Aztecs call Qualcomm home.

Where to Stay

RV PARKS

Campland on the Bay: If you like the water, you'll love this place. There's a private beach on Mission Bay, a marina where you can rent everything from paddleboats to motor boats, fishing, and more. It's adjacent to **Kendall Frost Wildlife Preserve.** All the basic amenities are offered, plus a grocery store, spa,

The Ultimate Tailgater's Travel Guide

restaurant/ice cream parlor, playgrounds, and more. There are 573 sites on the property, and they range from $44 to $120 for premium, private sites. (*2211 Pacific Beach Dr., San Diego, (800) 229-4386, campland.com*)

Chula Vista RV Resort: Located along San Diego Bay, the park has 237 full hookup sites, its own marina, a general store, and a waterfront restaurant. Sites will handle big rigs and have border landscaping to add a little privacy. The park has a pool, and bike rentals are available to explore the area. Rates run $49–$64 during the summer, $42–$55 in the winter. (*460 Sandpiper Way, Chula Vista, (800) 770-2878, chulavistarv.com*)

San Diego RV Resort: Convenient freeway access with 176 full hookup sites that can accommodate big rigs. Basic amenities, plus a pool and fitness center. Daily rates run $45–$75. (*7407 Alvarado Rd., La Mesa, (877) 787-6386, sdrvresort.com*)

For more information: For additional RV parks and campsites visit campingworld.com/campsearch.

HOTELS

La Valencia: In the 1930s and '40s, this La Jolla landmark was the preferred getaway spot for stars such as Charlie Chaplin and Greta Garbo. Today's stars such as Madonna and Martha Stewart have been known to stay here. With rooms, suites, and an ocean villa, La Valencia has all the amenities you'd expect in a luxury hotel, and the prices. Rooms and suites range from about $275 to more than $1,000, with most falling somewhere in between. (*1132 Prospect St., La Jolla, (800) 451-0772, lavalencia.com*)

Mission Valley Resort: Located in Mission Valley, near Old Town, this hotel has a sports bar, a hair salon, three pools, and a tennis and fitness club. Oh yeah, it has guest rooms, too. The rooms have standard hotel amenities and high-speed Internet, and will cost you $79–$149 based on the time of year. (*875 Hotel Circle S., San Diego, (800) 362-7871, missionvalleyresort.com*)

Pacific Terrace Hotel: Sitting on Pacific Beach, this hotel's rooms carry that care-free beach feel indoors—including a stocked mini-bar. Enjoy the beach-side pool. The hotel is walking distance from a number of shops, nightclubs, and restaurants, including waterfront dining. Rooms run $285–$485 for the family suite. (*610 Diamond St., San Diego, (800) 344-3370, pacificterrace.com*)

Park Manor Suites: Built in 1926, this Italian Renaissance-style building has a long history and was recently designated a historic site by the city of San Diego. With beautiful views of both **Balboa Park** (see page 169) and San Diego Bay, it's walking distance to the **San Diego Zoo** (see page 170). All rooms are suites (studio, one- and two-bedroom) and have a full kitchen. If you have a group, the two-bedroom

SAN DIEGO STATE UNIVERSITY
Qualcomm Stadium
San Diego, California
(619) 283-7378

Qualcomm Stadium is off campus, located on Friars Road. Parking surrounds stadium. Parking is free before 1 p.m.; after that it's $7. No alcohol allowed. Tailgating very family oriented; visit Fun Zone for children's activities, live music, live radio show.

Aztecs Media Partners: 1090-AM XPRS, Channel 4 San Diego (cable only)

Tailgating along the Outer Ring at Qualcomm Stadium. (Photo: Kenton Papacostas)

suites are 1,100 square feet. Rooms run $139–$199. *(525 Spruce St., San Diego, (800) 874-2649, park-manorsuites.com)*

For more information: To learn about more hotels in the area visit tripadvisor.com for listings and guest reviews.

B&BS

Balboa Park Inn: Not your typical B&B, this guesthouse is actually a complex of four Spanish colonial buildings housing 26 suites that are each a distinctive theme and decor. All rooms have private baths, refrigerators, and microwaves. The inn has a nice courtyard and patio, and is across the street from **Balboa Park** (see page 169) and the **San Diego Zoo** (see page 170). Suites cost $99–$219. *(3402 Park Blvd., San Diego, (800) 938-8181, balboaparkinn.com)*

The Beach Hut Bed and Breakfast: There's only one guest cottage here, but it's on Mission Bay and has a private pool. It also has a full kitchen stocked with utensils and other basics. The B&B is close to **SeaWorld** (see page 170) and steps away from a 6-mile bay walking trail. The cottage costs $119 per night, and there is a two-night minimum. *(3761 Riviera Dr., San Diego, (858) 272-6131, beachhutbb.com)*

Heritage Park Bed & Breakfast Inn: This restored Queen Anne mansion was built in 1889 and is furnished with pieces from that era. Secluded near historic Old Town, with manicured lawn and garden, the house has 12 rooms running $125–$280. Some rooms share a bath. *(2470 Heritage Park Row, San Diego, (800) 995-2470, heritageparkinn.com)*

For more information: To learn about more B&Bs in the area visit bedandbreakfast.com for a detailed directory.

Where to Eat

TAILGATER GROCERIES

Farmers' Markets: There's a farmers' market on every third corner in the San Diego area. Okay, not really, but there are a lot, so chances are you'll pass one on the way to the game. To find the closest to you, and learn when they're open, go to sdfarmbureau.org and click on "Farmers' Markets."

SPORTS BARS

McGregor's Grill and Ale House: Just across I-15 from Qualcomm Stadium, this pub has several TVs, including HD, pool, and darts. The menu has fish tacos to wings, salads to steak. They serve breakfast on Saturdays and Sundays, but breakfast for them starts at 10:00 a.m. *($, 10475 San Diego Mission Rd., San Diego, (619) 282-9797, mcgregors.signonsandiego.com)*

Nick's at the Beach: We could have put this in the restaurant section, but with 29 TVs, 16 beers on tap, and an ocean-view deck, "sports bar" won out. In addition to watching the game, you can play a game of pool. Downstairs you'll find a California-style restaurant, also with ocean views, which was voted "Best Neighborhood Restaurant" by *San Diego Magazine*. *($, 809 Thomas Ave., Pacific Beach, San Diego, (858) 270-1730, nicksatthebeach.com)*

Seau's The Restaurant: He may play for Miami now, but Junior Seau will always be a part of San Diego. His place has been named "Best Sports Bar" several times by the *Best of San Diego Readers' Poll*—but it's also been awarded "Best Happy Hour" and "Best Sushi." For the sports bar part, the place has 60 TVs and a 12-by-14-foot projection screen for game days. The food is, sushi aside, contemporary American. You can also watch radio broadcasts from Studio 55 (that's Junior's number). (*$, 1640 Camino Del Rio N., #1376, San Diego, (619) 291-7328, seau.com*)

Trophy's Sports Grill: It gets its name from its museum-quality collection of sports trophies and memorabilia, some dating to the 1930s. There's even a real World Series trophy. The food is better than most sports bars; one reviewer says, "Trophy's is a restaurant wearing a letterman's sweater." Located between **Fashion Valley** (see page 171) and Qualcomm Stadium. Three other area locations, too. (*$, 7510 Hazard Center Dr., San Diego, (619) 296-9600. trophys.tv*)

RESTAURANTS

Anthony's Fish Grotto: Sitting on the Bay, it offers great views accompanying fresh fish that's been voted the city's favorite by local publications. Seafood such as chowder, crab cakes, and seasonal fish dominate the menu, of course, but you'll also find steak and pastas. They also serve delicacies like frog's legs. (*$, 1360 North Harbor Dr., San Diego, (619) 232-5103, gofishanthonys.com*)

Bully's East: A local favorite for prime rib since 1967, Bully's also serves steaks and seafood. Bring the kids—there's a children's menu. The crowd is a little older during happy hour, but gets younger as the night moves on. The place is not far from Qualcomm Stadium. Sunday brunch is served before the game. (*$–$$, 2401 Camino Del Rio S., San Diego, (619) 291-2665, bullyssandiego.com*)

Donovan's of La Jolla: This San Diego original has the rich mahogany, leather, and white table-cloths you'd expect from a steakhouse. It has won awards for its food and its wine. Unlike similar steak-houses, vegetable and potato side dishes come with your meal. The menu also features lamb and seafood. (*$–$$, 4340 La Jolla Village Dr., La Jolla, (858) 450-6666, donovanssteakhouse.com*)

D.Z. Akin's: It might look like just another retail building, but inside is a local legend and an authentic "Jewish deli." The chicken and noodle soup is even called "Jewish Penicillin" on the menu. You don't get much more authentic than that. Specialties of the house include potato knishes and matzoh ball soup. They also serve 134 types of sandwiches. (*$, 6930 Alvarado Rd., San Diego, (619) 265-0218, dzakinsdeli.com*)

Fins Mexican Eatery: Started by three local boys, Fins prepares everything on its Mexican menu fresh and to order. The specialty of the house is traditional Baja California fish tacos, but the menu also has other Mexican favorites prepared with a San Diego twist. (*$, 8657 Villa La Jolla Dr., La Jolla, (858) 270-3467, fins.net*)

Woodstock's Pizza: This California original is an SDSU hangout. Built in an old Laundromat, the walls and wooden booths have Woodstock's history carved into them—literally. You can try one of their original pizzas, like the Firebird, or build your own. The pizza was voted "Best Pizza in San Diego" by the *Daily Aztec*'s Best of State Readers' Poll. (*$, 6145 El Cajon Blvd., San Diego, (619) 265-0999, woodstockssandiego.com*)

For more information: For a directory of additional places to eat in the area visit opentable.com. You can also book a reservation for many restaurants on the site.

What to Do

DURING THE DAY

Balboa Park: This is the nation's largest urban cultural park, and it's home to more than 30 attractions, museums, and gardens. You'll find the **Balboa Park Carousel** (hand-carved in 1910) here, along with the

San Diego Natural History Museum, San Diego Museum of Art, and the **Reuben H. Fleet Science Center** (with the city's only IMAX Dome Theater). The **San Diego Zoo** is in the park, as well (see below). (*Admission varies by attraction, 1549 El Prado, San Diego, (619) 239-0512, balboapark.org*)

Beaches: You're in San Diego, so you have to go to the beach. You just do. Go get your swimsuit. The weather's almost always nice, and the sand and water are part of what makes San Diego, well, San Diego. For listings of area beaches visit a-zsandiegobeaches.com or entersandiego.com/San_Diego_Beaches.cfm. In the meantime, here are a few to get you started:

Silver Strand State Beach faces both the Pacific Ocean and San Diego Bay. Here you can swim, boat, fish, and more.

Windansea Beach is a popular surfing spot facing the Pacific Ocean with sandstone cliffs and sandy beaches.

Torrey Pines State Beach and Reserve: This reserve is the home of our rarest native pine tree, for which the park is named. There are hiking trails that lead to the cliffs 200 feet above the ocean.

San Diego Zoo: Considered one of the nation's best zoos (at the very least you've seen their animals climbing all over Jay Leno on *The Tonight Show*), the San Diego Zoo is home to 4,000 animals from 800 species. The animal habitats are organized into 10 bioclimatic zones, from arctic tundra to rain forest. There are also exhibits and shows, dining and shops. Lots of activities for children are in Kid Territory. (*$$, 2920 Zoo Dr., San Diego, (619) 234-3153, sandiegozoo.org*)

SeaWorld: See Shamu and feed the dolphins. This theme park has shows, rides, and a slew of attractions. You can walk through a see-through tunnel surrounded by sharks, see more than 300 penguins in a snow-filled habitat, or hold starfish and sea urchins in the California Tide Pool. Your cocktail party trivia tidbit for the day: SeaWorld was an afterthought when its founders realized their first idea of an underwater restaurant wasn't technically feasible. (*$$$, 500 SeaWorld Dr., San Diego, (800) 257-4268, 4adventure.com/seaworld/ca*)

Presidio Park: Established as a military fort by the Spanish in 1769, the Presidio is the oldest European settlement on the Pacific coast of North America. Now the remains of this old fort and mission are a part of the 49-acre Presidio Park, which also includes the **Junipero Serra Museum,** statues, memorials, and several hiking trails. The museum celebrates San Diego's Hispanic and Indian cultures. (*$, 2811 Jackson St., San Diego, (619) 692-4918*)

The whale show Believe *makes a splash at SeaWorld. (Photo: SeaWorld San Diego © 2006 by Sea World, Inc.)*

Whale Watching: From December to April, whales swim by this part of the world during their migration. Watching them can be exhilarating. You can also see any number of other types of wildlife on whale-watching cruises, including sea lions and dolphins. There are several companies that host watching cruises, but here are a few to get you started. (*$–$$*)

Hornblower Cruises: (619) 686-8715, hornblower.signonsandiego.com/whale.html

H&M Landing: (619) 222-1144, hmlanding.com/whalewatch.html

Hike, Bike, Kayak San Diego: (858) 551-9510, hikebikekayak.com (Their whale-watching outing is by kayak.)

AT NIGHT

belo: This 20,000-square-foot club is divided into three rooms: red, green, and orange, designed in '60s retro. You can dance in the green room, or sit back and listen to music in the red room. The orange room is more of a lounge feel. The music runs from '80s, to dance, to mash ups. Full menu with items ranging from oyster shooters to pumpkin ravioli. (*$–$$, 919 4th Ave., San Diego, (619) 231-9200, belosandiego.com*)

Casinos: There are eight casinos in the San Diego area that offer Vegas-style gaming, off-track betting, shopping, dining, and entertainment. If you're under 21, call and ask the minimum age you are allowed to gamble—the answer varies casino to casino and ranges from 18 to 21. For a list of the nearest casinos, log on to seeyouinsandiego.com/casino_display.asp.

Pandas are a popular attraction at the San Diego Zoo. (Photo: © Zoological Society of San Diego)

Effin's Pub 'n' Grill: This is a college hangout, plain and simple. Near San Diego State University, they have pizza, wings, sandwiches, a big bar, and TVs (usually with games on). The kitchen stays open late and they deliver until 2:00 a.m. (*$, 6164 El Cajon Blvd., San Diego, (619) 229-9800, effins.com*)

The Gaslamp Quarter: This is one of San Diego's hottest districts for entertainment (there's also dining and shopping). The historic area features Victorian buildings built between 1873 and 1930, and dozens of nightspots from the Irish pub **Dublin Square,** to the hip **Onyx,** and just about everything in between. (*Bordered by 4th Ave., Broadway, and 6th Ave., San Diego, gaslamp.org*)

Lestat's Coffeehouse: Consistently on "Best of San Diego" lists, this Normal Heights coffeehouse has a diverse group of regulars. It's open 24 hours, so it's also a popular late-night place. Live entertainment nightly from open mic (Monday), to comedy (Tuesday), to music (most other nights). (*$, 3343 Adams Ave., San Diego, (619) 282-0437, lestats.com*)

Martini Ranch: Located in the Gaslamp Quarter, the Martini Ranch is a two-level club and has more than 50 martinis on its menu. There are several bars, private seating areas, a stage, and a dance floor. There is seating on a small patio, too. (*$, 528 F St., San Diego, (619) 235-6100, martiniranchsd.com*)

SHOPPING

Fashion Valley: Perhaps the area's best-known shopping center, the open-air Fashion Valley has more than 200 stores and restaurants. Many of the stores are famous, high-end ones; others are famous, not-so-high-end ones, but you'll find just about anything, and the atmosphere is probably nothing like anything you have at home. There's also a movie theater. (*7007 Friars Rd., San Diego*)

Ferry Landing Marketplace: Located across San Diego Bay in Coronado, this bayside center has restaurants and shopping. The Marketplace also has several art galleries. It's less than a mile from the Coronado Bridge, and you can rent bikes to explore the area, including the famed **Hotel del Coronado**. (*1201 1st St., Coronado*)

Normal Heights: Named for the San Diego Normal School—which later became San Diego State University—this neighborhood has antiques, books, clothing, art, and more. You'll also find places to eat as well as bars and nightclubs. Not far from Qualcomm Stadium. (*Adams Ave., San Diego*)

To learn more about things to do in the area visit cityguide.aol.com/sandiego.

San Francisco

The San Francisco 49ers were the first major league professional team on the West Coast. The team—whose name is a nod to the gold miners who rushed to San Francisco in 1849—was a charter member of the All-America Football Conference. If the Cleveland Browns hadn't been in the league, the 49ers would have dominated it.

But the AAFC collapsed in 1950, and the 49ers became an NFL team. A so-so NFL team. They stayed that way until the 1980s, when they began their domination of the NFL, including five Super Bowl championships.

The road to those championships often ran through Monster Park. Well, it wasn't Monster Park then (that name change came in 2004), but it was in the same stadium.

Built for baseball's San Francisco Giants, the 49ers moved in in 1971. Monster Park sits on San Francisco Bay and seats more than 64,000. Much of the parking around the stadium is reserved for season-pass holders, but there is some day-of-game parking for $25. The signage is pretty clear to get to those lots, so just follow them.

RV parking is $40, and the RV lot is at the corner of Gilman Avenue and Bill Walsh Way (take Third St. to Gilman, and turn right onto Bill Walsh Way). Limo parking is also near this lot and costs $40. Buses run $30, and motorcycles, which are parked in the main lot, cost $25 to park.

The 49ers run shuttles from the parking lots to the stadium, but they are intended for people who need assistance—not lazy ones.

If you didn't drive, there's public transportation to the stadium from all over the Bay Area. The best way to find out about routes and fares is to dial 511 before you're ready to head to the game. You can also log on to 511.org.

Once at Monster Park, in addition to your parking lot party, the team throws a couple of its own. The GOLDMINE is inside F Plaza, and if you have a game ticket you can get in. This is where the Gold Rush cheerleaders will be, and you'll find big-screen TVs, interactive games, DJs, and live entertainment. It opens 4 hours before kickoff.

If you amble over between Gates E and F, you'll find the Alumni Tailgater Area. Here former players hang out to sign autographs. There's a barbecue buffet and drinks. The catch is that you need to find a friend with tickets. They cost $10, but they sell them as season memberships.

The Ultimate Tailgater's Travel Guide

About San Francisco

The first Europeans to the Bay Area established settlements in the 1770s. But it was about 70 years later when the population boomed. Specifically, it was 1849.

That was the time of the California Gold Rush, which grew the San Francisco area population from about 1,000 to more than 25,000. A few made fortunes, but most found just enough gold to live day to day. Many couldn't even do that.

But the city continued to grow. In 1906 much of what they had built was destroyed. The 1906 San Francisco earthquake is one of the worst natural disasters to hit America. The quake and the resulting fires destroyed almost 80 percent of the city, including almost all of downtown. More than 3,000 people died.

The city was rebuilt, of course, and with the opening of the Golden Gate Bridge in 1936, and the San Francisco–Oakland Bay Bridge the next year, the city became more accessible. That, paired with the city's importance as a base during World War II and planned development after the war, has created the fourth largest city in the country.

But in a sense, the city is much larger than that. The Bay Area—with San Francisco and Oakland's metro areas to the north, and San Jose's to the south—is home to more than 7 million people and is the fifth largest metro area in America.

Put simply, this is one big area with lots to see and do. This is not one big book with lots of pages. Thus, we've had to condense this chapter some. There are six venues in six cities here, but we've kept most of the attractions (aside from the wine country) in San Francisco since it is the major tourist destination. But everything is close—San Francisco is 29 miles from Palo Alto, which is 16 miles form San Jose. Berkeley is 6 miles from Oakland, which is 11 miles from San Francisco. Sonoma is 45 miles out, so we've included a bit more detail for things to do there. Plus, heck, it's the wine country.

SAN FRANCISCO 49ERS
Monster Park
San Francisco, California
(415) 656-4949

All parking within main parking area next to stadium, all within walking distance. RVs have separate parking area; no overnight parking. Tailgate in front of or behind vehicle. One space per vehicle only. Must stay within your space. After game, shop at Pier 39, eat in Chinatown, walk Golden Gate Bridge.

Shuttle Info: Several Bay Area transit services provide transportation to Monster Park. When you're in the area dial 511 for details on routes and fares, or visit 511.org.

49ers Media Partners: 680-AM and 1050-AM KNBR, 107.7-FM KSAN

Where to Stay

RV PARKS

Candlestick RV Park: Candlestick has all the usual amenities, 165 full hookup sites, a game room, and sightseeing tours leaving from the park. But the best amenity is that it's right next to Monster Park. Like 40–50 steps away. Daily rates here run $52–$55, although it's higher on game day. (*650 Gilman Ave., San Francisco, (415) 822-2299, sanfranciscorvpark.com*)

San Francisco RV Resort: Park your RV along the cliffs overlooking the Pacific Ocean, and you'll see this park's main attraction. In fact, it's the only ocean-view RV park in the area. There are 51 ocean-

side sites, 182 sites in all. Close to Monster Park, the park has all the usual amenities as well as a convenience store, pool and spa. Rates here run $43–$61. *(700 Palmetto Ave., Pacifica, (800) 822-1250, sanfranciscorvresort.com)*

For more information: For additional RV parks and campsites visit campingworld.com/campsearch.

Monster grills get a workout at Monster Park. (Photo: Ed Rode)

HOTELS

Donatello Hotel: This European-style hotel boasts some of the largest rooms in the city. Decorated in a contemporary style, rooms have all the usual amenities. There's a restaurant, fitness center, and spa on-site. The hotel is one block from **Union Square** (see page 176). Rooms run $179–$295. *(501 Post St., San Francisco, (800) 227-3184, thedonatellosf.com)*

Executive Hotel Vintage Court: The "Vintage" in the name refers to wine. The 1912 building's decorations are inspired by the California wine country, and each of the 107 rooms is named for a different California winery. And it probably won't surprise you they have a wine reception in the evenings. Rooms have bay windows with window seats, stocked mini-bars, and all the usual hotel amenities. This non-smoking hotel is located on Nob Hill downtown. Rooms here will cost you $199–$229. *(650 Bush St., San Francisco, (415) 392-4666, vintagecourt.com)*

For more information: To learn about more hotels in the area visit tripadvisor.com for listings and guest reviews.

B&BS

Inn 1890: One block east of **Golden Gate Park** (see page 176), this Queen Anne built in 1890 has five rooms and one suite (the suite has a fireplace). The inn's full kitchen is open to guests 24 hours a day. Room rates are $89–$169. *(1890 Page St., San Francisco, (415) 386-0486, inn1890.com)*

The Inn San Francisco: This Mission District B&B occupies an Italianate mansion built in 1872 and a Victorian built in 1905. There are 10 guest rooms, eight with private baths. The Garden Cottage has a kitchen, fireplace, and whirlpool tub. There are antique furnishings inside, a sundeck and a hot tub outside. Rooms here run $105–$255, and the cottage is $295. *(943 S. Van Ness Ave., San Francisco, (800) 359-0913, innsf.com)*

For more information: To learn about more B&Bs in the area visit bedandbreakfast.com for a detailed directory.

Where to Eat

TAILGATER GROCERIES

Ferry Building Marketplace: Located along the Embarcadero at the foot of Market Street, this restored 1890s ferry landing and train depot is a shopping center for food. Here you'll find meat and fish, produce and breads, cheese and pastries. **The Farmers' Market** is here, as are cookware stores and restaurants. *(One Ferry Bldg., San Francisco, (415) 693-0996, ferrybuildingmarketplace.com)*

SPORTS BARS

Greens Sports Bar: A neighborhood bar with hundreds of sports photos decorating the place, 15 TVs (two big-screens), and pool tables is why Best of San Francisco called this the city's best sports bar. Eighteen microbrews on tap, but no kitchen. Instead, they provide menus, and local restaurants deliver to your table. (*$, 2239 Polk St., San Francisco, (415) 775-4287*)

Jack's Club & Sports Bar: Since 1978, Jack's has catered to 49ers fans in the Mission District. The bar offers five TVs, pool tables, free food on football Sundays, and karaoke on Thursdays. A basic bar menu is served. (*$, 2545 24th St., San Francisco, (415) 641-5371, jacks-club.com*)

RESTAURANTS

Alioto's: In 1925 Sicilian immigrant Nunzio Alioto Sr. opened a fresh fish stall. He sold lunchtime provisions to Italian laborers, and his business grew. In 1932 he constructed the first building on Fisherman's Wharf. Today Alioto's serves Sicilian recipes handed down through the family such as Potato-Crusted Halibut and Linguini with Frutti di Mare. There's also an outdoor crab market. (*$$, #8 Fisherman's Wharf (Taylor St. at Jefferson), San Francisco, (415) 673-0183, aliotos.com*)

The Cosmopolitan Cafe: A contemporary American menu is served in this restaurant, bar, and piano lounge. The dinner menu includes entrées such as Wild Mushroom-Potato "Lasagne" and Grilled Angus NY Steak. The café offers live jazz and specialty martinis in the bar. (*$, 121 Spear St., San Francisco, (415) 543-4001, thecosmopolitancafe.com*)

Crustacean: This Nob Hill restaurant has been hailed as the birthplace of Fusion Cuisine in the U.S. The philosophy here is food with clean and simple tastes, nothing heavy or fatty. That style shows up in the Seabass in Citrus and Vietnamese Crepes, among other dishes. (*$, 1475 Polk St., San Francisco, (415) 776-2722, anfamily.com/Restaurants/crustacean_sanfrancisco/displaypages/homepage.asp*)

For more information: For a directory of additional places to eat in the area visit opentable.com. You can also book a reservation for many restaurants on the site.

What to Do

DURING THE DAY

Alcatraz: This is "The Rock." From 1934 to 1963 this was a federal prison and an experiment. It was classified as a concentration model, where the worst prisoners were sent. Al Capone and "Machine Gun" Kelly were kept here, as were hundreds of lesser-known prisoners. There are several tour options that explore the history of the island as well as the prison. (*nps.gov/alcatraz*)

Cable Car Tour: San Francisco is famous for its cable cars (and not just because of the Rice-a-Roni commercials), so it's fitting to see the city from the seat of one of its landmarks. The tour hits city sights such as **Fisherman's Wharf, Chinatown,** and the **Golden Gate Bridge.** (*$$, Tours board at Pier 39, San Francisco, (888) 609-5665, allsanfranciscotours.com*)

Chinatown: The first Chinese immigrants—two men and one woman —arrived in San Francisco in 1848. Two years later, Chinatown was established, and today it is the oldest, and third largest, Chinatown in North America. Whether you enter through the famous dragon gate on Grant Avenue or from another direction, you'll find streets filled with restaurants, shops, and culture. (*Grant Ave. and Washington St., San Francisco, sanfranciscochinatown.com*)

Alcatraz, aka "The Rock."
(Photo: P. Fuszard/SFCVB)

Fisherman's Wharf: This is San Francisco's most popular tourist destination. Since the Gold Rush, San Francisco's fishing fleets have been based here. Today there is still fishing activity, along with restaurants and shopping. (*Ghirardelli Square to Pier 39, San Francisco, www.fishermanswharf.org*)

Golden Gate Bridge: The one image of San Francisco that stands out from the rest is the Golden Gate Bridge. It was built in 1937, and it was the longest suspension bridge in the world when it opened. You can walk, bike, or drive the bridge. (*goldengatebridge.com*)

Golden Gate Park: It once was sand dunes, but now it's covered with more than 1 million trees and is larger than New York's Central Park. But beyond the green space, the park includes the **de Young Museum of Art, the Japanese Tea Garden, Strybing Arboretum, the Conservatory of Flowers,** 27 miles of footpaths, and more. (*Bordered by Great Hwy., Fulton St., Stanyan St , and Lincoln Way*)

San Francisco Museum of Modern Art: This is the first museum on the West Coast devoted solely to 20th-century art. It includes works by Henri Matisse, Pablo Picasso, Georgia O'Keeffe, Frida Kahlo, Jackson Pollock, and Andy Warhol. (*$$, 151 3rd St., San Francisco, (415) 357-4000, sfmoma.org*)

AT NIGHT

Element Lounge: Located in the TenderNob District, this hip club offers several rooms designed to stimulate different senses. You can dance to mashed-up hip-hop music, sit and admire the art, or watch live performances. But, primarily this is a big party. (*$, 1028 Geary Blvd., San Francisco, (415) 440-1125, elementlounge.com*)

Plough and Stars: *San Francisco Weekly* named this the "Best Irish Bar" in the city. This authentic pub has a long, dark interior that leads to a stage where traditional Irish music is played most nights.

You can also play darts or shoot pool. The menu is, as you might expect, traditional Irish favorites. (*116 Clement, San Francisco, (415) 751-1122, theploughandstars.com*)

Blondie's Bar and No-Grill: They call themselves "A Swank Neighborhood Bar," and the crowd tends to back up that claim. There are big, round leather booths for sitting, and DJs and live music for dancing. The music ranges from '70s and '80s, to jazz and swing. There's a long list of martinis, too. (*540 Valencia St., San Francisco, (415) 864-2419, blondiesbar.com*)

SHOPPING

Ghirardelli Square: More than a century ago Ghirardelli Square was home to the Ghirardelli family's chocolate, cocoa, mustard, and box factory. Now it's home to more than 50 shops, galleries, and restaurants. **Fisherman's Wharf** is right here, too. (*900 N. Point St., San Francisco, (415) 775-5500, ghirardellisq.com*)

Union Square: In 1847 Jasper O'Farrell laid out a design for San Francisco with Union Square as the public plaza. In the 1880s it was a fash-

Golden Gate Park. (Photo: Jack Hollingsworth/ SFCVB)

The Ultimate Tailgater's Travel Guide

ionable residential area. After the earthquake of 1906, it became the city's premier shopping address. Today there are scores of shops, galleries, clubs, restaurants, and more. **Nordstrom, Saks,** and **Macy's** are the big stores, but there are many, many more boutiques and specialty shops. (*870 Market St., San Francisco, unionsquareshop.com*)

For more information: To learn more about things to do in the area visit cityguide.aol.com/ sanfrancisco.

PALO ALTO

The Stanford Cardinal—it's singular because it's in reference to the school color, not the bird—play down the road in Palo Alto. The city was founded because the township of Mayfield rejected Leland Stanford's request to reform the township, which was known for its saloons. Stanford, a business tycoon and politician who founded the university, supported Palo Alto and it grew to the size of Mayfield. In 1925 Palo Alto annexed Mayfield, which is why Palo Alto appears to have two downtowns.

This year the Cardinal will play in a renovated, smaller Stanford Stadium. Yes, you read that right. The school is downsizing the stadium. Fans weren't filling up the 85,000-seat stadium, so they're reducing the seating to 50,000, adding some suites, and upgrading the facility.

The changes to the stadium won't change the parking. There still won't be much around for people who don't have season passes. There are a few public lots nearby, and most are free. RVs, however, cannot park in them. RVs should park in the Stanford Shopping Center, and folks can then walk down Arboretum Road to the stadium.

Where to Stay

RV PARKS

Trailer Villa: This is a very basic RV park, but just a short shot down Highway 101 to Palo Alto. The park has 100 full hookup sites with community patios and picnic tables. In addition to the basic amenities, there is a dog run. Rates here run $35. (*3401 E. Bayshore Rd., Redwood City, (800) 366-7880, openspacecouncil.org/Camp/TrailerVilla.htm*)

For more information: For additional RV parks and campsites visit campingworld.com/ campsearch.

HOTELS

Cardinal Hotel: Built in 1924, this historic landmark has been updated with modern hotel amenities but keeps its vintage feel. Rooms have private or hallway baths, so ask when making your reservation. Located 5 minutes from Stanford's campus, the hotel charges $70–$145. (*235 Hamilton Ave., Palo Alto, (650) 323-5101, cardinalhotel.com*)

Stanford Terrace Inn: Across from Stanford University, this small hotel has spacious rooms with the usual amenities, heated swimming pool, free parking, and a workout room. Blue herons patrol the lawn. Rooms run $175–$195. (*531 Stanford Ave., Palo Alto, (800) 729-0332, stanfordterraceinn.com*)

For more information: To learn about more hotels in the area visit tripadvisor.com for listings and guest reviews.

STANFORD UNIVERSITY
Stanford Stadium
Stanford, California
(650) 723-1949 operations

Most stadium parking is for donors, season ticket holders. There are some public lots. No spaces for visiting RVs; park in Stanford Shopping Center, walk to stadium. Most parking lots are free; some charge fees. One space per vehicle. Dirt lots: discarded coals must be buried in ground.

Shuttle Info: Public transportation will get you close to Stanford Stadium. Call 511 when in the area or log on to 511.org for details.

Cardinal Media Partner: 910-AM KNEW

B&BS
Adella Villa Inn: Trees, a garden, and a pool set off this 1920s Italian craftsman-style B&B from the neighborhood. All five rooms have private baths and wireless DSL. No children under 12 are allowed. Rooms run $125–$165. (*122 Atherton Ave., Palo Alto, (800) 603-8105, valleyviewinn.com/tricia*)

For more information: To learn about more B&Bs in the area visit bedandbreakfast.com for a detailed directory.

Where to Eat
SPORTS BARS
The Old Pro: Voted "Best Sports Bar" in the area by several Bay Area publications and *CitySearch*, the Old Pro expanded in 2006, adding a larger bar, more TVs (including two 10-foot HD screens and plasma TVs on the patio), and "Bucky" the mechanical bull. The large menu offers everything from fish, to sandwiches, to steak, to po' boys. (*$, 2865 El Camino Real, (650) 325-2070 and 541 Ramona St., (650) 326-1446, Palo Alto, oldpropa.com*)

RESTAURANTS
Ming's: Since 1956, Ming's has been Palo Alto's premier establishment for dim sum (KGO radio says they have the best in the Bay Area) and other favorite Chinese dishes. You can cross cuisines, if you like, with margaritas here, too. The restaurant is close to the Stanford campus and to the Bay. (*$, 1700 Embarcadero Rd., Palo Alto, (650) 856-7700, mings.com*)

For more information: For a directory of additional places to eat in the area visit opentable.com. You can also book a reservation for many restaurants on the site.

What to Do
DURING THE DAY
Elizabeth Gamble Garden: This 2.5-acre estate was built in 1902 by Edwin Percy Gamble, the son of the cofounder of Procter & Gamble. His daughter, Elizabeth, lived in the house until she died in 1981 and it—along with its famed gardens—was left to the city. The grounds include a 1902 Georgian Revival house along with formal, woodland, and demonstration gardens. It's beautiful year-round. (*Free, 1431 Waverley St., Palo Alto, (650) 329-1356, gamblegarden.org*)

AT NIGHT
Blue Chalk Cafe: The Blue Chalk keeps its theme in decor with a pool table, and on the menu with the Blue Chalk Grill Combo and the 9 Ball Rib Eye. But the bar and menu both offer more. There are two

The Ultimate Tailgater's Travel Guide

bars here, DJs, and live music. The menu also offers fish, chicken, and pasta—as well as a Southern-style blue plate special each day. (*$, 630 Ramona St., Palo Alto, (650) 326-1020, bluechalk.com*)

SHOPPING

Stanford Shopping Center: This is one of the Bay Area's premier shopping areas. Here you can find the big boys like **Nordstrom** and **Neiman Marcus,** along with 140 other stores, and a European-style street market. (*680 Stanford Shopping Ctr., Palo Alto, (650) 617-8200, stanfordshop.com*)

Allied Arts Guild: This European-style crafts guild is a collection of unique shops and artists' studios in a Spanish-style complex with gardens and a restaurant. Sales also support the Lucile Packard Children's Hospital. (*75 Arbor Rd., Menlo Park, (650) 322-2405, alliedartsguild.org*)

For more information: To learn more about things to do in the area visit paloaltoonline.com.

SAN JOSE

On the south side of the Bay Area is San Jose, which calls itself the Capital of Silicon Valley. The city is home to Adobe Systems, Cisco, and eBay, among others. It is also home to the San Jose State Spartans.

The Spartans play at Spartan Stadium, which the school also uses for soccer, commencement, and concerts. Parking around the stadium is mostly reserved, but there is some game-day parking in Lot 5. A space here will cost you $15. RVs must park in the Fan Fiesta Lot along the fence line on 10th Street. Overnight parking is available in Lot 6A. The downside is that you must own a season parking pass. If you want to learn more about that, or other options, call (877) 757-8849.

Once you're in the lots, you're a short walk from the Tailgate Extravaganza the Spartans throw before every home game. The 6 acres of grass east of the stadium are transformed into a big tailgate party with food, drink, and entertainment. For $10 you can buy a Game Day Grill ticket that gets you smoked ribs and chicken, brats, tri tips, and more. The Game Day Grill ticket also gets you soft drinks or water; beer and wine are extra.

Where to Stay

RV PARKS

Trailer Tel RV Park: Just down N. 13th Street from SJSU, the park has 170 sites with all the usual amenities, along with a fitness room, pool, and car wash. Many of the sites are extended stay, so call ahead to reserve a spot. Rates here run $35. (*1212 Oakland Rd., San Jose, (408) 453-3535, trailertel.net*)

For more information: For additional RV parks and campsites visit campingworld.com/campsearch.

SAN JOSE STATE UNIVERSITY
Spartan Stadium
San Jose, California
(408) 924-7589

RVs, buses call ahead to reserve spaces. No reserved pass; you'll be charged by number of spaces you take. No overnight parking. Game day parking in Lot 5. No alcohol after kickoff time.

Shuttle Info: Public transportation will get you close to Spartan Stadium. Call 511 when in the area or log on to 511.org for details.

Spartans Media Partner: 1220-AM KNTS

HOTELS

Hotel De Anza: Built in 1930, this national historic landmark has been renovated in a Moorish style and has rooms, junior suites, and suites. Rooms have all the usual amenities plus a stocked mini-bar and high-speed Internet access. The hotel offers a restaurant on-site and live jazz. And you can raid their pantry 24 hours a day for deli snacks. Rooms here will cost you $119–$189, more for the suites. (*233 W. Santa Clara St., San Jose, (800) 843-3700, hoteldeanza.com*)

For more information: To learn about more hotels in the area visit tripadvisor.com for listings and guest reviews.

B&BS

The Briar Rose Bed & Breakfast Inn: This country-style Victorian mansion built in 1875 offers six rooms with baths, claw-foot tubs, and period furnishings. The yard features more than 100 rose bushes and walnut shade trees. Rooms here will cost you $100–$140. (*897 East Jackson St., San Jose, (408) 279-5999*)

For more information: To learn about more B&Bs in the area visit bedandbreakfast.com for a detailed directory.

Where to Eat
SPORTS BARS

San Jose Bar & Grill: Televisions line the bar, a big screen is on the wall, and there's an upscale sports bar atmosphere here. Located downtown, they subscribe to all the satellite packages, and on game day Sundays are open for breakfast at 9:00 a.m. The regular menu is heavy on burgers and sandwiches. (*$, 85 S. 2nd St., San Jose, (408) 286-2397, sanjosebarandgrill.com*)

RESTAURANTS

Señora Emma's: There are three places under one roof here. On the first floor is the restaurant, which serves Mexican basics. Place your order at the counter, and find a place inside or on the outdoor patio. Upstairs is **Club Miami** with live music and dancing. The **Miami Garden's** is the taqueria's full bar, open year-round, but it offers live music May–July. (*$, 177 North Santa Clara St., San Jose, (408) 279-3662, sanpedrosquare.com/senora.html*)

For more information: For a directory of additional places to eat in the area visit opentable.com. You can also book a reservation for many restaurants on the site.

What to Do
DURING THE DAY

Winchester Mystery House: Wealthy rifle heiress Sara Winchester kept building her home from 1884 until she died in 1932, because she believed spirits would harm her if she stopped. The result is a 160-room mansion with 47 fireplaces and elaborate details. The house gets its name because many of those details just don't make much sense—such as the stairs that lead up to the ceiling. (*$$, 525 South Winchester Blvd., San Jose, (408) 247-2100, winchestermysteryhouse.com*)

AT NIGHT

South First Billiards: Located in an area of clubs known as SoFA (South of First Avenue), this popular hangout is consistently on "Best of" lists. Jazz plays in the background as you play pool. They also have pinball machines, video games, and big-screen TVs. (*$, 420 S. 1st St., San Jose, (408) 294-7800, sofapool.com*)

SHOPPING

The Raider Nation in Oakland. (Photo: theraiderzone.com)

San Jose Japantown: More than 100 years old, this is one of the last three Japantowns in the U.S. The heart of Japantown runs along Jackson between Fourth and Sixth Streets, and it offers a wide variety of restaurants, gift shops, and specialty stores. There's also a **Farmers' Market** on Sundays. (*Between 1st and 7th Sts. in the Jackson and Taylor neighborhoods, japantownsanjose.org*)

For more information: To learn more about things to do in the area visit sanjose.org.

OAKLAND

When the AFL prepared for its inaugural season, there were eight teams in the new league. Oakland was not one of them. Minnesota was. But Minnesota decided, instead, to join the NFL and become the Vikings. The AFL was a team shy. Enter the Oakland Raiders.

The team played its first game in 1960, and within five years the team began to dominate the league, posting winning records in 19 of the next 20 seasons. But in more recent times, the off-field adventures of the Raiders have gotten more headlines.

In 1982 the team packed up and moved south, to Los Angeles. That's where the Raiders played for the next 12 seasons, during which time they won one Super Bowl (they had also won two Super Bowls before moving). Then in 1994 they packed up again and moved back to Oakland. Fans welcomed them home.

The Raiders play in McAfee Stadium, which they share with baseball's Oakland A's. This is also home to the Raider Nation. You won't miss it. This nation's citizens are the guys in the face masks and silver and black outfits who are the first ones to the parking lot to tailgate. They have become legendary. And you can tailgate with them. Don't worry, they won't bite.

The lots at McAfee open 5 hours before kickoff. Besides the usual stay-in-your-one-space rules, you can't have any glass in the parking lot, and kegs are not allowed. Parking is $15 for cars and $50 for RVs, buses, and limos. If you don't get there early enough, you'll end up in an overflow lot that costs $10.

If you want to leave the driving to someone else, the BART system runs trains to the Coliseum/Oakland Airport station near the stadium's Eastern Plaza (call (510) 465-2278 for schedules and fares). In addition, AC Transit runs buses to the Coliseum from a number of locations; call (800) 448-9790 for details.

Where to Stay

RV PARKS

Anthony Chabot Campground: Located in the Anthony Chabot Regional Park, this campground has 75 sites with minimal amenities, but nearby a 315-acre lake offers fishing, boating, and other outdoor

OAKLAND RAIDERS
McAfee Coliseum
Oakland, California
(510) 615-1888

Gates open 5:00 a.m. No overnight parking in stadium lots, but many do so across the street a day or more before game. No glass containers; no open fires. Stadium serious about banned items. Enjoy whole pig and barbecue.

Train and Shuttle Info: You can get to McAfee on the BART system; get off at the Coliseum/Oakland Airport station—call (510) 465-2278 for fares and schedules. AC Transit runs buses to the stadium from several locations—call (800) 448-9790 for fares and schedules.

Raiders Media Partner: 560-AM KSFO

activities. Boat rentals are available. There's no real street address, so call for directions. The daily rate is $25. (*Redwood Rd., enter Marciel Gare, Oakland, (510) 562-2267*)

For more information: For additional RV parks and campsites visit campingworld.com/campsearch.

HOTELS
Waterfront Plaza Hotel: This Oakland Harbor hotel offers great views of San Francisco and private docking facilities, if you came here by boat. Rooms and suites have all the expected amenities plus "On Demand" movies and Nintendo. The hotel has a fitness center, pool and spa, and charted boat service. A stay here will run you $199–$450. (*10 Washington St. (Jack London Square), Oakland, (800) 729-3638, waterfrontplaza.com*)

For more information: To learn about more hotels in the area visit tripadvisor.com for listings and guest reviews.

B&BS
Webster House Bed & Breakfast Inn: This Gothic Revival home was built in New York, then shipped around Cape Horn and assembled in 1854. It is Alameda's oldest home and was recently renovated and furnished with antiques. Most bedrooms feature fireplaces. A public restaurant is in the house, too; make reservations to eat there. Rooms run $95 to $175; discounts are available for longer stays. (*1238 Versailles Ave., Alameda, (510) 523-9697, websterhouse2.home.comcast.net*)

For more information: To learn about more B&Bs in the area visit bedandbreakfast.com for a detailed directory.

Where to Eat
TAILGATER GROCERIES
G.B. Ratto & Co. International Grocers: It's been here for a century and has all the food you'd expect from an Italian deli, and some you wouldn't. The shelves stock ethnic foods from around the world, too. (*821 Washington St., Oakland, (510) 832-6503, sfgate.com*)

SPORTS BARS
Ricky's Sports Theatre & Grill: Open since 1946, Ricky's is a hangout for Raiders fans—and often players. Even the sandwiches are all named for former players, although we don't know if Jim Plunkett

has ever eaten the Jim Plunkett. TVs are everywhere, including the bathrooms. (*$, 15028 Hesperian Blvd., San Leandro, (510) 352-0200, rickys.com*)

RESTAURANTS

Kincaid's Fish, Chop & Steak House: This is classic American cuisine served up on the waterfront. The menu includes dishes such as Braised Beef Shortrib and Roasted Tiger Prawns. The signature clam chowder is made from an 1885 recipe. (*$$, 1 Franklin St., Oakland, (510) 835-8600, kincaids.com*)

The USS Potomac.
(Photo: Barry Muniz/Oakland CVB)

For more information: For a directory of additional places to eat in the area visit opentable.com. You can also book a reservation for many restaurants on the site.

What to Do

DURING THE DAY

The USS *Potomac*: Built in 1934 as the Coast Guard Cutter *Electra*, it was renamed in 1936 and served as Franklin D. Roosevelt's presidential yacht until his death in 1945. This was the "floating White House" during the summer, when he cruised on the ship to avoid Washington, DC's hot summer days. It is docked at the Port of Oakland, and you can take dockside tours or a 2-hour floating tour around San Francisco Bay. (*$–$$, 540 Water St., Oakland, (510) 839-8256, usspotomac.org*)

AT NIGHT

McNally's Irish Pub: This authentic Irish pub has the oldest liquor license in Oakland (1933). A large bar, a fireplace, and a long line of beer taps makes this a popular place to hang out. There are pool tables and video games, too. Hope you're not hungry—they don't serve food. (*$, 5352 College Ave., Oakland, (510) 654-9463, irishpubsdirectory.com*)

SHOPPING

Jack London Square: The square anchors the waterfront district and is home to several shops, as well as restaurants, museums, and other attractions. (*311 Broadway Ave., Oakland, jacklondonsquare.com*)

For more information: To learn more about things to do in the area visit oaklandnet.com/visiting.html.

BERKELEY

Just up the road from Oakland, and across the Bay from San Francisco, is Berkeley. The University of California's history and the city's are intricately related. The city was founded, in part, to host the university. For many, Berkeley is the city of liberal—some would call it radical—political thought and actions. For others, it's the home of the California Golden Bears. Since we're talking about tailgating, we'll deal with the latter.

Cal plays its games in Memorial Stadium. The 80,000-seat venue is scheduled for renovations that

UNIVERSITY OF CALIFORNIA–BERKELEY

Memorial Stadium
Berkeley, California
(800) GO-BEARS
(888) CAL-ALUM

No RV lots for visitors. Parking starts 7:00 a.m. game day; cars cost $20 to park. Don't grill inside parking garage. No security in lots; lock up vehicle. Visit Fun Zone hosted by the school.

Shuttle and Train Info: Free shuttles are available from the parking lots, from stops around campus, and from Cal's main entrance on Oxford Street. AC Transit runs public buses to the game from the Rockridge BART station on College Avenue (call (510) 839-2882 for details). BART trains run to the Downtown Berkeley station one block from campus (call (510) 465-2278 for schedules and fares).

Golden Bears Media Partner: 810-AM KGO

will displace the team for a year, but they haven't set a date for construction yet.

When you arrive on campus, look for the University Hall, Genetics, and Clark Kerr softball field lots. Parking is first-come, first-served and will cost you $20. Once you've packed away your tailgate supplies for the game, just hop on the free shuttle to the stadium.

Shuttles also run to Memorial Stadium from a number of stops around campus, and the Bear Express loops from the West Crescent on Oxford Street (at the main campus entrance) to the stadium beginning 2½ hours before kickoff. All shuttles are free.

You can also take public transportation to the game. BART drops off at the Downtown Berkeley station, one block from campus (call (510) 465-2278 for schedules and fares), and AC Transit runs buses to the stadium from the Rockridge BART station on College Avenue (call (510) 839-2882 for details).

Like most universities, Cal has its own tailgate party. They call theirs the Fun Zone, and here you can have your face painted, listen to live entertainment, and play games. The Fun Zone is free, but food and drinks are not.

Where to Stay

HOTELS

Berkeley City Club: Founded in 1927 as a women's club, this building that mixes Gothic and Moorish influences is a California State Historical Landmark. Rooms have views of the San Francisco Bay, the Berkeley Hills, and the Cal campus. An indoor pool, access to the UCB Fitness Center, and an in-house massage therapist are some of the amenities. It's also an easy walk to campus. Rooms run $150–$250. (*2315 Durant Ave., Berkeley, (510) 848-7800, berkeleycityclub.com*)

For more information: To learn about more hotels in the area visit tripadvisor.com for listings and guest reviews.

B&BS

Rose Garden Inn: Comprised of two historic homes, the inn offers 40 guestrooms with private baths; some rooms have fireplaces. There are several outdoor spaces, a back patio, and a rose garden, but the name gave that away, didn't it? Rooms here cost $115–$185. (*2740 Telegraph Ave., Berkeley, (800) 992-9005, rosegardeninn.com*)

For more information: To learn about more B&Bs in the area visit bedandbreakfast.com for a detailed directory.

Where to Eat

SPORTS BARS

Bears Lair Pub: Housed in the Student Union since 1962, the pub is full of Cal students and memorabilia. You'll find 40 beers on tap, a full menu (pizza is the specialty), and big-screen TVs. *Sports Illustrated* named the pub one of the "Top 5 College Bars in the Country" and one of the "Top 25 Sports Bars." (*$, 2475 Bancroft Way, Berkeley, (510) 843-5247, bearslairpub.com*)

Chez Panisse Café & Restaurant.
(Photo: Berkeley CVB)

RESTAURANTS

Chez Panisse Café & Restaurant: This is Alice's restaurant. Alice Waters opened this legendary Berkeley eatery in 1971, and it has become a culinary legend. Alice champions organic, fresh, and ecologically sound ingredients, so the menu changes daily. Downstairs in the formal restaurant (reservations required) multicourse dinners are prix fixe; upstairs in the café, the ever-changing menu is à la carte, simpler, and less expensive. (*$–$$, 1517 Shattuck Ave., Berkeley, (510) 548-5525 restaurant; (510) 548-5049 café, chezpanisse.com*)

For more information: For a directory of additional places to eat in the area visit opentable.com. You can also book a reservation for many restaurants on the site.

What to Do

DURING THE DAY

Berkeley Art Museum & Pacific Film Archive: Founded in the 1960s, the Berkeley Art Museum has gathered an impressive collection that spans five centuries, although its contemporary art holdings are the centerpiece of the 13,000-object collection. On the ground floor, the Pacific Film Archive has programs of historic and contemporary films. (*$, 2626 Bancroft Way, Berkeley, (510) 642-0808, bampfa.berkeley.edu*)

AT NIGHT

Blakes on Telegraph: Originally a jazz and blues club, this Berkeley fixture now books more contemporary music acts—both local and touring. In its 50-plus years, Blakes has hosted everyone from Etta James to Train. The menu is basic bar food, but they do have weekday specials from lasagna to jambalaya. (*2367 Telegraph Ave., Berkeley, (510) 848-0886, blakesontelegraph.com*)

SHOPPING

Telegraph Avenue: Welcome to the '60s. Telegraph Avenue is very reminiscent of the era that Berkeley is perhaps best known for. The shops are a mix of the hippie era and modern-day trends. You'll also find street vendors and restaurants. (*www.telegraphshop.com*)

For more information: To learn more about things to do in the area visit visitberkeley.com.

INFINEON RACEWAY
Sonoma, California
(800) 870-7223

[P] [icons] [moon] [$] [shield]

[!] [box] [trophy] [flags] [figure]

[◄] [↯]

Camping allowed in designated campgrounds, not parking lots. Several RV campsites offer overnight and weekend parking. Prices run up to $1,585. Call ahead to get pass. General parking free. Camping rules: no open fires, barrel fires, or bad behavior. Pets must stay in campground. You're in wine country; go for winery tour while you're here.

Shuttle Info: The NASCAR "Ride the Bus" Program runs from Solano, Sonoma, Contra Costa, and Marin. The cost is $130 including a ticket to the race, $35 without a race ticket. Call (800) 870-RACE for more information.

SONOMA

A day at Infineon Raceway is different from a day at Bristol or Lowe's Motor Speedway. As we mentioned in *The Ultimate Tailgater's Handbook*, at Infineon the wine and cheese crowd rubs elbows with the blue-collar crowd. The result is tailgating that might expand your palate, but is still all racing.

Infineon is, arguably, the busiest track in America. On average the track is used something like 340 days a year. On race days, parking is free in the general lots, but there is no overnight parking.

For the overnighters, there are several campgrounds at the track. Prices vary based on what race you're here to see, but the most expensive race is, of course, the NASCAR NEXTEL Cup Series weekend. For that race, campground rates are $218 in the 50 Acres Campground (reserved) and the Cougar Mountain Campground (general admission). The Trackside RV Terraces run $930–$1,585, and the Carousel Campground costs $1,040–$1,585. The latter two are reserved and include four weekend passes.

The newest campground is the Turn 8 Campground, which is the closest to the track action, but is used for only Superbike and IRL races. This campground will cost you about $900, including four weekend passes.

If you'd rather just take the bus to the track, you can. For $130 you get a ticket to the race and the bus ride from pickup points in Solano, Sonoma, Contra Costa, and Marin. If you already have a race ticket, the bus ride is $35. Call (800) 870-RACE for more information and to reserve a spot.

Where to Stay
RV PARKS

Skyline Wilderness Park: This privately owned park offers hiking, horseback riding, mountain biking, and other recreational activities. The RV park has 39 spaces, so be sure you call ahead to book a spot. Nineteen of the spaces have full hookups, and there are restrooms and showers. Daily rates run $25–$27. (*2201 Imola Ave., Napa, (707) 252-0481, ncfaa.com/skyline/skyline_park.htm*)

For more information: For additional RV parks and campsites, visit campingworld.com/campsearch.

HOTELS

Sonoma Hotel: Located on the **Sonoma Plaza** (see page 188), this historic 1880 inn has been remodeled, and its 16 rooms have all the modern hotel amenities. Its location means you can walk to shops and wineries; there's also wine tastings in the hotel lobby. Rooms cost $95–$245. (*110 W. Spain St., Sonoma, (800) 468-6016, sonomahotel.com*)

The Ultimate Tailgater's Travel Guide

Inn at Sonoma: The 19 rooms here feature casual California decor and fireplaces. Most also have a balcony. The hotel has wine and hors d'oeuvres in the afternoon, bikes you can borrow to explore the area, and a rooftop hot tub. Rooms run $145–$250. (*630 Broadway, Sonoma, (707) 939-1340, innatsonoma.com*)

For more information: To learn about more hotels in the area visit tripadvisor.com for listings and guest reviews.

Tailgaters turn wine country to RV country on race day. (Photo: Joe Jacobson)

B&BS

Beazley House: This was the first B&B in Napa. Located in a historic Victorian neighborhood, the home has 10 guest rooms with private baths in the mansion and Carriage House. Some rooms have fireplaces and two-person whirlpool tubs. Spa services are available, too, at additional cost. Rooms here run $185–$299. (*1910 First St., Napa, (800) 559-1649, beazleyhouse.com*)

Victorian Garden Inn: This historic 1870 Greek Revival–style farmhouse has gardens with private patios and a swimming pool. There are five guest rooms, three with private baths. A massage studio is on the property, too. Room rates are $159–$289. (*316 E. Napa St., Sonoma, (800) 543-5339, victoriangardeninn.com*)

For more information: To learn about more B&Bs in the area visit bedandbreakfast.com for a detailed directory.

Where to Eat
SPORTS BARS

Stone's Sports Bar: Televisions are the primary decoration here, including 40-inch plasma screens and a 65-inch big-screen. In addition to watching the game or race, you can play pool and darts. There is a basic sports bar menu. (*$, 1679 W. Imola Ave., Napa, (707) 255-1633*)

RESTAURANTS

Girl and the Fig: Located in the **Sonoma Hotel,** this bistro offers a nouveau country menu with French nuances and an award-winning California Rhone wine list. The menu changes seasonally but always includes cheese and charcuterie platters. Outdoor seating is available. (*$–$$, 110 West Spain St., Sonoma, (707) 938.3634, thegirlandthefig.com*)

The General's Daughter: Housed in a Victorian home built in 1864 for General Mario G. Vallejo's daughter, this restaurant uses organically grown local produce and fresh meats and fish, along with Sonoma cheeses, to serve up New American cuisine like Slow Roasted Colorado Lamb Loin and Molasses and Soy Glazed King Salmon. (*$–$$, 400 West Spain St., Sonoma, (707) 938-4004, thegeneralsdaughter.com*)

For more information: For a directory of additional places to eat in the area visit opentable.com. You can also book a reservation for many restaurants on the site.

What to Do

DURING THE DAY

Napa Valley Wine Train: Ride a train through the wine country while you enjoy the scenery and gourmet meals. All meals are, of course, paired with wines from the area you're touring. Lunch, dinner, and Murder Mystery tours are available. Railcars range from "glass-topped" to traditional Pullmans. (*$$$, 1275 McKinstry St., Napa, trains board at depot at Soscol Ave. and First St., (800) 427-4124, winetrain.com*)

Benziger Family Winery: This Sonoma Mountain estate ranch forms a bowl in the landscape that produces beautiful views and the Benziger wines. Tours here include a tram ride through the vineyards and a tour of the facility. The tasting room—which has been recognized by *Best of Napa and Sonoma Valleys* as the area's "Best Tasting Room"—is open everyday except holidays. Seating is limited on the tours, so call ahead to make a reservation. (*$, 1883 London Ranch Rd., Glen Ellen, (888) 490-2739, benziger.com*)

Charles M. Schulz Museum and Research Center: Legendary cartoonist Charles Schulz's creations are featured at this interpretive museum. But this isn't just about seeing Charlie Brown; exhibits examine the evolution of the comics and their societal messages. You can also stroll through the Snoopy Labyrinth. (*$, 2301 Hardies Ln., Santa Rosa, (707) 579-4452, schulzmuseum.com*)

Napa Valley Balloons: Tour the wine country from above, gently floating about the hills and vineyards in a hot-air balloon. Flights include a picnic before take-off and champagne upon landing. (*$$$, 6525 Washington St. (call for directions to board balloons), Yountville, (800) 253-2224, napavalleyballoons.com*)

AT NIGHT

Carneros Bistro & Wine Bar: It's located in **The Lodge at Sonoma,** but don't let the location fool you. This bistro and wine bar has won awards for its food, wine, and atmosphere. Serving all local wines, along with a full menu, this bar has become a popular place to sit down and enjoy an evening. (*$, 1325 Broadway (Clay St.), Sonoma, (707) 931-2042, thelodgeatsonoma.com*)

SHOPPING

Sonoma Plaza: Sonoma's downtown square is a National Historic Landmark—in 1846, settlers raised the flag of the Republic of California for the first time here—and is a part of Sonoma State Historic Park. There are plenty of shops, restaurants, galleries, historic buildings, and more. (*sonomavalleyvisitors.com/html/Sonoma_plaza.php*)

For more information: To learn more about things to do in the area visit sonoma.com.

Seattle

The Seattle Seahawks entered the NFL as an expansion team in 1976. The city had wanted a team since 1957, when talk first surfaced of building a domed stadium.

The team played in the Kingdome until 2002, when it moved into the 67,000-seat Seahawks Stadium/Qwest Field (although it wasn't called Qwest until 2004). Its unique design provides a roof over the heads of 70 percent of the seating area, and the view out the north end zone is the Seattle skyline.

If you're going to tailgate, you have to do it on the east side of the north parking lot. Many of the spaces are sold out for the season, but there is some game-day parking for $25.

There are day-of-game lots nearby. You can try to snag a space at 1st Avenue South and Atlantic Street, 1st Avenue South and South Holgate Street, the WOSCO parking lot, or in the International District. If you can't find a spot in one of those lots, there are private lots in the area where you can tailgate. The cost of those spots varies from corner to corner, of course.

The city's regular bus service drops you off within three blocks of Qwest Field; there are several routes. Visit transit.metrokc.gov for details. Express Bus service runs from five Park & Ride locations in the city and costs $3 each way. The transit Web site also has details on the Park & Ride locations and shuttle times.

Sounder Rail Service runs trains to the King Street station, which is a short walk to the stadium. Log on to soundtransit.org for train routes and pricing.

Finally, Washington State Ferries run boats to locations near the stadium, including Pier 52, which is just a few blocks from Qwest Field. For ferry information, go to wsdot.wa.gov/ferries.

Once you've made it to the stadium, you'll want to build into your tailgating schedule a visit to Touchdown City. Located in the Qwest Field Event Center, on the south side of the stadium, Touchdown City has games and activities, the Linebacker Lounge sports bar with a projection TV, face painting, former players signing autographs, the Sea Gals cheerleaders, and more.

Tailgating at the University of Washington takes on a feel like nowhere else. It's sterngating! Husky Stadium sits alongside Lake Washington and thousands of fans arrive by boat, tie up to the moorings, and start their parties. Members of the school's crew team shuttle fans back and forth to land for the game. It is truly a sight.

If you want to joint the crowd on the water, moorage is based on the length of your vessel. You'll need a permit in advance. Call (206) 543-2234 or e-mail huskies@u.washington.edu.

There's tailgating on land, too, of course. Public parking around the stadium is in Lots E1 and E2 north of the stadium on Montlake Boulevard. They do stack parking

Parking is limited due to location. Visitors park on private off-site lots, located near the stadium, within walking distance. No overnight parking; only propane grills allowed; no alcohol. Visit Touchdown City at south end of stadium for music, food, and more; free admission.

Shuttle Info: Express shuttles run from five Park & Ride locations to the game; visit transit.metrokc.gov for locations and times. The cost is $3 one-way. Regular bus routes drop off within three blocks of Qwest Field; the transit Web site has that information, too. Sounder Rail Service runs trains to the King Street station (details at sound transit.org), and Washington State Ferries run boats to locations near the stadium (details at wsdot.wa.gov/ferries).

Seahawks Media Partner: 710-AM KIRO

in Lot E1, which is bumper to bumper, putting you in tight quarters, and you can't move your car until the one in front of you has moved. The west campus lots don't park cars this way. RVs park in E1 on game day—there's no overnight parking allowed on university property.

Parking costs $10 per car with three or more people, $20 per car with two or fewer people (they're trying to encourage carpooling). Buses pay $30 to park and RVs shell out $40. For details about general parking, call (206) 616-8710. If you want to ask about parking permits, call (206) 543-2234.

If you have a game ticket, you can ride the bus shuttles for free from eight Park & Ride locations (it's $4.50 round trip without a ticket). Buses board two hours before kickoff; call (206) 543-TIME to verify kickoff time. Log on to transit.metrokc.gov for Park & Ride locations.

If you're not tailgating in your own spot but still want to enjoy the pregame party, head to the Husky Huddle. This is the school's indoor tailgate party at Dempsey Indoor with food and drinks, and you can enjoy performances by the band and cheer squad.

Once inside the stadium, chances are you'll see the wave. A cheerleader invented it here in 1981. That cheerleader was Robb Weller. Yep, the same Robb Weller from *Entertainment Tonight*.

About Seattle

The first settlers arrived along the Puget Sound in 1851, and in 1869 Seattle was incorporated—named for Noah Sealth, chief of the Duwamish and Suquamish tribes. He was better known as Chief Seattle.

The Emerald City has weathered its share of booms and busts from fishing, to lumber, to shipbuilding, to plane building. (Boeing moved out a few years ago.) Microsoft is nearby, and hometown Starbucks is the largest of several coffee companies founded here. The city has also survived the Great Seattle Fire of 1889 and the 2001 Nisqually earthquake.

Seattle is also home to a diverse music scene, and it is the birthplace of grunge music, sometimes referred to as the Seattle Sound. Its popularity peaked in the mid 1990s while creating several hit bands such as Nirvana, Pearl Jam, and Soundgarden.

Where to Stay

RV PARKS

Bryn Mawr Beach & RV Park: On the south side of Lake Washington, this is a small park (27 sites) with just the basics, but a pretty quick drive into the city. The sites will accommodate big rigs. The daily rate is $25. (*11326 Rainier Ave., Seattle, (206) 772-3064*)

Seattle/Tacoma KOA: Adjacent to the Green River and next door to the **Kent Bird Sanctuary,** the feeling is decidedly rural, yet it's only 20 minutes from the city. The KOA has 138 sites and the amenities you'd expect, along with bike rentals and guided Seattle tours. Staying here will cost you $35–$57 a night. Kamping Kabins available. (*5801 S. 212th St., Kent, (800) 562-1892, seattlekoa.com*)

Trailer Inns: East of Seattle off of I-90, this park has 90 full hookup sites. Besides the standard amenities, they have LP gas (by meter), an indoor heated pool, saunas, and indoor hot tubs. Rates run $25–$40. The park is pet friendly. (*15531 SE 37th (near Exit 11A), Bellevue, (425) 747-9181, trailerinnsrv.com*)

Vasa Park Resort: On Lake Sammamish, this small park (22 sites) has the basic amenities as well as a boat launch, a swimming beach with waterslides, and other recreational options. There is easy access to downtown Seattle. The daily rate here is $22–$27. (*3560 W. Lk. Samm S.E., Bellevue, (425) 746-3260, vasaparkresort.com*)

UNIVERSITY OF WASHINGTON
Husky Stadium
Seattle, Washington
(206) 543-2210

RVs park in lot E1 ($40); cars park in E1 or E2 ($10–$20). "Sterngating": up to 5,000 people in Lake Washington tailgate on boats. Now that's fun!

Shuttle Info: Bus shuttles run from eight Park & Ride locations. It's free with a game ticket, $4.50 round trip without one. Buses board 2 hours before kickoff; call (206) 543-TIME to verify kickoff time. Visit transit.metrokc.gov for Park & Ride locations.

Huskies Media Partner: 950-AM KJR

For more information: For additional RV parks and campsites visit campingworld.com/campsearch.

HOTELS

The Alexis: This European-style hotel is on the National Registry of Historic Places, just a couple of blocks from the water and just up First Avenue from Qwest Field. Almost half the rooms are suites, some with whirlpool tubs or wood-burning fireplaces. The hotel is decorated in a mix of contemporary and antique furnishings. There's a wine tasting every evening, and the **Aveda Spa** is in the hotel. Rooms and suites range from $199 to $329. (*1007 1st Ave., Seattle, (800) 426-7033, alexishotel.com*)

Hotel Vintage Park: This downtown hotel celebrates Washington's wine industry. Each room is dedicated to, and named for, a local winery and vineyard. This luxury hotel has custom-made cherry furniture; the suites have fireplaces, flat-screen TVs, and oversized whirlpool tubs. All rooms have soundproof windows. The hotel is pet friendly, too. Rooms here will set you back $139–$289 depending on the season. (*1100 5th Ave., Seattle, (800) 853-3914, hotelvintagepark.com*)

Pioneer Square Hotel: Built in 1914, this Romanesque-Victorian building was a workman's hotel. It definitely has an Old West flavor, but has been restored and has modern amenities. Standard rooms and suites include WiFi service. The hotel is just a block from the waterfront and within walking distance of Qwest Field. Rooms go for $119–$169. (*77 Yesler Way, Seattle, (206) 340-1234, pioneersquare.com*)

University Inn: This renovated 1960s hotel in the University District is left over from when the World's Fair came to town. And while it might still look like a motel from the outside, the inside's been updated. The older rooms overlook the pool; newer ones offer scenic views. Basic amenities include an outdoor pool. The hotel is just a few blocks from campus. Rooms run $100–$145. (*4140 Roosevelt Way NE, Seattle, (800) 733-3855, universityinnseattle.com*)

Husky Stadium sits on the lake, but the nearby ocean is the theme for many tailgate menus. (Photo: Ed Rode)

Watertown Hotel: Many of this sleek, modern hotel's rooms offer views of downtown and Mt. Rainier. The hotel's glass sculptures, portholes, and entrance fountain reflect its nautical theme. Amenities include a complimentary exercise room, high-speed Internet access, loaner bikes, and the innovative "a la cart" program, which brings a themed cart (games, spa, bedtime, Web surfing) of supplies to your room. Rooms run $145–$205. (*4242 Roosevelt Way NE, Seattle, (866) 944-4242, watertownseattle.com*)

For more information: To learn about more hotels in the area visit tripadvisor.com for listings and guest reviews.

B&BS

The Bacon Mansion: This 1909 house in the Harvard-Belmont Landmark District is a classical Edwardian-style Tudor. There are nine rooms in the main house and two in the Carriage House that run $89–$179. Each room has its own character, decorated from antique to modern. There are minimum stays for certain times of the year, so call ahead. Close to Capitol Hill and downtown. (*959 Broadway E., Seattle, (800) 240-1864, baconmansion.com*)

Chambered Nautilus: One of Seattle's first B&Bs, it has six rooms and four suites, all with private baths. The suites are in a separate building across a garden walk, and they have a complete kitchenette. The inn is between the University of Washington and Ravenna Park, in a neighborhood, surrounded by trees. Rates run $89–$144 for the rooms, $104–$174 for the suites. (*5005 22nd. Ave. NE, Seattle, (800) 545-8459, chamberednautilus.com*)

Green Lake Guest House: Located just across from, you guessed it, Green Lake, this 1920 crafts-man-style B&B offers three rooms with private baths, jetted tubs, and lake views. There are also heated tiles in the bathrooms. You are very close to walking and biking trails at Green Lake Park, as well as to boating and other recreational activities. Rooms run $129–$199. (*7630 E. Green Lake Dr., Seattle, (866) 355-8700, greenlakeguesthouse.com*)

An Olympic View Bed & Breakfast Cottage: Like the name says, this is a cottage and there's only one on the property. It's nestled on a hill overlooking Puget Sound with great views of the Olympic Mountain range. The cottage is contemporary, with a full kitchen and private deck with an outdoor Jacuzzi hot tub. It's been named by *Arrington's Book of Lists* as "Most Scenic View for a B&B." You're about 15 minutes from downtown Seattle. Rates run $165–$210, and there's a two-night minimum. (*2705 SW 164 Pl., Seattle, (206) 243-6900, olympicviewbb.com*)

For more information: To learn about more B&Bs in the area visit bedandbreakfast.com for a detailed directory.

Where to Eat

TAILGATER GROCERIES

Pike Place Market: A stop here will get you whatever you need for your tailgate menu. Within the market is fresh fish (including that found in the famous **Pike Place Fish Market**), bakeries, meat, poultry, groceries, and more. See more details about the market on page 195. (*1531 Western Ave., Seattle, pikeplacemarket.com*)

SPORTS BARS

FOX Sports Grill: ESPN has a sports bar chain; now FOX Sports has one, too. The FOX Sports Grill has more focus on dining to draw casual fans along with the sports nuts. Contemporary American food on the menu includes St. Louis Ribs and Soy Ginger Salmon. On the other side of the building is a sports bar with hip styling and TVs everywhere. (*$–$$, 1522 6th Ave., Seattle, (206) 340-1369, foxsportsgrill.com*)

Inside Touchdwn City.
(Photo: Seattle Seahawks)

Pyramid Alehouse: Located across the street from Safeco Field (where the Seattle Mariners play) and a couple of blocks from Qwest Field, it's a popular pre- and postgame place. There are more than a dozen brews on tap (it is a brew pub after all) and a menu with everything from fish tacos to meatloaf. (*$, 1201 1st Ave. S., Seattle, (206) 682-3377, pyramidbrew.com/alehouses/seattle.php*)

Rocksport Bar & Grill: You can watch football or play interactive football. You can catch just about any game on their 16 TVs, including a 20-foot big-screen. Their menu is heavy on sandwiches and burgers, but you kind of expect that here. There is music on the weekends. (*$, 4209 SW Alaska, Seattle, (206) 935-5838, rocksport.net*)

Sport: There's a 130-inch HDTV, 15 42-inch HDTVs, and 28 other TVs (some HD) scattered around Sport. This is a serious sports bar that also has four showcases of Seattle sports memorabilia celebrating more than 100 years of Seattle sports history and champions. The menu is pretty typical bar food. There are lots of events, so check their calendar. (*$, 140 4th Ave. N., Suite 130, Seattle, (206) 404-7767, sportrestaurant.com*)

RESTAURANTS

5 Spot: This is a popular neighborhood hangout that claims its food is "all over the map." The map is America, and the menu changes every 12 weeks to feature a different regional cuisine. It's open for breakfast, lunch, and dinner. (*$, 1502 Queen Anne Ave. N., Seattle, (206) 285-7768*)

Agua Verde Café & Paddle Club: Mexican food served on the waterfront. You can watch the kayakers on Portage Bay, or they'll rent you one to join them. The entrées are mostly tacos, but while true to their Mexican roots they're prepared with a Seattle flair. You'll want to try the fish tacos. There is live music on Mondays. (*$, 1303 NE Boat St., Seattle, (206) 545-8570, aguaverde.com*)

Elliott's Oyster House: *Gourmet* says this is the place to go for oysters in Seattle. The 21-foot oyster bar certainly tells you they know what they're doing with them, and you can get yours served any number of ways. After all, they have more than 30 varieties. Elliott's is also known for its local Dungeness crab and other seafood. There's a great view, too, on Pier 56 overlooking Puget Sound. You'll want to make reservations here. (*$–$$, 1201 Alaskan Way, Seattle, (206) 623-4340, elliottsoysterhouse.com*)

Hing Loon Restaurant: Located in Chinatown/International District, you order off the wall here. We don't mean you just make something up, we mean look on the wall for the handwritten notes (in

GRILLED HALIBUT

Okay, you're in Seattle and one of the best fish markets in the world is here: Pike Place Fish Market (see page 195). Take advantage of that and add some fresh fish to your tailgate menu.

2 cups olive oil

Juice of 2 lemons

2 tablespoons lemon pepper

4 pounds fresh halibut fillets

For the sauce:

4 tablespoons butter

2 tablespoons chopped cilantro

Juice of 1 lemon

Before the game: In a medium bowl mix the olive oil, lemon juice, and lemon pepper. Pour the marinade into a large zip-top bag and add the halibut. Place in a refrigerator or cooler and marinate for at least 2 hours.

At the game: Preheat the grill to medium-high heat.

Remove the fish (discard the marinade) and place the fillets on the grill. Cook until done, 3 to 5 minutes per side depending on thickness.

Meanwhile, in a pan, combine the butter, cilantro, and lemon juice and stir until the butter has melted and the ingredients are combined.

Put the fish on a plate and pour the sauce over the fillets.

Makes 4 servings.

Cantonese and English) telling you the specials. You'll find them on paper place mats, too. It's a cafeteria-style place known for its hot pots and seafood. Remember, the red stars mean the dish is spicy. And they mean it. (*$, 628 S. Weller St., Seattle, (206) 682-2828*)

Paddy Coyne's Irish Pub: This is a fairly new place, but with a strong Irish tradition since the owner's a transplant. The casual pub grub menu is sprinkled with Irish favorites like bangers and mash, Guinness-braised beef stew, and, of course, shepherd's pie. There's a wood-burning fireplace inside, and seating outside. (*$, 1190 Thomas St., Seattle, (206) 525-2955, irishemigrant.net*)

Piatti Locali: Located in University Village, this casual dining restaurant serves up regional Italian fare from its exhibition kitchen that features a wood-burning pizza oven and mesquite grill. The menu has the pastas, chicken, and fish you expect, along with specialties such as Roasted Duck Breast Risotto. *Locali* means "community," and the chef uses many locally caught and grown ingredients. (*$, 2695 NE Village Ln., Seattle, (206) 524-9088, piatti.com/seattle*)

For more information: For a directory of additional places to eat in the area visit opentable.com. You can also book a reservation for many restaurants on the site.

What to Do

DURING THE DAY

Bainbridge Island: Take the 35-minute ferry ride from downtown Seattle across Puget Sound to Bainbridge Island. You'll enjoy spectacular views of the Cascade and Olympic Mountain ranges and the island's restaurants, galleries, museums, and unique shops. It's known for its beautiful residential gardens; you can tour one of the best, the 150-acre **Bloedel Reserve:** (*206) 842-7631, bloedelreserve.org. (bainbridgeisland.com*)

Chinatown/International District: One of the main businesses here is the **Uwajimaya** Japanese superstore, but there are also scores of Asian restaurants, herbalists, acupuncturists, antique shops, and private clubs for gambling and socializing, as well as plenty of green space. They added the International District name to this area, in part, because restaurants, clubs, and stores are no longer just Chinese, but also Korean, Japanese, Thai, and Vietnamese. Look for the diamond-shaped dragon signs in store windows: these establishments will give you a free-parking token. (*Bordered by Yesler Way and S. Dearborn St. and 4th and 12th Aves., (206) 382-1197, internationaldistrict.org*)

Pike Place Market: This is the place where they toss fish and where **Starbucks** was born. It is the soul of Seattle. It opened in 1907 with the goal of building one of the world's best markets. It worked. There are now more than 300 vendors on the market's 9 acres selling anything you need, from fresh fish to meats, to produce, to coffee, to crafts—the list goes on and on. You'll also find street musicians, fresh flowers, restaurants, gifts, and more. And, yes, the first Starbucks is still open, and **Pike Place Fish Market** is where they toss fish as part of their "show" (pikeplacefish.com). (*Market parking garage at 1531 Western Ave., Seattle, (206) 682-7453, pikeplacemarket.org*)

Pike Place Market.
(Photo: Seattle CVB)

Seattle Aquarium: An octopus welcomes you with darkened rooms and large, lighted tanks that brilliantly display Pacific Northwest marine life. The most impressive exhibit is the Underground Dome, a spherical undersea room with 360-degree views into a 400,000-gallon tank filled with fish. Kids will love the Discovery Lab, where they can touch starfish, sea urchins, and sponges. (*$–$$, 1483 Alaskan Way, Pier 59, Seattle, (206) 386-4300, seattleaquarium.org*)

Space Needle: Built for the 1962 World's Fair, this is undoubtedly Seattle's most famous landmark. At 605 feet tall, it was the tallest building west of the Mississippi River when it was built. There are 848 steps from the bottom of the basement to the observation deck. Not that you'd want to walk them. Instead, ride the glass elevator to enjoy spectacular views of Puget Sound and the Olympic Mountains from the observation deck or the restaurant. (*$–$$, 400 Broad St., Seattle, (800) 937-9582, spaceneedle.com*)

AT NIGHT

The Ave: Formally, it's University Way NE, but locals call it The Ave. No matter what you call it, it's the hub of the University of Washington social life, and it has great coffeehouses, cinemas, clothing stores, and cheap ethnic restaurants. Oh, yeah, there are several bars, too. That's what has the mostly young crowd up late. The major action along The Ave is between 42nd and 50th Streets.

Ballard Firehouse: It once was a firehouse, but now it's one of Seattle's top live music venues. They book local and national acts spanning rock, to blues, to alternative. Located in the city's Ballard neighborhood, it's close to restaurants, pubs, and shops. (*Admission varies, 5429 Russell St. NW, Seattle, (206) 784-3516, ballardfirehouse.com*)

The Space Needle.
(Photo: Seattle CVB)

SEATTLE

Cowgirls Inc.: This is Coyote Ugly for the country set. The all-female Cowgirls staff line dances on the 45-foot bar, shoots tequila from their boots, and sprays down anyone who asks for water. They've got a mechanical bull, too, not that it would surprise you. (*421 1st Ave. S., Seattle, (206) 340-0777, cowgirlsinc.com*)

Pioneer Square District: Seattle's oldest neighborhood is filled with galleries, boutiques, and restaurants. At night it fills will crowds heading to any of several clubs. Whether you're looking to dance, meet people, listen to music, or enjoy drinks by the water, you can do it here. (*pioneersquare.org*)

Spirit of Washington: For something a little different, board the Spirit of Washington Dinner Train. The train winds its way along Lake Washington's shoreline and includes a stopover at **Columbia Winery.** Yes, you get to taste. The trip lasts about 3 hours and leaves from Renton. (*$$$, 625 S. 4th St., Renton, (800) 876-7245, spiritofwashingtondinnertrain.com*)

SHOPPING

Bay Pavilion/Pier 57: Built in 1902, the pier is part of the city's Waterfront Park. Whether you want something with a team logo on it, a unique gift, or jewelry, you'll find it here. There are also restaurants on the pier, and you're within walking distance of other shops and attractions along the waterfront. (*1301 Alaskan Way, Seattle, (206) 623-8600, pier57seattle.com*)

University Village: Just north of campus, University Village is an open-air complex that features popular national specialty shops as well as local merchants. Attractive garden areas and several restaurants are also here. There is ample parking, including an 800-car garage on the north end. (*2673 NE University Village at 25th Ave. NE, Seattle, (206) 523-0622, uvillage.com*)

Ye Olde Curiosity Shop: Located on Pier 54 and open since 1899, the shop is considered a Seattle landmark. It sells everything from T-shirts to Native-American jewelry, plus some strange objects. For example, you can get a shrunken head here (no, you don't get to pick whose). (*1001 Alaskan Way, Seattle, (206) 682-5844, yeoldecuriosityshop.com*)

To learn more about things to do in the area visit cityguide.aol.com/seattle.

State College

If there were a Tailgating Hall of Fame, Penn State would be in it. Heck, it might even be in State College. About 50,000 fans are here 4 hours before the game to tailgate. More follow. Lots more. That's one reason why *Sports Illustrated* named Happy Valley the Ultimate Tailgating Venue.

Many also claim Beaver Stadium is the Ultimate Game Venue. It holds 107,282 and is the second largest college stadium in the country. On game days the stadium is the third largest city in Pennsylvania. And just about everyone is there to cheer on the legendary gridiron powerhouse in blue and white. Think they'd be as legendary a team sporting pink and black?

Those were the official school colors picked by students in 1887, and it was done by a unanimous vote. But the pink on hats and garments faded into white after exposure to the sun, and students decided they liked blue better than black. So in 1890 they officially changed the colors to blue and white. Thank goodness. "Joe Pa" just wouldn't look right pacing the sidelines in pink.

If you've come to join the crowd (and it is a very friendly crowd), you'll find several places to park. Your best bet is to buy your parking pass early (cars, vans, pickups $10; RVs $20; buses $40). If you have a pass, you'll be directed to a lot closer to the stadium. If you wait and buy your pass at the stadium on game day, you'll find yourself in one of the peripheral lots farther from the stadium.

Penn State is one of the few places where tailgaters can park their RVs overnight beginning as early as the Thursday before the game (beginning at 6:00 p.m.). You'll be directed to a designated parking area, and the cost is $50 per night. If you're pulling a travel trailer and have a car to park, too, there will be additional fees. Keep in mind tents are not allowed in the Blue or Yellow Parking Areas, and portable generators are not allowed anywhere. (For all the rules and other information, visit gopsusports.com or call (800) 833-5533.)

If you didn't drive or don't plan to set up your own tailgate, shuttle service begins 3 hours before the game. The shuttles run from the corner of Curtin Road and University Drive through downtown State College. There are also some shuttles that run to and from nearby hotels. The cost is $1.50.

And by the way, there's no such thing as a Nittany Lion. In 1907 the school picked the lion to be its mascot. Since Penn State is located at the foot of Mount Nittany, they decided to call the lion a Nittany Lion.

About State College

State College exists, basically, because there's a school here. But the name gave that away, didn't it?

PENNSYLVANIA STATE UNIVERSITY

Beaver Stadium
State College, Pennsylvania
(814) 863-3489

Penn State's overnight RV lots available for $50 per night, two nights prior to game day. Call ahead for same-day pass—prices can be cut in half! No open fires, charcoal grills, or fireworks. Some lots allow tents, others don't; call ahead to find out.

Shuttle Info: Shuttle buses run continually from the corner of Curtin Road and University Drive through downtown State College. There are also shuttles to and from many of the hotels along South Atherton Street. Buses begin running 3 hours before kickoff. Fare is $1.50. For more details visit catabus.com.

Nittany Lions Media Partners: 1450-AM WMAJ, 93.7-FM WBUS

The Shawnee and Delaware Indians were the first to live in the area. White settlers moved in around 1780, and in the 1800s iron furnaces sprang up in the region, using timber, ore, and flowing streams. (You can still see the preserved furnaces.)

But the town of State College was built to serve the needs of the fledgling Pennsylvania State Farmers' High School, which was founded in 1855. The school grew and became Pennsylvania State College. Then, in 1959, it became Pennsylvania State University. You know it better as Penn State.

The town of 38,000 sits in almost the exact geographic center of Pennsylvania—snuggled between the Appalachian and Allegheny Mountain ranges. Residents call their home Happy Valley, and it turns out they're right. In the 1980s *Psychology Today* surveyed America and named State College one of the least stressful places in the country. We're guessing they didn't take that survey with 2 minutes left in the fourth quarter, with Penn State trailing.

The area is primarily agricultural, with forestry, fishing/hunting, and mining also a large part of the economy. But, with a university of 41,000 in town, there are also a number of cultural centers and other activities similar-sized towns don't have.

Where to Stay

RV PARKS

Bellefonte/State College KOA: It's not exactly "George Washington slept here," but this campsite won the 2004 President's award for excellence. Okay, so it wasn't *that* president, but it's pretty good and a short drive down the road from Penn State. The park has 140 sites—the maximum pull-through length is 70 feet—and all the standard amenities, including dump stations, are available. RV sites run $26 to $42 depending on hookups. But, don't plan on this place for late-season games—they close up for the winter November 15. (*2481 Jacksonville Rd., Bellefonte, (800) 562-8127, koa.com*)

Fort Bellefonte Campground: It's the closest campsite to Penn State, with 100 sites and a full complement of amenities, including WiFi and dumping stations. Rates range from $32 to $38, including water, sewer, and hookups. (*2023 Jacksonville Rd., Rt. 26, Bellefonte, (800) 487-9067, fortbellefonte.com*)

Kearns Campground: It's bare-bones basic, but it's cheap. And it's close to campus. RV sites with electric hookups are $18 the first night, $17 each additional night. Hookups are powerful enough to run an air conditioner. Water hookups are available and the dumping station is free. Not much else. Except, for the herd of bison. Really. (*137 Kearns Rd., Spring Mills, (814) 364-1339, outdoorsunlimited.net/~jrkearns/index.htm*)

Seven Mountains Campground: This RV park has full camping facilities, TV hookups, cabins and rentals, a dump station, and other standard amenities. But be sure to call ahead to make sure you have a space. Of the 70 sites, 35 are available for travelers. Rates are $22 per night with water, sewer, and electric hookups; $20 per night for water and electric only. (*101 Seven Mountains Campground Rd., Spring Mills, (888) 468-2556, geocities.com/ sevenmountainscampground*)

For more information: For additional RV parks and campsites visit campingworld.com/campsearch.

Prepping the pregame meal at PSU. (Photo: Bradley Harris)

HOTELS

Atherton Hotel: Thanks to a multimillion-dollar renovation, this historic, Federal-style hotel looks next-to-new. The hotel offers pleasantly decorated rooms with basic amenities. The hotel's restaurant, **Tarragon,** serves everything from pasta, to Black Pepper Crusted Sea Scallops, to Napoleon of Grilled Lobster Filet. Prices for rooms range from $107 (for guests visiting the campus) to $128. (*125 S. Atherton St., State College, (800) 832-0132, athertonhotel.net*)

Nittany Lion Inn: You're not getting any closer to campus—the Nittany Lion is on campus. Listed in the National Registry of Historic Hotels, the inn is a graceful building with nice rooms, although they're a little on the smallish side. The inn does have the amenities you'd expect and dining. Rooms can be $118 in slower months, but they jump to $259 during home game weekends. (*200 W. Park Ave., State College, (800) 233-7505, pshs.psu.edu/nittanylioninn/nlhome.asp*)

For more information: To learn about more hotels in the area visit tripadvisor.com for listings and guest reviews.

B&BS

Great Oak Inn: Located about 2 miles from campus, this homey B&B (it even has a white picket fence) has three guest rooms with adjoining bathrooms. The Inn can either serve you a continental breakfast in bed, or a three-course hot breakfast, not in your bed. Home game rates run $163 to $217. Rates are lower at other times. (*104 Farmstead Ln., State College, (814) 867-1907, greatoakinn.com*)

Inn on the Sky: The Inn is part mountain lodge, part *Architectural Digest*, with three floors, an open floor plan, polished honey-colored wood, and exposed timbers everywhere. Every bed here is king-sized; every bedroom has its own bathroom and sports a great view. There are five rooms costing $260–$310 a night for home game weekends. Rates are lower at other times. (*538 Brush Mountain Rd., Spring Mills, (814) 422-0386, innonthesky.com*)

Keller House: This restored Victorian house, built in 1887, has two guest suites and two additional guest rooms furnished with many antiques. A full breakfast is served weekends; weekday guests receive a continental-style meal. To stay here will cost you $85–$115. A two-night minimum stay is required on home game weekends, but there isn't a rate increase. (*109 W. Church St., Centre Hall, (888) 554-2588, kellerhousebb.com*)

Reynolds Mansion: This place is a genuine stone mansion with a massive, ornately crafted main staircase right out of a history book—as are the carved wooden ceiling panels in the hallway. Rooms feature inlaid floors, high ceilings, and long windows. The Mansion offers six rooms that on home game weekends go for $185–$235 and require a two- or three-day minimum. Rates and stay requirements are different when there's not a game in town. (*101 W. Linn St., Bellefonte, (800) 899-3929, reynoldsmansion.com*)

For more information: To learn about more B&Bs in the area visit bedandbreakfast.com for a detailed directory.

Where to Eat

TAILGATER GROCERIES

State College Farmers' Market: This outdoor market sets up every Friday at 11:30 a.m. on Locust Lane, between East College Avenue and East Beaver Avenue, from the beginning of June to the middle of November. Everything offered is locally grown or made. If it's not in season, it's not for sale. (*Locust Ln., State College, statecollegefarmers.org*)

Stone Soup: A 2,500-square-foot, year-round community market, Stone Soup was created as a place to buy locally raised products. Here you can stock up on fruits, vegetables, dairy products, meats, poultry, fish, eggs, and baked goods. Participating farms practice sustainable agriculture, and most of the produce is organic. There are also homemade body-care products, specialty foods, and wares created by local artisans. (*1011 E. College Ave., Suite C, State College, (814) 234-3135, stonesoupmarket.org*)

A NOTE ABOUT BUYING BEER, WINE, AND SPIRITS IN PENNSYLVANIA

Pennsylvania has some of the strictest laws in the nation regarding the sale and distribution of alcoholic beverages. This gets confusing, so pay attention.

In short, the only places to buy beer are at a beer distributor or at a six-pack store (also called a bottle store). If you buy from a distributor, you'll find a larger selection than at the six-pack store and get a chance to discover some regional beers. You'll also be buying in quantity—they don't sell anything smaller than a case at a time. The bottle store lets you buy beer—you guessed it—a six-pack or two at a time. So if you have a big tailgate party, the distributor is your best bet. (Some bars and restaurants are also allowed to sell patrons a six-pack of beer.)

The only place to buy wine or "hard" liquor in Pennsylvania is from a state store. As the name suggests, these are owned and operated by the Commonwealth of Pennsylvania. And it is flat out the only way you'll be buying anything stronger than beer in this state, unless you're buying it by the glass at a bar or restaurant.

Purchasing alcohol on a Sunday also gets complicated. Beer distributors and bottle stores are usually closed on Sundays. However, some state stores are open.

SPORTS BARS

Champ's Sports Bar and Grill: It's really big, having doubled in size after some serious remodeling, so don't be afraid to bring a crowd with you. Inside you'll find 70 TVs and the type of menu you'd expect at a sports bar. (*$, 1611 N. Atherton St., State College, (814) 237-6010, champssportsgrill.com*)

The Sports Center Café & Grille: This is a pretty typical college town sports bar, with lots of games, six TVs, and plenty of inexpensive beer. They also offer cheap cheeseburgers. (*$, 244 W. College Ave., State College, (814) 234-2299*)

RESTAURANTS

The Diner: If you call this restaurant simply "The Diner," everyone will know what you're talking about. It's been that way for more than 70 years, and it's where you go for breakfast. Try the grilled stickies—a square, gooey sticky bun that's been split, brushed with butter, and then grilled. You'll also find plenty of breakfast dishes and comfort foods such as mac and cheese and meatloaf. (*$, 126 W. College Ave., State College, (814) 238-5590, thediner.statecollege.com*)

Duffy's Boalsburg Tavern: Here, you've got two places in one—the **Boalsburg Tavern,** which serves a more upscale menu, and **Duffy's Tavern,** with casual pub-style fare. The building itself is really cool—pun intended—with 22-inch-thick stone walls keeping summer's indoor temperatures around 68 to 70 degrees. Built in 1819, it operated continuously for 115 years, until a fire damaged it in 1934. Now carefully restored, this 186-year-old building's present appearance and condition are recorded in the Library of Congress. (*$, 113 E. Main St., Boalsburg, (814) 466-6241, duffystavern.com*)

Gamble Mill Restaurant: The combination of atmosphere and food here is something you just won't find anywhere else. First, this is a 219-year-old mill with exposed brick or fieldstone and mortar walls, with wood panels and some plaster. The building's massive timbers are exposed and set off, as are door frames, with bundles of birch saplings seeded with fairy lights. Second is the food, which runs from French (veal with cranberry bean ragout) to Asian (Ahi tuna appetizer with glass noodles and wasabi crème fraiche) and several countries in between. Award-winning wine list, too. (*$$, 160 Dunlap St., Bellefonte, (814) 355-7764, gamblemill.com*)

The Goppers: Penn State students and local residents are unanimous in their passionate love of Goppers' pizza, stromboli, pasta dishes, sandwiches, and subs. There's a hippie vibe to the place, and it offers takeout and delivery. (*$, 114 Hetzel St., State College, (814) 234-1606, goppers.com*)

The Hotel State College: So everyone wants something different, huh? Well, here's the place to stop the bickering. **Allen Street Grill, The Corner Room, Players Nite Club,** and **Zeno's Pub** are all

---

HAPPY VALLEY OMELET

Tailgating starts early at Penn State, so the ultimate tailgaters here don't just cook up a game-time meal. They often cook up breakfast, too. This omelet is our version of the Penn Stater you can find at The Diner on West College Avenue (see entry at left), but they add home fries and a World Famous Sticky.

1 tablespoon butter

3 large eggs, beaten well

1 ounce mild cheddar cheese, shredded

1 ounce aged provolone cheese, shredded

1 ounce aged Swiss cheese, shredded

2 to 3 strips of cooked bacon, diced

2 to 3 white mushrooms, diced

Melt the butter over medium heat in an 8-inch skillet. Add the beaten eggs. As the eggs begin to coagulate, sprinkle the three cheeses evenly over the eggs, then add the bacon and mushrooms. As the cheese begins to melt, but before the eggs get brown, fold over the eggs. Continue to cook until the cheese melts and the mushrooms are cooked, turning over the omelet once to cook and brown the other side.

Makes 1 to 2 servings.

Duffy's Boalsburg Tavern.
(Photo: centralPACVB.org)

located within the Hotel State College. The Corner Room on the first floor serves casual food; upstairs, Allen Street Grill has a more upscale menu. Players and Zeno's are popular places for a drink and dance. *($, 100 W. College Ave., State College, (814) 231-GRIL, allenstreetgrill.com)*

Penn State Creamery: A happy side effect of Penn State's dairy farming research, the Creamery is famous for its super-premium ice cream—all 110-plus flavors. How good is it? Ben and Jerry took a correspondence course through Penn State to learn about ice cream production. It's true. *($, 2 Borland Laboratory, University Park, (814) 865-7535, creamery.psu.edu/creamery.html)*

Zola New World Bistro: This mod/hip bistro has a menu "foodies" will love, with appetizers such as PEI mussels in coconut milk and lemongrass, crispy chickpea dumplings with a red chile beurre blanc sauce, and entrées such as double-breasted duck, wild boar ragout with pasta, and buffalo or (real) Kobe beef strip steaks. If you want the buffalo or Kobe beef you need to call ahead—both must be ordered a day in advance. Be prepared to spend real money for the Kobe beef—it's $97 for a 12-ounce steak. *($ (except for the Kobe beef), 324 W. College Ave., State College, (814) 237-8474, zolabistro.com)*

For more information: For a directory of additional places to eat in the area visit opentable.com. You can also book a reservation for many restaurants on the site.

What to Do
DURING THE DAY

Brookmere Winery: This isn't Napa, but there are more wineries around here than you might expect. Brookmere has one of the best tours, and it's a short drive from town. Wine tours, tastings and a wine/gift shop are parts of the package (yes, you can buy wine here). If you've got a larger group, call ahead and they'll prepare for you. *(Free, 5369 S.R. 655, Belleville, (717) 935-5380, brookmerewine.com)*

Caverns: Pennsylvania is loaded with caverns, thanks to its geological makeup. We've listed three that offer tours and a good time. (If you're interested in finding out more about the state's caves, log on to goodearthgraphics.com/showcave/pa.html.)

Indian Caverns: These caverns are a huge series of rooms, tunnels, and passageways with really stunning formations. The cave's history is fascinating with archeology, tales of robbers, and buried treasure. It's also the only known cavern in the world with a deposit of radium in the ceiling, which creates a visual effect that looks like a twinkling starlit sky, since the deposits glow in the dark. *($, 5374 Indian Tr., Spruce Creek, (814) 632-7578, indiancaverns.com)*

Lincoln Caverns: Lincoln Caverns is a smaller cave system than Indian Caverns, but it can make you rich. Okay, maybe not rich, but you can pan for real gemstones from mid-March through mid-November. *($–$$, U.S. Rte. 22, R.R. #1, Box 280, Huntingdon, (814) 643-0268, lincolncaverns.com)*

Penn's Cave: This cave system lies half-submerged by underground springs wending

The Ultimate Tailgater's Travel Guide

their way to the surface, so you tour it by boat. The hour-long motorboat tour winds through limestone corridors and rooms full of spectacular formations. The water itself is full of trout. There's also a wildlife tour available via safari bus featuring animals found in the Northeast—such as deer, elk, wolves, wild turkeys, bear, even a mountain lion. (*$, 222 Penns Cave Rd., Centre Hall, (814) 364-1664, pennscave.com*)

Columbus Chapel and Boal Mansion Museum: The Boal family was one of the first to settle this area, shortly after the Revolutionary War. Among their accomplishments was founding the school that became Penn State. The mansion itself, while not enormous, is well maintained, with rooms reflecting fashions from the late 1700s to the Gilded Age of the early 1900s. Perhaps the coolest room is the chapel of Christopher Columbus—it's not a replica, it's the actual chapel itself, moved piece by piece from Europe. (*$, Business Rt. 322, 163 Boal Estate Dr., Boalsburg, (814) 466-6210, boalmuseum.com*)

Fort Roberdeau: Altoona and Fort Roberdeau are about a half-hour's drive from State College. Fort Roberdeau puts on a good show, with costumed reenactors who are happy to tell you about clothing, tools, daily or seasonal chores, and general aspects of life during and after the Revolutionary War. It's open from May to October. (*$, Historic Sinking Spring, R.R. #3, Box 391, Altoona, (814) 946-0048, fortroberdeau.org*)

Palmer Museum of Art: The museum offers rotating exhibitions of its large permanent collection. With eleven galleries, a print-study room, 150-seat auditorium, and outdoor sculpture garden, the museum holds an impressive number of A-list European and American artists. (*Free, Curtin Rd., Penn State University, University Park, (814) 865-7672, psu.edu/dept/palmermuseum*)

The Sky's the Limit Balloon Company: Float around the Pennsylvania sky for a while. Flights last about an hour and conclude with a champagne toast; first-timers also get a flight certificate to prove they made it up and back. (Don't worry, they have a perfect safety record.) They charge $175 for the ride. (*$$$, P.O. Box 605, Lemont, (814) 234-5986, paballoonrides.com*)

Tours of Penn's Cave are by boat.
(Photo: centralPACVB.org)

AT NIGHT

The Crowbar: If you like live, loud rock music, this is the place to go. Most rock bands on the college circuit end up playing here, providing a steady stream of fresh, new sounds. And some of today's A-list bands honed their sound on the Crow's stage (Matchbox 20, Train, and others). They've also got a couple of pool tables and a laundry list of drink specials. (*$–$$, 420 E. College Ave., State College, (814) 237-0426, crowbarlivemusic.com*)

The Gingerbread Man: It's a restaurant by day, and probably the most popular bar in town by night. This is due to the G-Man's low prices on food (it's a pretty basic menu) and alcohol, plus many nights with no cover charge. There's a heavy Greek presence and seating for 200 people. They have a small dance floor. (*$, 130 Heister St., State College, (814) 237-0361, gmanstatecollege.com*)

Otto's Pub and Brewery: Not exactly a campus hangout—in fact it's in northwest State College—this microbrewery offers seasonally changing beer selections. Like many microbreweries, it has a full kitchen, too. (*$, 2105 North Atherton St., State College, (814) 867-6886, ottospubandbrewery.com*)

The Hotel State College.
(Photo: centralPACVB.org)

The Rathskeller: The favorite bar of Penn State alums the world over, the Skellar has been providing cheap beer and entertainment since 1933. It's your prototypical hole-in-the-wall joint—cozy, smoky, and full of memorabilia. It's also one of the few places you'll find where the dinner menu is an abbreviated version of the lunch menu. Go figure. (*$, 108 S. Pugh St., State College, (814) 237-3858, theskeller.com*)

Zeno's: One of the collection of places in the **Hotel State College** (see page 201), Zeno's has a dark and smoky atmosphere, and it's known for its wide selection of high-quality beers and ales. The bar shares the same kitchen as **The Corner Room**. (*$, 100 W. College Ave., State College, (814) 237-4350*)

SHOPPING

The Artisan Connection: Here you'll find unique items such as hand-blown glass, wooden boxes and bowls, paintings, one-of-a-kind clothing, ceramics, and even sculptures. (*35 E. Beaver Ave., State College, (814) 231-8989, artisanconnection.com*)

Family Clothesline: Themed clothing, gifts, and accessories for Nittany Lion fans are featured here. (*352 E. College Ave., State College, (800) 237-1946, familyclothes.com*)

The Gallery Shop: This shop features 50 local artists working in every medium you can imagine—wood, metal, jewelry, textiles, paper, and on and on. Much of the art shares Pennsylvania heritage. (*824 Pike St., Lemont, (814) 867-0442, gallery-shop.com*)

Old State Clothing Co.: Still looking for something with a Nittany Lion in it? In addition to the basic sweatshirts, jackets, and such, Old State also offers things such as men's dress shirts and a slew of gift items sporting the PSU logo. (*310 E. College Ave., State College, (888) 234-1415, oldstate.com*)

Plaza Centre Antique Gallery and Ritz Gift Mall: This is a co-op of merchants inside a restored, early 20th-century theater, selling antiques, collectibles, vintage clothing, and arts and crafts. There are also retail and gift shops. The adjacent **Ritz Theatre** houses an arts and crafts mall with even more shops. (*124½ W. High St., Bellefonte, (814) 357-4870, geocities.com/plazacentre*)

For more information: To learn more about things to do in the area visit : statecollege.com/tourism.

Washington, DC

The story of the Washington Redskins actually begins about 400 miles up the coast, in Boston. In 1932 George Preston Marshall was awarded the inactive franchise there and named his team the Boston Braves, since the team played at Braves Field, where one of the city's pro baseball teams also played. The next year the team moved to Fenway Park and became the Boston Redskins. In 1937 the team moved to DC and became the Washington Redskins. There's no recorded date for when the first guy wore a dress and a pig's nose to a Redskins game.

The Redskins now play at FedEx Field in Maryland. It's the NFL's largest stadium, with more than 91,000 seats. It's also home to some of the league's most spirited tailgating.

Tailgating is allowed in lots around the stadium. For most, you need a parking pass (call (301) 276-6050 for information, although be forewarned that season-ticket holders have them pretty locked up), but there are some cash lots across the street from Boulevard at the Capital Centre, along McCormick and Apollo Drives. If you want to meet friends and tailgate together, be sure to get to the parking lot more than two hours before the game; that's when parking attendants show up and start filling the lot from front to back.

If you're not driving, there is train and shuttle service to FedEx Field. By train, just ride on the Metro Orange Line to the Landover Metro station, where you can hop on the shuttle to the stadium ($5 round trip). You can also take the Metro Blue Line to the Morgan Boulevard station; from there it's about a mile walk to the game. (For more information, log on to wmata.com.)

Once you're there, you'll find some serious but friendly tailgaters. If you don't have your own tailgate party, and don't want to join someone else's, you can amble to the Budweiser Beer Garden along the exterior plaza of Gates F and G. Here you'll find food, drinks, and live music before the games.

If you have friends who are 'Skins fans, and they're members of the TailGate Club, hit them up for an extra game pass for you ($75 per person). This is tailgating at a whole other level: leather chairs and sofas, more than 100 TVs, two sports bars, autographs from former players, face painting, games, food, drinks—you get the point.

About 10 or 15 minutes from FedEx Field is Byrd Stadium, which seats 48,385 and is home to the University of Maryland Terrapins.

What's a Terrapin? Well, actually, it's a

WASHINGTON REDSKINS

FedEx Field
Washington, DC
(301) 276-6000

Tailgating permitted in all stadium parking lots. Tailgate in front of or behind your vehicle only; no buying extra spaces. Put out all flames and grills before game. Ash dumpsters available throughout lots. Stadium is 5 minutes from DC.

Train and Shuttle Info: Take the Metro Orange Line to the Landover station; from there take the shuttle to the stadium ($5 round trip). The Metro Blue Line stops at the Morgan Boulevard Station, which is less than a mile walk to FedEx Field. For more information, visit wmata.com.

Redskins Media Partner: 106.7-FM WJFK

diamondback terrapin, which is a small turtle—just 5 to 8 inches long—that makes its home in the waters around Maryland. While the University of Maryland has been known as the Terrapins since 1933, it became the official mascot in 1994, the same year it became the Maryland state reptile. The Terrapin you're going to see roaming the sidelines is much bigger and answers to the name Testudo.

The University of Maryland is in College Park, just 12 miles or so from Washington, DC (which is why we've combined the two cities in this chapter). In addition to the school, it's home to the oldest continuously operating airport in the country. Not that you'll need to use it to get to the game.

If you're not coming from Washington on the Metro (it stops at the College Park Metro Station on campus), then chances are you're driving. Most of the lots around the stadium are reserved for Terrapin Club members or other ticket holders, but the Mowatt Lane Garage (MLG), Lot 4i, Terrapin Trail Garage (TTG), Lot 11B, Lot 4B, and the Paint Branch Visitor's Lot are all cash lots on game day. Check about tailgating rules before you park. (You didn't expect to be able to fire up the grill in the garages, did you?)

Two hours before the game, fans gather along Terp Alley to cheer as the band, cheerleaders, and team walk to the stadium. If you want to join in, line up between the top of Field House Drive and the Gossett Football Team House, which is on the south side of the stadium.

About Washington, DC

Even the Founding Fathers played politics.

Washington, DC is where it is thanks to a dinner that Thomas Jefferson and Alexander Hamilton had. Where to put the capital was a hot debate. The northern states wanted someplace such as New York or Philadelphia (both served as the U.S. capital for several years), and southerners wanted it somewhere in their backyard.

Alexander Hamilton, the Secretary of the Treasury at the time, wanted something else. He wanted Congress to approve his financial proposals. The problem was he didn't have the votes.

So the southern Jefferson and the northern Hamilton sat down for that dinner. By the time they got dessert, Jefferson had pledged his support to pass the financial package, and Hamilton agreed the nation's capital could be in Jefferson's Virginia.

Okay, so that's oversimplifying it a bit, and Virginia *and* Maryland actually gave up land to form Washington, DC, which isn't even a state. It's a federal district whose residents couldn't vote for president until 1961.

Named for George Washington (who never referred to the city as Washington; he called it the Federal City), DC was burned down by the British in 1814 and rebuilt, and it really began to grow during

The Ultimate Tailgater's Travel Guide

and after the Civil War as the government expanded. The city itself has had its problems (remember Mayor Marion Barry?), but it's home to unforgettable monuments, a powerful atmosphere, and a pretty darned successful football team.

The Hogettes are the Redskins' best-known tailgaters. (Photo: TheHogs.net)

Where to Stay

RV PARKS

Cherry Hill Park: This park has 400 sites. There's a dump station, and all roads are paved. It is the closet RV park to DC, but sites tend to be small, and there are a fair number of long-term residents. Rates run $47–$62. Cabin and trailer rentals are also available. (*9800 Cherry Hill Rd., College Park, MD, (800) 801-6449, cherryhillpark.com*)

Duncan's Family Campground: This park is located about 20 miles outside of DC. Due to a fire in April 2005, parts of the park are newer. Besides the basic amenities, they offer cabins, cable TV, WiFi, mini-golf, and beach volleyball. A space with full hookups runs $38 during peak season (May–September) and $33 the rest of the year. (*5381 Sands Rd., Lothian, MD, (800) 222-2086, duncansfamilycampground.com*)

Lake Fairfax Park: Located about 21 miles from DC, this basic park has basic amenities, and 70 sites have electrical hookups only. Sites run $22–$24 after Labor Day—and that covers up to seven people. Lake Fairfax and the surrounding park are attractive and have campsites. (*1400 Lake Fairfax Dr., Reston, VA, (703) 471-5415, co.fairfax.va.us/parks/lakefairfax/fairfaxcamp/index.htm*)

Washington DC/Capitol KOA: Located about 30 minutes from Washington, and 12 miles from a Metro station, this KOA campground offers 120 sites with full hookups on 50 acres of land. While some of the sites are a bit uneven, they are generously sized. An RV campsite runs $38–$59. They also have tents and Kamping Kabins. (*768 Cecil Ave. N., Millersville, MD, (800) 562-0248, koa.com/where/md/20139/*)

For more information: For additional RV parks and campsites visit campingworld.com/ campsearch.

HOTELS:

The Fairmont: It's part of the Fairmont family of hotels, and not cheap, but if you want to be pampered, this isn't a bad place to do that. If you can swing it, stay on the Gold level concierge floor for larger rooms (including marble bathrooms), super-personalized service, and a slew of amenities. The hotel also houses restaurants and throws a Sunday brunch. All this will set you back $279 to $549. (*2401 M St. NW, Washington, DC, (866) 540-4508, fairmont.com*)

The Helix Hotel: This is a hotel Austin Powers would love. It's decorated in "yea-baby," groovy '60s decor, and offers some rather unusual room choices—such as bunk beds for adults. Rooms also come with themes. The Zone room is equipped with a plasma-screen TV, high-tech stereo system, lava lamp, and lounge chair. The Helix has WiFi (free) and Web TV (not free). The hotel is about six blocks from the **White House** and there's a free champagne Bubble Hour every evening. Staying here will cost you

UNIVERSITY OF MARYLAND

Byrd Stadium
College Park, Maryland

(800) 462-8377

University prohibits kegs and grilling inside garages. Alcohol patrols, along with campus police, keep things under control. Keep everything orderly and you won't have any trouble.

Train and Shuttle Info: Take the Washington, D.C. Metro to the College Park Metro Station, which will put you on campus. Shuttle service is provided for some games; visit transportation.umd.edu to see if it is for the game you're attending.

Terrapins Media Partners: 630-AM WMAL, 1300-AM WJFK, 105.7-FM WHFS

$289–$439 during the fall season. (*1430 Rhode Island Ave. NW, Washington, DC, (866) 508-0658, hotelhelix.com*)

Jurys Washington Hotel and Jurys Normandy Inn: If location is everything, these two places just might have everything. The hotel is right on **DuPont Circle,** a popular area full of art galleries, restaurants, museums, theaters, parks, and nightlife (see page 214). The inn is less than a mile up the road. As you'd expect from hotels in older buildings, both properties have good atmosphere, but smaller rooms. They have been updated with Internet service and other amenities. Rooms range from $125 to $350 (the hotel), and $109 to $205 (the inn), but book online and rates can dip as low as $89. (*Jurys Washington Hotel: 1500 New Hampshire Ave. NW, Washington, DC, (866) JDHOTELS (534-6835), washingtondchotels.jurysdoyle.com/jurys_washingtondc) (Jurys Normandy Inn: 2118 Wyoming Ave. NW, Washington, DC, (800) 424-3729, washingtondchotels.jurysdoyle.com/ normandyinn_washingtondc*)

Lincoln Suites Downtown: This downtown DC hotel has rather large rooms with a kitchenette and choice of one king or two double beds. The Executive Studio suite offers two queen-sized beds and a kitchen with pots, pans, dishes, and full-sized appliances. Free homemade cookies and milk every afternoon are a nice touch. Rates during football season range from $287 to $311, although specials and packages can lower prices by as much as $122. (*1823 L St. NW, Washington, DC, (800) 424-2970, lincolnhotels.com*)

For more information: To learn about more hotels in the area visit tripadvisor.com for listings and guest reviews.

B&BS

Adam's Inn: This cozy bed-and-breakfast spreads through three residential townhouses near **Adams-Morgan,** the **National Zoo,** and **Dupont Circle.** The Victorian-style rooms are small but comfortable. Of the 26 rooms available, 15 share baths but also have a washbasin in the room. Many rooms can comfortably accommodate four people. Rates run from $99 to $129 per night; weekly rates are $500–$570. (*1744 Lanier Pl. NW, Washington, DC, (800) 578-6807, adamsinn.com*)

Swann House: Here you can choose from nine rooms inside a turreted Victorian, red brick mansion. Built in 1883, the house has large rooms, many with fireplaces and whirlpool tubs; all with private baths. Located in the **Dupont Circle** neighborhood (see page 214), the Swann is walking distance to a slew of restaurants and attractions—including the **White House.** Rates run $150–$345 and vary based on season or special event. (*1808 New Hampshire Ave. NW, Washington, DC, (202) 265-4414, swannhouse.com*)

Victoria & Maxwell Art Studio Bed and Breakfast: The V&M offers just four rooms, three of which share bath facilities but are filled with American history. The houses along this block date to

The Ultimate Tailgater's Travel Guide

around 1887 and were given to Union Army generals after the Civil War in lieu of pensions. That's why they call this area "General's Row." Rooms cost $95 to $175. There is street parking available outside the V&M for an additional $15 per night. (*1705 Q St. NW, Washington, DC, (866) 483-4077, VictoriaandMaxwell.com*)

Woodley Park Guest House: Renovated in 2001, this 18-room B&B reflects history with antique furnishings, but has the amenities of the modern era, including WiFi. Close to the Woodley Park Metro stop, the Guest House tries to keep things peaceful and quiet for guests, but that means there are no TVs or radios. They have plenty of books, magazines, and newspapers. Laundry service is

DuPont Circle. (Photo: WCTC)

provided for a small fee. Rooms with private baths run $143–$210; rooms with shared facilities run $97–$132. No pets or children are allowed. (*2647 Woodley Rd. NW, Washington, DC, (866) 667-0218, woodleyparkguesthouse.com*)

For more information: To learn about more B&Bs in the area visit bedandbreakfast.com for a detailed directory.

Where to Eat

TAILGATER GROCERIES

College Park Farmers' Market: Vendors here sell only what they make and grow themselves. The market's open every Saturday morning from May to November. (*5211 Calvert Rd., College Park, MD (parking lot of Herbert Wells Ice Rink/Ellen Linson Swimming Pool), (301) 297-9370, veggilicious.com*)

H Street Market: Every Saturday, the farmers at H Street bring their local, seasonal bounty, including handmade cheeses, organic and grass-fed meats, produce, eggs, baked goods and sweets, native plants, flowers, and more. H Street is just a few blocks from FedEx Field. (*600 block of H St. NE, Washington, DC (parking lot between 609 and 625 H Street NE), (202) 362-8889, freshfarmmarket.org*)

Note: There're a bunch of farmers' markets in the DC area. For a complete listing, log on to ams.usda.gov/farmersmarkets/States/DistrictofColumbia.htm.

SPORTS BARS

Cornerstone Grill & Loft: This is a great sports bar, right in College Park. It features two levels, more than 20 beers on tap, and four big-screen TVs. The Cornerstone is a very popular pre- or postgame spot with University of Maryland fans. There is a real fireplace downstairs in the Grill; live music is upstairs in the Loft. The kitchen is open until half an hour before closing. (*$, 7325 Baltimore Ave., College Park, MD, (301) 779-7044*)

ESPN Zone: It's got a huge HD-projection-screen TV. It's got 150 other televisions. And it's got loads of games and such in the Sports Arena. What else would you expect from a bar the *Washingtonian* called a "sports-nut heaven" and one of its "Best of 2005"? (*$$, 555 12th St. NW, Washington, DC, (202) 783-3776, espnzone.com/washingtondc*)

The Exchange: A short walk from the **White House,** this might be DC's oldest sports saloon, but they have a new 6-by-4-foot, drop-down screen, HD-projection TV (complete with a state-of-the-art sound system). There are 11 other TVs scattered around the dining area, too. The menu is pub-style fare. (*$, 1719 G St. NW, Washington, DC, (202) 393-4690, theexchangesaloon.com*)

Joe Theismann's Restaurant: First we'll answer your question: yes, he really does come here— and pretty often. Now, the other stuff: they have three huge plasma TVs over the bar, plus three other TVs in two additional dining rooms. If you're not a huge Joe Theismann fan, come for the food. Try the seared Ahi tuna appetizer, the linguine with chardonnay cream sauce, or the 18-ounce Black Angus porterhouse. (*$, 1800 Diagonal Rd., Alexandria, VA, (703) 739-0777, joetheismanns.com*)

RESTAURANTS

The Caucus Room: While DC "power" restaurants rise and fall like political opinion polls, it's a safe bet the Caucus will be feeding the powerful for a long time. It's owned by a bipartisan group of top-dog politicos and entrepreneurs who wanted a neutral place to sit down and eat. And they do—during meals you'll find members of Congress, television newscasters, and corporate VIPs scattered about the main dining room. There are also private rooms. The menu is a mix of seafood, steak, and poultry with inventive appetizers and scrumptious desserts. (*$$$, 401 9th St. NW, Washington, DC, (202) 393-1300, thecaucusroom.com*)

Hard Times Cafe: Picture a beat-up 1930s Southwestern chili joint, with horse pictures, lassos, and photos of daily life covering the walls. That's the Hard Times Cafe, one of several in the Virginia/Maryland area, started by a couple of guys who just wanted to open a cool chili house. Hard Times is known for its chili—their Texas-style is said to be based on a 100-year-old family recipe. Monday through Friday all appetizers and draft beers are 40 percent off from 4:00 p.m. to 7:00 p.m. (*$, 4738 Cherry Hill Rd., College Park, MD, (301) 474-8880, hardtimes.com*)

Jaleo: Run by *Bon Appetit's* "Chef of the Year," José Andrés, and just a short walk north from the **National Mall,** this traditional Spanish restaurant serves more than 70 tapas, plus a few entrées, and an excellent list of imported sherries. Tapas come hot or cold, with or without meat, mild or wild in flavor, light or hearty. Mix and match for a great meal. (*$–$$, 480 Seventh St. NW, Washington, DC, (202) 628-7949, jaleo.com*)

Mama Ayesha's: Selected by *Washingtonian* as one of "Washington's 100 Best Bargain Restaurants," Mama Ayesha's serves up good food at a good price. The menu offers dishes such as *musakan* (a half chicken baked with onions, pine nuts, and sumac), stuffed grape leaves, kebabs of lamb, kibbeh, and hummus. Located in the **Adams-Morgan** neighborhood (see page 213). (*$, 1967 Calvert St. NW, Washington, DC, (202) 232-5431, mamaayeshas.com*)

Mama Lucia: Mama's is an old-style neighborhood joint that serves up standards such as baked ziti, veal Parmigiana, and pizza. The lunch menu offers items such as meatball sandwiches and stromboli. For dinner, dishes such as mushroom ravioli with Bolognese sauce and penne with eggplant take the spotlight. There are also some other locations in the DC area. (*$, 4734 Cherry Hill Rd., College Park, MD, (301) 513-0605, mamaluciamd.com*)

The Prime Rib: With black walls, black leather chairs, and leopard-print carpeting, the atmosphere is pretty carnivorous. Makes sense, it's a steak place. It's also very formal; men must wear jackets and ties. The dishes won't leave you hungry here. The prime rib comes in 1½-pound servings. While meat is the star, the kitchen also makes noted versions of crab cakes and crab imperial. Don't be surprised to find some of the DC power set here. (*$$$, 2020 K St. NW, Washington, DC, (202) 466-8811, theprimerib.com*)

Tony Cheng's Seafood Restaurant: If you're looking for Tony Cheng's Seafood Restaurant, go up the stairs to the second floor. The ground floor is **Tony Cheng's Mongolian Barbecue,** which is perfectly good, but nothing compared to the Seafood Restaurant. Upstairs, you'll find what's been called the most accomplished kitchen in Chinatown. The menu is mostly Cantonese, but there are some spicier Hunan and Szechuan dishes, too. (*$, 619 H St. NW, Washington, DC, (202) 371-8669*)

Zed's Ethiopian Cuisine: Washington's large Ethiopian population has brought to town some good restaurants. While Zed's feels very western, with white tablecloths and fresh flowers, the food is truly authentic. Try the *doro watt* (chicken stewed in a tangy, red chile-pepper sauce) or the *yeawase tibs* (beef sautéed with seasoned butter, fresh tomato, berbere, green pepper, and onion). Oh, don't let this surprise you: you eat it without utensils. (*$, 1201 28th St. NW, Washington, DC, (202) 333-4710, zeds.net*)

For more information: For a directory of additional places to eat in the area visit opentable.com. You can also book a reservation for many restaurants on the site.

What to Do
DURING THE DAY

Alexandria: Just five miles south of Washington, DC, Alexandria, VA, was founded by a group of Scottish tobacco merchants on a sunny day in July 1749. Today, you'll see more than 2,000 buildings dating from the 18th and 19th centuries in the city's historic district, **Old Town.** You can have a drink in the tavern where George Washington stood and reviewed his troops for the last time, walk past Robert E. Lee's boyhood home, or sit in the pews of **Christ Church,** where both men worshiped. Old Town holds an abundance of quaint shops, boutiques, art galleries, and restaurants. (*For information about attractions in Alexandria, visit funside.com*)

Cruise the Potomac River: It's a whole other perspective on the nation's capital, viewed from the Potomac River. There are several sightseeing vessels and tours available. Here are a couple of good ones. Keep in mind these tours run from spring to fall; call for exact dates.

DC Ducks: This is just cool. The 90-minute tour is in an authentic 1942 "Duck," an amphibious craft that travels both on land and water. Yep, it's a bus and a boat. (The military created them after Pearl Harbor to get supplies to places that didn't have ports). (*$$$, Tours depart from Union Station, Washington, DC, (202) 832-9800, historictours.com/washington/dcducks*)

Capitol River Cruises: These 45-minute cruises offer historical narration and refreshments. There aren't any frills, but it's also one of the least expensive of all the DC tours. (*Washington Harbour, Georgetown ($$, 31st & K St. NW, (301) 460-7447, capitolriver cruises.com*)

The International Spy Museum: What do these folks know about spying? Well, the Spy Museum's executive director was with the CIA for 36 years, and his advisory board includes two former CIA directors, two former CIA disguise chiefs, and a retired KGB general. The museum takes visitors through the history of spying (they say it's the second-oldest profession), shares *007*-style artifacts from around the world, shows videos of people being made up in disguise, sends you through secret tunnels and shares real stories of agents' adventures behind enemy lines, escapes and more. (*$$, 800 F St. NW, Washington DC, (866) 779-6873, spymuseum.org*)

The International Spy Museum.
(Photo: WCTC)

Mount Vernon: Eight miles south of Alexandria, VA, you'll find the home of George Washington, once an 8,000-acre working plantation, and now a national monument. The 500-acre estate features three gardens, workshops, kitchen, carriage house, greenhouse, and the slave quarters. Down the hill toward the boat landing is George and Martha Washington's tomb. For one of the most beautiful spots anywhere, go around to the back of the main house. Beneath a 90-foot portico is the home's dramatic riverside porch, overlooking an expanse of lawn sloping down to the Potomac. Even today, United States Navy and Coast Guard personnel salute as their boats pass by during daylight hours. (*$$, 3200 Mount Vernon Memorial Hwy., Mount Vernon, VA, (703) 780-2000, mountvernon.org*)

The National Mall: This lovely, tree-lined stretch of open space between the Potomac River and the **Capitol Reflecting Pool** (it extends from the **Capitol** to the **Washington Monument**) is a hub for museums, tourist attractions, restaurants, and hotels. The 300-foot-wide Mall is great for relaxing and visiting national treasures such as the **Lincoln Memorial.** (*Between Constitution and Independence Aves.*)

The National Zoo: The 163-acre zoo is set amid **Rock Creek Park,** in the heart of Washington, DC. It's open to the public 364 days a year and home to more than 2,700 individual animals of 435 different species. The zoo's best-known residents are giant pandas Tian Tian, Mei Xiang, and their cub, Tai Shan. Part of the **Smithsonian,** the National Zoo was founded in 1889 to study, celebrate, and protect the diversity of animals and their habitats. (*Free, 3001 Connecticut Ave. NW, Washington, DC, 24-Hour Information (recorded): (202) 633-4800, nationalzoo.si.edu*)

The Smithsonian Institution Museums: The Smithsonian's 16 museums located on and near the **Mall,** plus the **National Zoo,** make it the world's largest museum and research complex. It's also our nation's attic.

It all began in 1826 when British scientist James Smithson drew up his will, naming his nephew as beneficiary. Smithson stipulated that, if his nephew died without heirs (he did in 1835), the estate should go "to the United States of America to found at Washington under the name of the Smithsonian Institution, an establishment for the increase and diffusion of knowledge among men." No one is sure why he did this—he'd never even been to the States—but he did, and today this collection of museums and research centers, taken as a whole, gives us a comprehensive look at the ancient and modern world.

From the **American Indian Museum** and the **African Art Museum,** to the **Museum of Natural History** and the **Air and Space Museum,** we're able to see who we were, who we are, and, perhaps, where we're going.

It's also a lot of fun. You can gaze at the millions-of-years-old skeleton of a proto-whale, or touch a lunar rock with your bare hands. You can look at the art of masters, or look at Julia Child's kitchen. History, pop culture, fine art, science, and technology are all accounted for. And if you want to see everything, quit your job—it will take you several years.

For addresses, hours, and anything else you want to know about the Smithsonian's museums, log on to si.edu or call (202) 633-1000. For a listing and links to all the museums and other Smithsonian properties, visit si.edu/websites_a_z.

The Ultimate Tailgater's Travel Guide

AT NIGHT

Barns of Wolf Trap: Put a state-of-the-art sound system inside an acoustically gifted 200-year-old barn, fill it with just 382 seats, and you have one neat and unusual place to listen to live music. Part of **Wolf Trap Farms,** this cozy space features jazz, pop, country, folk, bluegrass, and chamber musicians from late fall until May. (*$$–$$$, 1635 Trap Rd., Vienna, VA, (703) 938-2404, wolf-trap.org*)

The Air and Space Museum. (Photo: Mark Avino, National Air and Space Museum)

Black Cat: National, international, and local indie and alt groups perform at this laid-back, comfortable club. The place is made for dancing, accommodating more than 600 people, most of them wearing black. Black not your color? Try the **Red Room Bar,** a big, red-walled lounge with booths, tables, a red-leather sofa, pinball machines, a pool table, and a jukebox. The Cat also hosts film screenings, and poetry readings in its ground floor room called **Backstage.** (*$–$$, 1811 14th St. NW, Washington DC, (202) 667-7960, blackcatdc.com*)

Habana Village: This club is one of the best places to salsa and merengue in the **Adams-Morgan** neighborhood (see below). Habana is a three-story nightclub, with a bar and restaurant on the first floor, a bar and dance floor with a DJ on the second level, and a live music space on the third floor. You can take a dance lesson Wednesday through Friday for $10. (*$, 1834 Columbia Rd. NW, Washington DC, (202) 462-6310, havanavillage.com*)

Madhatter: This wacky bar draws a diverse group of 25- to 35-year-olds each night. It gets its name—and theme—from Lewis Carroll's *Through the Looking Glass.* The Hatter's kitchen offers classic pub grub, a raw bar, and special entrées inspired by Carroll's book. Wear a sufficiently weird hat and you could get a free drink. (*$, 1831 M St. NW, Washington, DC, (202) 833-1495*)

Madam's Organ Restaurant and Bar: The club includes a wide-open bar decorated eclectically with a 150-year-old gilded mirror, stuffed fish and animal heads, and paintings of nudes. Every night features a different style of music. On the second floor, you'll find **Big Daddy's Love Lounge & Pick-Up Joint,** which pretty much says it all. The food is a combination of pub grub and Southern meat-and-three (otherwise known as soul food). (*$, 2461 18th St. NW, Washington DC, (202) 667-5370, madamsorgan.com*)

The Tombs: Believe it or not, this college bar, located near the **Georgetown University** entrance, is included on the campus meal plan. The Tombs has been a neighborhood institution since 1962, part sporting bar (that means sports like rowing and lacrosse, as well as football) and part college hangout for students and faculty alike. The look is classic saloon with high-backed booths, vintage crew and sporting prints, colorful sweeps, and antique leaded glass. On Sunday, brunch after mass at Holy Trinity Church is a longtime Georgetown tradition. (*$, 1226 36th St. NW, Washington, DC, (202) 337-6668, tombs.com*)

SHOPPING

Adams-Morgan Neighborhood: This is probably Washington's most bohemian, oddball neighborhood. Most of the shops you'll want to visit are on either 18th Street NW or Columbia Road NW. It has

Adams-Morgan neighborhood.
(Photo: WCTC)

no Metro stop, but it's only a 15-minute stroll from the Woodley Park/Zoo station. This probably isn't the place to find priceless treasures, but this is a bargain hunter's paradise. If you have a particular shop in mind, like **Miss Pixie's** (some great antique parasols and vintage clothes) or **Skynear and Company** (unusual stuff for the home), call ahead to make sure they're open. Folks in Adams-Morgan don't seem to live by the clock. (*18th St. and Columbia Rd. NW, Washington, DC*)

Capitol Coin and Stamp Co. Inc: Here's a great place to stop and browse. This store is full of political memorabilia from both sides of the aisle, along with coins and stamps. There's collectible stuff, such as signed letters from former presidents, to items with a fun "gee-whiz" factor, like a book of matches from Air Force One. (*1001 Connecticut Ave. N.W., Suite 745, Washington, DC, (202) 296-0400, capitolcoin.com*)

Downtown Area: The area bounded east and west by 7th and 14th Streets NW, and north and south by New York and Pennsylvania Avenues NW, is where to go if you want to shop downtown. Here you'll find high-end stores such as **Dean and DeLuca's** and **Chanel Boutique** alongside unique shops such as **Apartment Zero** (very cool design furnishings and accessories) and **Al's Magic Shop** (magicians Doug Henning and David Copperfield have shopped here).

Dupont Circle Neighborhood: With offbeat shops, specialty book and record stores, coffee houses, and a park, this area really is urban living. For something different, go to **The Chocolate Moose** and pick up oddball greeting cards, European chocolates, or just some plain old wind-up chattering teeth. If your focus is clothing, then stick to Connecticut Avenue NW from K Street north to S Street for traditional shops such as **Brooks Bros., Burberry,** and **Talbots,** discount bonanzas such as **Filene's Basement** and **Ann Taylor Loft,** or the haute couture temple of **Rizik.** The closer you get to Dupont Circle, the hipper things get. (*Connecticut Ave. between M and S Sts., Washington, DC*)

Georgetown: You'll find chain stores and one-of-a-kind shops, chic as well as thrift, in this neighborhood. Most stores lie to the east and west on M Street and to the north on Wisconsin. Stop into **Georgetown Antiques Center** and shop for art nouveau or art deco antiques, fireplace equipment, and silverware. At the other end of the spectrum, go to **Commander Salamander** for bizarre or retro clothes and candy-color makeup. (*Starts at the intersection of Wisconsin Ave. and M St. and fans out from there*)

Union Station: It's touristy, but fun. With more than 100 specialty stores, this combination railroad station and historic landmark is also a shopping destination. Stop into **Appalachian Spring** for hand-crafted items made by American artists, **Destination DC** for local souvenirs, or **Out of Left Field** for sports memorabilia. Union Station also has 45 eateries. (*50 Massachusetts Ave. NE, Washington, DC, (202) 371-9441, unionstationdc.com*)

For more information: To learn more about things to do in the area visit cityguide.aol.com/washington.

Also by Stephen Linn:

The Ultimate Tailgater's Handbook is filled with everything you need to know to be the envy of the parking lot. You'll find tailgating tips, recipes, and venue guides for every NFL, NCAA Division 1-A, and NASCAR stadium in the country—there's never been a more comprehensive book about tailgating!

It's the ultimate how-to for the tailgater who wants to do it all, have it all, and host the best party in the parking lot.

Available in stores and at
theultimatetailgater.com!

Also on **theultimatetailgater.com:** Watch and listen to Stephen and his guests on *The Ultimate Tailgater's 2 Minute Drill* video segments and *The Ultimate Tailgater's Podcast* for tips, news, and features from tailgate parties coast-to-coast!

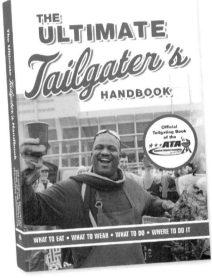

Plus you'll find recipes, *The Ultimate Tailgater's Blog,* and more!